Beer in Maryland

Beer in Maryland

*A History of Breweries
Since Colonial Times*

MAUREEN O'PREY

McFarland & Company, Inc., Publishers
Jefferson, North Carolina

ISBN (print) 978-1-4766-6773-7
ISBN (ebook) 978-1-4766-2882-0

LIBRARY OF CONGRESS CATALOGUING-IN-PUBLICATION DATA

BRITISH LIBRARY CATALOGUING DATA ARE AVAILABLE

Front cover: Employees of Fred Bauernschmidt's American Brewery,
circa 1905 (Historical Society of Baltimore County)

Printed in the United States of America

*McFarland & Company, Inc., Publishers
Box 611, Jefferson, North Carolina 28640
www.mcfarlandpub.com*

Table of Contents

Acknowledgments

The writing of history is a journey, one that is all encompassing for the historian. Without the unwavering support of my husband Chris, daughter Paige, and sister Tina I would never have been able to travel this path to its conclusion. They lend me strength and provide the safe harbor in a storm. They keep me grounded and smiling while I am tackling the complexities and frustrations of monumental endeavors like this one. It is with my sincerest gratitude that I thank the brewers and proprietors of Maryland for their time, willingness to share their stories, and access to their inner sanctums where the magic is created. It has been my honor to reveal these histories. My hope is that I have captured even a modicum of their dedication to the noble pursuit of craft and community.

There have been many people along the way who have been incredibly supportive and deserve many thanks: Hugh Sisson, Stephen Demczuk, Kasey Turner, Mark and Irene Duerr, Chris Anderson, Dominic Cantalupo and Lisa Lawson, Judy and Rob Neff, Ronald Roaché (Library of Congress), Vince Fitzpatrick (Enoch Pratt), the Maryland State Archives staff, the Maryland Land Records staff, Lawrence Handy (ECBA), Cross Street Irregulars, Society for the Preservation of Beers from the Wood, the Baltimore Beer Babes, and everyone who has offered their support and encouragement through the course of this journey.

This book is dedicated to all the brewers, past and present, their families, and their patrons. May their legacies live on, and may they always be remembered for their exceptional craft.

Sláinte!

Abbreviations

AHTA—American Historical Truck Association

BBT—Baltimore Book of Trade

BGE—Baltimore Gas and Electric

BMI—Baltimore Museum of Industry

BBLS—Barrels

BWBW—Baltimore Washington Beer Works

CCS—Crown Cork and Seal

DNB—Das Neue Baltimore

ECBA—East Coast Breweriana Association

HABS—Historical American Building Survey

HAER—Historical American Engineering Record

HSBC—Historical Society of Baltimore County

LOC—Library of Congress

MHT—Maryland Historic Trust

NARA—National Archives and Records Administration

SV—Seine Vergangenheit

USBA—United States Brewers Association

Preface

Beer in Maryland takes you on a journey through the rich tapestry of brewing history from the earliest settlers to our modern craft artisans. This pivotal history reveals the untold stories of brewers risking it all to provide for their families, build communities, and create brewing legacies. The brewers of Maryland not only helped to forge the cities and towns we call home but also fought for our freedoms, shepherded slaves on the Underground Railroad, challenged city hall, founded some of the most successful charities in the nation, all while working painstakingly long hours to provide us with the best possible brews they could produce. They embraced (and often cursed) the latest technology had to offer, adjusting with the ever-changing world around them. Not even Prohibition could stop them. In addition to creating some of the finest beer in the nation, our modern Maryland brewers, male and female, have taken up the mantle of brewers past and continue to build and support their communities in the most unexpected and critical ways, from charitable works to saving the Chesapeake Bay.

This is a history that must be revealed, not only to document the current craft beer explosion but also because many of their stories have remained hidden, like a diamond deep within the earth. After years of researching every facet of this enthralling subject and conducting exhaustive interviews with current and former brewers, their employees, and families, it is time to bring these unique stories to light. A host of sometimes scandalous tales from unpublished manuscripts detail everything from secret midnight brewery parties during Prohibition to family feuds and hidden gold. Every story is revealed and placed in the framework of understanding how Maryland was forged and the integral role the brewers played, and continue to play. It is a blessing to be able to share this intriguing history with you.

Introduction

The Historical Origins of Beer in America

Beer has been brewed for millennium. As far back as Neolithic Mesopotamia and Egypt, society has brewed beer as a staple of the diet.[1] In the ancient world bread and beer were often interchangeable; bread was frequently added to liquid, allowing the yeast to ferment the sugars into alcohol.[2] Not only was it delicious, beer was also a commodity to be bartered for and a symbol of wealth.[3] There is strong evidence suggesting that Neolithic people (post–hunters and gatherers) malted grain when they first began to cultivate wild grains 12,000 years ago. Very well constructed malting floors with evidence of careful and ongoing repairs have been found in the crude Neolithic adobe (sun-dried mud brick) homes from Syria to the Jordan Valley and beyond. The first farmers were indeed our very first maltsters. Within a few millennium, the malting floors became more elaborate, including the extremely complex task of lime plastering, demonstrating how very important the malting of grain was to our ancient ancestors.[4] The ancient Sumerians even had a goddess of brewing—Ninkasi, whose hymn details the process of malting grain for use in creating beer and notes that it was such a precious commodity it was guarded by dogs.[5]

Over the course of western history, the value of beer changed and wine was often considered a more valuable spirit. One thing that did not change was the need for beer as a nutritional staple. During the Middle Ages 50–80 percent of the grains harvested in feudal society were used for alcohol. Workers would drink beer and cider throughout the day instead of water. This stemmed from the often true belief that water was contaminated and only achieved non-toxic levels once fermented into alcohol. Alcoholic beverages were also believed to have many curative effects. Most ladies would take concoctions that included beer or spirits and were designed to cure a variety of illnesses and promote good health.[6] The grains used to make the beer were also integral to the medieval diet, much like in the ancient world. A loaf of bread would mold in a few days, where beer and other alcoholic beverages would last through a winter and beyond. It comes as no surprise that brewing technology was brought with the Europeans colonizing a very wild and unpredictable America.

Early colonists were also of the belief that water in America was just as contaminated as water in Europe. They had no information to disabuse them of that notion, and they relied heavily upon the production of cider and beer to sustain them. Cider was a bit easier to manufacture in the new world than beer, as the ingredients were fewer and more available. When it came to beer, the colonists relied upon the impor-

3

tation of beer as well as hops, and, for a time, grains (until they became viable crops in America). Colonists were advised to take malts with them to the New World. One of the biggest problems settlers faced in the early years was access to hops. Shipments were infrequent and hops quite expensive, so many colonists were forced to improvise. Some would substitute juniper or spruce to get the piney bite they were used to receiving from the hop cones.[7] Other improvisations took place in colonial brewing, from the substitution of wheat, Indian corn, or rye for barley to a variety of additions for flavoring beer like persimmon and molasses.[8] Another critical aspect of beer production brought to colonial America from Europe was the belief that it was solely the purview of women.[9] Colonial kitchens were designed for brewing, particularly if your tract of land was not large enough to build a separate brew house.[10] Every household was responsible for brewing their own. If beer was good, often neighbors would exchange batches or just share. If a household did not possess a knowledgeable brewer more trade was necessary. In Virginia none of the colonists had the skill to brew so an advertisement was placed in a British newspaper for two brewers to come to the colony and brew.[11] Historically, brewing prior to the industrial revolution (and the advent of technology and an understanding of yeast fermenting sugar into alcohol) was fickle with regard to consistency. Brewers would make a recipe and the result would be grand, and the next time they brewed the exact same recipe the beer would be abysmal. Thus was the nature of colonial brewing, which also prompted the desire to experiment widely with ingredients.

Colonial brewing technology was limited, however, and everything was done by hand. Most brewery items were made of wood: mash tun, forks, rakes, shovels, buckets, and barrels. Barrels would eventually see the advent of iron hoops to secure them, and copper brew kettles would become the norm for colonists. Most commercial colonial brew houses adjoined beer cellars.[12] These cellars were often below ground, as the temperature would be much lower and better for storing beer. Sometimes they were lined with cut stone for the same purpose, as well as structural reinforcement. A malting house would occasionally be constructed adjacent to the brew house and cellar where a horse would be used to grind the malt. This was atypical, however, as commercial malt production on a large or consistent scale would not be seen for a number of years. As the eighteenth century got underway brewers would see thermometers invented to gauge temperature and hydrometers to measure density.[13] All of these advances would help to make more consistent beers on a larger scale in America.

Beer was of such great import to colonists that even Harvard University included beer rations for all students. The president of Harvard from 1640 to 1654, Henry Dunster, commented on having to direct daily rations for students, which included two servings of beer twice per day.[14] Harvard had three breweries on campus that served two types of beer. This was not at all unusual for the time. In fact, it was common for students to pay for their board with malted barley or wheat to aid the rations.[15] This became characteristic for the early American colleges, as beer was considered necessary for the diet and curative in its effects. For those colleges that had more limited access to brewers, cider was often the drink of choice. This was true at Princeton University in New Jersey.[16]

Outside of the collegiate world brewing was integral to many differing professions. In Maryland during the colonial years when a new building was constructed and the first stones of a new wall were laid masons were given a case of brandy. One-half barrel of beer was given to carpenters for every beam placed. More beer was also dispersed among the other tradesmen working on the structure, demonstrating that beer was a critical part of the infrastructure of colonial Maryland society.[17]

Standard colonial beers fell into four general types: "small" beer (weakest beer with no cellaring ability), "strong" beer (strong in alcohol and taste and could be cellared for extensive periods without compromise), "table" beer (average alcohol and moderate flavor), and "ship's" beer, which was brewed with great strength fit for long seafaring journeys.[18] A distinction between beer and ale was in the yeast used, the temperature boiled, and the style brewed. Since yeast was not known in the colonial era as the cause of fermenting sugar into alcohol, this went more to taste. Most German- or continental-style brews were "beers" (with hops added) and English brews were "ales," owing to the malty nature and lack of hops.[19] Some credit the English king Henry IV (1399–1413) as being the first to make the distinction between ales and beer.[20] Porter would eventually become another popular style by the 1730s in American colonies.

Regulation of the brewing process in the colonies became a necessity as an attempt to guarantee quality beer production. One colonial law in New Netherland (New York) forbade less than four bushels of malt for a hogshead (54 gallons) of beer.[21] Some colonies restricted commercial sale of beer to those with "sufficyent skill and knowledge in the art or mistery of a brewer."[22] Along with regulation of brewing came taxation. Colonial governors were not shy in taxing one of the most popular commodities in the colonies. Other laws were eventually enacted to limit the amount of spirits consumed by colonists, in preference to the lesser alcohol content of beer.[23] Eighteenth-century laws also pressed colonists to buy American instead of importing beer or hops from England, once crops were established, to help boost the economies of the colonies.[24] In fact, Samuel Adams advertised his beer as an American product and stated the colonies should "no longer be beholden to Foreigners for a Credible Liquor, which may be as successfully manufactured in this country."[25] This sentiment may have been influenced in no small part by the growing fervor for American independence.[26]

1

Colonial Maryland Breweries

Maryland was chartered as a colony in June of 1632 by King Charles I with a colonial grant to George Calvert, Lord Baltimore.[1] The colony was settled in St. Mary's, the first location where the 140 settlers landed with accessible shores and suitable provisions in 1634. Maryland was settled for profit but also for religious freedom. In the case of the Calvert family that religion was Catholicism. The hope for Catholics was to escape the persecution they suffered for their faith in England. The native Indian tribes agreed to the colonists' settling the land in exchange for European goods like blankets and also showed the settlers how to plant and harvest native grains, vegetables, and legumes. The colony was situated in the middle of the eastern seaboard and the midpoint of the northern and southern colonies. Settlers believed this would position them in the center of trade for all colonies, which was in large part true. As more settlers arrived, inland exploration and settlement continued. The Chesapeake Bay provided an excellent location to ship and trade goods as well as to accommodate more settlements. The sandy loam provided a brilliant soil for planting a variety of crops, including tobacco. This accommodated the establishment of plantations throughout the Chesapeake region. As a result, counties were established and Maryland quickly began to grow, founding Anne Arundel County in 1650 and Baltimore County in 1660.

As previously noted, most brewing was done in the home or in an adjacent structure. As Maryland's population grew and more port towns were established there was an increase in the migration of peoples. Travelers who did not have family in the area would stay at a tavern (or "ordinary," as they were called) or take lodging with a private family who had room. They usually ate with the tavern owner's family and would partake of the beer brewed by the tavern owner's wife. Most wives were responsible for running the tavern. Some women even owned their own taverns, since that was considered a respectable occupation for women in the New World. Licenses to operate taverns were held in the husband's name in the case of married women, but magistrates knew who was ultimately responsible for the management. As the population increased, so did the import of taverns. Taverns connected colonists separated by plantations and became the social and economic centers of localities. Town meetings would be called and gossip, news, and political conversations were held over cider or ale. Often taverns served as mail stops for local residents, games were played, court was held, and lost and found posters were hung. Taverns eventually became more social centers than accommodations, and the trade in spirits, among other goods, was high.[2] Importation of goods from England was quite expensive and often untenable for colonists. The lack of a manufacturing industry to make goods provided the impetus for legislation to be passed in 1704 prohibiting the importation of bread, beer flower (hops), malt, etc., to promote the growth of industry and stimulate the economy of the colonies.[3]

This population increase and newly created legislation fashioned an opportunity for the establishment of the first industry in Maryland—a brewery. The first commercial brewery built in Maryland was Benjamin Fordham's Brewery in the state capital of Annapolis in 1703 on Prince George's Street. Other than the charter by Queen Anne and the notices in the *Maryland Gazette*, we have no clear understanding of whether Fordham's beer was popular or how much he produced. Fordham was a native of London and started the brewery with his brother James. James quickly turned power over to Benjamin in 1704. Anne Arundel County land records indicate that in March 1705 Fordham was deeded the land, by Charles Carroll for 150£, where Fordham operated the brewery.[4] Business must have been strong enough not only to sustain the brewery but also to grow the business and Fordham expanded operations in 1713. He needed the brewery to thrive since his wife Lydia bore him eight children, quite a number of mouths to feed for the Quaker and his bride. Fordham also became quite prominent in Annapolis, taking the position of alderman in 1708.[5] Despite the dearth of information today pertaining to the business, his venture into brewing must be deemed a success due to the vast land holdings bequeathed to his heirs upon his death just one year after closing the brewery in 1716.[6]

Contrary to what was expected of Annapolis, the capital city did not thrive and

Annapolis, a lithograph of the city, ca. 1800 (NYPL).

population remained stagnant for many decades. Despite these limitations another brewery opened in the capital city on what appears to be the same location as Fordham's—Mark Gibson's Brewery in 1746. Gibson's was the first brewery in Maryland to advertise. Prices appeared reasonable at sixpence per gallon and twelve shillings per barrel of table beer.[7] Although Gibson's advertisements sounded appealing, he was not successful, and it has been speculated that competition was his undoing. This rivalry came from John Muschett of Charlestown (Charles County), a contemporary of Gibson, providing competition that may have drained an already weak market. Muschett purchased the Port Tobacco lot #28 for his brewery from Samuel Luckett on September 28, 1745.[8] Brewing operations commenced rather quickly. It appears he also malted his own barley, but even that was not enough to keep his business viable. As a result, Muschett was attempting to sell his brewery by 1748.[9]

Approximately a year later Patrick Creagh attempted to run a brewery in Annapolis, with perhaps a greater measure of success. Creagh was a third-generation Irish immigrant whose family settled on the Chesapeake Bay in Annapolis. He made his way with initially very little—just his wit and a small inheritance from his grandfather and parents amounting to less than 14£. Despite difficult circumstances, Creagh was industrious and savvy and turned his small bequest into a legacy. Initially working as a painter, he eventually ran his own business contracting workers out to a variety of projects. He was an industrious shipbuilder and was also responsible for constructing Bladen's Folly—the governor's house. He was integral to the building of Annapolis as a large port city. Wisely he used indentured servants and some convicts for a fair amount of his labor and located skilled expert craftsmen when necessary for important jobs that required them. "Industrious" is an understatement when describing Creagh.[10] Among many other ventures he opened a brewery on Maryland Avenue in Annapolis. The brewery was quite a vast operation that included a large brick brew-house, a malt kiln, a copper brew kettle and still, and brewing utensils, along with lots of land and tenement housing.[11]

Since Creagh was malting his own barley, consistency would have been established in at least part of his brewing process. Even if a brewer had no malting experience, many malting recipes were available at the time. With the proceeds of his business ventures Creagh was able to purchase three lots on Prince George Street in Annapolis for 190£. One would become his home residence, which he shared with his family. This home at 156 Prince George Street still stands today and is a noted historic landmark, demonstrating exquisite eighteenth-century craftsmanship and the perseverance of a motivated Irish immigrant bent on success and building his community.[12] Although Creagh would attempt to sell the brewery after only six years of operation, it was a testament to his ability to capitalize on his business acumen. But he also knew when to get out.

A tavern eventually opened on the site of Creagh's former brewery in March of 1773. Patrick Tonry advertised a tavern operation that provided stables for customers' horses, a weekly wagon service to and from Baltimore town, and many types of liquor to choose from like Geneva (gin). When purchasing the property Tonry had the copper brewing kettle, distillery, and tools at his disposal. Although he advertised for bushels of rye and barley, he requested delivery to his home, not his business. It is speculation to assume he was brewing at the tavern, but it is clear from the advertisements he was

Patrick Creagh House, Annapolis (HABS)

distilling.[13] Unfortunately for Tonry, he was deeply indebted and petitioned the county for relief in less than two years. Denied this relief, he began selling off his brewing and distilling equipment and closed the tavern.[14]

Despite the lack of success for the breweries in Annapolis and the surrounding area, brewers continued to try their hand at the brewing business. John Juedy opened his brewery on Prince George and East streets in Annapolis in 1764. Juedy not only malted his own barley and rye but was also a cooper, sold yeast, and grew his own hops on brewery lands (the first known in colonial Maryland). He advertised his strong beer for thirty-two shillings per barrel and his table beer for fifteen shillings per barrel, a great deal by today's measure but a price increase over what Gibson had been charging.[15] Within a year the brewery property was up for sale. Once again there is not enough extant historical information to determine the reasoning for the closure, but inferences can be made as to population, quality, and competition.

The meager success of the colonial breweries in and around Annapolis was not a deterrent to some eager brewers. Just south of Annapolis in South River (near London-towne) James MacKubbin (great-grandson of Patrick Craegh) attempted brewery operations prior to 1772.[16] Operations for MacKubbin appear to be short lived. By 1772 the brewery was taken over by another brewer hoping to make a success of it. By 1774 it was unclear if MacKubbin was still operating as a brewer or working a few careers at once. Correspondence between British exporter Joshua Johnson and James MacKubbin in April 1774 suggests MacKubbin was at this time just a merchant (no longer a brewer) in Annapolis selling British goods. This also provides insight into how difficult things were after the Boston Tea Party and the impending Intolerable Acts of Lord North and the British Parliament under King George III, as Johnson warned of the potential loss of funds and shared concerns over whether Americans would resist or submit.[17] Since no letters address MacKubbin prior to 1774, it appeared to be a recent arrangement. It was unclear why MacKubbin ventured out of the brewing business but the plant was being operated by John Broderick beginning in 1772. Broderick ventured into substitutes (Indian corn and rye) in addition to the barley malt brews.[18] This too would be a short-lived venture. No postings indicate if he was successful or carried out brewing operations beyond 1772. Scholarly inference suggests either the inclusion of substitute ingredients was unfavorable or the beating of drums toward the fight for American Independence played a role in the closure of the brewery.

A more successful brewery during the colonial period can be found on the Eastern Shore, in Queen Anne's County at Wye Island. The brewery was established in 1770 by John Beale Bordley. Bordley did not build the brewery for commercial purposes per se but did construct it for use by his family, servants and slaves. He developed an interest in the growing of hops while on his farm in Baltimore. He inherited half of Wye Island through his wife Margaret Chew, and when he moved to Wye Island he continued to dedicate his studies to rural agriculture and considerations of hop farming and productivity. Bordley was an innovative thinker when it came to agriculture. He eschewed standard agricultural practices for more untested but sound operations. He experimented with soil improvements using gypsum and marl, in addition to planting an eight-field system.

The eight-field system replaced the European standard three-field system, which left one field fallow each year while rotating seasonal crops on the other two to replenish the soil. Bordley experimented with a variety of potentially harvestable plants like hops.[19] It is interesting to note that he was engrossed in the study of hop production as it related to his understanding of the preferential taste of beer over spirits and wine.[20] He detailed much with regard to his experimentation with beer and temperance, including recipes and methods of brewing. He also promoted the idea of self-sufficiency for farmers with his eye toward the impending revolution. Bordley practiced his preachings. His farm was completely self-sufficient, as he not only produced his own beer and wine, he also owned a tannery to make leather, processed wool for cloth, and manufactured salt from the Wye River.[21] Many of Bordley's agricultural experiments became the standard for farming in America after the Revolution. After twenty-one years at Wye Island, Bordley closed the brewery and moved north.[22] This appeared to be a personal decision related to where he chose to spend his retiring years with his second wife, Mrs. John Miffin of Philadelphia.[23] Consequently, production of the brewery was not a relevant factor in his decision making, although he continued his agricultural pursuits.

Other colonial-era breweries that opened in Frederick, Maryland, met with much greater success. The Charlton family of Frederick was granted land in 1736 by Governor Ogle.[24] This land was located west of the Susquehanna River in disputed territory between Frederick and Baltimore counties. The family was essential to the burgeoning town of Frederick. John Charlton was a defining factor in the fomenting of Frederick when he began brewing operations in his mother's tavern. The brewery adjoined the tavern and was operational beginning in 1746. The tavern on Market and Patrick streets served as the ersatz courthouse until the original courthouse was eventually erected in

1756. Charlton also played a critical role in growing Frederick when he was appointed overseer of the road from Frederick to Dulaney Mills while at the same time running the brewery. He purchased quite a bit of land around Frederick, amassing wealth and the opportunity to rent and sell the property.[25] Unlike the Annapolis breweries, Charlton successfully ran this English-style brewery in the heart of German-founded Frederick, until his death in 1766, perhaps appealing to the divergent palates found across the city. The family continued to prosper in Frederick quite prominently, although none were known to be brewers other than John.[26]

Another successful Frederick brewer was Balser Heck, a German immigrant believed to have opened his brewery in 1760. The Charles Carroll papers indicated that Heck supported his brewery with other business operations that included selling horses, as he was noted to have sold a horse to Charles Carroll in 1771 for 14.10 £ Sterling.[27] Heck must have produced a fine product, perhaps even a luxury one considering that an Annapolis merchant, James Dick & Stewart, included Heck's beer prominently in their advertisements along with fine Madeira from New York and other luxuries.[28] Heck successfully continued brewing until his death in 1790, a testament to the quality of the beer produced. Neither his widow, Eve Margaret, nor his children (all under the age of 21) chose to continue brewing operations and instead sold the brewery.[29] A staple of the community for three decades, the brewery proved a great loss for Frederick consumers at the time.

The most successful colonial-era breweries were to be found in Baltimore. Estab-

Baltimore town as it appeared in 1752 (NYPL).

lished in 1729, the town of Baltimore was initially a small town made up of sixty one-acre lots surrounded by a stockade fence with three gates and situated on a tract of land known as Cole's Harbor. Within a few years the territory was expanded to include access to freshwater sources, and this area was named Jonestown. Eventually this area would be joined to Baltimore as one unified town.[30] The town would continue to be enlarged every few years as wharves were constructed to manage shipping trade. Lots were offered for reasonable prices, and the population began to grow. Western settlements that planted grain directed greater commercial activity to the Chesapeake. The building of the Monocacy Road from Frederick to Baltimore solidified Baltimore's role as a commerce center in the latter half of the 18th century. Cecil County also began to transfer its industry to Baltimore after a devastating hurricane in 1769 left Charlestown with shallow-water ports that no longer supported the large ships filled with cargo.

Baltimore was not meant to be the main hub of activity for Maryland shipping and industry but became so by default. The long route along the Patapsco River to Baltimore was considered to be less than ideal by early merchant vessels, thus making for an unsuitable port. Elkridge Landing was the prime location settlers believed would be the center of commerce, as envisioned by the Dorsey brothers. Unfortunately, strip mining and deforestation contributed to erosion silting the harbor at Elkridge Landing, rendering it no longer navigable by large ships, thus forcing trade and shipping to Baltimore's harbor.[31] The growth of Baltimore as a major commercial hub combined with the increase in German immigrants from Europe into Baltimore (and Pennsylvania) due to the War of Austrian Succession, the desire for religious freedom, and the promise of cheap land.

In 1748, John Leonard Barnitz, a German immigrant from Falkenstein, Germany (by way of York, Pennsylvania), established Baltimore's first industry—a brewery on the corners of Hanover and Baltimore streets. Barnitz was a brewer in York, Pennsylvania, who had run a brewery in Hanover, Pennsylvania, before moving to Baltimore and building a brewery there.[32] Taking into consideration the standard practice of home brewing and the failure of so many breweries in colonial Maryland, it was a great risk for Barnitz. Despite these potential obstacles to success, the brewery was a winner. The Barnitz family produced good quality beer demanded throughout the town. This was due in no small part to Barnitz's extensive brewing experience and proven record of operating successful breweries in America.

Not only did the Barnitz family establish the first brewery in Baltimore but they also helped to establish one of the earliest churches in Baltimore, Zion Church in 1755.[33] The Barnitz family would not be the only family of brewers to congregate at the church throughout its storied history. Zion Church became known as the "brewer's church" due to the large number of German brewers who attended services there over the centuries. Prior to the formation of the church, families were worshipping alone or together in homes. Sometimes they would congregate at St. Paul's Parish, which was the Anglican Church. Since Maryland was an English colony, all citizens, regardless of denomination, were required to pay taxes to support the Anglican Church, a situation that also entitled them to the use of the church.[34] The worshippers had to pay for their own pastor to tend to their flock, but they could afford only occasional traveling reverends.

A split grew, however, between the Anglican Church and the German Lutherans, in part due to the unscrupulous nature of a few of the traveling pastors. The Germans were forced back to worship in private homes. Eventually an honorable German pastor, John George Barger, came down regularly from Pennsylvania to tend to the flock beginning in 1755.[35] This is when the congregation officially formed. The Germans of Baltimore at this time were split between the Lutherans and the Reformed (Calvinists), and the plan was to build one church they would share. This would never come to pass, as tensions flared between the groups. Zion was constructed by the Lutherans alone.[36] Lots were acquired and plans for construction were underway in 1758. Since the process had taken so long, it was necessary to hire a new pastor, and the Reverend Johann Kirchner tended the flock until the church on Fish Street and the Jones Falls was finally constructed in 1762.[37] It was John Leonard's son Elias Daniel Barnitz who helped to found the congregation and the church after the death of his father.[38] The Barnitz brewery would continue operations throughout the trials of establishing the first Lutheran church in Baltimore. The brewery remained in the hands of the family through the Revolutionary War and beyond.

The second brewery to open in Baltimore town was that of Andreas Granshet, who was also of German birth. He positioned his brewery near the Jones Falls to take advantage of the fresh water and a location considered to be the edge of the town on Frederick and Lexington streets (not too far from Zion Church, although Granshet and his wife were Reformed Lutherans who attended the First German Reformed Congregation).[39] After twenty-five years of prosperity, and having survived the Revolutionary War, Granshet sold his brewery, cellars, and tanyard in 1783. The reason is unknown but he became the deacon of his church the same year.[40] Perhaps he shifted his focus in his later years to more spiritual obligations.

The last colonial brewer in Baltimore established his brewery at the juncture of Gay and Lombard streets. An Irish immigrant, James Sterett learned brewing in Lancaster, Pennsylvania, and opened his own brewery in Carlisle, Pennsylvania before moving to Baltimore in 1761 shortly after the death of his father. Sterett not only established a brewery with a malt house but he also established a bank and partnered in a shipping business in Baltimore. As the third brewer in Baltimore, it would seem Sterett hedged his bets for success. In addition to his business pursuits Sterett helped found the First Presbyterian Church on 519 Fayette Street (the graveyard of this historic structure would serve as the initial burial site of Edgar Allan Poe a century later).[41] Sterett's diverse business activities proved to be a saving grace when the first brewery succumbed to an intentional fire on February 4, 1779. He immediately rebuilt a second brewery on Water Street shortly thereafter. This second brewery was also burned down, on November 4, 1783, but it was not rebuilt.[42] It was a testament to Sterett's brewing and business capabilities that the brewery continued operations during some of the most difficult periods of the Revolutionary War, sadly only to be destroyed a few years later.[43] The Sterett family would thrive in Baltimore as merchants, bankers, shipbuilders, and heroic officers in the country's military. None of them but James Sterett chose the path toward a profession in brewing, however.

BREWERY LISTINGS

Breweries are arranged in chronological order by region. When a brewery was sold during the covered time period the new owners are listed below the previous ones and the address appears as "same."

Anne Arundel County

Brewery	Proprietor	Location/Neighborhood	Years	Peak Production (if known)
Fordham Brewery	Benjamin & James Fordham	Prince George Street Annapolis	1703–1716	
Gibson Brewery	Mark Gibson	Annapolis	1746	
Creagh Brewing	Patrick Creagh	Maryland Avenue Annapolis	1749–1755	
Tonry Tavern & Brewery	Patrick Tonry	Same	1773–1775	
Juedy Brewery	John Juedy	Prince George & East streets Annapolis	1764–1765	
McKubbin Brewing	James McKubbin	Londontowne	1772	
Broderick Brewing	John Broderick	Same	1772	

Baltimore

Brewery	Proprietor	Location/Neighborhood	Years	Peak Production (if known)
Barnitz Brewery	John Leonard Barnitz & Daniel Elias Barnitz	Hanover & Conway	1748	
	Daniel Elias Barnitz	Same	1749–1780	
Granshet Brewery	Andreas Granshet	Baltimore	1758–1783	
Sterett Brewery	James Sterett	Water Street Baltimore	1761–1783	

Frederick County

Brewery	Proprietor	Location/Neighborhood	Years	Peak Production (if known)
Charlton Brewing	John Charlton	Frederick	1746–1766	
Heck Brewery	Balser Heck	Frederick	1760–1790	

Queen Anne's County

Brewery	Proprietor	Location/Neighborhood	Years	Peak Production (if known)
Bordley Brewery/Distillery	John Beale Bordley	Wye Island	1770–1791	

Charles County

BREWERY	PROPRIETOR	LOCATION/ NEIGHBORHOOD	YEARS	PEAK PRODUCTION (IF KNOWN)
Muschett Brewery	John Muschett	Lot 28 Port Tobacco	1745–1748	

2

Revolutionary War Breweries

As the Intolerable Acts of King George III became even more untenable, the colonists responded by creating an "Association" that would later become the Continental Congress. These acts came on the heels of previously imposed tariffs like the Townsend Act, which taxed tea, glass, oil, paint, paper, and lead. In 1773 the Tea Act gave a monopoly to the British East India Company as the only supplier of tea to the colonies, resulting in substantial resistance from the colonists.[1] The result was the Boston Tea Party, where colonists disguised themselves as native Mohawks, snuck aboard the British merchant vessels and dumped 92,000 pounds of tea into Boston harbor. The Acts of 1774 were a punishment imposed on colonists who participated in the Tea Party. These acts included the Boston Port Act, which closed the port of Boston until losses from the tea were repaid; the Quartering Act, which required colonists to house and feed British troops; the Administration of Justice Acts, which granted British officials immunity from prosecution in the colonies; the Massachusetts Government Act, prohibiting democratic assemblies and instituting a military governor (by appointment not election); and the Quebec Act, granting all territory from the Mississippi River to the Ohio River to Quebec (French Catholic controlled) and thus taking away valuable fur trade from protestant colonies. The Association would enact legislation to counter that coming out of Britain.

As relations and laws grew more contentious, colonists began to consider a revolution, and changes came to the brewing industry in Maryland. It was greatly encouraged for Americans to grow their own hops and barley instead of importing any British ale. With the notable progress of brewers like Bordley, Barnitz, and Sterett, who were not only brewing quality beer but malting their own barley and growing their own hops, this was met with the hope of great possibility. With the nonconsumption agreement of December 1, 1774, made by the First Continental Congress, colonists agreed to abstain from consuming any British goods, including beer. Unfortunately, shortages of beer became a byproduct of the agreement and the push was on to increase production from breweries in Maryland and the colonies. This is when there began to be a distinct change in brewing in Maryland.

The rise of commercial breweries was a result of demand and of the war. Beer served not only as a regular beverage of the colonists, it was also the incentive for men to enlist! Each man who enlisted was promised a daily ration of beer.[2] Standard rations were a quart per day of spruce beer (or cider). Beer, of course, was preferable to colonial rum, as the alcohol was lower and the troops as a result were (usually) more orderly.

Maryland, it turned out, would play a critical role not only in the production of beer for the army but also in the Revolution itself! When Boston was besieged in March of 1775, it was Maryland riflemen (2 companies from Frederick Town) who were integral in breaking the siege. A year later the riflemen again defended the American position against the much larger force of Hessian troops in the Battle of Fort Washington.[3] In the Battle of Brooklyn in August of 1776, four hundred Marylanders under the command of Col. Smallwood helped to stave off the British onslaught so the Continental Army could make its retreat safely. They paid with their lives. While we do not have an account of all of those brave men, we do know they fought valiantly.[4] This battle was one of the many reasons George Washington called Maryland the "Old Line State": the soldiers' courage in the Revolutionary War.

As during most of the Revolutionary War, America (Maryland in particular) was always short on supplies. French military advisors hired to train the men for combat noted the Maryland troops did not even have proper uniforms but instead had blankets "elegantly turned about them." This lack of supplies also extended to beer, and the demand to manufacture beer in large enough quantities to supply the Continental Army with their beer rations was a priority. George Washington was, of course, holding up his end of the ration supply by (whenever possible) establishing his encampments near breweries or taverns that had a large supply of beer! In Maryland, brewing came out of the kitchen and into commercial breweries to aid the war effort. The Barnitz family in Baltimore was still producing beer commercially, although by the end of the war the brewery was left in the hands of John Hammond, Elias Daniel Barntiz's son-in-law, who renamed the brewery John Hammond & Co.[5] By 1794 Hammond was no longer operating the brewery and had moved on to farming.[6] The brewery was then operated by partners John Kendall and Thomas Kerr until 1796, when it became the sole operation of Thomas Kerr for more than decade.[7]

The Granshet brewery was operational and producing, along with James Sterret's brewery, throughout the war. In addition, in Baltimore there was the formation of another brewery to aid in the war effort, that of Peter Littig. Born in America to German parents, Littig opened his brewery on Eastern and Central avenues in 1779. Situated next to a source of water, ideal for the brewer,[8] the brewery met with some measure of success, as it remained operational for a decade, perhaps because of the war effort. The postwar years were not good to Littig's business and he was foreclosed upon in September of 1789 by his creditors.[9] Like other German Baltimore brewers Littig was a member of Zion Church and was even appointed to the vestry two years prior to his foreclosure.[10]

More new breweries were constructed to aid in supplying the Continental Army with beer. One notable brewery was established by Isaac Perkins prior to 1780 in Kent County on the Eastern Shore of Maryland. It was ideally situated on Morgan Creek, which provided water and transportation of goods. Although fighting had almost ended, the war was not technically over until the Treaty of Paris was signed in 1783 recognizing America as a sovereign nation separate from Britain. Perkins was a captain in the war and was known for caring for soldiers at his plantation, which contained grist mills, a brew house (capable of brewing over 30 barrels per week) and a distillery. It was noted that Perkins would brew for the men, just as he would supply flour to the Continental

Army.[11] His beer was advertised by Maryland merchants, touting the lack of the common "smoky taste" to his beer.[12] This may be the result of a number of things that were common for the time. Many beers took on smoky notes because of the malting process, in which direct heat over wood or coals would lend the smoky aroma to the finished beer. Perkins would continue the successful business, and even attempt to bring on partners or sublets in 1785.[13] The brewery would continue operations until at least 1792, when the brewery was passed on to his sons and their partner Ward, who may have come into the business in response to the 1785 advertisement.

One significant but previously unknown brewery was the only one in Prince George's County. It was located on a plantation known as Darnall's Delight, which was commonly referred to as the Woodyard. The plantation was named after its first owner, Colonel Henry Darnall. Eventually the property was sold to Stephen West and his wife Hannah. West was an industrialist with a mind to capitalize on the tension between America and Britain. He purchased Darnall's Delight in 1765 and immediately got to work adding a brewery to the large brick home nestled among the vast gardens and sprawling acreage.[14] This would be one of many breweries that supplied troops during the Revolutionary War and beyond. Stephen West, Esquire, served as postmaster and the Woodyard was his county seat. West, however, was also responsible for the production and distribution of linens to Continental soldiers, which made the Woodyard even more valuable to the soldiers.[15]

Another brewery of great significance would be constructed in Baltimore by Thomas Peters. Peters also served in the Continental Army and understood the great import of the beer ration. He wrote his memoirs a few decades after the war both as a commentary on his service and in hopes of starting a successful brewery. Retiring from service shortly before the end of the war, he believed in the necessity of constructing the largest brewery in America to supply American and French troops with their beer rations. His intent to use water transport for delivery was a good fit with Baltimore's harbor area,[16] and he constructed his brewery on East Lombard (formerly called King George Street) on the Jones Falls in 1784 after relocating from Philadelphia. Initially it was not on the scale he anticipated, but eventually meeting with success serving ale, strong, table, and small beers he expanded the brewery in 1785 and brought on more employees, including maltsters.

Based on advertisements from the time, it is also clear that Peters needed to bring on partners to help finance expansion and operations. Periodically these partnerships dissolved and were re-formed. In 1792 the brewery was called Peters, Johnson, and Company and was considered the largest in America at the time according to the *Maryland Journal*.[17] It appears Peters was eventually ousted from his own operations by the Johnson family in 1810, and began distilling operations in Bowley's Wharf. Doctor Edward Johnson, the mayor of Baltimore, continued brewing operations without Peters during the height of his own political career.[18] Johnson would help Baltimore City in many ways, from guiding them through a yellow fever epidemic to founding the House of Industry (which would eventually become the Maryland School for Boys) to sitting as a judge on the Orphans Court. His career as a brewery owner would come to an end, but his public service would continue to flourish. The brewery succumbed to fire in 1812 at a loss of $80,000 and brought an end to brewing operations by the Johnson family.[19]

Other brewers in Baltimore attempted to jump-start their businesses immediately after the war as well. Some met with great success while others did not make enough of a mark to leave reasonable historical data. Conrad Helmer Hoburg was an interesting case to note, particularly due to his changing breweries with the seasons. In the summer he would operate in Hampstead Hill (Eastern Baltimore Towne, not yet incorporated into the city) making strong beer.[20] In the winter he would operate near Griffith's Bridge in a brewery on Gay Street (formerly Bridge Street) adjacent to the Jones Falls owned by Captain Joshua Gorusch.[21] It is not clear why Hoburg operated in seasonal locations, but a logical explanation would be that he had access to cellars at his Hampstead Hill summer location when his beer would need cooler temperatures during Baltimore summers. Hoburg was of German heritage, and like many German brewers he was also a member of Zion Church. It is unclear if he ever used the Hampstead Hill brewery in the summer months after 1791—due to the lack of extant advertisements—but it is interesting to note that his wife Sophia operated a small brewery on Broadway and Fairmont in 1791, perhaps obviating the need for the Hampstead Hill brewery. It has been established that Hoburg was completely out of the brewing industry by 1796.

Another brewer of the time with a far more limited historical footprint is that of John Schriner. His only record is the line in the *Baltimore Directory* of 1796 where he is listed as operating a brewery on Liberty Street. He is registered as a baker just a few years later. Another Baltimore brewer who set up shop at least briefly in 1800 was Andrew Hoffman, at 17 Union Street. It appears he was operational until his death in 1810.[22] Little else can be determined as the records are scarce.

It is important to note that changes took place in perfecting and transporting beer at the same time as new methods of gauging and measuring beer were created in the late eighteenth and early nineteenth centuries. In a self-published work, *A Treatise of Practical Gauging*, Thomas Sullivan not only provides calculations for gauging the volume of ale and beer barrels but also goes to exhaustive lengths to walk the reader through problems in gauging these volumes and then takes them through the mathematical process of solving them.[23] The work Sullivan engaged in along with the technological advances of the thermometer and the early development of the hydrometer in the latter half of the eighteenth century demonstrate the import of the brewing industry in Maryland and America. Additionally we see the rise of glass manufacturers in Maryland by the end of the eighteenth century specifically for beer bottling (which at this time was often green glass).[24] Many glass manufacturers opened shop in Frederick, Maryland, most of them German immigrants who relocated from Pennsylvania. Just prior to the Revolutionary War until the turn of the century, six separate glass manufacturing houses were opened in Frederick.[25] This was much needed considering the lack of glass available as imports, particularly during the war, and advertised requests for glass bottles by brewers. One Frederick glass manufacturer was Johann Friedrich Amelung of Hettlingen, Germany. Amelung had eleven years of experience working in his brother's factory prior to relocating to America to establish his own factory. In 1783 Amelung barely escaped seizure by the British en route to America from Bremen with several dozen glassworkers. He carried with him letters of introduction from John Adams and Benjamin Franklin, which quickly helped him find investors with capital.[26]

John Frederick Amelung opened New Bremen Glass Manufacturing works on the

John Frederick Amelung House, Frederick (HABS).

site of the former Foltz glass factory in Frederick County. Immediately he acquired over two thousand acres of land around and including the glass factory. In part it stemmed from his experience in Germany where not enough housing meant few qualified glass blowers. Amelung began construction on the homes quickly and even built a school for the children of the workers where English, German, and French were taught. In large part, the factory was far too small and did not afford him the opportunity to produce the types and quality of glass he wanted to offer. Therefore he began construction on another factory on the expanded property by 1786 and followed this with a third factory shortly thereafter.[27] Amelung acquired his quartz locally from Sugarloaf Mountain and employed between 400 and 500 workers.[28] This also made things difficult, as it was not what he or his men were used to in Germany.

Amelung was mastering the business in America and even presented George Washington with custom goblets Washington raved about. Shortly after the presentation, Washington raised tariffs on imported glass in America, encouraging citizens to embrace the beautiful glassworks made in their own backyard.[29] Amelung provided all the necessary bottles for the breweries, from point bottles to hogsheads, in addition to tableware.[30] He was a renowned glass producer throughout the Mid-Atlantic. Unfortunately, he suffered great setbacks, one from the flooding of the Monocacy River and another from the fire that destroyed one of his glass houses. These disasters were financially devastating and Amelung was forced to take on a partner in 1793 to pay his debts to suppliers and investors. James Labes of Baltimore took controlling interest in three of the four factories. This was not enough and Amelung and Labes were forced to offer the New Bremen Glassworks for sale in 1794. This proved too much for Amelung and he suffered a stroke in 1794 that resulted in paralysis. He closed up shop in 1795 after he could not find a buyer for his factory, and he and Labes then petitioned for insolvency. Amelung died in 1798 in Baltimore, where his son Frederick had relocated.[31] Frederick opened Baltimore Glassworks with partners, including Lewis Reppert, in 1799. This would be a successful venture, carrying on the Amelung legacy and supplying glass bottles to brewers and distillers throughout Baltimore and Maryland for nearly a century.[32] As the 19th century dawned, bottle production increased sharply and grew beer type-specific. For example, Porter's distinctive bottle was shaped differently from ale or beer bottles.[33] Glass would quickly become the standard for transport second only to barreling.

A more successful and notable brewer of the early post–Revolutionary War era was Irish immigrant Marcus McCausland. He opened a brewery in 1800 on Holliday Street on the Jones Falls. McCausland had engaged in many businesses prior to opening the brewery: contracting, candlemaking and shipping, among other interests. He entered the brewing industry with vigor, advertising for 30,000 bushels of barley and large quantities of hops to begin production at the newly constructed brewery.[34] McCausland malted his own barley, limiting his external resources and cost. A series of ads ran regularly offering Porter, strong beer, pale ale, and table beer. He seemed to produce a fine product as he conducted his business well, and his prices were reasonable for the time: $1.25 for a dozen bottles of ale and $1 for porter. The ale was his most popular brew. The only issue came in the form of the flooding of the Jones Falls in 1801 that destroyed his brewery.[35] McCausland rebuilt the brewery and maintained operations until his death in 1827.

During his ownership of the brewery McCausland had many opportunities for bottling his beer, including Samuel Green, who began advertising his bottling cellar in 1795, a few years before McCausland's opening. In addition, the establishment of the Baltimore Glassworks in 1799 would have positioned McCausland to take advantage of the availability of glass in the region. Glass was still a precious commodity and he advertised the return of his bottles for a fee. McCausland did have competition from the other Baltimore breweries; a result of this was often the changing of brewmasters as they left one brewery for another in hopes of a better opportunity (this revolving door of brewmasters between breweries apparently hasn't changed over the centuries). One brewmaster who worked for McCausland, Samuel Lucas, would later operate the brewery after his death, keeping production at its peak of 7,000 barrels per year.[36]

Further competition in the postwar Baltimore brewing business came in 1804 from the Henry Saumenig family, who had immigrated to Baltimore from Germany. The brewery was established by Henry at 129 Camden Street (on the corner of Camden and Eutaw streets). He advertised strong beer, table beer, and malt.[37] Saumenig had the advantages a Baltimore brewer would have enjoyed at this time: access to bottling and a steady supply of grain and hops. He was an experienced brewer who had worked for other Baltimore brewers prior to opening his Camden Street brewery. Henry would eventually take on a partner, Johann Altvater, in 1804, a relationship that lasted until 1808, when Altvater left to open his own brewery. Saumenig continued brewing operations alone on Camden Street until his death in 1819. Considering the length of operation of the brewery by the proprietor and the competition from other much larger breweries in Baltimore, the quality of the product appears to have been enough to sustain a regular clientele.[38] None of Henry Saumenig's children chose to continue the brewery. Altvater thrived in his own operation, located at 44 Wagon Alley, not far from that of his former partner. Altvater was an accomplished brewer and also created a success of his small business. He remained in production with his sons until his death in 1819, and the family continued operations until choosing to sell the plant in 1827.

Post–Revolutionary War breweries were also established by former soldiers in Washington County, Maryland, specifically Hagerstown. The first of record was founded by a nephew of Jonathan Hager, founder of Hagerstown. The Hager family hailed from Germany and arrived in what was Elizabeth Town by way of Pennsylvania. Jonathan Hager (the founder) purchased 200 acres of land and established Hager's Fancy. He built the town around his property as he acquired more land, thus the town was renamed Hagerstown. Eventually Hager's nephew and Revolutionary War veteran Jonathan arrived in Hagerstown and established brewing operations in the late 18th century. He partnered with a former captain in the war, George Shull.[39] It is unknown if this was strictly a commercial brewery or the brewery affiliated with a tavern owned by Hager and Shull. The brewery operations lasted until 1800, when the records indicate the brewery was sold to Jacob Rohrer, Jr.[40] The intertwining of families and brewery operations was remarkable to note in Hagerstown as well as other cities in Maryland. Jonathan Hager, the founder of Hagerstown, sold his estate, Hager's Fancy, to Jacob Rohrer's father (Jacob Rohrer, Sr) for 200£. The Rohrer family would eventually establish the town of Rohrersville, south of Hagerstown, Maryland.[41]

Conrad Crumbach was also listed as a brewer in Hagerstown from 1800 to 1805.[42] John Cake was also listed in the *Maryland Herald and Advertiser* as a brewer from 1805 to 1815. It is uncertain if he took over brewery operations from Crumbach or started a brewery of his own. Crumbach was no longer listed as a resident in Hagerstown after 1805.[43] Other members of the Cake family are mentioned in Hagerstown, but none were noted as brewers. The most prominent Hagerstown postwar brewing family was that of the Gelwicks, Charles and John. The Gelwicks family emigrated from Palitinate country in Germany starting with Frederick Gelwicks, Jr., and his brother in 1735. They settled in York County, Pennsylvania, and eventually the family spread into Maryland in Washington County and beyond. Charles opened his brewery in 1805, and his brother John operated another brewery in Williamsport beginning in 1810. Charles successfully ran brewing operations in Hagerstown well into the War of 1812, when he turned operations over to his son-in-law George Brumbaugh in 1815 (Brumbaugh had married Charles's daughter Louisa in 1778).[44] Since he was already affiliated with the brewing industry as a tavern owner and Charles was still operating the brewery, the transition was easily made.[45] Charles's brother John did not seem to have nearly as much success in brewing operations. After seven years in business, John sold his brewery to Jacob Weaver (1817).[46] Records do not reveal the fate of Jacob Weaver's brewery nor of his family, although there are a remarkable number of Weavers in the region.

Another member of the Gelwicks family who opened a brewery in Maryland was Frederick Gelwicks. This branch of the Gelwicks family settled in what became Emmitsburg, Maryland, in Frederick County. Born just prior to the Revolutionary War,

Frederick purchased one of the lots originally owned by Samuel Emmit, the city's founder.[47] Frederick helped to guide the building of Emmitsburg as one of the three original trustees governing the city until its incorporation in 1825. Gelwicks was recognized as a strong leader and subsequently was named one of the town burgesses in 1841.[48] As with many of the early brewers, Gelwicks fomented the growth and expansion of his community, making it a strong city where people wanted to settle and raise their families. All the while, Frederick Gelwicks owned and operated the brewery that served the town of Emmitsburg, from 1800 until he died in 1851. Frederick's son Mathias continued the brewery for a few more years until it became unprofitable.[49] The Gelwicks family's roots are deep in Washington and Frederick counties. Many Gelwicks descendants continue to reside in the region to the present day, although none of the current family members have been known to continue the tradition of brewing as their predecessors had.

BREWERY LISTINGS

Baltimore

Brewery	Proprietor	Location/ Neighborhood	Years	Peak Production (if known)
Peter Littig Brewery	Peter Littig	Eastern & Central	1779–1789	
John Hammond & Co.	John Hammond	Baltimore & Hanover	1780–1794	
Barnitz Brewery	John Kendall & Thomas Kerr	Same	1794–1795	
Kerr Brewery	Thomas Kerr	Same	1796–1809	
Thomas Peters & Co. Brewery	Thomas Peters	Lombard Street & Jones Falls	1784–1792	
Peters, Johnson, & Co. Brewery	Thomas Peters, Edward Johnson	Same	1792–1810	
Edward Johnson Brewery	Dr. Edward Johnson	Same	1810–1812	
Hoburg Brewery	Conrad Hoburg	Hampstead Hill	1791–1792	
Gorusch/Hoburg Brewery	Gorusch & Hoburg alternating summer/winter	Back St & Griffith's Bridge	1792–1796	
Ms. Sophia Hoburg Brewery	Sophia Hoburg	Farimont & Broadway	1791	
Andrew Hoffman Brewery	Andrew Hoffman	17 Union & Penna	1796–1810	
Schriner Brewery	John Schriner	42 North Liberty	1796	
McCausland Brewery	Marcus McCausland	Jones Falls	1800–1827	7,000 bbls/yr
Hague Brewery	John Hague	55 Jones	1802	
Saumenig Brewery	Henry Saumenig & Alvater (1804–1808)	129 Camden	1804–1819	
Altvater Brewery	Johann Altvater & sons	44 Wagon Alley	1808–1827	

Frederick County

BREWERY	PROPRIETOR	LOCATION/ NEIGHBORHOOD	YEARS	PEAK PRODUCTION (IF KNOWN)
Gelwicks Brewery	Frederick Gelwicks & son Matthew (beginning 1845)	Emmitsburg	1810–1851	

Kent

BREWERY	PROPRIETOR	LOCATION/ NEIGHBORHOOD	YEARS	PEAK PRODUCTION (IF KNOWN)
Perkins Brewery	Isaaac Perkins	Morgan Creek	1779–1785	
Perkins & Ward Brewery	Issaac Perkins & Ward	Same	1785–1792	

Prince Georges

BREWERY	PROPRIETOR	LOCATION/ NEIGHBORHOOD	YEARS	PEAK PRODUCTION (IF KNOWN)
Darnell's Delight	Stephen West & family	The Woodyard	1768–1814	

Washington

BREWERY	PROPRIETOR	LOCATION/ NEIGHBORHOOD	YEARS	PEAK PRODUCTION (IF KNOWN)
Hager & Shull Brewery	Johnathan Hager & George Shull	Hager's Fancy	1792–1800	
Rohrer Brewing	Jacob Rohrer	Same	1800–1815	
Crumbach Brewery	Conrad Crumbach	Hagerstown	1800–1805	
Cake Brewing	John Cake	Same (most likely)	1805–1815	
Gelwicks Brewery	Charles Gelwicks	Hagerstown	1805–1815	
Gelwicks Brewery	John Gelwicks	Williamsport	1810–1817	

3

The War of 1812 and the Rise of Industrial Breweries

After the Revolutionary War there were notable shifts in Maryland to facilitate trade in the major port of Baltimore. Baltimore County funded the building of turnpikes west from the city to increase trade. The port of Baltimore developed into a major granary for sugar cane production from the Caribbean and South America. The overland route (via the National Road) across the Appalachian Mountains brought grain east to Baltimore, subsequently making it one of the major exporters of grain and drawing in more merchants and even more trade. Wheat, corn, and raw materials were brought to Baltimore from as far west as Ohio. The city blossomed, and her potential to become a major port in the United States was palpable. But it was not without challenge.

Although America had won its freedom as a sovereign nation, Britain was not done harassing it quite yet. Impressment (by English naval press gangs) was taking a toll on America, families, and trade. Beginning shortly after the Revolutionary War, British navy ships that encountered American merchant vessels at sea boarded them and seized any sailors they suspected might have been born in Britain, forcing them into British naval service. They claimed that since these men were British born they had by law an obligation to give service to the king, even if they resided in America as American citizens. Inquiries were often established with regard to many of these men that were "pressed," including quite a few from Maryland.[1] Britain had the largest fleet in the world but a sailor's pay was minimal and the work was grueling; therefore it was unsurprising there was a shortage of experienced sailors in the British fleet. At the time, the British were at war with France, and the British Royal Navy was the cornerstone of a successful defense as well as the linchpin for offensive moves against Napoleon (by the constant ushering of supplies to troops). America had formed only a nascent navy during the war of independence against Britain (the official Department of the Navy was formed in 1798 with Maryland merchant Benjamin Stoddert becoming the first secretary of the navy).[2]

The United States was incensed by the actions of the British Royal Navy and the attacks on American vessels. Both Norfolk and Portsmouth, Virginia, passed legislation refusing British naval vessels the opportunity to use their ports to resupply or repair. The rest of the country quickly followed suit. America was acting as a unified nation. An embargo act was quickly passed in 1807 to deny exports to Britain or any other country. It was disadvantageous, as it prevented American ships from leaving port except for those engaged in coastal trade with other American ports. This was exceedingly detrimental to the U.S. economy and far less harmful for the intended targets—Britain and France. The Embargo Act was repealed in 1809 after eighty million dollars was lost to America in exports.[3] The repeal—entitled the Non-Intercourse Act of 1809—stipulated that the embargo would be lifted with all countries except Britain and France. The act also banned imports from Britain and France and prohibited their ships from entering U.S. ports. This may have eased economic stress for Americans but it certainly did not stop the press gangs. American President James Madison needed to determine a course of action whereby Americans were no longer seized from their vessels and the United States was not being used for leverage by France or England in their continuing war. By 1812 there seemed no other alternative but to request a declaration of war from Congress, at the same time the British Royal Navy began to blockade American ports.

Once again Americans braced for war and worked in earnest on industrial beer production in order to supply the troops. America had a small fleet but quickly made her mark against the British. In August of 1812 the USS *Constitution* (Old Ironsides) had been refitted and prepared for battle. She set sail out of Annapolis commanded by Capt. Isaac Hull. After capturing a number of British vessels near the Bay of Fundy she eventually encountered the British warship HMS *Guerriere*, on the 19th of August. The *Guerriere* attempted to sink the *Constitution* with a barrage of fire. Capt. Hull waited it out, drew close to the enemy vessel and destroyed the *Guerriere*'s three masts with

HMS *Shannon* waiting to board USS *Chesapeake* to "press" men into British naval service (LOC).

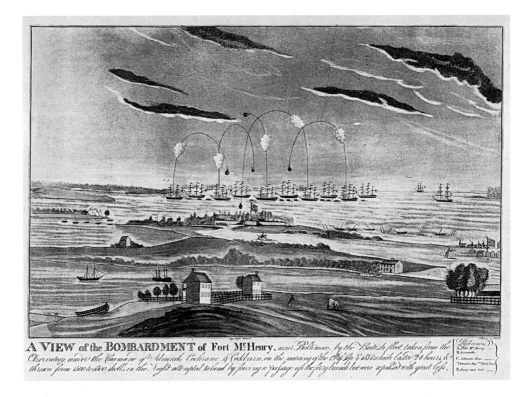

The Bombardment of Fort McHenry (LOC).

an onslaught of fire. Captain Dacres was forced to surrender the *Guerriere*.[4] This was a decisive victory and a morale boost for the Americans, squelching the voices of opposition to the war. Although America would suffer heavy losses during the war, including the burning of the White House and several government buildings, she would also find a way to persevere.

Maryland would once again play a critical role in the defense of America by thwarting the British. By 1814 Britain had defeated Napoleon and could focus all of its energies on the war with America. The Battle of Bladensburg on August 24, 1814, exposed the weakness of the Americans' defense when 2,600 British troops moved north on the Patuxent River towards Washington. Although the American troops far outnumbered the British forces, they were mostly militia, not regular troops, and were consequently unprepared for battle. The British quickly outflanked those troops that did not retreat and Washington, D.C., was left abandoned and exposed to destruction. The city and capitol were burned severely but not destroyed. The next target of Major General Ross was Baltimore. Baltimore was believed by the British to be the harbor that based many privateers inflicting corrosive damage on British shipping interests.[5]

Ross, under command of Vice Admiral Cochrane, planned a two-pronged attack on Baltimore. Ross would land at North Point on September 12, 1814, and head overland with his army, while Cochrane would head up the Patapsco River with his fleet to bombard Fort McHenry and breach the defenses to advance on Baltimore. Ross came ashore at North Point with approximately 5,000 troops. America's General Stricker was sent to delay the British Army with his 3,200 troops while defenses were reinforced and arrangements were made to head off the fleet. Stricker sent forward a small contingent of riflemen to scout Ross and his troops and disrupt their operations while he established his line of defense with six cannons on Long Log Lane (now North Point Road) near the Bouldin farm.[6] Stricker's crew spotted Ross and his advance guard out ahead of the main British troops, who happened to be finishing their breakfasts at the Gorusch farm. American riflemen opened fire, killing Ross. Two snipers, Henry McComas and Dan Wells, were credited with killing Ross, but both snipers were killed themselves in the subsequent volleys.

Ross's second in command, Colonel Brooke, advanced toward the American defensive line, readied cannons, and exchanged fire. The Americans were able to hold their position for much of the day but slowly retreated as night approached. By this time Major General Smith had Rodger's Bastion defended and prepared, with one hundred cannons and 12,000 men ready to engage the British. The next morning the British advanced towards Rodger's Bastion. Upon seeing the superior forces and defensive lines, Brooke chose to retreat, noting the number of casualties he had suffered when facing far fewer Americans the day before.[7]

This left the defense of Baltimore against the British fleet in the hands of Fort McHenry, with Major George Armistead in command of 1,000 men. On September 13, 1814, Ft. McHenry was bombarded. For twenty-five hours the British, hoping to gain access to the Northwest and Middle branches of the Patapsco River and the city of Baltimore, fired upon Ft. McHenry, which guarded access to these branches of the Patapsco River along with Forts Covington and Babcock. The fort withstood 1,800 rounds of mortar shells and fire from Congreve rockets, all while the British ships were out of range of Armistead's cannons due to the shallow waters surrounding the fort. When the British attempted to advance or send rowboats forward on the river, thinking the fort had sustained too much damage to retaliate, they were fired upon and suffered heavy losses.[8] After 25 hours the British fleet retreated back down the Chesapeake, having made no progress toward their objective.

Francis Scott Key was present during the bombardment of Fort McHenry. Key was a Washington lawyer aboard one of the British vessels to negotiate the release of a prisoner and witnessed the bombardment and the American flag flying high above the fort afterward. This particular flag was contracted to Mary Pickersgill by Major Armistead in the summer of 1813. Mary owned a flag-making business she ran out of her home after her husband had died. She was commissioned to sew two flags for Fort McHenry; one was a garrison flag and the other a storm flag. Mary lived adjacent to the former brewery of Thomas Peters and Mayor Edward Johnson. The brewery burned down in 1812; it was purchased by George Brown for $65,000 and renovated in 1813.[9] The storm flag, at 13 feet by 25 feet, was easily completed by Mary within the confines of her home. The garrison flag was much larger, 30 feet by 42 feet, making it very difficult to complete without additional space, as it required over 400 yards of bunting.[10] Mary asked permission from George Brown to use the floor of his brewery to sew the stars on the flag. He consented. Mary, her daughter Caroline, her nieces and an indentured servant worked diligently to complete the flag in the brewery over the course of six weeks.

After the bombardment on September 13/14, as morning dawned and the smoke cleared, Key saw Mary's garrison flag flying high above the fort and knew the fort had survived the onslaught. He took pen to paper and wrote "The Star Spangled Banner," originally titled "The Defense of Fort McHenry." This would eventually, in 1931, become our national anthem and our symbol of freedom. Although much has been made of the location of Key during the bombardment, the flag would have been large enough to see over four miles away. Additionally, there has been ample conjecture regarding which flag was flying during the bombardment. Due to the heavy rains during the bombardment it most likely would have been the storm flag. With the bombardment ending near one o'clock in the morning, and the rains easing, the garrison flag would have been raised before dawn.[11]

The war would officially end with the signing of the Treaty of Ghent in December 1814. The defense of Baltimore was the turning point of the war for the British. The flag-famous brewery of George Brown, unlike Pickersgill's garrison flag, would not last, however. Brown, a veteran of the war, sold the brewery to another War of 1812 veteran, Eli Clagett, in 1818. The brewery would bloom under Clagett's stewardship. He was the first in Baltimore to install a steam engine, a little one of six horsepower, which he used to grind malt. This helped increase capacity to a whopping 10,000 barrels per year. Clagett continued operations with son, William Clagett, at the helm until William's death, and then it was left to his widow and children. It became more than the widow could manage and an investing partner, John Danels, was brought aboard in 1849 to help save it.

John Danels was a renowned clipper ship commodore famous for both helping secure South American independence from Spain and terrorizing the British fleet prior to the war. He was acquainted with the Clagett family by marriage.[12] Family was the erstwhile commodore's primary purpose for investing in the brewery and helping prevent bankruptcy, and the brewery was turning a substantial profit with thirty employees once Danels came on board.[13] Danels' son became instrumental in plant operations and remained so for the rest of his life, eventually purchasing William Clagett's shares. The Danels family contributed to the success of the brewery by selling porter in porter bottles, as was the fashion and preference of the time, as well as selling ale, and beer. The brewery also sold malts, hops, and yeast daily, realizing an extra income stream from those still brewing at home.[14] By 1860 the brewery employed fifty men and was turning out over 16,000 barrels per annum, with total sales hovering around $100,000.[15]

Clagett and Company was well known for employing free black brewers and workers, even before the outbreak of the Civil War. One gentleman, Benjamin Carroll, was employed until 1842, when he was injured on the job, losing his foot when it became caught in a wheel driven by a steam-powered engine. Medical attention was quickly sought and Carroll survived. In addition, from 1856 to 1859, Clagett's employed Pompey Williams and Asbury Bullet, also free blacks.[16] Thus Clagett's Brewery was one of the earliest incarnations of an equal opportunity employer. The brewery truly thrived under the joint venture of the Clagett and Danels families until successive floods (1837, 1868) and fires (1860, 1861) claimed the brewery towards the latter half of the century. The flood damage was extensive and the Danels family blamed the city for the failure of a retaining wall it had constructed when the city improved the Jones Falls. After two trials, the judge found in favor of the city and awarded no damages.[17] The brewery was no longer operational and closed in 1879, leaving a legacy of great service to America by her proprietors.

By 1820 Baltimore's population had grown to 62,738 inhabitants, a 120 percent increase from 1776. The War of 1812 did not discourage many brewers in Baltimore, and in fact encouraged the trade a number of them had already undertaken and attracted many to the city to build businesses. One such brewery was that of Captain Joseph Leonard. In 1808 Leonard operated what was the oldest brewery in Baltimore, on Hanover Street, the former brewery of Thomas Kerr (the original brewery of the Barnitz family). Leonard built his residence adjacent to the brewery and in 1816 erected a new, modern, and substantially larger brew house on the northeast corner of Hanover and Conway streets.[18] This new brewery extended beyond the Barnitz brewery, as Leonard purchased more lots on Hanover Street to expand. This brick structure housed a malt house, mill, brew house, cooperage, stables, and brick, vaulted cellars deep below the street. Steam power was used as well to cook the malt.[19] Leonard was responsible for constructing one of the larger breweries in the city of Baltimore, at that time second only to McCausland's. Leonard sold his English-style ale, porter, and beer until his death in 1820.[20] It appears the family attempted to keep the brewery operational, but they were forced to sell by 1822.

After the death of Captain Leonard and the failure of the family to continue operations, the brewery changed hands repeatedly. The next purveyor of malt beverages at the plant was Peter Gloninger. He renamed it the Washington Brewery. Under his direction the brewery did not thrive and he was forced to take on a partner to prevent insolvency in 1827. This familiar brewery operator was none other than Dr. Edward Johnson, who quit Thomas Peter's brewery after it succumbed to fire in 1812. With a modernized and far larger operation, Johnson perhaps saw his final opportunity at brewery success. This, however, was not meant to be, as the brewery was sold to John Krouse in 1829. Dr. Johnson divested himself from operations and fully invested in his political and philanthropic endeavors at that time.

Gloninger found a much greater measure of success in business with George Freinscht when he joined him as a partner in 1831 in his brewery on Camden Street west of Eutaw. Freinscht was an emigrant from Bavaria who arrived in Baltimore in 1826. He opened brewing operations a year later producing ale, beer, and porter at the former plant of Henry Saumenig on 129 Camden Street.[21] It is not clear why Freinscht decided to accept Gloninger as a partner, but prior to the affiliation he was involved in a court case against Christian Kauderer for the title to the lot the brewery was located on. Speculation would suggest a small influx of funds from Gloninger may have aided his efforts and fostered the pairing.[22] This was a small brewery, producing only about 1,000 barrels annually, but it was prosperous. Freinscht fruitfully continued operations after Gloningers' death in 1835.[23] Freinscht was also a founder and stockholder of the Baltimore and Rappahannock Steam-packet Company, which formed with the approval of the Maryland General Assembly in 1829.[24] This corporation monopolized transportation on the Rappahannock River between Baltimore and Fredericksburg for both passengers and merchandise. Like many Baltimore brewers, Freinscht explored divergent business interests with an aim toward prosperity. This steam-packet interest provided additional income until 1838, when he sold the brewery to Frederick H. Brandt.

Brandt was a member of the German Guard and a colorful character who operated the Camden brewery until it succumbed to fire in 1842. The scuttlebutt was that Brandt paid for the brewery to be burned to collect the insurance money. He had been investigated in February of 1838 for swindling money and gold from a Dutch gentleman but was eventually released without prosecution.[25] Considering his involvement in questionable activities, the police took a close look at the fire that destroyed the brewery and charged Brandt with perjury and obtaining money under false pretenses but not arson. A witness, Joseph Minwegen, testified that brewmaster George Heiner asked him to set the fire because Heiner just couldn't do it himself. He also testified that he saw very few bushels of malt and bales of hops in the days preceding the fire. Several witnesses discredited Minwegen's account and his testimony was eventually thrown out by Judge Snyder.

Heiner swore an affidavit to the police that Brandt requested he set fire to the brewery and lie about the amount of malts and hops to collect a maximum insurance payment. Heiner later retracted his statement, stating he was "pressured" by police officer John Zell to confess. He also stated that he did not set the fire and that the voluminous amount of hops and malts in Brandt's statement was indeed accurate. Judge Snyder released Brandt and held Heiner for perjury.[26] The brewery was rebuilt fully and placed in the hands of trustees for immediate sale.[27] The destroyed brewery and ensuing scandal proved more than Brandt could overcome, and he filed for bankruptcy in November of 1842.[28]

Another notable brewer of the time in Baltimore was Samuel Lucas. He worked as a brewer for Marcus McCausland and purchased the Holliday Street brewery after McCausland's death in 1827.[29] Lucas would conduct that operation until 1833, when he took over the former brewery of John Krouse on Hanover and Conway streets.[30] Lucas quickly brought the brewery up to modern standards, installing a 6-HP engine to grind malt in an attempt to keep pace with Clagett's Brewery, which was producing over 10,000 barrels per year. Lucas brought production quickly up to the levels of his former brewery on Holliday, reaching 7,000 barrels in annual production by 1837.[31] He brewed beer, porter, and ale much like his competition but concentrated sales in his section of the city. He continued to malt his own barley, facilitating lower operational costs and greater concentration on the final products. Lucas came from a prominent family in Baltimore made up of lawyers, publishers, tailors, and seaman.[32] He alone chose brewing among the diverse interests of his family members, and his brewery thrived until his death in 1855, when it was sold to Francis Dandelet.

Francis Dandelet was a native of France who relocated to America with his wife Lucille.[33] He began in the import business in Baltimore, offering dry goods brought in from France, Germany, and Britain, and partnered with a variety of different merchants to sell his goods. He drew no satisfaction in his position other than the guarantee that America was now his home, as he became an American citizen in 1852.[34] Looking forward to an additional investment and more prosperous opportunity, Dandelet purchased the brewery of Samuel Lucas in 1855 and began operations with a partner, Enoch Wood.[35] Dandelet named it the Baltimore Brewery, producing his XX Ale, porter, stout, and beer.[36]

Dandelet moved his family, along with a few domestic servants and the brewery laborers, into the home adjacent to the brewery and sponsored some of his workers who emigrated from France specifically to work in his businesses.[37] Taking advantage of the advanced machinery that pumped and cooled the beer, as well as the steam power used to sanitize the casks and, of course, the 600 feet of vaults below the property, he worked to maximize the quality of his product and its storage. He had the foresight (perhaps from his previous experience) to dig subterranean wells below the vaults to gain access to clean water, which helped create the finest quality brew. Dandelet adapted quickly to the new venture and was said to make some of the finest domestically produced ale in America. One visitor to the brewery suggested this was due to his use of western hops grown in America.[38] Dandelet also had access to the malt house at the rear of the property. Although malting was widely written about, it was a process that required as much experience as finesse and was something Dandelet needed to learn. For the next decade he perfected his craft while raising five children and continuing his investments in other business practices. It was only the beginning of his long career in the industry.

Joshua Medtart relocated to Baltimore in 1816 from Frederick, Maryland, after serving in the War of 1812 as a 1st lieutenant. He was the son of German immigrant Jacob Medtart, a farmer in Frederick. Joshua's brother Jacob was a tavern owner in Frederick. When Joshua arrived in Baltimore he joined the Zion Church congregation, the "brewers church," but eventually helped to found another Lutheran (English) church, in 1824 on Howard and Pratt streets. Having begun his career in Baltimore as a merchant before entering the brewing industry in 1833 on Saratoga Street, he made brewing a family operation when he brought in his brother Jesse as brewmaster.[39] They embraced new technology and added a 10-HP engine to grind malt. In addition to the malting floor and lagering cellars, most of the operation was run by hand, allowing for a production of about 5,000 barrels annually, second only to Lucas and Clagget's breweries.[40]

Joshua was politically active as a committee member of the General Assembly of Maryland.[41] He ran for the legislature in 1829, and in 1838 he ran for mayor of Baltimore while serving as a general in the Maryland Militia.[42] After Medtart passed away in 1841, his brother Jesse and his son Jacob continued brewing on Saratoga Street.[43] The plant thrived, despite Jesse's leaving the business in 1847 to join up with brewer John Zwansger (another German-born brewer), who operated the former Brandt brewery on 129 Camden Street. This partnership lasted only until 1851, when Jesse quit the business, leaving Zwansger quite successfully to his own devices for the next fifteen years.[44] Jacob, as sole proprietor, saw great success, with ten full-time employees and the ability to charge almost $4 per barrel, until 1857, when he sold the brewery to enter into government service.[45] It was speculated that he was indebted and forced to sell the brewery despite malting his own barley and consistently operating as a top producer in the city. The new owners, Bayley and Blakely, expanded operations to increase production, but the brewery would succumb to fire in 1859 and close permanently.[46]

By mid-century, breweries were popping up all over the city. The first brewery known in Fell's Point in Baltimore was opened by German brewer John Laekauf in 1847.[47] Laekauf made small beer at the plant for almost two years, tapping into a local market directly on the point. Fell's Point was rife with sailors and others who either worked on the wharf or were new immigrants arriving off of passenger ships and looking for both work and a refreshing brew. There were numerous boardinghouses to accommodate them and the beer flowed. Lekauf's German beer operation was profitable enough to hire three full-time workers to aid production. The 1850 census has Lekauf's brewery sales valued at $3,400 per annum, more than a decent intake, but he wanted more. Due to the limited size of the brewery and the desire to expand operations he quickly relocated to a larger property in 1850 in what is today known as Little Italy. The Fell's Point brewery was eventually sold in 1851 to another brewer, Adam Lurz, who continued operations on Fell Street until 1857.[48]

At the new location Laekauf took on a partner, a brewer named John Ludwig who was already operating in the area, albeit less successfully than Lekauf.[49] Ludwig operated a small brewery on East Pratt with only one worker to help him. Although his brew was apparently quite good, the annual sales amounted to less than $1,000. This was not enough for Ludwig and he eagerly partnered with Lekauf in the joint venture producing small beer. The brewery operated well for three years until 1853, when Ludwig moved on to operate his own Berlinerweisse brewery on North Frederick.[50] Lekauf's business survived only one more year once the partnership dissolved. Ludwig, however, would do quite well despite a potentially devastating fire that struck his brewery in 1853. Fortunately a quick response by the fire department mitigated damage and allowed Ludwig to operate unhindered until his death in 1867.[51]

Fell's Point remained a desirable location for brewers, and Conrad Herzog was a brewer that would make a go of it and succeed. The largest challenge brewers on the Point faced was the lack of cellaring ability. The water table was too high due to the proximity to the river and the geography of the Point, making cellaring impossible. Herzog began brewing operations in 1850 in Fell's.[52] Although space was a challenge he was making decent money selling about $5,000 of beer per annum with two full-time employees, feeding the demand that was clearly present in the neighborhood.[53] He made an excellent product but wanted more than what he was able to produce in Fell's Point. He also wanted to change what he was producing. For that he had to move, which he did in 1853, just a bit eastward on the border of Canton where Burke met Essex Street.[54] This was where he would find success as a brewer for the next twelve years. Although he still had no underground vaults for storing and ageing his beer at the new location, he leased property from the nearby Canton Company for a site on O'Donnell and Conkling streets and hired a well digger in 1854 to create deep cellars 114 feet below the street.[55] This was all Herzog needed, brewing beer close enough to the market in Fell's Point while merely a stone's throw from the cool, deep cellars waiting to age his beer. So what was this new product he was making? Lager beer, of course!

One more Fell's Point brewery was that of German immigrant John Schwingler of Bavaria. After immigrating with his wife he began his brewing operation as part of a saloon he operated at 20 Shakespeare Street in 1853.[56] The diminutive size of the brewery and the lack of vaults prohibited production and variety, and Schwingler sold only common beer in his saloon.[57] With a desire for more profitable options he looked to move elsewhere and in 1858 moved to South Bond Street in Fell's Point. This was a vastly larger brewery than his previous plant, with potential for greater manufacture, including an area for picnicking consumers and their families on the lot, which backed all the way to Dallas Street.[58] Schwingler sold his former brewery to John Ramming, an

Canton Lager Beer Brewery, Sachse's bird's-eye view, 1869 (LOC). This was originally the brewery of Conrad Herzog, which later became the brewery of George Wiessner and John Miller. Wiessner left the partnership and eventually opened his Fort Marshall Brewery. William Stab (Wilhelm Staeb) took over operations of the Canton Lager Beer Brewery.

experienced brewer from Bavaria. Although the increased size of the new brewery allowed for more production and variety, Schwingler still could not produce the brew of his homeland—lager beer, as the ground was unsuitable to excavate vaults. He followed in the footsteps of many other Fell's Point brewers and leased land, in Canton in 1865 near O'Donnell and Fifth streets, where he dug out and properly reinforced lagering cellars. He rented out space to other Fell's Point brewers who wanted to venture into lager brewing as extra income. Schwingler prospered until his death in 1874.

John Ramming, the purchaser of Schwingler's former brewery, also made common beer at Shakespeare Street.[59] Although a native of Bavaria and a brewer by training, Ramming did not choose to enter into lager beer production. He decided that the Fell's Point brewery was far too small for his growing family and moved in 1860 to a new location at the northern boundary of the city on Harford Road. Here he built a general store with a small brewery in the rear of the shop. This served to foment the growth of the population to points north and provided a more than sufficient income.[60] Ramming continued to make common beer for his customers and family while also acting as a major force in expanding the city. He was noted to have been on many projects that helped to build and expand Baltimore resources, including Druid Lake and the Montebello aqueduct.[61]

The Rise of Baltimore Lager Beer Breweries

Baltimore was rife with breweries in the mid-nineteenth century and many brewers like Herzog took their chances at success in the growing industry. Occasionally brewers moved their operations to maximize visibility and sales. Some ventured into new territory—lager beer. This was what Herzog sought. With the construction of the clipper ships and the opening of the port of Bremen, Germany, large-scale changes came to the brewing industry in America. Since these ships could carry passengers directly to Baltimore in less than 30 days, German immigrants could bring with them lager yeast. This was quite significant, as lager was a staple of the southern German brewing industry and had not been previously available in America as it was viable for only thirty days and could not survive the journey across the Atlantic. Traditionally, lager beers were produced in southern Germany, specifically Bavaria from Würtzburg to Rosenheim. With the speed of the clipper ships and German immigrants from Bavaria lager beer became a reality, and Maryland embraced it thoroughly.

One such brewer was Conrad Hoffman, a Bavarian immigrant who began operations in 1847 at a small plant located on West Mulberry Street in Baltimore. Hoffman chose to relocate to 53 Pennsylvania Avenue in 1849 after leasing acreage from lawyer and early Baltimore land speculator Henry Shirk.[62] Taking advantage of the viable yeast, Hoffman made his lager well and his prices competitive. Although he started off small, with only one employee, making barely enough to survive in 1850, by 1859 he was fetching $1.50 per keg.[63] This demand for quality lager beer also explained his arrest for selling liquor on the Sabbath, charges of which he was later acquitted. Despite legislation to the contrary, arrests were commonplace for brewers selling their wares on Sunday. If they were not acquitted they were usually let go with a fine, the proverbial slap on the wrist.

Hoffman was a fixture in the community and began to expand his real estate holdings as demand increased for his lager beer.[64] Another property he purchased from Henry Shirk in 1854 was located along the Jones Falls, near the first tollgate. This location was optimal for building vast lagering cellars, and eventually, by 1859, Hoffman would transfer full brewing operations to that location.[65] The strategy apparently succeeded, as he remained in business until 1860, operating what may arguably be the earliest lager beer brewery in Baltimore.[66] He was careful not to distance himself from city affairs and frequently hosted the meetings of the Homestead and Land Association at his brewery.[67] He served as a member of the Taylor Light Dragoons, demonstrating his willingness to heed the call of his adoptive country if need be. He was much respected in the city. When he died in 1860 it was a testament to his life that his funeral was so well attended.[68]

John George Hoffman leased the land and brewery from his father, Conrad, beginning in the fall of 1859 for $600 per year.[69] He continued lager operations, renaming it the Mount Royal Brewery, and sold grain at 10¢ per bushel to supplement his brewing income. He, like his father before him, was arrested and acquitted for selling his beer on Sunday.[70] Many German brewers who came to Baltimore got their start in the Hoffman brewery, from Franz Schlaffer to John Schultheis, who later opened their own brewing operations in the city. Hoffman, despite his successes, struggled to profit from the brewery and fell into deep debt with maltsters H. Straus Brothers & Bell for more than $12,000. This was a sum too vast to recover from and his brewery was taken by the malting company. Those who knew Hoffman stated that he succumbed to the grief of losing the brewery and took his own life in 1877.[71] The brewery, however, would forge ahead in several incarnations after the Civil War.

George Röst operated breweries in several locations in the city prior to the Civil War, including the brewery of John George Hoffman. Röst was a brewer by trade who emigrated from Bavaria to Baltimore. He started his first brewery on South Bond Street in 1849. This small brewery supplied lager beer to his brothers' (John and Anthony) taverns, both of which were located on South Bond. The lager beer was extremely well received in the region. Röst was considered quite successful, and as word of his product spread his operation grew. By 1850 he was paying the premium monthly wage of $75 for three full-time employees, raking in $6,000 per annum.[72] He had strong competition from five other breweries in his ward including Herzog. He was also competing with Gustave Stuerlein, Michael Warner, Joseph Ruppert, and John Grauf. Only Grauf was turning out more beer annually than Röst.[73] Ruppert, it would seem, not only produced lager beer but also dug artisan wells, was a cooper by training (in Germany) and was extremely involved in the pickling business—a true jack of all trades. All of his businesses were located next to one another on a strip of Eastern Avenue, and all were successful among the growing competition.[74]

Despite this rivalry, Röst's lager was in strong demand and he eventually opened a much larger brewery on Belair Avenue in 1853 to avail himself of a greater audience. The location on Belair was ideal for Röst to build and expand at his own pace on vast acreage at the very edge of Baltimore. There was plenty of business, as it was the first large production lager beer brewery in the city, annually turning out around 15,000 barrels at its peak. Several other businesses were beginning to relocate to this remote corner of Baltimore.[75] Röst constructed massive lagering cellars extending over seventy feet in each direction to accommodate growth. To insure that travelers would come to the brewery and stay for the day Röst provided them with a shaded park, a concert arena, a bowling alley, and both indoor and outdoor dance halls for their pleasure. His patrons were served by white-aproned wait staff, lending both an air of class and an assumption of quality.[76] Röst's lager beer was of extremely high quality, fetching a full $6 per barrel, and he spawned an entire generation of German brewers in Baltimore over the course of two decades who wanted to learn from one of the best.[77] Röst, as was typical of the German brewers in Baltimore, often gave arriving immigrants from Bremen their first brewing job in the city. These brewers would go on to open their own plants after gaining the necessary expertise from one of the best, if not the very best, lager beer brewers in the state. Unfortunately, after Röst's death from heart failure in 1871 his wife Sophia struggled to maintain the quality of the beer, profitability dropped, and indebtedness to the maltsters brought about foreclosure in 1881.[78]

George Rossmarck also emigrated from Bavaria in 1837, not to Baltimore but to Philadelphia. He relocated to Baltimore in 1842 to open his own brewery after years of working for others. He had family in the region and acquired enough loans via family and friends to open a very small brewery at the juncture of Liberty and Saratoga streets.[79] His intent was to produce lager beer, but the first brewery in 1846 had no cellar appropriate for lager, and Rossmarck had to seek alternatives. He found in Federal Hill a very small production brewery owned and operated by Jacob Wohlleber, who produced ales. It was extremely suitable, however, for the construction of large underground lagering vaults. In 1849 Rossmarck was able to strike a deal with Wohlleber and the latter relocated to 68 North Liberty, while Rossmarck began operations at the Federal Hill plant

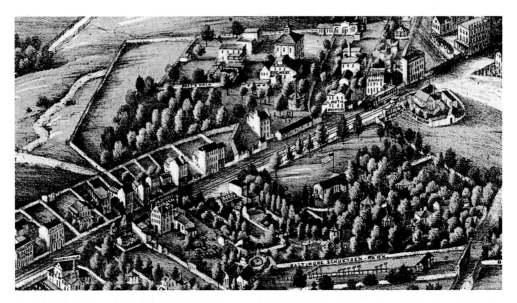

Belair Road Breweries, Sachse's bird's-eye view, 1869. The Wiessner, Röst, Engel, Muth, and Bauernschmidt breweries can be seen lining Belair Road, with Schuetzen Park situated behind Wiessner's brewery (LOC).

located at the intersection of Cross and Covington streets.[80] Rossmarck would succeed in the new location but Wohlleber would not. He was forced to sell, although he continued to work as a brewer at other plants in the city for years after.[81] The Wohlleber brewery was purchased in 1849 by the Auer and Lauer families, who retitled it the Auer & Lauer Brewery.[82] It is likely that the brewery was far too small to compete in the growing market and the Auer family left the operation, opening separate taverns by 1853.[83] George Lauer, however, chose to remain in business alone, removing himself to another location to brew lager beer at 128 North Howard Street.[84]

Immediately after relocating, Rossmarck got to work excavating the vaults fifty feet below the ground, using some of the natural underground caves of the area as vaults he reinforced. These massive cellars were connected by a network of tunnels accessible across from the brewery on Cross Street, allowing easy access to the lagered beer.[85] The same tunnels were used over the course of the next several decades for lager beer brewers, the military during the Civil War, and of course bootleggers during Prohibition.[86] By 1852 Rossmarck purchased another new brewery with his cousin Christian on 23 North Frederick, where they also operated a tavern.[87] The family, including Andrew, floated between the two properties. It appeared the Rossmarck family was attempting to corner the market in the city.[88] Unfortunately it was more than the family could manage and the Frederick brewery was foreclosed upon in 1858 and sold at auction.[89] After a fire claimed the Cross Street brewery in 1858, the cousins rebuilt and invested in yet another brewery, this time in Fell's Point on Aliceanna Street. Since Fell's Point provided no opportunity for lagering cellars, Christian hauled his beer to Canton and cellared under O'Donnell Street in Schwingler's vaults. Christian retained primary ownership at this new location, which his wife Anna took over after his death in 1864. George continued operations at the Cross Street location once it was completely rebuilt.

He too was repeatedly arrested for selling beer on a Sunday. In 1878 the brewery was finally forced to close. The Rossmarck family left their mark, however, and the use of Federal Hill and its viability for underground lagering certainly sparked others to open lager breweries in the neighborhood over the next several decades.

Edward Stiefel emigrated from Bavaria with a dream to construct a brewery in Baltimore. He partnered with Theodore Seeger and built a brewery in 1854 in Federal Hill. The lure of the lagering capabilities drew them there, along with the ease of constructing vaults within the numerous underground caves. Unfortunately, politics would eventually drive them out. A third political party arose in Baltimore in 1854, known as the "Know-Nothing Party." It represented a viewpoint outside of the standard two-party system. In the 1854 Baltimore mayoral elections Samuel Hinks, Know-Nothing candidate, won the election. The party also started to gain ground in state elections. The legislature of Maryland however was of a differing opinion. The Know-Nothing party was known for using gang-style tactics on Election Day, with gangs like the Plug-Uglies, the Rough-Skins, and Blood-Tubs either intimidating voters into voting for their party or scaring them away from voting altogether.

By the October 1856 election things had reached critical mass between the Know-Nothings and the rest of the state. Although Baltimore police were posted to control threats against voters, they supported the Know-Nothings and chose not to act. As a result, eight men were killed and two hundred fifty were wounded. The governor at the time was a Democrat, Thomas Watkins Lignon, but the legislature was increasingly controlled by the Know-Nothings, resulting in a stalemate.[90] It seemed as if the entire state was now in the hands of ruffians, and a resolution was not in sight. It eventually took the upstanding citizens of Maryland to undo the damage. They marched en masse through the streets with banners decrying the murder and violence of the Know-Nothing Party and their gangs. Polling places were surrounded not by gangs, but by

SEEGER & STIEFEL'S LAGER BEER BREWERY CARROLLTON, BALT. CO.

Seeger & Stiefel's Lager Beer Brewery, Sachse's bird's-eye view, 1869 (LOC).

CORNER PRATT STREET & FREDERICK ROAD, OFFICE No.25 GERMAN ST.

Jacob Seeger Brewery, Sachse's bird's-eye view, 1869 (LOC).

citizens demanding the safety of casting a vote free from coercion. Many Know-Nothings were voted out of office order restored, and new resolutions enacted.[91]

For Seeger and Stiefel, the ordeal forced a move to new quarters, on Frederick across from Mount Olivet Cemetery. Here they maintained operations together, selling the highly touted "Buck Beer," which was a misspelling of the German "Bock Beer," until 1872 when Stiefel began operations alone.[92] He improved the brewery, expanded slowly and brought in brewmaster John Knecht from Bavaria to orchestrate the lager process. Steifel never produced more than about 4,500 barrels per year of his lager. This was not only due to the competition but also to his political ambitions distracting him from the brewery. It appears the negative political experience inspired him toward civil service. The sale of his renamed Carrolton Brewery in 1892 was the result. The brewery was fairly technologically advanced for the time, with two steam boilers and two 20-HP engines helping to run the plant; but a large percentage of his overhead went to the eight full-time employees, and he wasn't recouping his capital investment.[93] Stiefel did continue operations at his inn, which was also located on the property, for a few years more. Although his brewery may not have been the success he envisioned, he was considered one of the foremost brewers of his day as well as being responsible for founding the Brewer's Association of Maryland in 1871 to protect and promote the interests of brewers and their industry in Baltimore and beyond.[94]

An area of Baltimore that was extremely promising for lager beer brewers was slowly drawing attention for the opportunities it afforded for lager beer production. One of the very first brewers to actually move brewing operations to Canton instead of just lagering the beer there was Johann Baier.[95] Baier was born in Bavaria in 1823 and immigrated to Baltimore at an early age. He had learned the brewing trade in Germany before arriving in Baltimore and quickly found work in the city in the same capacity. In 1850 he was noted to have been a brewer living at 30 Fell Street in Fell's Point. This is the same address for the Conrad Herzog, who also opened a brewery in Fell's

Point just prior to 1850.[96] Baier learned of the vast lagering cellars in Canton through this work for Herzog, realized he needed to make a move and began preparations before Herzog crossed the city line into Canton.

Baier looked to Canton as an unrealized opportunity for actual brewing instead of just lagering. Canton was so named because the original owner of the land, John O'Donnell, called it that after a port in China he conducted trade with. When the land was acquired by the Real Estate Company organized by charter in 1828 it was aptly named the Canton Company. The company purchased thousands of acres of land around Baltimore with the intent of developing the land for residences, manufacturing, railroads, schools, etc. Many of the names of the streets in Canton are named after the founding members, like Baylis, and of course its first owner, O'Donnell. It was not officially part of the city of Baltimore and technically was still on the outskirts of the city. It did demonstrate potential for a very specific manufacturing industry—that of brewing. This was due not only to the vast opportunities to create underground vaults for cellaring beer but also to the quality of the water, another critical component in the production of fermented beverages.[97] Several other industries were thriving from shipbuilding to iron and copper works, and Baier decided to take a gamble on success in Canton.

Fairly early on Baier had cellars dug on property he leased from the Canton Company in 1850 at the corner of O'Donnell and Third (now Conkling).[98] He eventually opened his own brewery in 1853 on Canton Avenue, east of Chester, and lived and worked at the Canton location.[99] The distance to the lagering cellars was still great, although shorter than when he operated in Fell's Point. With the excellent quality of his lager beer, he was quickly forced to expand. Baier would continue to expand his plant, eventually hiring Franz Schlaffer, a German immigrant from Bavaria as brewmaster. With the expansion, he also required more vaults to lager his beer. In 1863 he again took a lease from the Canton Company for property abutting his space on O'Donnell and Conkling. This space ran eastward from the property all the way to the next block. Sadly, the only way to finance the new lagering cellars involved taking out a mortgage to pay his maltster, Francis Denmead, in 1863. Denmead owned the City Malt House on West Falls that supplied malt to several of the city's breweries. This expansion allowed him to exceed 10,000 barrels of lager beer per annum.[100] It appears that for a time Baier's son Paul also worked in the brewery with his father, learning the craft of a brewer. Paul was married in 1866 at St. Michael the Archangel Catholic Church on Wolfe Street in Fell's Point to a Teresa Meiring.[101] Sadly his father would not live more than a few months afterward, perishing in June 1866.[102] Johann Baier's widow, Anna, was left to pay debts and operate the brewery. She quickly remarried, in 1869 to Frederick Wunder, a brewery worker who took charge of the plant. Paul eventually left the family business after the marriage of his mother, partnering with other brewers like Frederick Altevogt in his Canton brewery on Trappe Road.[103] This wouldn't be the first family to have a falling out over the disposition of the family brewery, and it most certainly would not be the last in Maryland.

George Pabst was yet one more in the influx of German immigrants seeking success in Baltimore in the brewing trade. He arrived from Pfalz, Germany, with his wife, Katie.[104] Pabst saw his future in Canton, the heart of manufacturing in Baltimore and the epicenter of the burgeoning railroad industry in Maryland. He had experience in the production of lager beer before his arrival and invested in the production of the most delicious brew at a location that provided the best opportunity for lagering—Canton. He purchased property from the Canton Company in 1859 on the corner of O'Donnell and Second streets, with offices on Elliott and Clinton.[105] Pabst was immediately engaged in excavating lagering cellars in the deep earth below O'Donnell Street. His brewery was quite prosperous, and his family eventually immigrated to Baltimore to join him in the business.[106] Pabst's Lager Beer Brewery continued to flourish as a family-run business, even through the War Between the States, which forced many breweries out of business.[107]

The western reaches of Baltimore City were fast becoming an attractive location to establish a brewery. Mathias Brandel was an active businessman within the city of Baltimore and decided the timing was appropriate for a new lager brewery in western Baltimore near the city limits. Brandel believed the new lager brewery would offer an alternative to the ales and small beers sold in that neighborhood. In 1850 he built his plant at 554 West Saratoga Street, where he employed seven full-time workers producing lager beer, ale and porter. It became the second most profitable brewery in the city in 1850, taking in $11,000 per annum. Brandel used a mixture of steam and horse power. He too constructed massive underground vaults with stone arches and walls to securely lager his beer.[108] He employed his brothers George and Frederick in his brewery. As with many of the German immigrants, families worked and often lived together until such a time as they could survive separately, even then they never strayed far from one another. At times the Brandels struggled greatly, from losing the brewery to fire in 1851 to misplaced deeds and succumbing to gangs attacking Brandel, his family, and workers at the brewery.[109]

No better example can be provided than the murder of his employee Balthazar Groeninger at the brewery. Shortly after 8:00 on the night of May 15, 1853, a young man and his compatriots entered the barroom adjacent to the Brandel brewery. George Brandel warned the man and his rowdy group to behave themselves, but things quickly escalated. The group shouted anti–German expletives, extinguished the candles in the barroom, and then pulled George Brandel down to the floor, where they proceeded to beat him mercilessly. Mathias Brandel and a few brewery workers grabbed swords hanging behind the bar and attempted to defend George and themselves from the onslaught. George was dragged out into the yard, a garden area of the brewery, by the gang, with Mathias Brandel and a few brewery employees in pursuit. Shots were allegedly fired by a man named Henry Winyard, resulting in the death of Balthazar Groeninger and the wounding of Mathias Brandel. Several witnesses on both sides testified at the trial. Despite identification from several witnesses, family members of Winyard testified he was not at the brewery at the time but on another street corner in the area. He was acquitted of all charges and released.[110]

Mathias Brandel was constantly under attack, even at home with his wife where they were randomly fired upon, prompting him to take out an ad in the *Sun* paper to warn off future attackers as he did in 1853, no doubt in response to the unsolved murder at the brewery.[111] Other defendants were eventually tried in the murder case when it was decided by prosecutors to move the trial out of Baltimore in an attempt to find an

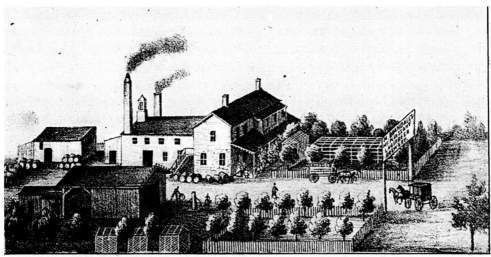

MATH. BRANDALL'S MOUNT PLEASSANT LAGER BEER BREWERY.
GARRISSON LA. N. OF FREDERICK R.

M[athias] Brandall's Mount Pleasant Lager Beer Brewery, Sachse's bird's-eye view, 1869 (LOC).

impartial jury, which translates to this: one that was less hostile to the German population in Baltimore.[112] Despite attempts to solve the case, only two of the defendants were found guilty of manslaughter, one of which was immediately pardoned by the governor.[113]

Brandel eventually succumbed to debt to his malt supplier, and the extremely busy brewery was seized by the maltster and sold at auction, including the famed "haunted vaults" below it.[114] Brandel constructed a new smaller brewery a bit further west, on Bloomingdale (Baltimore and Franklintown now) near Western Cemetery and the Cattle Yards—at the time known as Butcher's Lane due to the large-scale string of slaughterhouses lining the block. Brandel called it the Mount Pleasant Brewery, as, despite the surrounding businesses, it backed onto Gwynn Falls, where he created a lovely beer garden for the patrons.[115] Unfortunately the same financial burdens haunted him at the new location and it was turned over to maltsters in 1871. Brandel died a few years later, in 1877, when he slipped at the stream and hit his head on a rock.[116]

Another Seeger (no relation to the aforementioned) who immigrated to America seeking success was Jacob. He was born in Reutlingen (Württemberg), Germany, in 1809. He was the son of a silver-plater and trained as an apprentice in his father's business. By 1831 he was ready to strike out on his own and he sailed to Baltimore with a stout heart and empty pockets. For three years he worked as an indentured servant for a silver-plater, amassing all the money he could save. In 1835 he opened his own silver plating business on German Street, married the lovely Barbara Beck, and started his family. To say Seeger was industrious would underestimate his drive and determination to succeed.[117] By 1854 he had purchased a property on West Pratt near Smallwood and Frederick and opened a brewery, all while continuing to operate his silver plating business.[118] Seeger engaged in the lager brewing business in the far western part of the city, sensing a need to serve those in the hinterland betwixt city and county.[119] He built a malt house to begin malting his own barley. This prevented indebtedness to any malt-sters and provided consistency to his brews. Seeger embraced technology and installed a large steam engine to help not only grind the malt but also transfer malt from the mill to the vat. He constructed several massive lagering vaults with three-foot thick walls and two-foot thick reinforced archways below the brewery that included excellent ventilation for the lager beer. He had one vault dedicated to his winter beer that was capable of holding 1,800 barrels. It was his lager beer however that was highly praised. Seeger used a historic German brewing process known as triple decoction. This process enhanced the sweeter, stronger malt flavors in his lagers that the public clamored for—that taste of home. Seeger also constructed a beer garden where families could spend the day, as well as a saloon.[120] This was quite the draw for those in the city and the county.

Seeger was financially independent by this time, and as a result he was able to close his silver plating business in 1866 and focus primarily on the brewery.[121] He hired the best possible plant manager directly from Germany, Conrad Klaus. Klaus worked at the top breweries in Munich, München, Augsburg, and Prussia and was extremely familiar with the decoction method Seeger employed. As the brewery thrived, homes were constructed closer to it, and the stunning gardens drew many patrons. Together with his son Paul August, Seeger ran the brewery smoothly until he suffered an illness and became housebound. Paul was more than capable of running the operation, as he not only learned valuable lessons from his father, but he had also been sent away to New York to formally train in the brewing arts. Paul actively ran the brewery while Jacob, still possessing his mental faculties, orchestrated operations until his death in 1877. That was when Paul took sole control over the plant and continued the fine brew-ing tradition until 1888.[122]

An entrepreneur who opened his brewery in the western region on Baltimore Street and Calverton Road was a German immigrant from Holland, Thomas Beck. Beck arrived in Baltimore in his early twenties and set to work at a dye factory just a stone's throw from Clagett's Brewery. He eventually opened his own carpet manufacturing business on North Gay and ran it quite successfully.[123] Apparently it was his days near Clagett's or perhaps his German roots or a combination of the two, but Beck desired to earn his way only as a brewer of lager beer! The western end of the city was just the place to get it done. Beck moved his family to Calverton Road and built the brewery on a former amusement park and (appropriately) former beer garden. Access to the Gwynn Falls was ideal, and a fresh spring ran beneath his brewery, which Beck called the Rock Spring Brewery. He employed his sons August and Thomas Junior, who was sent off to Bavaria to train as a brewer.[124] Beck employed many Old World techniques to craft his lager beer, but he wisely produced ale, stout, and porter to appeal to the divergent tastes of western Baltimore. He also brought in other family members and brewery workers from Germany, providing them room and board in his home with his growing family on Calverton Road.[125]

Beck crafted a family legacy with the brewery, despite the fortune amassed in the carpet and dye industry prior to his brewing venture. He provided security and stability for future generations, enough so that he was able to retire from the business in 1874, leaving his sons to run operations while he consulted and enjoyed time with his grandchildren. The brewery, despite the lack of major technological advancements, was still a vast operation in Baltimore. The location was a selling point in 1884 when it finally changed hands. Thomas Beck made his mark on Baltimore, becoming a pivotal player in helping to build the western portion of the city. Baltimore however, was expanding beyond its city limits and many brewers aided in the redevelopment of its boundaries. Other areas of the city still held great appeal for new breweries.

George Neisendorfer was born in Baden Germany in 1820. He traveled with his wife (Mary) to America, as did many of his fellow countrymen, in search of cheap land and lots of opportunity.[126] In 1856 he purchased the former lager beer brewery of Orth & Olnton off of South High Street near Pratt.[127] The former brewer at the plant, Peter Krieg, was happy to sign on with Neisendorfer for continued employment in the lager beer operation.[128] He would remain only a year, as the brewery was located in far too residential a neighborhood and business was not enough to sustain his family. Despite this, Krieg continued operations at the plant after Neisendorfer's departure.[129] Like many, Neisendorfer considered locating at the northern boundary of the city, which was filled with travelers and in proximity to many other German immigrants. George Röst's brewery was located in that area and the word quickly got to Neisendorfer that the brewery of John Huebner (opened in 1852) was available for purchase. Neisendorfer quickly occupied the brewery on the 4400 block of Belair Road. The brewery was in no way advanced, and was in fact crude. The "vaults" were dug into a hillside with little to no reinforcement, and Neisendorfer set about improving both the vaults and the process, making the small brewery into a greater success than it had been under its previous stewardship.[130] It still was not enough.

In 1859 Neisendorfer purchased a lot on Erdman Avenue and Bowley's Lane, much further north and slightly east of his Belair Road location. As the population was expanding, so were the homes, the travelers, and other industries. Neisendorfer wanted to capitalize on this and build a proper lager beer brewery where he could take advantage of a greater number of consumers. He took his time creating a brewery that met his needs for lagering and potential expansion. He excavated "proper" and well-reinforced lagering cellars beneath the brewery and built a brew house grand enough to enlarge as necessary to accommodate demand and increase capacity. Neisendorfer continued operations at the old brewery on Belair while his new plant was under construction. Within a year or so he was operating only out of the new brewery and business was booming as anticipated. The product was more dependable and Neisendorfer embraced technology to create more consistent brews. By 1860 he was turning out around 1,900 barrels annually. He also housed the brewery workers with his family, paying the travel fees for those that emigrated from Germany. One very young couple, the Hamms, arrived together, the young wife serving the family while the young husband learned the brewing trade.[131] This was what Neisendorfer longed for—success and the opportunity to help others while building a community on the outskirts of town. By 1865 he was producing at maximum capacity and was ready for yet another expansion. Unfortunately he did not live to see the next phase of his plant, and his wife took the helm upon his death in 1866.

One of the few brewers to produce small beer as well as lager chose to locate centrally within the city. George Beck immigrated with his wife, Margaret, to America with some training as a brewer in Bavaria.[132] Beck worked for Joseph Keller, who had a small plant on Pennsylvania Avenue near Pitcher for about two years before taking over the brewery in 1860.[133] Beck quickly brought production up to around 500 barrels annually, more than half of which was lager. He paid attention to his consumers and met their desires quite well. It was a fine living he crafted for himself and his family, and he began to bring over brewery workers from Bavaria. He was paying two full-time employees by 1860 and was expanding the plant as growth and demand allowed.[134] The brewery was successful enough to survive the Civil War and continue operations until 1876, when Beck retired from the plant.

Throughout this period the population of Baltimore continued expanding, and a realization that the infrastructure was not supportive of the growth prompted change. By 1850 the population had more than doubled, to 169,054. The first concern was that the water supply was not enough to meet the needs of the inhabitants. In 1858 the construction of Lake Roland, a five-hundred–million gallon capacity reservoir, was completed followed by Hampden Reservoir, Mount Royal Reservoir, and finally Druid Hill Lake, which was a bit more ornamental than was practical. Also, in 1858 the old volunteer fire departments were abolished and control handed over to a board of commissioners overseen by the city. New steam fire engines were purchased and processes were revamped. Very few fires of magnitude were noted after the reorganization of the fire departments in the city.[135] Baltimore was doing everything in its power to meet the needs of the merchants, manufacturers, and citizens who populated the city. This promoted the success of Baltimore breweries, but those were not the only breweries operating in Maryland and many would provide stringent competition to the major port of the Chesapeake.

Carroll County

In Carroll County, we see the very first commercial brewery open in Westminster. The territory was once in dispute between Frederick and Baltimore counties. In 1827 Carroll County was established as a county unto itself. One of the citizens integral to the process was also the first brewer of record in Carroll County, Michael Barnitz. The name should sound familiar, as he was the great-grandson of Baltimore's first commercial brewer, John Leonard Barnitz. Michael Barnitz opened his brewery on 211 East Main Street in Westminster in 1821.[136] Just a few years prior to the brewery opening, Westminster was incorporated as a town, in 1818. Barnitz's brewing operations seem to have prospered with Westminster as it grew. He dabbled in wheat beer (*weissbier*) as well as the expected barley-based malt beers and most likely supplied the neighboring hotel and taverns with his products.[137] His was the only industrial brewery between Baltimore, Frederick, and Gettysburg, filling the supply gap of a much needed commodity.

By 1839 Westminster was adding neighboring towns of New London, Winter's Addition, New Elenburgh, and Pig's Addition to its limits. Barnitz was designated as one of the judges to hold the first elections of this expanded town.[138] It is in this same year that Barnitz sold his brewery after eighteen years of operation, perhaps due to his additional responsibilities as judge of the Orphan's Court, although advertisements for the brewery suggest that his health was not good.[139] Westminster was officially incorporated as a city on February 28, 1850, and Barnitz was once again designated as a judge to hold the elections.[140] Highly regarded in the community, Barnitz was active as a founder of the Westminster Academy in 1839 and a Freemason in the Door to Virtue Lodge, no. 46, in Westminster.[141] Shortly after his service in the Orphan's Court, Barnitz purchased 227 East Main Street, where he lived out his years. This home remained in the Barnitz family until 1939.[142]

After Barnitz's retirement, the brewery was operated by the member of another significant family in Westminster, the Zepps. They were not only integral to incorporating the Westminster Academy but also were deacons in the church and significant in the development of the city as lawyers and judges. Solomon Zepp was the only brewer known to be in the family. He consulted with Barnitz regularly on brewing operations to keep up the quality Barnitz established. Unfortunately, he could not manage the brewery and it was placed in receivership and listed for sale a mere five years after his taking possession.[143] It can be surmised that Zepp sought his fortunes in Baltimore after his failure with the brewery based upon this advertisement in the *Baltimore Sun* of January 1, 1844:

> A valuable brewery in Westminster for sale. The Beer is unrivalled in Norfolk, Richmond, or Baltimore. Brewery was not used to capacity. The former owner (a practical brewer) will give one month's instruction to the purchaser teaching the art of making this very superior article. Was $5,000, now $2000. The owner moved to Baltimore and retired. James Tracey, House and Land Agent.

Whatever fortunes Solomon Zepp sought in Baltimore, his family continued to thrive in Westminster. Solomon eventually relocated to New Windsor and occupied his time farming.[144] Carroll County entered a time following Zepp where no breweries existed within the county until after the Civil War.

Frederick County

In Frederick there was a more permanent establishment of the industrial breweries and far different challenges for Frederick brewers than those in other regions of Maryland. In 1817 Frederick County passed a law prohibiting the sale of intoxicating liquors on Sundays.[145] This legislation was primarily aimed at limiting whiskey consumption on the Lord's Day, as whiskey was preferred by most German settlers and was far more prolific throughout the city and county of Frederick. The breweries bore the hardship of selling enough beer the rest of the week to make up for the loss of revenue on Sundays, a time when many families took the day for picnicking (often at the breweries) and relaxation after morning church services. This was a greater challenge in an area where consumers preferred imbibing a more potent liquid.

John G. Lipps was born in Württemberg, Germany, in 1803 and like many immigrated to America with hopes of freedom and success. Lipps chose Frederick, Maryland, as his destination with dreams of a grand family business that would make an impact on the growing community. He was appointed justice of the peace in 1846 in Frederick.[146]

Serving the community was something very important to Lipps, almost as significant to him as building a large family and a successful business to support them. Like other brewers of the time he saw opportunity in the town located on the National Road between Baltimore and the west. As the population saw steady growth, more potential customers mingled with the travelers to provide ample sales for a burgeoning brewery. This was what Lipps sought when he opened the brewery on West Patrick Street near the bridge crossing Carroll Creek, a wise choice, as it was situated on the main road (turnpike) through town that would receive the most traffic from travelers.[147] It also offered a central location, easily supplying those residing within the community. This was facilitated by Lipps' purchase in 1848 of a large tract of land known as Long Acre, which was formerly held by the Steiner family. This property was part of Taskers Chance, a German immigrant-settled section of the town of Frederick originally planned and outlined by Daniel Dulaney in 1745.[148] Dulaney offered quite reasonable prices for the land in Frederick in the latter half of the 18th century, which had great bearing on the Lipps family's decision to reside there.

Lipps married a young German lass from Bavaria, Catherine Ritchie (from the same family as esteemed future governor of Maryland Albert C. Ritchie). Together Lipps and Catherine had seven children, and the eldest son, John, joined the family business with his father when he was of age and capable of contributing to the operation.[149] The entire family, along with three full-time employees of the brewery, resided in the family home, as was the German tradition. The children all attended school and were by all measures well educated.[150] In addition to operating the brewery, Lipps often helped out other Germans in Frederick who were in need, either by cosigning surety bonds or offering reasonable mortgages on properties he owned.[151]

The Lipps brewery was incredibly prosperous, despite peak production never exceeding 700 barrels a year.[152] This was in part due to the dearth of consumers in a whiskey-driven region, but Lipps was able to develop a customer base in spite of it. He began operations selling common beer and ale and continued across nearly the first three decades of brewing operations. Eventually he began offering lager as the yeast became available and consumers demanded the option. As expected, the brewery became Lipps & Son when his son John became a brewer at the plant. Upon the death of the father on November 2, 1881, the son became the sole proprietor. Like his father before him, John served his community quite well, giving back to those who needed him, thus establishing a lasting legacy.

One of the Lipps family competitors was Jacob Markell. Markell, who was born in 1786 in Pennsylvania to German parents.[153] Jacob had fought in the War of 1812 before relocating to Frederick, and this service had a great impact upon him, prompting him to advocate for both veterans and their families. He was integral in creating and maintaining a survivor's committee to enable legislation to grant soldiers or their minor children land as a benefit of their service.[154] Markell, like most of his family in Maryland and Pennsylvania, was an established merchant prior to entering the brewing business. He married twice and consequently had a child from each marriage: a daughter, Sophia, from his first wife, and a son, Frederick, from his second.[155] He saw a chance to move beyond his current vocation in 1852 when he operated his brewery in the former plant of William Small in Brewer's Alley on the corner of Carroll Street and West All Saints.

Small had opened his brewery in 1846 and was ready to move on in the tough economic times. It was a minuscule brewery, with Carroll Creek positioned behind it to carry away the wastewater from the plant.

Like many German brewers before him, Markell was quite active in the community he served. In 1856 he was appointed commissioner of the Frederick Female Seminary, but this was not his only role.[156] He was quite active in real estate investments in Frederick, thus providing additional income to fill the family coffers. He was incredibly enterprising, operating the brewery without completely extricating himself from his merchant business selling dry goods and persihables, in addition to all of his other responsibilities. This was sage reasoning, due in part to his advancing age coupled with the realization that after six years in business the more profitable enterprise was not the brewery. Markell sold the brewery to Peter Baer and spent the remainder of his life immersed in his real estate investments and his merchant business.[157]

Peter Baer was born in Weinheim, Germany, on Christmas Day 1822 to parents who were farmers and vintners in Baden. Baer successfully graduated from Weinheim City College in 1844 and immediately chose to sail to America and stay with his uncle while planting his feet in the fertile soils of Pennsylvania. He worked at the Upton Washabaugh Brewery in Chambersburg, Pennsylvania, and learned everything he needed to start his own brewery, from brewing processes through management. By 1857 he was ready to operate a plant of his own and sought out just the right opportunity. He found it in Hagerstown, Maryland, with another German brewer, Peter Middlekauf.[158] Together they operated the brewery on East Franklin Street for a full year. By September of 1858 Baer had saved enough money to purchase the Markell Brewery in Frederick. Recognizing the outdated condition of the plant, he invested in "first class machinery" to update the plant and maximize his advantage.[159] He accomplished what he set out to do. Not only did he operate the plant for fifteen years, he also expanded operations, bringing on two full-time employees within his first two years and pumping out more than 800 barrels per year. He quickly eclipsed the Lipps Brewery in production, with fewer employees.[160] Baer capitalized on his success and ventured into real estate, purchasing several houses that he leased to other German immigrants in Frederick. The time came, however, for him to focus on his family of four children and his French wife, Salome, he had met upon his arrival in America.[161] His additional real estate holdings were enough for him to manage quite well financially.

A seemingly renowned brewery in Frederick County at this time was that of Dr. William Zimmerman. The Zimmerman family was well known throughout Frederick County as not only leading figures but also purchasers of large tracts of land, helping to develop the region. They were among the earliest settlers in Frederick, aiding in the establishment of the German Reformed Congregation in 1746 in Frederick and later in Creagerstown in 1787.[162] Dr. Zimmerman purchased a large tract of land in Creagerstown in 1848 on Church and Main for $500.[163] The property was greater than four acres, providing ample opportunity for the construction of a large brick brewery on it.[164] Since Creagerstown was more than twelve miles from Frederick City, where most of the breweries in the county were located, the local population in Creagerstown was ecstatic at the thought of a locally produced beer readily available in such close proximity. Zimmerman opened the brewery in 1849, providing for his own family and the surrounding public, all while serving as a mentor for the University of Maryland Medical School.[165] As with many brewers of the age, Dr. Zimmerman embodied the role of multitasking while building his community.

Allegany County

Allegany County was another territory rich in the operation of breweries, and an influx of experienced brewers that wanted to establish themselves as the main supplier of beer in the community. Unlike in Baltimore and Carroll counties, the immigrants were not primarily German. In 1842 William and Michael Gessner of Switzerland founded a common beer brewery together on the National Pike, which ran through Cumberland.[166] It was an ideal location on the heavily traveled east/west route between Baltimore and Ohio. William arrived in 1841 with a plan to make his mark on Cumberland and the western portion of the state. His brother arrived a short time later. The location was ideal, as the beer was stored in the caves of an abandoned stone quarry for the summer just over the hill from the brewery.[167] Perhaps the desire for common beer was not quite what they anticipated or perhaps the quality of theirs was not what consumers sought. The brothers remained, operating the brewery together, only until 1850, when they would seek their fortunes separately, Michael in Pennsylvania and William in Baltimore to train at a lager beer brewery. After nearly a decade of training, William returned to brew in Cumberland. This time, however, he would locate in the center of the city, where his beer was accessible to all inhabitants, not just travelers. If success can be measured by barrel count, William achieved it. His new establishment, named the Washington Brewery, was producing over 900 barrels per year by 1860.[168] This was exceptional for the area and the time. He also began producing lager beer, a sign of his training and willingness to reach local consumers with the brew they desired. Gessner continued production until his passing in 1863.

Gessner was not the only Swiss brewer who relocated to Cumberland to pursue his brewing fortunes. Nicholas Hodel of Switzerland studied brewing at length before emigrating from his homeland to America with hopes of staking a claim in Maryland. In 1845 he began purchasing tracts of land in what was known at the time as Gebhart's Addition, located in the center of the town of Cumberland. Hodel took on a partner, Daniel Ash, to help purchase adjoining lots and expand the brewery he began in 1850.[169] The success of the brewery was such that Hodel continued to purchase adjoining lots and eventually buy Ash out of his contribution.[170] Hodel was always tinkering with new ideas and inventions to improve the brewing process and the final product. He used steam-powered machinery in addition to manual labor. By the continued expansion of the brewery to more than 1,000 barrels by 1860, whatever he was doing most certainly worked![171] He was able to charge more than $5 per barrel, which was a good price for the time and a testament to the quality of his ales. Hodel employed his sons in the brewery, as they were old enough and capable. He sent his eldest son, John, to Switzerland to train professionally as a brewer. For Hodel it truly was a family business, one that he passed on to the next generation when he died in 1861 at the age of 70. His sons successfully took the reins and continued brewing, constantly improving process and quality, until 1882.

It was not only Swiss brewers who enjoyed the fruits of the brewing industry in the ever-growing city of Cumberland. In 1850, German immigrant Bartholemew Himmler also opened a brewery in the city.[172] Himmler established himself in Maryland by 1844 with his sights set on brewing. He purchased a lot in Gebhart's Addition much as Hodel had done.[173] Bartle's Brewery, as it was called after Bartholemew's nickname, was located on Broad (eventually Centre) Street near Knox and Hay streets. It appears the water and foot traffic within the expanding city provided ample opportunity for parched beer drinkers. The topographical features were ideal and Himmler excavated vaults into the slope adjoining the brewery to store the beer through summer. It appeared as if everything was aligned toward prosperity.

Himmler had other plans, however. and chose to rent the brewery to his brother-in-law John Zink in 1854. Zink had been working at the brewery since its inception and knew operations like the back of his hand.[174] Himmler decided to pack up his family and move across the state line to West Virginia to open a distillery. Zink excelled as a brewer, while Himmler chose not to. Zink purchased the brewery from Himmler in 1858 once profits were enough to justify the expense.[175] Unfortunately his tenure was short lived, as he died that same year, leaving brewery operations to his second wife, Anna. Anna stuck with the brewery for about two years and was one of the top producers in the city, knocking out over 1,000 barrels in that year.[176] She brought in a brewer from Germany to aid her, Lewis Wolfe.[177] Eventually Anna retired and rented the brewery out to Gustav Stucklauser in 1860.

Stucklauser was also a German immigrant and worked for the Zink family in the brewery as a teenager when he first arrived in America. As with many German brewers it was common to sponsor a brewery worker by paying travel expenses to America when they came to learn the trade. Stucklauser stayed with the Zink family in their home. Since he was so young when he immigrated it is safe to assume this was indeed the case. He learned the craft of making common beer under the Zink tutelage, earning his room and board. It would appear that Anna Zink ran the brewery just long enough to allow Stucklauser to prepare for the managerial responsibilities of operating it. By 1860 he was ready and took control. He renamed it the City Brewery, happily taking advantage of the storage vaults adjoining the brewery. By all measure his training proved a success, as Stucklauser's brewery thrived until 1872, when he packed up and moved mere blocks to accommodate expanded brewing operations.

Allegany County was home to many immigrants from varying backgrounds who chose to operate breweries as their major source of income. One such immigrant was James McNulty of County Kildare, Ireland, a bright man who graduated from Maynooth College in Dublin before coming to America to escape the starvation of the Great Hunger (also known as the Potato Famine) in his homeland. He worked at the B&O Railroad for seven years until hampered by an injury he suffered when a train jumped the tracks. It was this very injury that sparked his desire to open a brewery, in 1859 in Mount Savage. He dug into the hillside adjacent to his home, where he operated the brewery, to build vaults to store his beer, ale, and porter. The unique and wonderful aspect to McNulty's process was how he embraced his heritage and brought the taste of Kildare to his brews by adding a kiss of Irish moss to his beer at the end of the boil for clarity.[178] His venture in brewing proved enough to supply and support his family of six for several years. In 1867 he chose to pack up his family, sell his brewery and home and return to the B&O Railroad to accept a much sought after position as a dispatcher in Pittsburgh, Pennsylvania.[179] The growing competition in the brewing trade in Mount Savage may have held sway in his decision to return to the railroad, although stories were rampant that it was a personal feud with a neighboring brewer.[180]

Another German immigrant who chose Cumberland as his prime location for a brewery was Frederick Beck of Württemberg. Surprisingly, Beck was a common beer producer instead of a lager beer producer despite his deep roots in Bavaria's lager beer country. The small brewery he built was located on Valley Road near Chestnut and opened in 1858. The location was ideal, and, much like Himmler, Beck excavated vaults of stone rubble into the slope adjacent to the brew house. In an effort to keep the consumers close by and spending money on his fine common beer, Beck also constructed a saloon on the lot near the brewery. To help produce larger quantities of beer that were also of extremely high quality (Beck fetched $5 per barrel) he used steam power to grind his malt, providing consistency in the grain size and hence the final product. Frederick Beck was an expert at his craft and mentored his entire family in the business. This accommodated a seamless transition when he died in 1861, and his wife, Sophia, and eventually his sons (and son-in-law) kept the plant operational for another fifty years! The brewery continued to expand and eventually began producing lager beer by the 20th century to accommodate the range of tastes in the community.

Henry Hanekamp was one more German immigrant who came to America to seize cheap land and realize big dreams. He and his brothers, with the entire family in tow, including Henry's mother-in-law and mother, settled on opening a brewery in 1859 in Allegany County.[181] The men held other jobs as butchers and railroad conductors while the brewery got off the ground.[182] As money and time permitted, the most advanced technology was brought in to aid the brewing process, including a 15-HP engine to grind malt and turn out ten bushels of malt per hour.[183] The brewery charged slightly less than the top breweries in the county, coming in around $4 per barrel.[184] This was by no means unprofitable or a determinant of poor quality but more a result of the brewery's location outside of the major city of Cumberland, where the population was smaller and less transient. The Hanekamp brewery made common beer and ale from its inception but over time added lager to the stable of brews. Henry eventually became the sole proprietor of the brewery, passing it on to his children and hiring managers like Charles Fredericks of Pennsylvania to run operations while he pursued other dreams. In 1879 Henry Hanekamp became sheriff of Allegany County and served proudly in that capacity for two years. But without Henry the brewery closed after serving the surrounding community for two decades.[185]

Washington County

Margaret Geak Butz was a brave young woman. Born in Hesse-Darmstadt, Germany, in 1815, a region well known for its weissbier, she traveled alone to America in search of a new life and to marry a suitor. She married John Geak of Frederick, Maryland, and bore him one son, John. Life did not turn out as she expected, however, and her husband died quite young. Margaret gathered herself, prepared her son and relocated to Hagerstown, where she would meet her second husband, Jacob Butz of Baden, Germany.[186] In 1840 she bore Jacob a daughter, Mary, and within a year opened her own weissbier brewery adjacent to her home on South Potomac Street. Margaret brought the traditional beer of her homeland to Hagerstown and it was an unprecedented success. It was a family business, as her husband Jacob also took part, and her son, John, sold the beer throughout Washington County.[187] Over the next decade, the German population of Hagerstown increased, along with the sale of Margaret's traditional wheat beer, which she produced year round to accommodate avid consumers. Margaret and her brewery on Potomac Street were a fixture of Hagerstown for decades, even as she outlived both her husband and her son. She continued to operate her brewery until 1868, remaining a resolute woman who risked it all to thrive in America, albeit not without heartache. Her daughter and grandchildren carried on her legacy through the memories and stories of Margaret and her weissbier brewery.

As mentioned in previous chapters, the Gelwicks family was quite established in western Maryland with regard to both land holdings and breweries. The Hagerstown brewery the family had previously sold to son-in-law George Brumbaugh was repurchased from the trustees of his estate for $5,000 in 1841 by a Gelwicks family transplant from Pennsylvania by the name of George C. Gelwicks.[188] George relocated his established family to Hagerstown at the prospect of new business opportunities, reasonably priced tracts of land, and a desire to help further establish the burgeoning city. He purchased almost ten acres in Hager's Delight, where he settled his family.[189] At the age of fifty-seven George took over operations of the Brumbaugh brewery, renaming it the Hagerstown Brewery. His son Charles was also trained as a brewer and worked diligently at crafting good-quality ales and common beer to serve both travelers and the erudite local population. A quick examination of the 1850 census for Hagerstown is quite revealing. There were innumerable lawyers and scholars residing within the city, and far fewer skilled tradesmen. Keeping the brewery open was paramount for the population at the time, as well as an accommodation to travelers between Baltimore and the west who would pass the brewery en route. George's family tree being rooted in the brewing industry was certainly a help, as he was able to fetch $4 per barrel of ale from the populace. He employed two full-time workers in addition to his son Charles.[190]

Gelwicks constructed massive vaults below the brewery to store the ale during the hot summer months, which aided in the quality of the brews and the price he could charge. He continued to purchase land around the brewery and the city and lived up to the expectations of his family and the community by building homes that he then sold or rented to new families settling in the area. The family productively continued operations at the 7 Franklin Street brewery for more than thirteen years. By 1854, at the tender age of seventy, George Gelwicks finally decided to retire and offered the brewery for sale, along with the substantial acreage, stables, and a dwelling more than sufficient for a brewer and his family.[191] Slowly the Gelwicks family sold off lots from the main property and manumitted several slaves, all in anticipation of retirement, until the brewery itself was finally purchased on September 11, 1855, for $3,450 by Daniel

Startzman.[192] Sadly, that same year George C. Gelwicks died, never enjoying the retirement he desperately sought. Startzman, a potter by trade, began operations immediately
since the brewery was fully operational. He needed only barley to get underway at this
new enterprise producing Old Time Beer and ale.[193] Competition with the thriving
Witzenbacher Brewery, located a block away, was more than he could handle, however,
and the brewery quickly changed hands. Perhaps it was his intention all along, to buy
it and sell quickly to an experienced brewer, but that remains unknown.

The brewery was next taken over by Peter Middlekuaff in 1857. The Middlekauff
family had been well established in Washington County for over a century, mainly as
farmers. Middlekauff was also a farmer prior to entering the brewing business.[194] He
took full advantage of the vaults beneath the brewery. Initially he brought on a partner,
Pater Baer, who later opened his own brewery in Frederick. The partnership lasted just
a year, long enough for Baer to earn enough money to open his own operation. By 1860
the brewery was valued at over $10,000 and fifty-two year old Middlekauff embarked
upon a lucrative real estate development career, purchasing additional plots of land in
Hagerstown. Some of the lots came from former Hagerstown brewery operator Daniel
Startzman, who had vast land holdings in the region and served as county commissioner
for a time.[195] Perhaps this was Middlekauff's idea of retirement planning. Retirement
from the industry would come quickly and he had returned to farming by 1864.[196]

In part it was competition in the budding town that made Middelkauff's venture
more risky. Andrew Leibold and Lewis Heist were trained brewers from Germany who
immigrated with their wives to America in search of opportunity, Leibold seeking his
future in Maryland and Heist in Pennsylvania. Both men grew their families while brewing for others until they decided to pool their resources. In 1849 they purchased a small
tract of land in Hagerstown on 112 South Potomac Street and built their brewery. Leibold had two children with his wife, and Heist had three sons with his bride. They all
lived together in the same home while the brewery was opened, until it became financially sound.[197] By all measures it was quite a success, fetching $5 per barrel of ale while
maintaining three full-time employees' wages at $60 per month.[198] Perhaps it was the
close quarters of two families sharing one home, although not unusual for the time,
that split the families apart. Whatever forced the tension between them, in 1854 Leibold
purchased Heist's share of the brewery and ran the plant alone until his death in 1862.
At that time his wife continued the family business with her son for another nine years,
providing strong competition in the limited market.[199]

One prominent Hagerstwon brewery traces its roots to yet another German immigrant who sought his fortunes in Washington County after departing Middlestadt, Germany, near Frankfurt. This gentleman was quite a departure from many of the German
brewers discussed thus far. William Witzenbacher was a linguist. He was fluent in both
written and spoken German, French, and English. This skill set served him well upon
arriving in America in 1848 at the adventurous age of twenty-five.[200] He opened his
first brewery adjacent to the home he occupied in Clear Spring, about fourteen miles
west of Hagerstown. Although Clear Spring had a relatively small population compared
to Hagerstown the road was traversed by those journeying between Cumberland and
Baltimore, as well as those building the railroad to accommodate them. Witzenbacher
produced ale in the spring and summer, demonstrating to consumers his brewing acu-

men. He resided in Clear Spring for only two years, a rather interesting accident prompting his move. His daughter told the story often that one day in 1850 when Witzenbacher was riding to the brewery loaded down with malt bags, his old white horse bucked him off down a hill. It was supposedly at that moment he had the epiphany to relocate his home and brewery to Hagerstown.[201] In 1851 he did just that, renting a lot on East Washington Street in the center of town. The brewery was still located on the main thoroughfare through town but was much more accessible to a larger population within his own city and could realize greater profits. Witzenbacher was offering what Margaret Butz was not, lager and ale. In addition, he was located at the opposite end of town from Butz and Leibold, assuring that his product would not lose out to excessive competition. His strongest rivalry came from the George Gelwicks brewery, which was located just a block north.

Demand for Witzenbacher's beer was more than enough to sustain his plant. He established a reputation for making ale so good it was known as far as Baltimore. As business picked up he purchased the adjacent lot to the brewery to build a larger home to accommodate his growing family.[202] He built massive underground caves below his new house to store his beer and accommodate the lager beer he began to produce each winter, becoming a full-service brewery year round to meet the financial needs of his expanding family. Witzenbacher's lager beer was described as dark (much darker than his ale) and sparkling, leading one to believe he was most likely brewing Bock beer.[203] This also provided an alternative product to his competitor, the Hagerstown Brewery.

All of Witzenbacher's children but his eldest daughter, Lillie, were sent to school, as education was critically important.[204] After his schooling his youngest son, Frederick, was sent off to Baltimore to train in the latest methods of brewing beer at the behest of his mother, Catherine. Once he returned, his father, William, refused to listen to what modern brewing "chemists" were suggesting and instead chose the traditional methods he had learned in Germany. His eldest son, William Junior, was also a gifted linguist, speaking Spanish and reading both Greek and Latin in addition to the languages his father knew fluently. The younger William graduated from Johns Hopkins University and taught at McDonogh School for a few years before passing the bar and entering fully into the legal profession. He eventually served as Hagerstown city attorney and held several governmental offices, including a judgeship in Hagerstown while also acting as an interpreter for the court.[205] The Witzenbacher Brewery would flourish in the growing city of Hagerstown until 1888. The family was integral to the establishment of libraries and the building of the governmental infrastructure, as well as making their mark on the brewing industry for decades. This was just one of many legacies left by the early brewers in Western Maryland.

All of the brewers, merchants, and citizens of Western Maryland benefited from what had begun in Baltimore decades before—construction of the railroad. To foment the growth of Baltimore as an epicenter of trade in the East and support the mounting population, there was great concern on behalf of the public that canals and railways be constructed to advance commerce and manufacturing. This prompted the creation of the Baltimore and Ohio Railroad at a private meeting of the most influential men in Baltimore on a clear night in February 1827 at the home of George Brown.[206] Ground was broken in April 1828 (with the last living signer of the Declaration of Independence in attendance, Charles Carroll). By 1830, the line was completed to Ellicott Mills and by 1835 to Washington, D.C. It took quite a bit more time to complete the rail to Cumberland in 1851, and eventually West Virginia in 1853. The construction of the railroad did not immediately impact commerce and manufacturing, but once it reached Wheeling the effects were tangible and everyone in Maryland was benefiting. The Baltimore and Ohio Railroad constructed a massive grain elevator at the port of Baltimore that facilitated this. The "Queen of the Chesapeake," as Baltimore had come to be known, was the center of both foreign and domestic trade. It all came to a screeching halt as the specter of war loomed yet again. This time it would not come from outside invaders threatening the sovereignty of America but from within, tearing the country apart, destroying the very fabric that bound her together.

Brewery Listings

Allegany County

Brewery	Proprietor	Location/ Neighborhood	Years	Peak Production (if known)
Gessner Brewery	William & Michael Gessner	National Pike Cumberland	1842–1850	900 bbls/yr
Bartles Brewery	Bartholemew Himmler	Knox & Hays & Broad (Center) Streets Cumberland	1850–1854	
Zink Brewery	John Zink	Same	1854–1858	
	Anna Zink	Same	1858–1860	1,000 bbls/yr
City Brewery	Gustav Stucklauser	Same	1860–1872	
Hodel Brewery	Nicholas Hodel & Family	193 North Centre Street Cumberland	1850–1882	1,000 bbls/yr
Beck Brewery	Frederick Beck	57 Valley Street near Chestnut Cumberland	1858–1861	700 bbls/yr
Beck Common Beer Brewery	Sophia Beck & Family (John F., Julian, George, John D.)	Same	1861–1911	
Washington Brewery	William Gessner	32 South Paca Street Cumberland	1859–1863	900 bbls/yr
Hanekamp Brewery	Henry Hanekamp & Family	Jackson Street Lonaconing	1859–1877	700 bbls/yr
McNulty Brewery	James McNulty	Mount Savage	1859–1867	

Baltimore City and County

Brewery	Proprietor	Location/ Neighborhood	Years	Peak Production (if known)
Captain Joseph Leonard Brewery	Capt. Joseph Leonard & Family	Baltimore & Hanover Streets extended to Conway Street 1816	1808–1822	

Brewery	Proprietor	Location/ Neighborhood	Years	Peak Production (if known)
Washington Brewery	Peter Gloninger & Dr. Edward Johnson (partner in 1827)	Same	1822–1829	1,000 bbls/yr
	John Krouse	Same	1829–1831	
	Graham & Silvey	Same	1831–1833	5,000 bbls/yr
	Samuel Lucas	Same	1833–1855	7,000 bbls/yr
Baltimore Brewery	Francis Dandelet	Same	1855–1871	10,000 +/- bbls/yr
George Brown Brewery	George Brown	Water Street (now Lombard)/Jones Falls	1813–1818	
Clagett's Brewery	Eli Clagett	Same	1818–1848	10,500 bbls/yr
William Clagett & Co.	William Clagett & Family; John Danels & Family partnered in 1849	Same	1848–1879	16,000 bbls/yr
Camden Street Brewery	George Freinscht & Peter Gloninger (partnered in 1831)	129 Camden Street	1827–1838	1,000 bbls/yr
	Frederick Brandt	Same	1838–1842	
	John Zwanzger & his son John in 1866	Same	1842–1868	
Samuel Lucas Brewery	Samuel Lucas	Holliday & Saratoga/ Jones Falls	1827–1833	7,000 bbls/yr
Medtart's Saratoga Brewery	Joshua Medtart & Family	Saratoga Street near Cove (now Free-mont)	1833–1857	6,000 bbls/yr
	Bayley & Blakey	Same	1857–1859	
Wohlleber Brewery	Jacob Wohlleber	Cross & Covington Streets	1838?–1849	
Geo. Rossmarck's Excelsior Lager Beer Brewery	George Rossmarck & Family	Same	1849–1878	4000+/- bbls/yr
George Rossmarck's Brewery	George Rossmarck	68 N. Liberty Street near Saratoga	1846–1849	
Wohlleber Brewery	Jacob Wohlleber	Same	1849–1850	Less than 500 bbls/yr
Auer & Lauer Brewery	Auer Family & George Lauer	Same	1850–1853	
Lekauf Brewery	John Lekauf	10 Fell Street	1847–1850	500+- bbls/yr
	Adam Lurz	Same	1851–1857	500+- bbls/yr
Hoffman's Brewery	Conrad Hoffman	West Mulberry	1847–1848	Less than 500 bbls/yr
Hoffman's Lager Beer Brewery	Same	53 Pennsylvania Avenue	1849–1859	600+- bbls/yr
Frederick Ludwig Brewery[207]	Frederick Ludwig	Belvedere near Greenmount	1848–1852	Less than 500 bbls/yr
	Frederick Weber	Same	1858+- 1862	1,500 bbls/yr
Baumgartner's Brewery	Andrew Baumgartner	29 Granby	1849–1854	1,000 bbls/yr
Ludwig & Lekauf Brewery	John Lekauf (1850–1854) & John Ludwig (partner 1849–1853)	28 East Pratt near Albermarle	1849–1854	500+/- bbls/yr
George Röst Brewery	George Röst	303 So. Bond Street near Hanover	1849–1857+/-	500+ bbls/yr
Brandel Brewery	Mathias Brandel & Family	West Saratoga	1850–1857	3,000+ bbls/yr

BREWERY	PROPRIETOR	LOCATION/ NEIGHBORHOOD	YEARS	PEAK PRODUCTION (IF KNOWN)
Fell's Point Brewery	Adam Sugg	Fell's Point	1850–1851	500+ bbls/yr
Geger & Frohlinger Brewery	Geger & Nicholas Frohlinger	269 Ann Fell's Point	1850–1851	
Grauff's Brewery	John Grauff	Near South Bond	1850–1851	1,000+ bbls/yr
Gustus German Beer Brewery	Erniest Gustus	Fell's Point	1850–1851	500 bbls/yr
Herzog's Brewery	Conrad Herzog	Fell Street	1850–1853	500 bbls/yr
Ruppert Brewery	Joseph Ruppert	213 Eastern	1850–1851	500 bbls/yr
Stuerlein Brewery	George Stuerlein	South Bond Street	1850–1851	500 bbls/yr
Warner Brewery	Michael Warner	South Bond Street	1850–1851	500 bbls/yr
Weiss Brewery	Conrad Weiss	37 Thames Street	1850–1851	
Huebner Brewery	John Huebner	4437 Bel Air	1852–1857	500 bbls/yr
Neisendorfer Brewery	George Neisendorfer	Same	1857–1859	500 bbls/yr
George Rossmarck Brewery	George Rossmarck & Family	23 North Frederick	1852–1858	
Adolphe Auer's Lager Beer Brewery	Adolphe Auer	Frederick Road near Calverton	1852	
George Auer Lager Beer Brewery	George Auer	128 No. Howard Street	1853–1854	
Baier Brewery	Johann Baier & Family	Canton Ave near Chester	1853–1866	10,000 bbls/yr
Canton Lager Beer Brewery	Conrad Herzog	Burke & Esssex Streets Canton	1853–1864	
Grasebenader Mead and Beer Brewery	John Grasebender	89 Lee Street	1853–1854	
	Mary Grasebenader	Same	1855–1856	
Gortler's Brewery	Francis Gortler	Canton & Choptank	1853–1854	
Hager's Brewery[208]	John Hager	Bel Air near North	1853–1854	
Ludwig's Berlinerweisse Brewery	John Ludwig	53 North Frederick	1853–1867	Less than 500 bbls/yr
Röst Lager Beer Brewery	George Röst	Bel Air (under construction beginning in 1853 for several years)	1853–1871	15,000 bbls/yr
Schemm's Brewery	George Schemm	Light Street near Barney/Federal Hill	1853	
Schwingler's Brewery	John Schwingler	20 Shakespeare Street	1853–1858	
Ramming Brewery	John Ramming	Same	1858–1860	325 bbls/year
Seeger and Stiefel Brewing	Edward Stiefel & Theodore Seeger	Federal Hill	1854–1856	
Jacob Seeger's Brewery	Jacob Seeger & Son Paul August	1045 West Pratt	1854–1888	10,005 bbls/yr
Orth & Olnton Brewery	Francis Orth & Hermann Olnton	59 S. High	1855–1856	
Neisendorfer Lager Beer Brewery	George Neisendorfer	Same	1856–1857	
Krieg Lager Beer Brewery	Peter Krieg	Same	1857–1859	
Hager's Brewery	John Hager	East Lombard St	1856–1857	
Bauernschmidt Brewery	John Bauernschmidt	71 Camden & Paca	1856–1857	
Rossdeuscher Brewery	John Rossdeuscher	Same	1857–1860	1700+/- bbls/yr
Thomas Beck's Rock Spring Lager Beer Brewery	Thomas Beck & Family	Baltimore St & Calverton Rd.	1856–1884	9,000 bbls/yr
Mount Pleasant Brewery	Mathias Brandel	Baltimore & Franklintown	1857–1871	

BREWERY	PROPRIETOR	LOCATION/ NEIGHBORHOOD	YEARS	PEAK PRODUCTION (IF KNOWN)
Carrolton Brewery (1872–1892)	Stiefel & Seeger (Stiefel operating alone 1872–1892)	Frederick & Franklintown Road	1857–1892	4,500 bbls/yr
Bauernschmidt Brothers Brewery	George & John Bauernschmidt	281 West Pratt	1858–1864	
Keller Brewery	Joseph Keller	360–362 Pennsylvania Avenue	1858–1859	500 bbls/yr
Beck Brewery	George Beck	Same	1859–1876	500 bbls/yr
Leaderer Brewery & Saloon	Henry Leaderer	341 S Charles	1858–1860	3800 bbls/yr
Raumfts Brewery	Alois Raumfts	105 West	1858–1860	1800 bbls/yr
Christian Rossmarck's Lager Beer Brewery	Christian Rossmarck & Family	239 Aliceanna	1858–1864	
Schwingler's Brewery	John Schwingler	317 South Bond & Dallas Streets	1858–1874	
Hoffman's Mt. Royal Brewery	Conrad Hoffman	Shirk & Jefferson/ Jones Falls 1st Tollgate	1859–1860	600 bbls/yr
	John George Hoffman	Same	1860–1877	
Kohles Brewery	John Kohles	92 S. Wolfe Street	1859–1864	
Neisendorfer's Brewery[209]	George Neisendorfer	Bowley's Lane & Erdman	1859–1866	10,000 bbls/yr
Engel Brewery	Otto Engel	59 North Exeter	1860–1865	
Frenie Brewery	George Frenie	146 Pennsylvania Avenue	1860–1863	350 bbls/yr
Grimmer Brewery	Valentine Grimmer	277 South Ann & Thames Fell's Point	1860–1863	
Krieg Lager Brewery	Peter Krieg	247 Aliceanna	1860–1865	
Loehr Brewery	John Loehr	260 E Pratt	1860	
Pabst Lager Beer Brewery	George Pabst	O'Donnell & 2nd Street Canton	1860–1868	2,000 bbls/yr
Ramming General Store & Brewery	John Ramming	2706 Harford Road	1860–1882	400 bbls/yr

Carroll County

BREWERY	PROPRIETOR	LOCATION/ NEIGHBORHOOD	YEARS	PEAK PRODUCTION (IF KNOWN)
Barnitz Brewery	Michael Barnitz	211 East Main	1821–1839	
	Solomon Zepp	Same	1839–1844	

Frederick City and County

BREWERY	PROPRIETOR	LOCATION/ NEIGHBORHOOD	YEARS	PEAK PRODUCTION (IF KNOWN)
John G. Lipps Brewery	John G. Lipps	West Patrick Street near the Bridge	1840 +/- to 1880	700 bbls/yr
Small Brewery	William Small	Brewer's Alley/South Carroll Street cor West All Saints	1846–1852	

BREWERY	PROPRIETOR	LOCATION/ NEIGHBORHOOD	YEARS	PEAK PRODUCTION (IF KNOWN)
Markell Brewery	Jacob Markell	Same	1852–1858	
Baer Brewery	Peter Baer	Same	1858–1873	800 bbls/yr
Zimmerman Brewery	Dr. Willilam Zimmerman & Family	Church & Main Streets (Creagerstown)	1849–1875	
Grundel Brewery	John Grundel	Market & Fifth	1859–1860	150 bbls/yr

Washington County

BREWERY	PROPRIETOR	LOCATION/ NEIGHBORHOOD	YEARS	PEAK PRODUCTION (IF KNOWN)
Butz Weiss Beer Brewery	Margaret Geak Butz	220 South Potomac Hagerstown	1840–1868	
Witzenbacher Brewery	William Witzenbacher	Clear Spring	1848–1850	
	Same	18–20 East Washington Street Hagerstown	1851–1885	126 bbls/yr
Hagerstown Brewery	George C. Gelwicks & Son Charles	7 East Franklin Street Hagerstown	1841–1855	300 bbls/yr
	Daniel Startzman	Same	1855–1857	
Middlekauf Brewery	Peter Middlekauf (& Peter Baer for one year 1857)	Same	1857–1864	
Leibold & Heist Brewery	Andrew Leibold & Lewis Heist	112 South Potomac Street Hagerstown	1849–1854	500 bbls/yr
Leibold Brewery	Andrew Leibold	Same	1854–1862	
	Katherine Leibold	Same	1862–1871	

4

The Civil War and the Flourish of Late 19th-Century Brewing in Maryland

All the benefits of the railroad were just beginning to be felt by the manufacturing industries in Maryland, specifically the blossoming brewing industry, when Abraham Lincoln was elected as the first Republican president of the United States in November of 1860. The country was on its way to recovery from the financial crisis of 1857, and the railroad was helping industry to get back on track. This aided both employment and opportunity across the state. Properties slowly regained value, and the exorbitant (bordering on usury) loan rates declined. Although concern for the health of the banks, securities, and real estate was still prominent, the country was beginning to breathe as financial stability was within reach by 1859. Unfortunately, after the election of Lincoln, tensions were high when state after state began to secede from the Union, beginning with South Carolina in December 1860. Six more states followed suit by February 1, 1861. Maryland was not one of them.

What was all the hubbub about? It was about slavery and economics, as well as the continued struggle for states' rights versus that of the federal government, problems that had existed since the founding of the United States. The northern states over time had abolished slavery, and many Irish and German immigrants provided cheap labor that easily replaced slave labor. In the southern states the majority of laborers were still slaves and this helped drive the economy of the agrarian states. Where did Maryland stand in all of this, situated as it was below the famous Mason and Dixon Line dividing north from south? Although agrarian production was strong in areas of the state, industry was arguably supplanting it as an economic driver with the outbreak of the Civil War. Maryland had sympathetic leanings toward the South, and business relationships were intensely strong, as were family ties. Maryland, however, never voted to secede despite these bonds. In fact, Maryland was a unique state in that there was much criticism levelled against it by her southern neighbors for more than a century due to her "lax" attitude towards slaves.

In the eighteenth century, travelers noted that, unlike in many southern states, slaves in Baltimore and surrounding areas had greater freedom and more power. For example, slaveholders left their slaves to their own devices once the workday was complete. The only requirement was to be back the next morning on time for work. Even Frederick Douglass commented upon this anomaly.[1] Many slaves and free blacks worked additional jobs selling produce and cooked foods and held other such positions to more quickly save toward buying their freedom or just to aid in the care of their families. For those slaves this was more akin to indentured servitude than it was to traditional slavery.[2] Although legislation would change in the nineteenth century that more strictly regulated these activities, the precedent was set in Baltimore and parts of Maryland and served as an example of what could be. Maryland always had a history of handling things uniquely, like interracial marriage taking place during the colonial years, although legislation was enacted to prevent it beginning in 1664.[3] Molly Welsh was a white indentured servant from England. Once her servitude ended she bought land and eventually married the black slave she had procured to help her farm the property. Her daughter followed suit, marrying a black slave she owned. Molly's grandson Benjamin Banneker, child of her daughter Mary's union with her (former) slave Robert, became a famous mathematician and astronomer who corresponded with, and was well known by, Thomas Jefferson.[4] The families were also property owners. Neither Molly nor Mary were ever prosecuted for violating the law, and all of their children remained free, although according to later amendments to the law they should have been forced into servitude.

This by no means was indicative of the entire state, although there was a large percentage of free blacks living in Maryland, notably Baltimore. Attitudes—and legislation—waxed and waned toward slavery in the state. Maryland at times adjusted legislation to stop the physical abuse of slaves and mitigate penalties on interracial marriage, and other times it increased penalties for slaves for a variety of perceived "negative" actions, as well as creating legislation to maintain control.[5] Not surprisingly, and in spite of some of the legislation, there was a rising population of free blacks in the state, and Baltimore led the way. But clearly not all of Maryland wished for an end to slavery. Tobacco plantation owners, for example, relied heavily on slave labor, and many fought vehemently against abolition. As that industry began to die off, a decline in the slave population was seen. By 1860, 49.1 percent of Maryland's black population was free, and only 1 percent of the population of Baltimore was made up of slaves.[6]

When looking specifically at the brewing industry in Maryland, one can see that they too had a unique perspective on slavery and free blacks. As mentioned in previous chapters, breweries hired free blacks as both laborers and brewers. Clagett and Company was notable for their equal opportunity hiring. What also must be mentioned is that many brewery owners voluntarily freed slaves and indentured servants long before the Civil War. Brewers like George C. Gelwicks in Hagerstown manumitted slaves in the decade before the war, while brewers like John G. Lipps of Frederick used his own home for transporting slaves on the Underground Railroad.[7] These men were indicative of the brewing culture and its attitude toward slavery. The question is why? Perhaps it came from their origins and reasons for their own immigration, such as escaping compulsory military service or imperialism that for many equated to the loss of freedom. Most likely it was an understanding that everyone who was willing to work hard could make their own way, just like these immigrants did for themselves in the brewing industry in Maryland. This perhaps was their way to pay it forward. And why not? Like the German and Irish immigrants, free blacks fought in the Revolutionary War (they were drafted) and the War of 1812. If they had fought for the land, shouldn't they too have a

Freedmen arriving in Baltimore, 1865 (NYPL).

right to it? Whatever the reasons, the brewers leaned in strong favor of emancipation, even though Maryland as a whole would waffle noncommittally, struggling to maintain neutrality at the dividing line of the warring territories.

Once the first shot was fired at Fort Sumter on April 12, 1861, by Confederate troops, Maryland became a deciding factor for both the federal government and the war. Three more states would secede and two more passed ordinances to do so. The country was truly at war with itself. Even though Maryland had not yet voted on secession, Baltimore would be the first place blood was spilled in the Civil War. While Baltimore was a bit of an anomaly in the South for its attitude toward slavery, it by no means meant that everyone supported abolition. When Lincoln called for volunteers, many from Massachusetts, Pennsylvania, and other northern states answered the plea. What that meant for Maryland was most certainly Union volunteers traveling through Baltimore on the rail lines to get to Washington, D.C., to fight for Lincoln and the Union. Mayor Brown of Baltimore anticipated potential problems from Southern sympathizers and those who openly demanded secession. Brown asked citizens to remain calm and allow the passage of soldiers through Baltimore. This worked on April 18, 1861, when Brown and police chief Kane met Pennsylvania artillerymen at Bolton Station and helped secure their way to Washington.[8]

That same evening a group of prominent men from Baltimore known as the "States Rights Convention" met to discuss and demand from the governor that Union troops no longer be allowed to travel through Baltimore on their way to Washington. Governor Hicks had taken the position that Maryland would not send soldiers to fight but would help to defend the capital if it came down to that. This did nothing to appease the convention, nor did it appease the citizens. What happened in Baltimore the next day,

April 19, 1861, dictated the course of the war and many legal actions Lincoln would take in Baltimore and the country. Lincoln could not afford for Maryland to secede, as Washington would officially be behind enemy lines, and that weighed heavily upon him.

On April 19, 1861, the fully armed Sixth Massachusetts, complete with 16-piece band, and Union volunteers from the Philadelphia Brigade, totaling around two thousand in all, headed through Baltimore.[9] Both the mayor of Baltimore and the governor called for order and peace. Those orders were not heeded. Mobs gathered at the President Street Station, where Union troops were forced to disembark and walk to catch the only train south from Cam-

The 6th Massachusetts at Monument Square after the occupation of Baltimore, 1861 (LOC).

den Station. Two miles separated the stations and by law railcars had to be pulled by draught horses from President to Camden Station down Pratt Street.[10] Union commanders decided it was best not to walk openly down Pratt Street and instead kept soldiers in the railcars and had the horses drag the full railcars to Camden Station. The mob quickly grew rowdy and brazen and increased swiftly in numbers. As the first seven railcars proceeded the mob acted to block rail lines with sand, tools, anchors, and whatever they could muster, preventing any more Union soldiers from arriving at Camden Station. The eighth car was derailed by an anchor on the track. Once back on track the car was pelted with stones, debris, and literally anything the growing horde could find to halt its progress. It was stopped near Howard Street, where the mob had torn up the track. Soldiers were forced to march precariously to Camden Station.

The remaining Union soldiers at President Station, along with the band, were told they would not be progressing to Camden Station because of the melee and they should return to Pennsylvania with the next train. One Captain Follansbee decided to march his men along the tracks to Camden Station anyway. This was a terrible idea, as the bridge had been intentionally damaged over Jones Falls, making the crossing incredibly dangerous; in addition they faced a wall of rioters who blocked their path down Pratt Street. The angry mob began hurling projectiles that included bricks, rocks, and anything heavy and damaging they could find. Union soldiers were injured, some dropping their rifles, which rioters quickly grabbed, loaded and used against the soldiers, who by this time were firing into the crowd often with no aim or concern for friend or foe. Mayor Brown made his way to the fracas, ordering men to clear the tracks so rail cars could be moved. Shopkeepers, concerned about the chaos moving down Pratt towards their stores, quickly shuttered their businesses. Mayor Brown risked his own life to try to personally escort the soldiers to Camden Station, thinking it would prevent the crowd from firing upon them. He was mistaken. Police chief Marshal Kane arrived with a small, armed contingent of police and protected the rear of the column. The Union soldiers and volunteers who survived or were uninjured boarded the train south, but not before firing off one last shot toward the crowd, hitting an innocent bystander and prominent citizen of Baltimore, Robert W. Davis.[11] Three soldiers were dead, and eight rioters and one bystander were killed by the time the train cleared Baltimore. The remaining Union soldiers and band members fared no better, as the rioters had set upon them as well. The Pratt Street Riot was over, for the moment, but things were just getting kicked off.

The dichotomy of the situation was that many Baltimoreans tended to the injured Union soldiers who were left behind, despite the personal risk from angry rioters. Some were secreted into private homes, others were pulled into shuttered shops on Pratt Street. By nightfall, rioters dispersed but things were getting even more heated. Chief Kane, who fulfilled his pledge of office by protecting the soldiers, was a secessionist who intentionally stirred tempers to anger, pushing for secession once the riot stopped. Despite the efforts of the mayor and governor to quell the rage and violence, gangs roamed the streets singing "Dixie." Secessionists from across the state gathered in Baltimore to stop further Union attempts to pass troops through the city. Northern rail lines and railroad bridges into Baltimore were systematically and efficiently destroyed. Curiously, most of the demolished track belonged to competing (not Baltimore-owned) railroads (Pennsylvania, PW&B, and Northern Central). Major roads and telegraphs lines from the north into Baltimore were also destroyed.[12] After the unrest, no Union troops attempted to go through Baltimore. Lincoln had determined that he would bombard Baltimore into submission if necessary but he would not let them secede, as the rail lines and the geographic location of Maryland were too important to the Union cause.

A rather brusque personality, lawyer Benjamin Butler was in charge of the Eighth Massachusetts militia. He made his way south, skirting Baltimore, and seized control of Annapolis (another stronghold of southern sympathizers) and the United States Naval Academy without firing a shot. Slowly his men repaired damaged rail lines, and things came to a head with the governor. With the capital of Maryland occupied, a legislative meeting was held in Frederick, where Governor Hicks succumbed to pressure to hold a vote on secession. Virginia was pressing Maryland to become her ally, while Hicks was a card carrying member of the Know Nothing Party. He was also pro–Union but possessed no backbone for the weight of his burden. Paradoxically, Maryland voted not to secede but held the right to do so if deemed suitable and appropriate in the future.

It was the time for Butler to act, albeit with no authority whatsoever from Lincoln or the War Department. Butler believed that Maryland was going to vote to secede, and he had no time to waste. Once the rail lines were completely repaired, he took his troops north by rail and snuck into Baltimore's Camden Station in the dead of a stormy night. He set up six cannons and crude fortifications on Federal Hill, assigning the Sixth Massachusetts to protect it. When Baltimore awoke it was to Union troops controlling the city and its coveted railways and ports. Maryland was Union by force. Lincoln, although displeased at the risk Butler took, was quite relieved to have control over Maryland and her obstructionist population. Sadly, Butler was immediately relieved of his command for acting without authority, although he did exactly what needed to be done for the Union.[13]

Lincoln by this time had already suspended the writ of habeus corpus and instituted martial law in Baltimore and Annapolis through his General Executive Order 100 on April 27, 1861. Now with Butler in position it could be enforced, beginning in May 1861. No longer was a body of proof required to arrest someone, the military could arrest anyone for any reason or no reason at all. Ignoring habeus corpus was one of the many reasons for the Revolutionary War and America's separation from England. In office for less than a month, Lincoln, without support or authority from Congress, issued an executive order carrying out the suspension of the rights America had fought so hard for. Article 1 Section 9 of the Constitution prohibits the suspension of habeus corpus except in the case of invasion, rebellion or if maintenance of public safety requires it, but only Congress (not the president) holds the authority to suspend those rights.[14]

Living in Baltimore was oppressive under martial law. Many were arrested and sent to Fort McHenry, which was under Union control and acted as a federal prison. Mayor Brown was arrested, despite his self-sacrifice to save Union lives during the riot. Many shopkeepers who aided Union soldiers were also arrested, along with police chief Kane and many secessionists. Things were only getting worse, and many Southern sympathizers fled the city to join the Confederate army. Some tried to keep a low profile but still fell victim to retaliation by Union soldiers who had barely survived the riots and wanted payback. Soldiers took what they wanted, and citizens had absolutely no recourse. Eventually, Lincoln lifted martial law and reinstated habeus corpus, but only briefly. By that time, the damage had been done to both families and businesses. Lincoln once again suspended habeus corpus, this time legally, in September 1862 at the behest of Congress, across all of the Union states. This was preparation for his Conscription Act passed in March 1863 forcing citizens to fight for the Union.[15] Many riots broke out in New York and other places challenging this, but soldiers quickly arrested rioters and anyone refusing to serve. This was fortuitous for Lincoln, however, when Northern reinforcements were sent to Maryland to prevent the threat of General Lee and his Confederate army from taking Baltimore. Union soldiers found Baltimoreans barricading the city to protect themselves but from what? Considering the Pratt Street Riots, Union soldiers assumed they had a fight on their hands and were shocked to discover it was General Lee and the Confederate Army Baltimore was trying to stop. Baltimore fought side by side with Union soldiers. Quixotic indeed.

How would the breweries respond to the chaos and warring factions within Baltimore and Maryland? Surprisingly they would for the most part attempt to operate normally. Advertisements for lost cows and dogs from various breweries would still be

FRED'K WIESNER'S LAGER BEER BREWERY BEL AIR AVENUE.

Fred'k Wiesner's Lager Beer Brewery, Sachse's bird's-eye view, 1869 (LOC).

posted in newspapers, along with charges and fines for operating breweries on Sundays, which was forbidden by law. Breweries would continue to go into receivership for debts unpaid to maltsters and creditors, and claims would be made against the estates of deceased brewers, causing great difficulties for survivors. A key difference of operations during the war was whether or not the brewers would serve in the military. Many brewers chose to pay other men to serve in their stead so they could remain at home operating their breweries and looking after their families. This became common practice. The greatest difficulty breweries would face involved acquiring supplies needed to make their products, from barley and wheat for malting, to hops. All sources were questionable once the railroad was under the control of the Union army and would remain so until hostilities ended and a new president was installed in office.

Baltimore

One of the breweries that most demonstrated the mutability and precarious nature of the brewing industry in the latter half of the nineteenth century was the Albion Brewery. Originally built in 1848 by Frederick Ludwig, it passed through the hands of six separate brewers and a foreclosure by a maltster (Francis Denmead) and finally landed with the most successful brewer at the location, Bernard Berger. Berger was born in Ellwangen, Germany, and immigrated to America as a brewer in 1868. His first stop was St. Louis, Missouri, where he was employed in the practical art of brewing. He then traveled to Maryland, where he was engaged as a brewmaster at the brewery of Jacob Seeger.[16] There he married his wife, Creszentia, who was from his hometown, and together they had three boys.[17] He was also brewmaster at the plant of Joseph Schreier. It was here that he learned of the opportunity to operate his own brewery in 1878, when Denmead was looking for a buyer for the Albion Brewery. Berger quickly

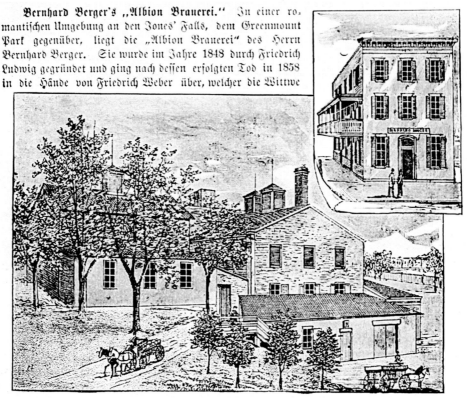

Bernhard Berger's „Albion Brauerei." In einer ro-
mantischen Umgebung an den Jones' Falls, dem Greenmount
Park gegenüber, liegt die „Albion Brauerei" des Herrn
Bernhard Berger. Sie wurde im Jahre 1848 durch Friedrich
Ludwig gegründet und ging nach dessen erfolgten Tod in 1858
in die Hände von Friedrich Weber über, welcher die Wittwe

Bernhard Berger's „Albion Brauerei."

Albion Braurei of Berhard Berger, ca. 1885 (SV).

realized the prospect was more than viable, with a four-story brewery, deep cellars, and
a magnificently advanced machine to aid in the cooling and lagering of the beers he
produced. Berger also appreciated that it was nestled on just over two acres of land,
where he could take advantage of constructing a proper beer garden with glorious views
of the city. It was here Berger would push the brewery to its 15,000 barrel annual capacity, with fourteen men employed, creating his future and subsequently securing the
future for his sons.[18]

It was his son John who would continue operations when his father passed on in
1893. John renamed it the John Berger Brewing Company. He had been in the business
with his father for a number of years when he became the sole operator but his tenure
was not without difficulty. John's younger brother Richard was merely nineteen years
old when his father died and Richard wanted to participate in the brewery business.
Bernard sold the brewery property to John shortly before he expired. Richard sued John
over the sale a few years later, claiming it was fraudulent (not an arm's-length transaction
or fair-value purchase). Clearly Richard wanted to be a part of the brewery. Perhaps he
hoped to operate the plant with his brother, but that never materialized, and any hope
was strangled when Richard added insult to injury in his lawsuit by claiming that John
was not even the biological child of Bernard Berger. Richard lost the lawsuit when
notable men of prominence in Baltimore testified on John's behalf.[19] Since there was no

DNA testing at this time and ABO typing of blood was still a decade off, it is unclear how these men "knew" that John was indeed the biological child of Bernard, but their words sufficed. John rebounded despite the scandalous implosion of his family and took the liberty of making the brewery his own, not only renaming it but also adding a bottling plant and selling his own unique brews, including Bijou. His employees adored him, even getting together to purchase a high end "Morris" reclining chair for him at Christmas in 1898.[20] He fulfilled his position as master of the brewery by creating a smooth operation that was close-knit, productive, and affable. The quality of the beer was outstanding and John Berger took full advantage when he sold the extremely profitable plant in 1899.

As many brewers of the era learned, profitability was not guaranteed but greatly improved with the invention of "ice machines." Dr. John Gorrie created the first patented ice machine in 1851, in Florida, but died a few years later. By 1860 Ferdinand P.E. Carre of France received a United States patent for an ice machine that was a closed, ammonia-absorption–based system that would become the standard for ice machines across the world. It would take decades for these ammonia-based systems to become commercially available for breweries. Eventually, the ice machines replaced the various incarnations of chilling beer that came in the centuries before. Lager beer was often made only in the winter because the yeast needed cooler temperatures to ferment the sugars into alcohol, unlike ale, which could ferment at higher temperatures. Ice became the standard component to help cool the beer to the necessary temperature. This was also one of the reasons for the deep lagering cellars below the earth—to cool the lager beer for four weeks, allowing the yeast to ferment the sugars. With the invention of ice machines it was no longer required to excavate the deep cellars but to just chill the air in the rooms where the lager was stored. This changed everything, including profitability. Breweries that could afford to do so took full advantage of this. Was this the determining factor for success where others had failed? Perhaps. It was definitely a component.

Frederick Weber, a former, albeit brief, owner of Albion Brewery, attempted to find success in 1862 by constructing a lager beer brewery off of nearby Harford Road and Hall Springs. It was still in Baltimore County at the time and most certainly wild and untamed. It was also close enough to Belair Road and the other German brewers, friends and community Weber was an integral part of but allowed him to make his mark in a relatively uncharted area for breweries. Weber cleared the forest and constructed a brewery, complete with a dwelling for his family and storage vaults for his beer. Unfortunately the brewery burned a year later while children played with matches near a bale of hay inside of the brewery. The loss totalled $6,000.[21] Luckily for Weber, he had insurance, and the most valuable property, the home and vaults, were untouched by flames. He rebuilt immediately, increasing the size of the brewery and clearing a beautiful picnic area with a pavilion and a tavern for visitors. It was a tranquil location that served Weber well for almost two decades before the brewery fell into decline and sales dropped off. Weber chose not to update the brewery when ice machines and more advanced technological innovations became available. Sadly, this would compromise the quality and consistency of his lager beer compared to local, competing breweries. Additionally it was well known that a homeless man, William Thiener, killed himself in Weber's Brewery in 1881, which did not help attract more customers.[22] This became more visceral when the poor man's body was dug up to verify that it was indeed placed within the coffin at the time of his burial. Business fell off and Weber went into receivership in 1889. He did, however, salvage his property and his livelihood. Weber closed the brewery but kept the park and tavern open and built a hotel. He added amusements to the park and found an extremely fruitful second career.

John F. Frederick Wiessner emigrated from Uhlfeld, Bavaria, in 1853 for the opportunity of a better life and a job with George Röst in his new brewery on Belle Air Avenue. An experienced brewer, Röst had emigrated from Bavaria with his brothers years earlier and opened a plant on Bond Street. After seven years of work at the Röst plant, Wiessner married Sarah Rupprecht and became a naturalized citizen in 1860.[23] Although happy building his family and honing his skills, Wiessner desired more for himself and his growing family. There was quite a bit of land south of the brewery in which he worked. This land was known as the Greenwood Estate and was owned by the Rogers family. It was an ideal location for his brewery with access to water and plenty of room for expansion. Wiessner needed one thing to get it underway—money. He was woefully short and decided to take a trip to the homeland to find family members willing to invest. This was a difficult proposition with the Civil War well underway in America and great uncertainty for all in Maryland.

Dr. John Gorrie, "Ice Machine," patented 1851. This was the very first of its kind and spawned a generation of ice machines that aided in brewing beer in Maryland (LOC).

Despite the risk, Wiessner was able to secure funds to lease land on Belair Avenue (Gay Street today). The small brewery was finally completed in 1863 and opened for business in the face of the raging war. Maryland was a border state where citizens fought for both sides, increasing peril even for those who remained neutral or paid men to serve for them. Wiessner's wife, Sarah, noted that she had to carefully place money in her apron when departing the brewery or the Union soldiers would steal it as they did the beer![24] Wiessner's brewery survived the war and thrived, even with the competition immediately surrounding him, including George Röst, George Bauernschmidt, Viet Butschky, and George Brehm, to name only a few. Wiessner was a tough taskmaster, as those things go, and demanded a level of quality far above most of the other breweries in the city. He understood his competition and kept pace but never at the cost of quality, and all of his workers adhered to this.[25] Like other German brewery owners, Wiessner housed his twenty-four workers within his own home, fomenting the growth of his community and Baltimore. Many of the workers were immigrants from Germany. These workers participated in church services at Zion Church and competed in the shooting matches held regularly at Schuetzen Park, which was conveniently located directly behind the Wiessner brewery and near the Röst, Bauernschmidt, Von der Horst, Engels, and Muth breweries.[26] Many games were available for the attendees (both German and American) including archery, pole climbing, bowling, and dancing. Beer and food were supplied by the organizers and great fun was had by all at these regular festivals.

Schuetzen Park festivities helped to instill that sense of community in newly arrived immigrants, as well as forging stronger relations with already-established immigrants and natives alike. Prizes for winning the marksmanship competition usually reached $500; some winners were even provided gold watches or fine china. Children were entertained by magicians, clowns, and games, which drew audiences as large as 60,000 for some of the festivals! Souvenir tokens were available to all attendees and continued to gain value since the park closed at the end of the nineteenth century when the city purchased it to develop the land.[27] Other *schuetzen* (shooting) parks were established in the city by German immigrants but none seemed as popular as the one organized by the breweries off of Belair (Gay street). The eight hundred members of the Belair Schuetzen Park rallied for the community whenever something was needed, particularly for the children. Wiessner personally accepted a leading role in the community as an Odd Fellow, a member of the Baltimore Liederkrantz (choir), and a member of Zion Church. He understood his role as an employer, mentor, and founding member of this Baltimore community located at the farthest reaches of the city. Regardless of the competition among the brewers they came together for community, as they did at Schuetzen Park, and worked together diligently to support the United States Brewer's Association. This was most notable when the Brewer's Congress was hosted in Baltimore, with Wiessner taking the helm on many preparatory projects.[28]

As Wiessner aged, he prepared his sons to take over the brewery. He instilled in them a great love of animals and taught them to care for the brewery horses with great love. He also taught them to keep the neighborhood in a good state of repair, taking pride in the streets, the homes, the businesses, even going so far as to pay crews of men to pick up debris in the streets around the brewery and the family home.[29] He also groomed them to take over the business. Shortly after his eldest son, John Frederick

Wiessner, Jr., returned from studying in Germany to learn the brewing trade from the masters, he became brewmaster at his father's brewery.[30] His brothers eventually joined him in finance and managerial roles and the brewery was renamed John F. Wiessner and Sons Brewing Company.[31]

Wiessner's plan was to provide for his family and their future, and he most certainly did that. The brewery was expanded in 1887, as Wiessner had completely outgrown the fledgling facility he built in 1863. He wanted to increase capacity from 40,000 barrels per year to well over 100,000. In part this was to keep up with the heavy competition in Baltimore, particularly that of his brother-in-law George Bauernschmidt, who was a year behind Wiessner in constructing his brewery but ahead of him in expansion. Wiessner adapted to the latest technology, purchasing two Von Linde refrigeration machines. He was also the first to use steam power to heat the mash instead of a copper kettle over open flame. The gravity-fed grain elevator was a critical component of the technological advances he embraced, along with a new bottling line to bottle on the premises instead of sending the beer out. These were the things that set him apart from his competition. This was also why he fetched $2 more per barrel than any other brewer in the city, at $6.50.[32] The Wiessner brewery became iconic to Baltimore and its brewing heritage with the rebuild into what has since been called the "Tuetonic Pagoda," which still stands as one of the most recognizable buildings in the state of Maryland. Wiessner died within a decade of the rebuilding, passing on the running of the brewery to his incredibly capable sons.

John F. Wiessner's older brother George also emigrated from Bavaria to chance success in the brewing industry in Baltimore. George, with partner John Miller, initially took over an older brewery in Canton from Conrad Herzog. Within three years, George decided he needed to expand operations due to his success and that he no longer needed a partner. After cutting ties with Miller he opened his Fort Marshall Brewery in Highlandtown in 1869. The brewery was located on Eastern Avenue and First Street on part of the site of the abandoned Civil War fort located on Murray Hill. George kept the initial brewery small with hopes of expanding as business increased. Sadly, he was not long for this earth and passed away in less than two years. George's widow married

GEORGE BAUERNSCHMIDT'S GREENWOOD PARK & LAGER BEER BREWERY, BEL AIR AVENUE.

George Bauernschmidt's Greenwood Park & Lager Beer Brewery, Sachse's bird's-eye view, 1869 (LOC).

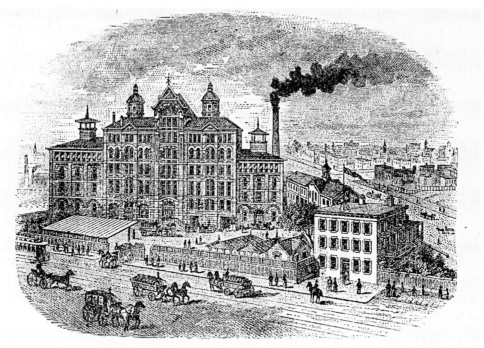

George Bauernschmidt's Brauerei.

George Bauernschmidt's Brauerei [Brewery] after complete remodel, ca. 1885 (SV).

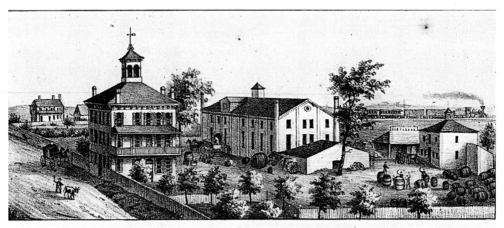

JOHN BAUERNSCHMIDT'S LAGER BEER BREWERY FOOT OF RIDGELY ST.

John Bauernschmidt's Lager Beer Brewery, Ridgley, Sachse's bird's-eye view, 1869 (LOC).

brewery worker Andrew Hoenervogt and kept the brewery operational until the sons were old enough to run it. Christopher (son of George) did train as a brewmaster in New York before returning to brew for his mother after his stepfather's death. John (George's son named after his uncle John Frederick) left his work as a firefighter and joined the family operation in 1876 after traveling to Germany to study under expert brewmasters in the German tradition.[33] The brewery was renamed the John F. Wiessner and Brother Brewing Company.[34] John continued operations after the death of both his mother and brother Christopher. Eventually, he sold the brewery to the Maryland Brewing Company in 1899.

In Baltimore there was another Wiessner from Bavaria operating a brewery within the city but not an immediate family member of the aforementioned Wiessner clan. A John Frederick Wiessner (a very common name in that region of Bavaria) also operated a lager beer brewery in Canton on the corner of Second Avenue and Highland.[35] He too was integral to the community around him, and was a member of the Brewer's Association charged with aiding the preparation of the Brewer's Congress in 1878.[36] Other than a slight mistake made on a beer keg stamp and a spot of trouble with the IRS resulting in a fine, little is known of the brewery beyond its more than ten years of operation in Canton.[37]

Belair Avenue was rapidly becoming the place to build a brewery for many German immigrants. Those who trained at the Röst brewery noted the location, suitability for lagering cellars (before ice machines) and proximity to Schuetzen Park and other important community functions. By the close of the Civil War the roads had greatly improved, as had amenities and the water supply. Baltimore was expanding and Belair Avenue was the ideal place to locate a brewery and a family. One such family was that of George Bauernschmidt.

The Bauernschmidt family has a storied history in the brewing industry of nineteenth century Baltimore. Three brothers emigrated from Bavaria to America to find opportunity and land. The Bauernschmidt brothers grew up north of Nuremburg as "hillbillies" in a caste system and kept animals in the basement just to keep them warm at night. The family business was brewing and carpentry, and more specifically they were coopers. In addition to the harsh circumstances at home, the brothers emigrated to escape the virtual slavery of Prussian military service and their impending conscription.[38] America was an opportunity they could not pass up. George Bauernschmidt came to Baltimore in 1853 and worked as a farmhand before his apprenticeship began at the George Röst Brewery.[39] George married John Frederick Wiessner's sister Margaretha. George and his wife were quite frugal, conditioned for loss and difficult financial circumstances. They purchased a small tract of land near Belair Avenue in Baltimore in 1855, for which the city later claimed eminent domain and paid George five times what he had invested in the property. This was money George would use to weather difficult financial times and to open his own brewery.[40] As he met with success in the brewing industry, George acquired $14,000 in gold coins that he later secretly buried beneath the front steps of his home on North and Belair just in case of emergency![41] Life taught him to be prepared for any eventuality, but he lived well and gave back to the neighborhood that embraced him. He was extremely active in his community, using his farm on Harford Road for meetings of the German Society of Baltimore, both for the Riding Club and the Maennerchor (men's choir). George was also a founding member of the Brewers Exchange, created to protect the interests of all the brewers in the region through the negotiation of commodities.

George's brother John Jacob Bauernschmidt, Jr., also arrived in America in 1853 and quickly relocated to Cincinnati to work for Christian Morlein's Brewery, where he gained valuable trade experience. John J. moved to Baltimore in 1856 and operated an extremely small brewery on Camden Street for a year until he sold it and went into the tavern business. Fairly quickly John J. convinced George to enter into business together and they opened a plant on Pratt Street in 1858. The youngest of the brothers, John T. Bauernschmidt, was also employed in the brewery when he arrived in Baltimore in 1864.[42] The brothers dug out cellars on a leased property on Ridgley Street to lager their beer. They met with a fair amount of success despite the damaging Civil War and predicted a swift end to the war resulting in an increase in business. George, like many businessmen at the time, paid another to serve in his place as a soldier so he might continue brewing operations.[43] The brothers decided upon independence from one another in 1864 to accommodate the impending demand and went their separate ways. George opened a brewery on Belair and John J. Jr. opened his brewery on Ridgely above the lagering cellars. Both breweries had room for expansion and were situated in different parts of town, thus limiting family competition.

John J. Jr.'s brewery was originally located in Baltimore County when it opened; shortly thereafter it was incorporated within the city limits. John Bauernschmidt's Lager Beer Brewery opened for business in 1866. John J. produced lager and, according to family members, a hoppy, yeasty, strong in alcohol, dark ale.[44] Everything in John J.'s brewery was hand operated. He never sold a bad batch of beer (he would dump any substandard brews) and saw the need for expansion relatively quickly. He renamed the plant John J. Bauernschmidt's Spring Garden Brewery after the expansion and rebuilding were completed. Business blossomed and by 1879 the Spring Garden Brewery was producing close to 12,000 barrels per year. Although the brewery was productive, profitability was limited, and the family struggled. In June 1879, John J. passed away of apoplexy (stroke) at the age of forty-nine.[45] His wife, Elizabeth Marr, and her brother succeeded him in the business, wich was renamed the Bauernschmidt and Marr Brewing Company.

George Bauernschmidt's Greenwood Brewery on Belair was fairly small, smaller than the home he shared with his family and his employees. He hired his youngest brother, John T. Bauernschmidt, as his brewmaster soon after opening. He produced around 5,000 barrels at his peak, yet he struggled to turn a profit. That all changed when he decided to rebuild the brewery and incorporate the latest technology available at the time: ice machines. George built this vast new structure in 1887 facing Belair and installed a Von Linde refrigeration machine to cool the beer. No longer were cellars needed for fermenting and lagering. The new brewery became a model of efficiency and quickly eclipsed the multitude of other breweries in Baltimore producing over 50,000 barrels per annum. George renamed the brewery George Bauernschmidt's Brewing Company. Not only was he incorporating the latest steam-powered equipment (and dealing with some of the problems new technology created) he was also experimenting with new styles.

George sent his son John off to Chicago to train as a brewmaster. John learned the art of working with yeast to create a pale, light beer, which met with great success and made the expansion of the brewery possible. George Bauernschmidt also had the distinction of beating out his brother-in-law John Frederick Wiessner and become the very first brewery in Baltimore to bottle its own beer on the premises. With production exceeding 60,000 barrels in 1887 when the bottling line opened, it was a phenomenal achievement. All of this was critical not only to George's success but also to his survival, as competition among the Baltimore breweries created a price war that, along with indebtedness to maltsters, was forcing the closure of many breweries in the 1880s. George's brewery was so prosperous he was offered $1,000,000 for it. He chose not to sell and instead incorporated the brewery, with his family holding most of the shares. This was one of the first stock breweries in Baltimore.

John Thomas Bauernschmidt grew weary of working for his brothers and longed to open his own brewery. In 1873 he opened a small brewery on West Pratt, John Bauernschmidt's Mount Brewery. It was literally a one-wheelbarrow brewery with a tiny brew kettle that could produce up to one-half of one keg daily.[46] The quality of the beer produced allowed John to expand operations in 1875. He finally achieved success like his brothers. By 1889 he was producing around 20,000 barrels per year and establishing a name for himself apart from his brothers. He operated a lovely beer garden on the property for families to relax in and enjoy after a long day of travel. He sent his son John Thomas, Jr., off to Chicago to train as a brewmaster and eventually take over the plant from his father. This would not come to pass. John T. Jr. became a brewmaster but would do so only for a short time at Mount Brewery. John T. Sr. took advantage of his success and sold his brewery to Baltimore United Breweries Ltd. to help cover the cost of an $80,000 mortgage to his maltster. Unfortunately his former brewery was not well operated and he was asked by Baltimore United to return as general manager to oversee quality production of beer among those breweries. He was also afforded the

Baltimore Street scene, 1853, a bustling city before the Pratt Street Riots (NYPL).

opportunity to secure the former brewery of his deceased brother John Jacob—the Spring Garden Brewery. It was also purchased by Baltimore United Breweries, was well run and produced excellent beer. John Thomas was much like his brothers, an active member of society engaged in philanthropic endeavors to help the growing community. A member of the Freemasons and the Odd Fellows, John Thomas worked tirelessly to not only foster a sense of belonging and home for many German immigrants but also to aid families in need of lodging, money, medical care and the like. He engendered this community spirit in his six children. John T. Bauernschmidt passed away at the age of fifty-nine years in 1897. Two years later his former brewery was sold and operations were discontinued, as the plant was considered out of date for the times.

John Von der Horst constructed his brewery on Belair shortly after the cessation of hostilities in 1865. He too was an immigrant, born in Gehre, Hanover, Germany, in 1825. When John (Johann) was twenty-one years old he decided to travel to America to build his future and, he hoped, his fortunes. He arrived in Baltimore penniless and took a position in the bakery of Mr. and Mrs. Dougherty on the corner of Howard and Fayette streets.[47] This position he would continue for decades, scrimping and saving every available penny. He found love with Johanna Beditz, also from Hanover, Germany, and they married in 1851, producing five children together over the next several years.[48] Von der Horst also branched out into other business ventures, like buying trusts in older homes to save money for what he truly wanted to do, which was to build a brewery. It took him two decades, but he finally constructed his Eagle Brewery, with a little help from a partner, Andreas Rupprecht. Rupprecht remained with the brewery just over a year, until he died in 1867, and Von der Horst was left to continue operations alone.[49]

The brewery was slowly constructed as finances allowed. Needless to say, output was very low in the early years. When Von der Horst consistently reached about 2,800 barrels annually, the sales allowed for the construction of a five-story malt house. The

ODENWALD & JOH'S LAGER BEER BREWERY, 7. CALVERTON ROAD.

Odenwald & Joh's Lager Beer Brewery, Sachse's bird's-eye view, 1869 (LOC).

reduced expenses for malt allowed the construction three years later of vast storage cellars and splendid icehouses. Von der Horst completed his brewery expansion and advancements by 1880. By then he was equipped with the most modern improvements available, including three steel steam boilers, two de la Vergne refrigeration machines, and Baudelot wort coolers. The plant was completed for the production of superior lager beer. The brewery ran with thirty-six full-time employees, producing around 40,000 barrels of lager beer and 100,000 bushels of malt annually. Von der Horst created the future that he dreamed of for his family, leaving a legacy for his son and the community.[50] The family were members of Schuetzen Park, supplying beer for the shooting competitions and fairs that took place with regularity across from his brewery. The community was integral to his success as a brewer but was also very close-knit and supportive of one another and the challenges of immigrants in Maryland. Von der Horst allowed neighborhood children to ride his brewery horses and spoke to them only in German. Von der Horst always kept an angora goat in the stables with the horses, claiming the horses liked the smell and it kept them healthy![51] This was a legacy anyone growing up on Von der Horst Lane was familiar with. His family was going to create yet another legacy, one that would smash the record books.

John's son Harry (Heinrich) was learning the family business and trained professionally as a brewer. It was not his passion, however. Like his father, he also saw the opportunity to expand family holdings beyond the brewery. Like his father, he wanted to carve his own path in life. For Harry that path led him toward his favorite pastime—baseball. The Von der Horst family, and more specifically the Eagle Brewery, began sponsoring the Baltimore Orioles baseball team. Harry possessed an excellent eye for talent and quickly invested in the team to make it competitive. Along with a little financial inducement he convinced Edward Hanlon, the Pittsburgh coach, to make the move to Baltimore in 1894.[52] Hanlon brought in the best players, and Harry paid them well. Harry had already forced the switch from the American League to the National League in 1892, vying for an opportunity at the title. The team was as impressive as it was aggressive, taking the National League Pennant in 1894, 1895, and 1896. They even

1894 Orioles: Willie Keeler, John McGraw, Hughie Jennings, Joe Kelley.

VON DER HORST'S LAGER BEER BREWERY BELL AIR ROAD.

John Von der Horst's Lager Beer Brewery, Sachse's bird's-eye view, 1869 (LOC).

won the elusive Temple Cup (an earlier version of the current World Series) in 1896 from their most intense rivals, the Cleveland Spiders, and the most formidable pitcher in history, Cy Young.

Harry Von der Horst filled the stadium for the games, particularly those against the Spiders, but the seats remained empty for the Temple Cup and ticket prices were consistently slashed year after year. Fiscally this was nearly impossible to maintain. Harry engaged in a few unorthodox practices for the regular season series, including overselling tickets to the point where fans were standing behind the catcher and in the outfield to watch the games. In 1897, Harry claimed attendance at over 23,000 fans in a 9,000+ seat stadium![53] This was not always the case, however, and fans were often content to show only for the heated series, not the regular games. Unfortunately, Harry's lack of ability to keep the seats filled, coupled with America's entry into the Spanish American War, resulted in the loss of several strong players from the team. This forced his hand into some questionable shenanigans in the National League. Harry decided to hedge his bets and tried to consolidate the Baltimore franchise with his ownership in a New York franchise—the Brooklyn Superbas. The Orioles' last season in the National League was 1899, as the league had grown unwieldy under the burden of too many teams and gave the boot to several teams. Many of the best Orioles players, and the renowned manager John McGraw, became Brooklyn Superbas.

When Harry became more interested in baseball than brewing new brewmasters were brought in to manage the operations and the brewery thrived despite the death of patriarch John Von der Horst. When the Orioles left the National League, Harry Von der Horst divested himself of the team and the brewery. No longer having interests in Maryland, he moved his family north to Brooklyn.[54] Harry Von der Horst eventually sold the majority of his interest in the New York club but stayed on as secretary of the National League. He died just a few years later after a protracted illness, in 1905.[55]

The acreage on Belair was attractive for several brewers looking to find profitability. One such brewery was that of George Brehm. Brehm took over the Neisendorfer plant just off of Belair on Erdman Avenue and Bowley's Lane, situated northeast of the Wiessner, Von d er Horst, and Bauernschmidt breweries. Brehm, too, was a German immigrant who worked at the Seeger Brewery, as well as the Engel Brewery, before taking a position at the Neisendorfer Brewery. He trained as a brewer in Bavaria and was head of a Russian brewery in Lithuania prior to immigrating to America.[56] He saw the opportunity to create the brewery he greatly desired and married the widow Neisendorfer. Not only had he become stepfather to three children but he also set about producing three more with the widow.[57] He sent his stepson off to train as a brewer in Germany, but a tragic accident prevented his installment at the brewery and Brehm had to bring in a brew-master from Bavaria. Within a year of Brehm's taking control of the plant, a devastating fire ripped through the structure, destroying the brewery, the stables, and the carriage house for a loss of $30,000. Fortunately he was insured, and took the opportunity to rebuild and expand the brewery, increasing capacity, and technology.[58]

The rebuilding of Brehm's Brewery fit nicely with the grounds of the brewery, which sported a beer and flower garden, a bandstand, a tavern, and a bowling alley. It was a lovely way for families to spend a Sunday afternoon. Brehm even set up Friday night bowling leagues and eventually improved the alleys to accommodate the duckpin rush.[59] The brewery was also in close proximity to Schuetzen Park, where Brehm happily supplied his One Grade Only lager beer, which was in high demand.[60] Brehm, like all of the German brewers in Baltimore, enjoyed creating the magnificent annual parade at Schuetzen Park, where all inhabitants of the city were welcome. It was always quite a spectacle, and Brehm used the opportunity to shine. Where brewers like George Bauernschmidt might create a float demonstrating the brewing process, Brehm would go to elaborate lengths to create floats with a rock grotto and beer waterfalls, or some-thing extreme, difficult, and breathtaking each and every year.[61] Competition didn't stop at the doors of the breweries; the good-natured rivalries extended well beyond, providing a lasting impact on all in attendance. The Brehms often took rival brewers (friends actually) on hunting trips to Middle River, returning with wagonloads of game for all to feast upon.[62]

However, it was not all fanfare for Brehm, and as the century wound down, he found himself on the short end of trouble with the growing unions. To help run oper-ations, he brought his son Henry into the business. Henry was a promising engineer who was pulled into his father's service when his twin brother perished. Although not trained as a brewer, Henry picked up the business quickly and became an exceptional administrator and operator. By 1894 he engaged in a complete rebuild of the brewery, installing an extra-large Case ice machine and building a massive storage house, a new bottling house, and stables with automatic feeders to accommodate the ten teams of horses needed to deliver Brehm's beer. Brehm's boasted thirty-five full-time employees for the state-of-the-art brewery, which became one of the largest in the region.[63] As the century drew to a close, Brehm, like other brewers, would be faced with the life-altering option of selling the extremely successful family brewery.

Another brewery on Belair that was once owned by Neisendorfer was that of Gott-fried Hertlein. In 1866 Hertlein, former brewer for Wiessner (on Belair), would create success where two previous brewers failed. The first order of business was to dig deep, large lagering cellars instead of using the poorly constructed vaults. He also set to work installing a pump to pipe water from the fresh spring on the property into the brewery. After this he enlarged the brewery for greater production capabilities. He also built a

LEWIS MUTH, LAGER BEER BREWERY, BELAIR AVENUE.

Luis Muth, Lager Beer Brewery, Sachse's bird's-eye view, 1869 (LOC).

saloon for thirsty customers to take refuge in on a hot day. The brewery was modestly successful until a fire claimed it in 1874. Hertlein still produced beer for sale at another brewery of a dear friend and competitor, Frederick Weber. Although the arrangement was not entirely unheard of, it was unusual. It was also a testament to the close-knit German community existing in the northern reaches of Baltimore. Once Hertlein's brewery was rebuilt, he continued operations only for about four more years before selling the brewery to yet another German immigrant who worked for the breweries on Belair, Otto Woerner. Woerner too struggled and ended up once again as a brewery worker on Belair for Wiessner.[64]

Luis Muth, an immigrant from Prussia, also attempted to operate his weissbier brewery on Belair near the aforementioned breweries. Muth had a greater chance at success, catering to an entirely different audience than did the brewers he was surrounded by. He was competent, but also knew how to appeal to consumers through added attractions. Muth borrowed funds from the maltsters to construct his brewery and brought in enough revenue to pay off his debt fairly quickly. So what was it that lured customers if it wasn't just fabulous beer? It was a perfectly sculpted garden with a building containing a sunken "bowl" in the lower level where men could gather, drink, gamble, and partake (as it was rumored) of the ladies who frequented the garden. Affectionately known as the Hornet's Nest it certainly was an attraction. It was a family business and in 1880 Muth's son Louis became brewmaster for the plant, easing his father toward retirement.[65] Muth Junior came in at a difficult time, as indebtedness once again took its toll and the brewery was handed over to trustees.[66] They would continue to operate the brewery under the reorganization until 1888, when it was closed and Louis Junior took on another position to feed his family.[67] The brewery could not profit without the technological advancements of an ice machine, among other necessary updates that the younger Muth did not implement. Gambling and loose women were not enough to keep him in business after all.

Although some of these breweries met with failure, they had years of success before going under. Many Baltimore breweries struggled to make it more than year or so. These brewers often went into business elsewhere or returned to work for another more successful brewery. Sometimes they found brewery widows to marry as a practical means of owning a brewery without the huge outlay of cash or need for credit. The increasing quality of the competition, aided by advanced refrigeration and machinery, was the linchpin to success, although not a guarantee. Joseph Schreier, a German immigrant and Civil War veteran, took this approach with the former brewery of Otto Engel on Belair, a stone's throw from Muth's brewery. Engel died in 1869 after only three years in business. Schreier, who previously ran a saloon, married the widow Anna Engel within a year and took control of the plant. Schreier was savvy enough to hire veteran brewmasters to create his beers instead of attempting the feat with no experience. Eventually the Engel sons began to work in the brewery, establishing it as a genuine family business. Beer gardens adjoined the brewery, and it was updated with relatively advanced technology but no ice machines. Engel could not keep the brewery from falling into receivership to his maltster, and the brewery closed. Schreier died the same year his brewery went into foreclosure—another hard lesson learned on Belair in the age of sweeping technological change in the industry.[68]

The western portion of Baltimore also saw an increase in breweries during and immediately after the Civil War, no doubt brewers were drawn to the water and scenery of Gwynns Falls, despite the numerous butchers in the area. One such brewery was that of Philip Odenwald and Ferdinand Joh. Both were German immigrants seeking refuge in America. Odenwald, a colonel in the Bavarian artillery regiment, fled after the German revolution, as did Joh, the son of a bürgermeister (mayor), on the losing end of the revolution. Odenwald came to Baltimore, while Joh went to Pennsylvania before relocating to Baltimore.[69] They met one another in Baltimore, where the German community was very close. They were in the Germania Maennerchoir (German Singing Society) together and formed a friendship that turned into a business partnership.[70]

The two friends constructed a brewery on Calverton Road. It was unremarkable, simply constructed with a saloon and deep lagering cellars below and no outside attraction adjoining it to lure consumers other than a saloon. The partners added a malt house to the brewery to maximize profit and steer clear of heavy debt to any of the Baltimore maltsters. It appears their lager brewery was popular enough to stay profitable and care for their families. The brewery was valued at just over $100,000, small but productive.[71] Despite locating in the western portion of the city the men stayed active with their families in the German societies and other organizations they supported. Odenwald perished in 1872, and Joh was left to run the brewery alone (although Odenwald's widow, Julia, held ownership in half the brewery, she was not a participant). It was more than Joh wanted and he found an investor in Julia's brother John, who had also emigrated from Bavaria. John Sommerfeld was a wealthy liquor dealer who wanted to branch out into the brewing industry and this was his opportunity.[72] He immediately set to work improving the brewery, building a four-story malt house capable of processing up to 30,000 bushels of malt annually. He also enlarged the brew house to maximize production. Within a few years Julia sold her share of the brewery to her brother and moved from her home on the brewery grounds. Unfortunately, Sommerfeld had taken on more than he could manage and found himself unable to pay the debt for the expansion. The brewery was placed into receivership and sold in 1881 for $34,000.[73]

This would not be the end of the story for Sommerfeld and the brewery, however. The Odenwald children would end up in court after the death of their mother, claiming her brother never paid for the Odenwald family interest in the brewery. Eventually the case was settled and the trustees of Julia Odenwald's estate were found to have not dispersed the funds to the children as directed. Sommerfeld ended up partnered with the new brewery owner to keep the beer flowing on Calverton Road. Eventually Sommerfeld bought out his partner and operated alone. He invested in the latest technology to create the best beer possible on a consistent basis. He added boilers and an ice machine to accompany the new brew house. This seemed to work, as Sommerfeld's lager beer was finally a hit. Unfortunately, a devastating fire coursed through the brewery and Sommerfeld was once again forced to rebuild. This time he did so on a grand scale, with a new two-story ice house built to accompany the three-story brew house and three-story fermenting house. All of this was run by a 60-HP steam engine and an 80-HP boiler.[74] Sommerfeld took full advantage of the rebuild, and the city took notice, as did neighboring towns. The expense of the rebuild on such a scale was more than he could manage and when he struggled to make mortgage payments he was forced to take on a partner, his brewmaster, August Wehrle, in 1892. This partnership devolved pretty quickly when the brewery was not profitable enough to pay dividends. Sommerfeld stopped making mortgage payments and the plant was put in receivership with liabilities far outweighing assets.[75] The fully equipped plant was purchased in 1895 but remained operational only until 1899. The brewery was proof that even with the latest machinery there was no guarantee of profitability. Competition was tough in Baltimore.

Some of that competition came from Sommerfeld's brother-in-law Ferdinand Joh.

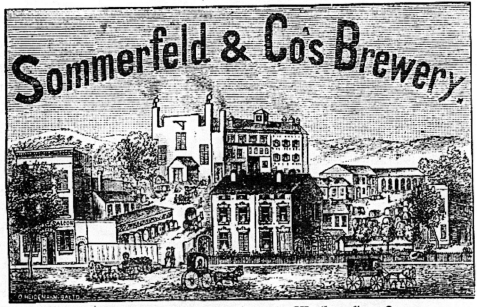

Sommerfeld's Lager Beer Brewery & Malthouse, *Der Deutsche*, 1878.

Joh opened a brewery further west on Wilkins Street (now Wilkins Avenue) after the sale in 1873. It was potentially far enough away from the western breweries that he could function with less competition. Here he made lager beer in a brand-new structure, with the latest machinery and a 12-HP engine fueling production. Joh died and the brewery was his daughter Louisa's to run. She, however, chose to marry a machinist by the name of Henry Eigenbrot. It was her husband who took control of the brewery in 1876 after the death of the founder. Eigenbrot's family had a long history in Baltimore, having emigrated from Germany in the early nineteenth century. He availed himself of his sprawling family's presence and brought them into the business. Although comments from the time refer to him as a lager beer brewer bent on perfection with a reputation for making beer of the best purity and health-giving qualities, there was a vast learning curve.[76]

Louisa retained ownership of the brewery, while her husband ran the day-to-day operations and brewed the lager beer. They engaged in an expansion of the brewery without investing in the most critical piece, an ice machine. This led to their downfall and indebtedness to Straus Malthouse. Instead of foreclosure, Straus took the opportunity to take the reins of the brewery, update it, and place his son Alexander in the brewery with Eigenbrot in 1892. The arrangement allowed Louisa to keep part ownership and to incorporate the brewery (for protection and investors).[77] The turnaround under the Straus family was remarkable. Production more than tripled, and the critical technological updates were installed, including a state-of-the-art refrigeration machine. The lager was flowing, and finally the reputation of being one of the better offerings in the region was deserved. The Eigenbrot brews Adonis Pale and Stock Lager were in high demand, so much so that Straus had to double the size of the brew house and build more cold-storage facilities to house it all. Western Baltimore brewing had finally come to life, and buyers came calling in 1899 with a price Straus and Eigenbrot could not resist.[78]

August Beck opened his brewery at the end of the Civil War in the western section of the city as well. An immigrant from Germany born in Rottenburg, Württemberg, Beck arrived in Baltimore with his wife, Christina, and two sons to work at the brewery of his brother who emigrated from Rotterdam.[79] America was rife with opportunity if one worked hard enough, and his brother's success was proof that it was possible to have financial freedom. Gauging the mood of the country, Beck thought hostilities were coming to an end and knew the time was right for him to venture into the brewing business. August's half-brother Thomas had his own brewery, the Rock Spring Lager Beer Brewery, nearby. Thomas was supportive of August's plan to locate in that portion of the city, where very few breweries operated to serve the growing population. The German community as a whole supported one another and were happy to support another brewery that would create jobs and help Baltimore move beyond the trials of an intense occupation and civil war.

In 1865 August broke ground on Garrison Lane (now Franklintown), constructing deep lagering vaults below the brewery. He built a dwelling to house his family and the workers he brought from Germany. The front of the home doubled as a tavern for patrons. Fairly quickly Beck's expertise and assiduous nature proved the key to success. Within the first year he was already indicted on three counts of selling lager beer on a

Sunday![80] He would be indicted several more times on that particular charge over the course of the fourteen years he operated the brewery. If he showed up for his hearing and confessed, he was charged a nominal fee (usually around $68) and was free to go.[81] Many brewers like Beck weighed the cost of the fine against the profits for selling beer on Sunday and found it reasonable to take the risk of getting caught. By 1870 his operation was valued at $60,000.[82] That was not at all bad for a relatively new plant, and based upon his court record his lager beer was very much in demand. Beck's eldest son, August Beck Jr., was a brewer at his father's plant and was officially brought on as a partner in the business in 1871.[83] Beck continued to develop his interests from there. He constructed a grand home for his family in 1876 coinciding with the outbreak of a fire at the brewery.[84] This beaux arts mansion was a three-story, red-brick wonder with a mansard roof. Extravagant for the neighborhood, perhaps, but Beck earned it through his hard work. He also expanded the brewery, adding a new 25-HP engine, storage buildings, and a concert hall to his beer garden.[85]

While things seemed ideal, they were far from it. Even though the German community was close-knit everything was not always copasetic. Beck and son were charged with slander by the not-so-distant neighboring brewery of Odenwald and Joh.[86] The case was nolle prossed (charges vacated) and the Odenwald & Joh Brewery was sold the following year, perhaps in part due to the conflict, which extended beyond the court and into the community. Beck was also brought before the court to explain charges of using grape sugar instead of malt in his beer. Nothing came of the charges, but it did impact sales for a time, harming his reputation. Beck knew how to recover his reputation for being a man of integrity, and that was done by helping the community he called home—the neighborhood that supported him and his family through their patronage. A difficult winter struck Baltimore in 1876, and the poor were the most affected. Beck purchased four hundred loaves of bread along with a vast quantity of meat and took it

AUG. BECK'S LAGER BEER BREWERY GARRISSON LA. N OF FREDERICK R.

August Beck Brewery, Sachse's bird's-eye view, 1869 (LOC).

to the Western Police Station for distribution to the poor.[87] This was typical of the German brewers in Baltimore, and perhaps expected, as their philanthropy saved many over the course of the years. Nevertheless, there was yet one more scandal that was going to break concerning the Beck family, and it was by far the more damaging.

The Beck Brewery grew stronger with each passing year until August Beck Senior grew ill one September and did not recover. In 1879 the elder Beck passed away, leaving the entire operation to his son. August Senior had remarried in the year preceding his death, to a younger woman named Fredericke Ruhle. Upon his death, she was paid $4,000 as stipulated in her prenuptial agreement with August Senior when they married and forfeited any future claim to the will or estate. It also stipulated that she remain in the dwelling house at the brewery until such time as she remarried. Suspiciously, just over a year after August Senior's death in April of 1880, the sons of August Senior were sued by the guardian of the alleged child of Fredericke Ruhle and August Senior, contesting the will. The child, Henry August Adolph Beck, was born eight weeks after August Senior died, yet the sons of August Senior had no inkling that Federicke was pregnant and nearly full term at the time of their father's death. Naturally the brothers contested the claim that the child of Fredericke was actually a Beck. They demanded proof of paternity, particularly in light of the fact that the widow Fredericke had already remarried since the death of August Senior.[88] Strangely, within a month Fredericke had taken the child and boarded a ship for Württemberg, Germany. The lawyer representing the sons filed letters offering evidence in support of the illegitimacy of the child. Since Fredericke had fled (or just left, depending upon one's interpretation of her actions) the documents had to be given to the president of the United States (Rutherford B. Hayes) to be delivered to the Emperor Wilhelm I of Germany so he could appoint a tribunal to take depositions and investigate the legitimacy of the child.[89]

The Beck family problems were about to get far worse. A few days after their response to Fredericke's suit was filed, the circuit court judge for Baltimore County placed the entire estate of August Beck Senior in the hands of trustees for immediate sale, due to the nullification of the will. The other component that made matters unbearable was the fact that the brewery was mortgaged to the hilt to H.L. Straus Bro & Bell Maltsters and was insolvent. Brewing operations were allowed to continue (supervised) until the brewery was sold. Adolph Beck took a job at a brewery in Pennsylvania, while August worked locally. Things were going to take yet one more dark turn before it was all settled. On September 10, 1881, Adolph Beck succumbed to heatstroke and died.[90] August Beck Junior was alone, fighting for the family legacy, fighting for survival, and fighting for his future.

August Junior regained control of the brewery in 1881.[91] After everything of his father's was sold and funds dispersed, and even after the lawyers from both sides sued one another over the commission of the estate and brewery sale, it finally came to an end. Almost immediately he made improvements to the plant, installing two large ice houses for storing up to 12,000 barrels of lager beer, a larger stable for ten draught horses, and new brew house, boiler, and steam engines.[92] Beck was back to doing the one thing he knew, brewing high quality lager beer, not quite in the quantities he once did with his father but enough to remain solvent. Beck ran the brewery built by his father until 1899, when he sold it to John Marr. Beck passed away only three years later.

After a life of hard work and difficult circumstances, he was a testament to perseverance. Sadly, he bore no children to whom he could pass on his legacy of creating brilliant craft beer through a family well known for their skill and dedication.

Another western brewery was established by the young Bavarian John Schultheis. His first position was that of brewer in the John George Hoffman Mount Royal Brewery. Schultheis not only grew into a fine brewer of lager beer but he also married Hoffman's daughter Maggie. Together they produced three daughters and two sons to be groomed for the family business.[93] When he proposed his own brewery, the idea was met with support from his family and a silent partner, Martin Kratt, to provide much needed financial help.[94] Schultheis wanted to construct the brewery near a viable source of water and liked the western region, particularly Gwynns Falls. He was able to appropriate an already functioning brewery from the Straus Brothers & Bell Maltsters, who had taken possession of the Brandel Brewery in 1871.[95] He immediately got to work brewing lager beer, after deepening the lagering vaults beneath the small brewery. Business was strong enough to force expansion in 1876. At this time he upgraded the machinery and enlarged the brew house. He continued on as brewmaster even when he hired employees to help with the brewery and the tavern. By 1882 he was churning out 30,000 barrels of superior lager beer.[96] He did not skimp on the quality of the malt, which was what caused trouble for Schultheis. In 1885 he and Maggie found themselves facing a lawsuit from their malt supplier, Gottlieb, Hobelman, and Wehr.[97] It took a year to sort out and a new partner for an infusion of cash. In addition to the partner, the brewery got a new name, Union Brewing Company.[98] The partnership lasted only a year, and Union Brewing got yet another partner; but that too would fail, leaving the brewery in the hands of trustees, as was typical of the times.

Perhaps one of the most notable brewers to establish a brewery in western Baltimore County was Thomas Murphy Dukehart. The Murphy Dukehart legacy in Maryland and the nation was tremendous and embodied all of those exceptional qualities of both German and Irish immigrant descent. Thomas Murphy Dukehart was the son of Mary Ann Murphy and Henri von Arden Dukehart, representing the merging of the Irish and German when they married in Baltimore. Mary Ann's father, John Murphy, emigrated from Northern Ireland to Halifax and on to Baltimore; he was lost at sea in 1809. Mary's uncle Thomas Murphy emigrated with his parents from Northern Ireland in 1797. Unfortunately, the parents died of yellow fever. Thomas made his own way in Baltimore. Once his brother was lost at sea and his sister-in-law remarried, Thomas took custody of his nieces and raised them as his brother would have desired. Mary Ann named her eldest son after her uncle and surrogate father, Thomas. Thomas not only made his own way but also was a founding member of the *American Commercial Daily Advertiser* in Baltimore. When the War of 1812 broke out, Thomas stepped away from the newspaper and joined the sharpshooters in the Battle of Northpoint. He was the first to print Francis Scott Key's "Defence of Fort McHenry" in his newspaper.[99] This was the stock that Thomas Murphy Dukehart came from. This was the stock that would carry him through one of the most precarious times in American history, the Civil War.

Murphy Dukehart was born in Baltimore in 1834. He was well educated, with a penchant for chemistry and engineering. After Dukehart received his degree from the

Wehr, Hobelmann & Gottlieb's Malzhaus.

Wehr, Hobelman, Gottleib Malthouse, ca. 1885 (SV).

prestigious Milton Academy, his uncle Murphy sent him on to Philadelphia for training for an officer's commission in the navy in 1858. His service was nothing short of heroic. Not only was he an integral member of the crew in search of the missing ship *Lavant* but he also was key to aiding the Union navy in the Civil War. Murphy Dukehart received a citation for gallantry for his actions aboard the *Tacony* and a citation for valor for his actions aboard the *Katahdin* from Secretary of the Navy Gideon Wells.

He served the entire duration of the war, forty-three engagements with exemplary service, even fighting against his brother Captain John Murphy Dukehart, who served in the Confederate navy. After the war, he was ordered to serve as professor of natural and experimental philosophy and engineering and chemistry as a commodore at the U.S. Naval Academy. This coincided with the academy's institution of the new Department of Steam Engineering. It was here that he first became engaged with the Medtart Brewery, off of Franklin, which he would eventually take ownership of. Murphy Dukehart took a leave of absence to work through some methods of improving concrete using the (Medtart) Maryland Brewery as his base of experimentation in 1866. This is where he learned the art of brewing and secured his future. When Jacob Medtart died,

Commodore Thomas Murphy Dukehart received a citation for valor for actions aboard the ram *Katahdin* during the Civil War (LOC).

U.S. Naval Academy, 1861, with USS *Constitution* (LOC).

Murphy Dukehart seized the opportunity and resigned from the navy, purchasing the brewery as his last position before retirement.[100] With a strong background in chemistry and engineering, coupled with knowledge of the brewing process, Murphy Dukehart was perfectly situated for prosperity in the brewing industry.

Dukehart carried on some of the more successful brews of his predecessor and friend, including the Medtart Ale, and renamed the porter the Dukehart Porter. He was

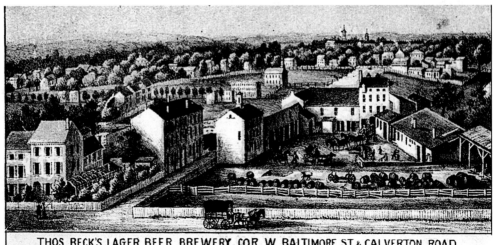

THOS. BECK'S LAGER BEER BREWERY, COR. W. BALTIMORE ST.& CALVERTON ROAD.

Thomas Beck's Lager Beer Brewery, Sachse's bird's-eye view, 1869 (LOC).

off to a great start, making porter, ale, and brown stout. He used modern machinery, including a 35-HP engine to facilitate the production of his brews, which were in demand in Virginia and parts of the south as well as Maryland.[101] Unfortunately, like most brewers, Dukehart fell into financial difficulty, not due to his inability to produce quality beer but more due to his need for malt. By 1884 he needed to downsize and moved to the former Rock Spring Brewery of Thomas Beck on Baltimore Street. It was smaller but perfectly suitable for porter, ale, and brown stout. Dukehart brought in partners to help run the business end of things, as his gift was engineering and brewing, not finance. The plant was updated to the latest technological needs but still struggled with debt to the maltsters.[102] He maintained operations as the Dukehart Brewing Company in various partnerships and incarnations until 1903, when receivership forced his hand and he was ousted from an ownership position in the business. Murphy Duekhart continued on as an employee until his death in 1912, his true legacy of heroism and engineering untarnished.

All of the western Baltimore breweries were competing with the former plant of Jacob Seeger. The operation was taken over by son Paul August when the founder died in 1877. Paul Seeger, although a talented brewer and competent manager, saw a decline in business over the decade after

Medtart's Ale.

—:0:—

Maryland Brauerei,

ALE,

PORTER,

BROWN STOUT.

—:0:—

Thomas M. Dukehart,

Eigenthümer.

Holiday, nahe Centre-Straße,

Baltimore, Md.

Thomas Murphy Dukehart's Maryland Brewery, *Der Deutsche*, 1878.

his father's passing. Desperately in need of upgrades to the plant, Seeger made the informed decision in 1888 that if he wanted the plant to survive he would need investors to finance the upgrades. The Baltimore Brewing Company was formed in 1888 out of a group of investors that saw the potential of the storied plant.[103] Tens of thousands of dollars came into the brewery over the course of years and Seeger used it to invest in refrigeration machines, new boilers, steam engines, and anything that potentially aided the production and quality of the beer. He took the help presented from the investors in everything from accounting to operations. He also began offering more than just the lager his father was so famous for. He began to offer pale, dark, and "special" brews, which most likely were akin to the seasonal beer selections of modern breweries.[104] It was clearly a sales tactic—and one that did not always pay off. Seeger moved on to new brewmasters, investors, and managers but still struggled to compete in the nearly saturated market. By 1898 things had become desperate financially and Seeger chose a risky path, introducing new beers at substantially lower prices that he could afford. An advertisement in the *Baltimore Sun* from November 28, 1898, outlined his last play to make a go of it in the brewing industry:

> Pale Export
> The **Baltimore Brewing Co.'s** new
> brand of pure, rich, and delicious BEER.
> In kegs $8.00 per Barrel.
> In bottles $1.25 per case of 2 dozen pints.
> **Brewery West Pratt Street & Frederick Ave.**

The ploy didn't help matters one bit, but Seeger found his way out of the failing plant in 1899. An offer was made to purchase the operation more for the advanced equipment than for the product it turned out. Seeger jumped at the chance (as did his investment partners) to extricate himself from his father's legacy. Some say his heart wasn't in the brewery once his father passed away, and that may have been true. He found a second career after the sale, in banking, which by all accounts was his true calling and his most successful venture in life.

Like the western portion of Baltimore and the Belair Avenue breweries, Canton and eventually Highlandtown became a hotbed of brewing. What began as merely the place for lagering became ideal for brewing by the time of the Civil War. Some brave souls, sensing a pending end to the conflict, chose to take advantage of the opportunity to seize the market and the prices in such an unsettled time. Occasionally it worked, as it did for George Wiessner; for many it was short lived, liked Michael Nitzel, whose business folded in two years.

Anna Baier, as previously mentioned, was married to the brewer Johann Baier. After his death she remarried brewery worker Frederick Wunder. A few years later, in 1872, they decided to move brewing operations to the location of the lagering cellars in Canton on Third and O'Donnell streets—a logical choice but an expensive one. The old brewery on Canton Street was valued at over $87,000 and Anna was forced to pay for it since it was not being given to the children of Baier.[105] Anna also appointed her husband to run the brewing operation, which not only caused the previously mentioned rift with her son Paul but also drove away their seasoned and exceptional brewmaster, Franz Schlaffer. The new brewery consisted of a three-story brick brew house, boilers,

Fred'k Wunder's Brauerei [Brewery], Trappe Road Canton, *Der Deutsche*, 1878. He married the widow Baier and took over the brewery, causing a deep rift in the family.

30-HP engine, stables, two wagons, a dancing pavilion on the grounds, and eight employees.[106] Of course those famous lagering cellars were beneath the block the brewery was erected upon.

It seemed as if the Wunders had everything in order. That was not the case, however, as the loss of brewmaster Franz Schlaffer, the cost of the move, and the need for malt financially stretched the Wunders. Additionally, production was half of what it had been at the previous location. Anna grew more deeply in debt with each passing year, with few compliments coming from the usually fawning writers of the time regarding the quality of her lager beer. In 1881 her second husband, Frederick, died, leaving everything in her hands, from the brewery operations to the debt to the broken relationships left in the wake of her hurried marriage. Soon the maltsters came to collect. Straus Bros. & Bell saw the potential of the brewery and took possession in 1885.[107] Anna passed away the following year and was buried with her second husband, Frederick Wunder.

The Straus brothers looked at the Wunder Brewery as a potential brewing gold mine because of the cellars, 30-HP engine, and expansive brew house. They saw a profitable future and moved operations away from the other breweries they controlled to direct all of their efforts towards maximizing production out of the Wunder plant. They decided to call it the National Brewing Company. Immediately they began a program of investment, updating beyond what the Wunders had done the decade before. Within two years they had invested $125,000. One of the first additions was a massive Von

National Brewing Company ad, 1887 (USBA).

Linde refrigeration machine to cool the two icehouses that held 10,000 barrels of lager beer. More buildings were constructed, including expanded brick and stone stables that could hold up to thirty draught horses to haul fifteen wagons filled with National Beer. The pavilion was destroyed and rebuilt on a far grander scale. By the time the Straus brothers were finished the entire structure spanned two complete blocks.[108] The brothers also brought in the finest brewmasters and paid them well to produce the best possible pilsener and lager for the time. The company was incorporated and became yet another stock brewery in Baltimore, allowing an influx of cash via stockholders but in limited runs, enabling the Straus family to maintain the controlling interest.[109] Unfortunately, it was all for naught. The brewery was destroyed by a devastating fire in 1892 that gutted the entire three-story brew house, sparing only the refrigeration machine, with a loss totalling $300,000.[110] The brewery was completely rebuilt. The Strauses made lemonade out of lemons and chose to completely expand operations with the rebuild.

The new brewery was completed in 1894 and boasted four boilers of 500-HP capability adjoining the brew house and refrigeration rooms. Brand new De La Vergne refrigeration machines were installed and connected to massive storage vaults capable of holding 14,000 barrels. New structures were also added, including a refrigerated hop storage room, sanitization/cleansing house, bottling plant, mill house with grain storage elevator, and an expanded stable to hold the forty-five horses necessary to deliver the product to Maryland, Pennsylvania, Virginia, Florida, and Texas. National was the most well-equipped brewery in the region and was producing National Pilsener, Bohemian, Bavarian, Braunschweiger, and Mumme.[111] Capacity was 150,000 barrels, although sales didn't reach beyond 70,000 in the nineteenth century.[112] By the end of the century the company hired renowned brewery architect Otto C. Wolfe to remodel the brewery in hopes of expanding production beyond the 100,000 barrels, with perhaps double storage capacity. And that was when everything changed. National, as one of the most successful breweries in the state, received an offer to sell in 1899 that was too good to pass up. The brewery was sold for the impressive sum of $500,000.[113]

Franz Schlaffer, when he first left the Wunder plant, took a position as a brewer in the Bayview Brewery on Eastern Avenue and Ponca. The Bayview Brewery was established just after the war in 1865 by the Baltimore County Brewing, Malting, & Distilling Company. It was one of the first stock breweries in Maryland, with each share valued at $25. Ground was broken immediately and the new brewery was completed and ready for operation by 1867.[114] Since anyone could buy the stock, there were a variety of "owners" of the brewery, from butchers to milliners. Most were German immigrants establishing themselves and new business interests. Investments ran the gamut from several thousand dollars to $100 or less. This divergent ownership managed well by hiring extremely well-qualified brewmasters. The brewery was consistent, the debt was well-controlled, and there were regular profits paid to investors, although in fairly modest amounts. At times the brewery operated at a loss, but it was nothing the officers could not overcome.

Bayview-Brauerei, 3.- und O'Donnell-Strasse.

190

Bayview Brewery, 1905 (DNB).

V. GRIMMER'S LAGER BEER BREWERY COR.LANCASTER&THIRD STRS., CANTON.

V[alentine] Grimmer's Lager Beer Brewery, Sachse's bird's-eye view, 1869 (LOC).

It was turning out twice as much as most other breweries in Baltimore. One of the reasons included brewmaster Franz Schlaffer's incorporation of summer beer into the brewing schedule instead of producing beer only in winter. It freshened up the souring winter beer when added to it (as was the common practice) and also provided a fresh alternative on its own. This was a procedure he first introduced when working at the Baier plant.[115] The profits, however, were not enough, simply due to the need for expansion of the business and the narrow profit margin of plants like this one that were not technologically advanced. Some years they were producing more than they could sell.[116] This led to the sale of the brewery in 1876 to a private group of investors, Hect, Miller, & Company. The new owners were in the fruit packing, clothing, and coffee businesses in Baltimore, among other diverse financial interests, and thought it an opportune time to invest in a brewery. They called it the Bayview Brewery.

One of these investors was Joseph Friedenwald, from the Orthodox Jewish Friedenwald family of Hess-Darmstadt, Germany. They immigrated to America in 1830 with nothing to their name, but Joseph's father was quickly able to earn a living in the umbrella business and then the junk business, until his interests were diversified enough to retire financially secure, having amassed a fortune through hard work and ingenuity. At that time the elder Friedenwald chose to engage in acquiring the education he never before was able to obtain, as it was never too late to learn. Joseph was a benefactor of this hard work and determination but also a participant by collecting, as a child, bent nails and straightening them out to sell at a profit. All of this had an impact on Joseph, and he too sought an education; but he never denied hard work was necessary to achieve one's goals. In addition to being the first Jewish owner of a brewery, Joseph was also a president of the Bay View Asylum and involved in land speculation and the clothing business.[117] The entire family gave back to the city that embraced them. The elder Friedenwald helped build the Lloyd Street Synagogue, as well as provided for the poor quite regularly. All of the family donated clothing, food, and goods to the victims of the horrific 1868 Baltimore flood and the 1871 Chicago Fire and provided homes for the orphans when the Hebrew Orphans Asylum burnt down in 1874.

Joseph Friedenwald helped build the Bayview Brewery into more than it had been under the previous ownership and into what the community needed. The Bayview Brewery would never reach its full potential, as it was in dire need of "mechanical refrig-eration" and other technologically advanced machinery it never received. This was due to the separation of the partnership in 1887, about the time the majority of the larger breweries were remodeling and seizing the latest technology had to offer. The brewery would continue on with only the Miller brothers left to run things, and they chose not to update the plant, rendering them unable to compete for greater profitability. As a result, the plant was sold in 1889 to a British company attempting to regain economic prosperity in America a century after the Revolutionary War.

After his brief stint at the Bayview Brewery, Schlaffer moved on to his own brewery in 1872, first on Belair in a somewhat primitive brewery built by German immigrant Viet Butschky in 1863 and then back to Highlandtown, where he took ownership of a brewery on Lancaster and 3rd originally built by Valentine Grimmer in 1868. The High-landtown brewery changed hands quite a few times before Schlaffer took it over, but he was happy to be back in the eastern quadrant of the city with the lagering cellars he loved and a vastly larger operation in 1881. Schlaffer brought his sons Carl (Charles) and George into the business with him, as they had also been in the brewing industry for years. Carl had trained as a brewmaster in New York before returning to help his father at Belair and then Highlandtown Brewery.

Schlaffer learned from the mistakes made at plants he worked at and from his own struggles at the Belair plant with a viable water supply and limited production capabil-ities. He installed all modern brewing equipment, from boilers to engines to a very large icehouse that could hold 3,000 barrels. The ice machine was a state-of-the-art Rankin Refrigeration Machine at the Lancaster plant (unfortunately it was a bit defec-tive). He also had a large stable with twelve draught horses to deliver the tens of thou-sands of barrels he produced annually.[118] Schlaffer, as business allowed, expanded his Oriental Brewery to meet demand, as the quality of his lager beer was among the best in the eastern portion of Baltimore. By 1890 a bottling plant was added for bottling their most desired brews: Ambrosia, Standard, and Orient Ginger Ale.[119] The brewery was the success Schlaffer hoped for, but he was ageing. He had been in the industry in Baltimore for many decades, making changes to brewing practices everywhere he went. He was one of the first to brew "summer" beer in the eastern plants, and he was also responsible for inventing an iron ice cone called a "swimmer" to drop into the ferment-ing tubs to cool the beer before mechanical refrigeration. Even after artificial cooling was introduced, Schlaffer never shortened the lagering time for his beer as most other plants did, preferring to let it rest and age for 6 weeks (as opposed to the two weeks other brewers adhered to). This was how he and his sons turned out quality beer year after year. This was also why suitors came calling in 1899 to buy his brewery.[120] He was by that stage in agreement with his sons that it was time to retire, as he had made his mark on Baltimore and the industry in his illustrious career.

In Highlandtown Schlaffer was competing not only with his former plant, the Bayview Brewery, he was also contending with another renowned brewery on Lancaster Street, Sebastian Helldorfer's Star Brewery. Helldorfer purchased the failed brewery of Gottlieb Bauer and Frederick Buechler in 1874. The brewery was operational for only a year when Helldorfer took ownership. Born in Bavaria, he was the son of a brewer. He emigrated from Germany to Baltimore in 1854 with dreams of opening his own brewery, but that dream had to wait. Helldorfer initially made his way as a cooper and then a grocer, but most people considered him a gifted musician. He was nestled into the German community in north Baltimore awaiting his opportunity to open a

Sebastian Helldorfer portrait, ca. 1885 (SV).

Sebastian Helldoerfer's Brauerei, Ecke Clinton und Lancaster Str.

Sebastian Helldorfer Brewery, ca. 1885 (SV).

brewery. It took two decades, but Helldorfer was patient and seized the moment when it arrived. The location was ideal, with a lovely scenic and shady backdrop to the brewery, with sweeping views of the Chesapeake Bay and the city, from the green hills up north to the myriad monuments and churches of the city to the west. Travelers commented on how one could stand inside the upper floors of the brewery and see the magnificent excursion steamers, small sailing vessels, and even the colossal German and English ships packed with immigrants arriving in Baltimore.[121] This was where Helldorfer built his future with his family.

Helldorfer made an excellent beer and got to work modernizing the plant. Unfortunately, after its update in 1880 it was razed by a quick and destructive fire, forcing Helldorfer to start again from scratch.[122] He equipped the remodeled plant with all of the modern amenities necessary to make quality competitive lager beer. It was completed by January of 1881 and ready for production. In addition to the boilers and steam engines exceeding 100 HP, Helldorfer added an Eclipse refrigeration machine once it became available, easily keeping pace with the most advanced breweries in the region. Storage with the new refrigeration machine reached 5,000 barrels, easily enough to serve Highlandtown and beyond.[123]

Of the eight children he had with his wife, Regina, Helldorfer brought four of them—sons, who also hailed from Bavaria—into the business. All of the Helldorfer children were educated, as Helldorfer instilled in his brood the need to educate oneself in order to progress in life and achieve goals.[124] He did not limit his engagement in the community to his brewing interests but also was actively involved in the German banking interests in the city as well as the Francis Denmead Malting Company and the Brewers Exchange. He was set on protecting the interests of those not only in the brewing industry but also those starting out new businesses, trying to support their families. It may be said that the work he did with the Sacred Heart Beneficial Society was the most rewarding, as he was honoring his community in ways that were immediately visible and beneficial. He set quite an example for his children and for those in the city he served. This allowed his children to make the right decisions once their parents passed on. Regina predeceased her husband, and Sebastian Helldordfer died in 1893 after a month-long struggle with illness.[125] His sons continued operations for another six years, carrying on the legacy in the brewery and caring for the community until they chose to sell in 1899.

George Guenther emigrated from his home in Wertheim, Germany, in 1869. Guenther apprenticed as a brewer and cooper in Germany and wanted to try his fortunes in America after his life had taken a turn. After a few years as a brewer in New York he was offered a position in the brewery of George Röst. This required a move to Baltimore. By this time Guenther had married Katherine, also from his hometown in Germany. She became his wife and partner, with whom he would create a robust family, although only four of their eight children lived to adulthood.[126] His children were well educated but were also taught the value of hard work. Guenther's reputation preceded him and his gift for "sweetening" the lagering cellars was one of the reasons Röst hired him. Sweetening the cellar involved the adding of lime or other additives to rid cellars of a sour odor that would permeate wood and ruin the beer as it fermented deep beneath the earth.[127] The cellars were located in Canton, far from the Röst brewery on Belair and Patterson Park. It was not uncommon to locate cellars a distance from the brewery if the depth and structure were better elsewhere. Röst believed Canton was ideal for lagering vaults and was uncertain of his Belair location.

Guenther continued work with Röst until an opportunity presented itself to partner in a struggling brewery and saloon in Canton, near the lagering cellars Guenther knew so well. In 1878 he joined Christian Gehl in brewing operations at 3rd Street (now Conkling). Gehl operated alone and was in a financial pinch that required an influx of cash and a very good brewer. In less than two years the partnership dissolved and Guenther owned the brewery and Gehl the saloon on Belair. There was much speculation about the nature of Gehl's departure from the brewery, since it happened abruptly and quite unexpectedly in 1880. Many thought Gehl was

26

Geo. Guenther's

Lager Bier Brauerei,

CANTON.

Bayerisches **Lagerbier.**

Schon von Weitem fallen die Gebæude der Guenther'schen Brauerei jedem Besucher des œstlichen Stadttheiles in's Auge. Dieselben wurden durch den genialen Architekten Herrn Otto C. Wolf in Philadelphia fuer den jetzigen Besitzer Herrn George Guenther aufgefuehrt, eine Musterbrauerei die dem œstlichen Stadttheile zur Zierde gereicht.

Die Gebæænlichkeiten mit Granitfundament und aus gepressten Backsteinen aufgefuehrt, sind mit den modernsten Einrichtungen versehen und enthalten unter Anderem eine der neusten De La Vergne Eis Maschinen.

Das Hauptaugenmerk des Herrn Geo. Guenther ist darauf gerichtet ein reines, gesundes Lagerbier zu brauen, welches sich ebenbuertig den deutschen Bieren zur Seite stellen kann und dass er diese Aufgabe geloest hat, wird ihm von Niemand abgesprochen.

Die Brauerei hat eine Capacitæt von 80 bis 100,000 Fass.

George Guenther's Brewery ad, 1887 (USBA).

forced out by Guenther with a little assistance from the German American Bank on Broadway, which served many in the German community and held more than a few mortgages on local breweries.[128] It would seem, as some have said, a cautionary tale of going into business with a savvy business partner who understood the industry well.[129] The bank clearly trusted the brewery to Guenther more so than Gehl and nudged him into buying out Gehl with the bank's assistance. It appears to have been the wise choice. Gehl ended up with the saloon and cash for his pockets, which he used to return home to Germany for a visit.

Guenther set to work on brewing. He purchased all of his hops and malts locally, from the Straus Malthouse, which helped provide consistency in the brews he produced. Fairly quickly he realized that he needed to expand operations to accommodate the vastly increased demand. This was not something he took lightly. Guenther brought Otto C. Wolfe, noted Philadelphia brewery architect, down to Baltimore in 1886 to design a new state-of-the-art brewery with updated refrigeration, boilers, and machinery at a cost of around $50,000. The previous brewery had been considered a bit of an eyesore and neighbors were happy to see one of the most renowned brewery architects in the east design the new structure. Wolfe was later responsible for parts of the magnificent design of John Frederick Wiessner's tutonic pagoda brewery on Belair. The

Guenther reconstruction was magnificent by all accounts and was considered by many the pride of Canton, boasting a five-story brew house on a base of heavy-duty granite, with a richly decorated ornamental façade of elegance and color.[130] He installed two De la Vergne refrigeration machines, steam boilers, and iron vats. Machines for processing and weighing malt were set up to mitigate the risk of fire, as was so common in malt houses of the day, and a rather massive ventilator was set up in the middle of the structure that could be seen from just about anywhere in the building. Malt storage capacity was increased to hold 6,000 bushels at any given time. Once the rebuild was complete in 1887 Guenther was capable of brewing lager beer three times per day (unheard of at the time), producing 600 barrels per day, which equated to between 80,000 and 100,000 barrels per annum. The point that many Germans coming to Baltimore noted was that flying high above the marble letters "George Guenther Brewery 1887" was the American Star banner (as it was referred to) in all of its glory.[131]

Guenther also purchased the land across the street from his brewery that used to house the George Pabst Brewery. There he built a row of homes for himself, his family, and his workers to live in comfortably. He invested heavily in real estate, either through direct purchase or private loans in exchange for promissory notes for real estate. This strategy seemed to pay off and Guenther either collected very reasonable payments with interest or he acquired highly desirable property.[132] He certainly appreciated the opportunity of hard work and realizing his dreams in his adopted country. He could now easily produce the beer in such demand of the local populace and export as needed for the next few decades. Guenther was proof of that German entrepreneurial spirit; coupled with an iron willpower, the careful management of assets spelled financial independence.[133]

All was not smooth sailing for the Guenther family, however. On one occasion of note Mr. Guenther's brewery and family were threatened by a seemingly unhinged man seeking money. The man, writing under the assumed identity of an anarchist leader, threatened to blow up Mr. Guenther's home or brewery if an incredibly large sum of cash was not delivered to a stated address forthwith. Guenther hired private detectives to handle the transaction and uncover the heinous blackmailer. They in turn marked the cash, delivered it as instructed, and promptly followed the marked money to a home on Fourth and Pratt, where they found and detained for arrest a Mr. Rudolph Mahlstedt, who was in no way an anarchist.[134] He seemed to be taking advantage of the times and the anarchist fervor to disguise his crimes. Fame has a price, and a brewery as successful as George Guenther's was most certainly famous. Perhaps this was one of the factors Guenther considered when an opportunity to sell his brewery for an exorbitant sum of money presented itself. No brewery meant no money seekers threatening his life, or perhaps it was just a prudent business deal. Whatever the reason, George Guenther sold his plant to the Maryland Brewing Company for $900,000 in 1899.[135] He regretted his decision almost immediately.

One of the greatest lessons from Canton/Highlandtown applicable to all nineteenth-century brewers could be learned from William Kemper. William Kemper was also a German immigrant who trained as a brewer in Berlin before coming to America. Once he settled in Baltimore he took positions at various breweries in the city, including the brewery of Ferdinand Joh and the Bayview Brewery. Kemper, like many, desired greatly to open his own brewery. After raising enough money, he took over the former brewery of George Miller on O'Donnell and 2nd streets in December 1876. Although he fared well making lager beer and slowly paying off his $30,000 mortgage to Straus Brothers, by 1879 he needed to take out a second mortgage with the maltsters for 10,000 bushels of malt. His plant was not updated and profitability was low, particularly because he had to pay for lagering cellars across the street since the brewery did not have its own.[136] This eventually forced William Kemper to sign his property over to the H. Straus Bros & Bell for indebtedness in 1880.[137] In the same year, he arranged to relocate to the former brewery of George Vogt on Eastern and Third. This brewery, unlike his previous one, had deep lagering cellars excavated below the brewery, which cut down on his expenses.[138] Kemper seemed to flourish where he could not at his former plant, but something else awaited him beyond more-fruitful production: disease.

Kemper was known to enjoy the cool air of the lagering cellars, especially in the heat of summer. Often, according to his workers, he fell asleep in these deep underground vaults. As mentioned, lagering cellars are cool, excellent for lagering and storing beer, but there are drawbacks. Deep in the earth are bacteria, fungus, mold, and gases. That is why Guenther and other specialists were called upon to sweeten the lagering cellars and rid them of the contaminants that could compromise the beer. Kemper spent so much time in his lagering cellars during the hot Baltimore summers that he contracted tuberculosis and perished in 1885. Mycobacterium tuberculosis thrives in environments devoid of fresh air and sunlight, and lagering cellars of the nineteenth century provided the perfect environment.[139] This was a hard lesson learned but an important one. As much as lagering cellars were desired by brewers, it was a relief when ice machines became available and the cellars were no longer needed. In addition to the work of sweetening the cellars, it was preferable to lager beer in them and remove it quickly to refrigerated storage, as that was known to stop the fermentation, whereas lagering cellars allowed fermentation to continue, resulting in higher alcohol beer that was prone to spoil more quickly. Refrigerated storage allowed beer to last longer and less product was wasted, saving brewers both money, and time. Those that could afford ice machines were better off. Unfortunately, Kemper died before he too could avail himself of the lifesaving technology.

In addition to the great successes witnessed in Canton/Highlandtown there was another growing group of brewers that also saw success. In part it was based on geography and in part on the product. Henry Beck was born in Prussia in 1838. He came to Baltimore looking for an opportunity for his family to thrive. He found it with his wife, Ernestine, when they opened the Celebrated Weiss Beer Brewery on east Fayette near Patterson Park in 1876.[140] As mentioned, weissbier was not the most in-demand brew made in Baltimore at the time but it had a devoted and specific audience good brewers knew to cater to. The Beck family certainly found their niche and their stride. The brewery and saloon served the community for over three decades, without indebtedness to maltsters and without producing more than 500 barrels in any given year.[141] What was the secret? The wiessbier certainly was celebrated!

Another weissbier brewer, John M. Berger founded his brewery in Fell's Point at Thames and Bond Streets in 1868. Berger was also a Bavarian immigrant, but his profession was not that of brewer but stonemason. Berger worked in Frederick Maryland for a time before relocating to Baltimore to become a bottler.[142] He found a wife and began his family in Baltimore. He also had some knowledge of weissbier, in part from his bottling partner, August Fick, prompting him to turn his bottling business into a brewing operation. Within a year he took on a new brewery partner, Andrew Dittman, replacing Fick in the brewery but continuing the bottling partnership. Dittman perhaps offered better insight into weissbier brewing and or brought in an influx of cash.[143] It was a wise decision, as was his decision to continue operating as a bottler while he got his feet wet with brewing. By 1870 it was inevitable that he discontinued the bottling business and partnership to focus solely on the brewing trade.[144] It was tight space however, and Berger was gaining a strong reputation. He decided to relocate to a larger brewery within a decade of opening. He was not running into the problems that many other brewers faced, much like Henry Beck.

Berger took over the former brewery of John Beh on South Bond Street. He was loathe to leave Fell's Point and seized the opportunity once that brewery became available. Berger continued the business with Andrew Dittman, but he was growing at a pace rapid enough to need more hands in the brewery. He hired six workers, four Bavarian immigrants including Louis Pabst, who like the other workers shared the Berger home with his employer. Pabst was an excellent student under Berger, enough so that he opened his own wiessbier brewery five blocks away after Berger's death. Berger, however, had a secret to his success. He bottled mineral water along with his weissbier to stay profitable. This seemed a key to staying out of debt, particularly when his neighbors brought forth frivolous lawsuits in hopes of easy money.[145] After Berger's death from asthma in 1883, his widow, Elizabeth, attempted to keep things running, installing her son John in the brewery to help. She called it the Fell's Point Brewing Company. But the family just could not keep things above water, even with the mineral water, and she found herself indebted to the maltsters Wehr-Hobelman-Gottlieb by 1887. Try as she might, she could not turn a profit, and when she doubled down on her investment to make the brewery work she lost everything, including her home.[146] Fortunately her daughter Mary took pity and helped her mother by purchasing the family home from the maltsters.[147] Elizabeth was not homeless. Her son John attempted to open and run his own brewery to no avail, while Louis Pabst saw much greater success in his venture.

Other weissbier breweries would also find tremendous success, notably that of Frank Sandkuhler, who founded his operation in 1886 and operated right up until Prohibition. Sandkuhler trained under the Beck family at the celebrated Weiss Beer Brewery for many years prior to setting off on his own, operating in the back of a saloon he owned on McElderry Street. He learned well, and his business was a success, enough so that he was forced to move to a larger facility in 1895. He still operated by hand in almost every aspect of brewing, from the mash tun to bottling. This had no impact upon his success, as it had with so many other breweries that were not technologically advanced by the end of the century. Sandkuhler operated until 1919, and even then he chose not to believe Prohibition would last and planned to reopen his business at that time.[148] What made his weissbier so good when it was made so primitively? Sandkuhler had a secret to his wiessbier—he did not use wheat! He used only the finest barley and hops but no wheat. Traditionally we think of weissbier, or "white beer," as wheat beer, as many know it today. The entire process of manufacture differed from that of the lager beer that had become prolific during the nineteenth century.

Weissbier followed a simple process. If one was to produce weissbier as it was originally produced in Berlin beginning in the seventeenth century wheat and barley malt were used together. It was a product that was "top fermented," meaning ale yeast was used and fermentation occurred at warmer temperatures than with lager yeast. In addition, lactic acid bacteria was incorporated in balance with the yeast. The strains were just being understood by scientists at the turn of the century, however, and the researchers still had a long way to go. They were still experimenting with the optimal way to add the lactic acid for safety while retaining flavor.[149] Of course the beer was not pasteurized at all. It was placed in kegs and then the beer was hose syphoned (by mouth) from the kegs and into bottles made of baked clay. Bicarbonate of soda was added into the bottles with the beer. It was inside of these clay bottles that the beer fermented once sealed. The bottles were then sold to the public, usually within a few days, requiring the empties to be returned for reuse. It was a simple process, really, and one that required a very specific audience used to the taste. Far less room was needed for weissbier brewers and much less equipment.

Sandkuhler, though, did things a little bit differently. As mentioned, he never used wheat, only barley malt, as he desired more clarity in his beer. He stirred the mash by hand and used an electric pump only to transfer the beer into the cellar to cool it after initial cooling in primitive, shallow, cooling pans known as *kühlshiffs*. Sandkuhler then allowed his beer to ferment in the kegs (in a temperature-controlled environment) for at least a week before it was bottled to give it greater strength and clarity. The alcohol content was low, around 2.5 percent, as was typical.[150] This probably explains why he was the largest producer of weissbier in Baltimore—his process was more refined, with less guesswork. This also explains why so many weissbier brewers failed so quickly; too much bacteria was left to chance and spoilage was quick and easy. Sandkuhler fetched 5¢ per eight-ounce bottle and $1.05 per case (thirty-six bottles). His salesmen earned $15 per week and the brewery workers $10 per week, excellent salaries for the time. Weissbier was something that was an acceptable alcoholic beverage—so much so even children partook—and it was not forbidden during Lent. This was one of the reasons Sandkuhler thought it would survive Prohibition.[151]

Another Baltimore region that maintained a strong presence of breweries was located on or near Pennsylvania Avenue. One notable operation was the Phoenix Brewery. The name conjured the image of a brewery rising from the ashes of some former outdated plant, and that wasn't too far off reality. One of the earlier postwar breweries was that of John Nagengast, which was founded in 1867 and located at Pennsylvania and Pitcher. The family hailed from Bavaria, Germany, and found success, with many of them participating in the operations of the plant.[152] The Nagengast family became well established in Baltimore in the brewing and other trades.[153] The brewery seemed to thrive despite the competition but was in need of expansion to meet growing demand. When the founder died in 1878, another brewer, Henry Werner, availed himself of the opportunity and married the widow Nagengast, taking control of the plant.

Henry Werner recognized the need for expansion and brought in a partner for a quick influx of cash to make necessary adjustments to the brewery. Within a year the partner was out, and Henry retained control of his Phoenix Brewery.[154] The resurgence of the brewery under Werner was much like a phoenix rising mainly due to the technological

Heinrich Werner's Phoenix = Brauerei.

Werner's Phoenix Brewery, ca. 1885 (SV).

upgrades installed. Not only was the brewery expanded but Werner also installed a brand-new Ferguson Ice Machine, one of the first in Baltimore. Additionally he was the first to rely upon the Zell water-tube boilers, a quantum leap in the brewing industry that would come to be the norm for efficiency in heating.[155] Werner also increased the size of the stables to accommodate the twenty horses he needed for beer distribution in Baltimore, along with an increase in staff to thirty employees. He was always considered a friendly man who went out of his way to engage with every patron who came out to the brewery.

Bustling business forced him once again to expand, and he added Eclipse refrigeration machines and three new cellars within a decade of taking control. It had been a long journey considering Werner's beginnings. He was the son of a businessman in Mainz, Germany, when he emigrated with no job and not a nickel in his pocket. He landed in New York City and took a job in a bakery for about a year before he decided to go to Baltimore for more promising horizons. It was in Baltimore that he married widow Nagengast and learned the art of brewing.[156] It was quite the story. Unfortunately, his gift was for brewing not for fiscal management like his father. The brewery fell into receivership for indebtedness to Straus Brothers maltsters and was sold to maltsters from New York in 1888. Beginning in 1892 it lay dormant for eight years of wasted potential and production, like a diamond hidden beneath the coal.

Another Pennsylvania Avenue and Pitcher Street competitor to the Phoenix was the brewery of John Mueller. Mueller constructed his brewery in 1869. He lived modestly and produced a good beer but in extremely limited quantities, much like the Nano breweries of the 21st century.[157] Mueller operated at his own production pace, which was apparently enough to sustain his family without fear of receivership, a rare feat indeed in those times. He died in 1880, and within a few years his wife took Robert Handloser, owner of a nearby saloon, on as a partner. The widow may have known the brewing end of business but was unequipped to handle the management side of things, a trait Handloser apparently possessed as well. They remained in partnership together until she died in 1890. At this point it had become clear that Handloser fared no better than any other brewery at staying debt free from the maltster. The plant was reorganized and Handloser renamed it the Western Maryland Brewery, a curious choice for a Baltimore brewery.[158] He performed no better and ended up in receivership to Straus Bros. once again in 1894. The maltsters reorganized and continued the brewery for only three years when the reality of limited profitability for the primitive brewery demonstrated the need to shut it down in 1897.

Who was the Straus family? To begin with, they controlled a monumental portion of the brewing industry in Baltimore. The family had emigrated from Bavaria in stages over the course of the nineteenth century and were very active in the city and county in a number of businesses from dry goods to clothing manufacturering. It was the maltsters, however, who really had power in the city. Without malt no beer could be brewed. Henry and Levi Straus saw an opportunity to extend beyond grocery items and get into the more lucrative endeavor of malt. When they entered the business during the Civil War there were only a handful of malt suppliers in Baltimore and only one of magnitude, Francis Denmead.[159] Denmead, like the Straus brothers, has been mentioned repeatedly as both maltster and brewery owner. He owned the City Malt House on West Falls Avenue, an ideal location, close to the docks and the railroad for grain shipments and central to getting malt to breweries across the city in all directions. The competition was minimal from the other maltsters, including John Boyd, who was in the bottling business prior to entering the malt trade. Denmead was well established but there was certainly room for another steady malt shop in the city. The Straus brothers wanted to close the gap with Denmead and also position themselves to replace him, as he was ageing. Steadily, through the end of the war, they brought in malt from Pennsylvania and New York to feed the breweries that were popping up across the city in the postwar years.

By 1870 there were a total of three malt mills in Baltimore's twenty wards that employed forty-eight men, with a value of $339,500, almost twice the value of all breweries operating within those same twenty wards![160] Within two years there were six malt houses operating within the twenty wards, and vast grain shipments were also coming from western Maryland and beyond. Malt houses in Baltimore were valued at over $1,500,000, employing over three hundred souls.[161]

Solomon Straus Malt House ad, 1887 (USBA).

The Straus brothers entered the malt industry just in time, and they maximized profits. Their malt house was located in the northern reaches of the city on North and Saratoga, supplying many of those Belair and Pennsylvania Avenue breweries.

The Straus brothers and their partner Alexander Bell achieved what they desired. Although the malt business seemed like easy money, it was not. When a brewery did not pay its malt bill, it either reorganized, often with the help of the maltster to manage finances and efficient operations (which required skills beyond malting and management) or they were foreclosed upon, as demonstrated numerous times thus far. In the early years of the malt business for both Denmead and the Straus brothers and Bell, plants were easily updated for profitable production or sold at foreclosure. As the latter half of the century arrived it became far more difficult to sell the plants, principally those that were not technologically advanced. The weissbier brewers certainly fit that bill.

The malt industry was tight, and the Straus family was quickly claiming much business from the newer breweries. Denmead was thriving, and John Boyd maintained an even keel when he took on new partner Ricketts to bring an influx of cash.[162] Another Straus chose to enter the malt business, Solomon Straus, who opened his malt house on Central and Fawn. Some breweries built malt houses to avoid the overhead of paying a maltster (and avoid receivership). Those are the breweries that most often met with great success. The maltsters faced a difficult challenge in what to do with seized breweries that were not productive. One example was the Darley Park Brewery, as the Straus brothers called it. The brewery on Harford Road was operated first by George Miller and then by Conrad Siegman. It was a small plant that was expanded with hopes of the investment turning a profit. The proprietor, Siegman, died before that could happen and Straus Bros. seized the property as mortgagers because of unpaid malt bills. The brothers placed their sons in charge of the brewery, which was an ideal facility in many ways, as there was a bowling alley in addition to a saloon and shaded picnic grounds with a pavilion. The maltsters ran the brewery to make it profitable and recoup their losses until it could be sold. Fortunately it was a great location and a quality brewmaster was hired to operate the brewery. Production increased to nearly 13,000 barrels by 1879, within the first year of operations.[163] The brewery stayed under the ownership of Straus Bros. until an offer was placed that would more than make up for the time, labor, and expense of the foreclosure and subsequent operations. In 1889 the brewery was sold to Baltimore United Breweries, the British syndicate reclaiming economic prospects in America.

Standard Brewery, located on Belair, was the former plant of George Röst and then Sophia Röst. The Straus's foreclosed on the brewery in 1881 but found no buyer. It was more profitable to let it remain dormant than to operate it. The brewery remained untapped potential until 1888, when the Straus family decided that an operating brewery was more likely to sell. They placed an experienced brewery manager in charge and concentrated on the Phoenix Brewery, another plant they had foreclosed upon (as previously discussed). Investors from New York, the Manning family of maltsters, leased both the Phoenix and Standard Brewery at the same time, trying to maximize their investments in Maryland. Quickly they cancelled the lease on the Phoenix and stuck with the more viable brewery, the Standard, which they purchased in 1895. The plant changed hands within a year to a corporation that decided John Marr, formerly of the Bauernschmidt & Marr Spring Garden Brewery, should run operations. He remained in that capacity until 1899. The brewery would continue into the next century.

The drama of the maltsters foreclosing on breweries played out across the country. In Baltimore many brewery owners tried to avoid this fate by making different deals with different maltsters for their malt and hops. This provided a bit of competition and room for other maltsters to enter the industry—but only if those maltsters were reliable with timely delivery of a quality product. A new malt house would pop up where it all began in Baltimore—at the site of the very first brewery, the Barnitz Brewery. In 1876, John Butterfield purchased the brewery on Hanover and Conway streets from William English, his partner in the malt and hops trade, from Wheeling, West Virginia, and the man with whom he was working to create a viable plant in Baltimore.[164] Butterfield, an immigrant from England, came from a family of brewers and maltsters and hoped to extend his business holdings across state lines.[165] He wanted in on the brewing and malting industry in bustling Baltimore while maintaining his business interests in Wheeling.[166] To make this both efficient and profitable, he brought in a partner, his son-in-law Frederick Gottlieb. Gottlieb was a Hungarian immigrant who had come to America as a child with his family, landing in New York.[167] Gottlieb, an accomplished flautist and an excellent bookkeeper, found a job in Wheeling and thus came to know Butterfield and his lovely daughter Christine.

Butterfield's Baltimore Brewery produced ale and porter, not lager. As expected of a family in the malting business they malted their own rye and barley. Butterfield operated as brewmaster of the plant for four years before choosing to concentrate on the Wheeling businesses. The Baltimore plant was old and in dire need of updating to be a truly productive brewery. Butterfield wanted out, and Gottlieb purchased his shares. Gottlieb by this time had met Herman Hobelman and now chose to take him on as a partner. The plan was to demolish the brewery and operate a malt and hop house in its place. By 1881 construction was completed and the gents had taken on a third partner, Fred Wehr, to help finance the venture. The "commodious structure" was seven stories high and had the most technologically advanced machinery to process and malt the grain. The operation was capable of malting 200,000 bushels annually, making it one of the largest malt houses in the country.[168] Wehr, Hobelman, and Gottlieb established themselves firmly in the malting business. They were part of Baltimore's growing brewing industry, and tey wanted to do more. Gottlieb helped to organize the Brewers and Maltsters Association of Baltimore, which eventually morphed into the Brewers Exchange. Those in the industry in Baltimore needed a voice, and Gottlieb made sure it was heard. He served as president of the Brewers Exchange for two years as well as trustee for four. Without fail he always operated in the best interests of the industry, even going before the state legislature in defense of the breweries.[169]

Although malting was Gottlieb's business, it was not enough for the three partners, as competition with the Straus family businesses was tough. Another member of the Straus family (Solomon) opened a Malthouse on Fawn and was outproducing H. Straus Brothers & Bell by three to one, not to mention Francis Denmead and smaller dealers like John Boyd.[170] The partners decided it was time to build a brewery and turn the plant into a malting and brewing operation. They definitely had the malt supply to accommodate the brewing process. In 1888 they began construction of a massive brew house and storage facility to begin production of beer. Otto C. Wolf was the architect, and the new business was called Globe Brewery. It was fitting to rebuild the brewery on the site, as it was located where the very first brewery in Baltimore had been situated one hundred and forty years before. It was an homage to the founding brewery. Another homage, if you will, was that Herman Hobelman was an active member of Zion Lutheran Church on Lexington, the church Daniel Barnitz, the son of the very first brewer, helped build. It had come full circle.[171] Perhaps they chose to use the name of a famous tourist hotel on Howard Street not far from the brewery—Globe.

The brewery was up and running by the end of 1889, with a capacity of 120,000 barrels per year. The four-story brew house was furnished with state-of-the-art equipment including a fifty-ton Weisel and Vilter refrigeration machine, an immense Corliss Engine, and a 350-barrel brew kettle. The four-story rear building kept a constant 40 degree temperature to maintain the amber lager once it was brewed.[172] This too became a stock brewery, in which many eager investors partook. All was good in the industry for Globe as they struck the perfect balance with their Munich, Goldbrau, and Imperial brews, while malting operations pressed on supplying their own and many other breweries across the city. The Globe was performing so well that it was sold along with sixteen other Baltimore breweries in 1899.[173]

Baltimore, in addition to seeing the rise of breweries and malt houses, also laid claim to the origin of the brewery workers union at the same time Gottlieb was organizing the Brewers and Maltsters Association, subsequently the Brewers Exchange. Although Baltimore was the birthplace of the National Labor Union in 1866, there was little impact on the industry for more than a decade. In 1883 the Baltimore Federation of Labor was formed. By 1885 the German Central Labor Union was created, and in 1886 the American Federation of Labor, but none of these applied specifically to brewery workers.[174] Gottlieb helped brewery employees claim their voice, but they needed the protection of the union, not just a rapt audience. Many independent regional unions had already formed in several states, usually organized by job title, not by the brewing industry as a whole. On August 29, 1886, the brewery workers of Baltimore, at the behest of Adolf Biswanger, assembled at Neidhart's Hall and agreed to form the National Union of Brewers of the United States. Five local unions chose to merge with them, and membership soared to four thousand by the end of 1886.

What is it that they wanted protection from? As with most unions, workers wanted to work fewer hours with better pay. A brief look at the Manufacturers Census of 1850, 1860, or 1880 will often reveal sixteen-hour workdays most brewery employees were expected to work, with the only reduction (by half) coming on the Lord's Day. That of course was a large part of it, but there was more that was strictly related to their welfare, both mental and physical.[175] Conditions in nineteenth-century breweries were dangerous even after the ice machines and engines became standard. The temperament of the proprietor could be just as deleterious to a worker as machinery or a boiling vat. Conrad Eurich, proprietor of the Germania Brewery in Baltimore, was famous for his temper. He was known to be a severe taskmaster who was not only prone to rudely dominating his German workers but also held no reservations about subjecting them to a horsewhip as he felt the need.[176] Often brewers suffered permanent injury that cut their lives short,

Germania Brewery, 1895 (BBT).

like Rudolph Bohnstengel. Bohnstengel was working at the Eingebrot plant when he suffered a head injury on the job and later died due to mental derangement caused by that same head injury. Unfortunately, injury on the job was commonplace. But once the union was organized, hours were limited to ten per day—two on Sundays—with an increase in wages, while health and safety became priorities. The ability of the workers to strike for better treatment played no small part in the improvement. This desire to unionize was something that was seen predominantly in major cities like Baltimore, Chicago, Milwaukee, and New York, but it was far from the minds and breweries of less densely populated cities in Maryland. Brewery workers were behind in places like Carroll County and Washington County, but they too would hear the call and answer.

Carroll County

After decades of its inhabitants relying upon Baltimore beers to quench their thirst, a new brewery finally opened in Westminster. Born in Hesse-Kassel, Germany, William Liedlich immigrated to York, Pennsylvania, seeking a future that would provide for himself and his wife, Elizabeth, help sponsor his family, and perhaps provide more immigrants with jobs in America.[177] Liedlich worked as a cooper before fighting in the Civil War. After the cessation of hostilities he relocated to Westminster, which was a city on the rise and a fine place to raise his family. Liedlich became the first lager beer brewer in Carroll County, in 1869.[178]

The lager trend quickly caught on in Baltimore and took a decidedly western turn following the immigrants who brought the lager yeast and the knowledge as they migrated. Liedlich primarily brewed lager, but he also brewed ale. Although trained and employed as a cooper in Germany before (and after) arriving in the states, he clearly knew the brewing business quite well. Even so, he hedged his bets by bringing over an experienced brewer from Prussia, Frederick Myres. He offered his goods by the keg as well as bottled to provide beer directly to residents and businesses alike, with an attached saloon to keep patrons spending money just a bit longer.[179] Situated next to the Montour House, his business was in an attractive, central location ideal for a lager brewery. As planned, he was able to bring his younger brother Peter to America, and both Peter and Myres lived with Liedlich, his wife, and their three sons.[180] Tragically, his business would not survive, as he suffered a stroke in 1871 at the tender age of forty-two and perished.[181] It is not clear why Myres did not continue the business after the death of Liedlich, but he was more than a decade older than Elizabeth and it seemed no marriage was destined to take place between them, as so often happened with brewery widows. The equipment was sold and the brewery closed.

German immigrant Valentine Zeller also opened a brewery in Westminster, concurrently to Leidlich, in 1870. Zeller had worked at a brewery in Virginia prior to his Westminster move. In Westminster his brewery was located on Green Street. Zeller produced ale, not lager beer, as that was his purview.[182] He and his wife and six children were fully invested in the industry in Carroll County, hoping business would thrive where there were too few brewers. His operation failed, and he was forced to move his family to a location where he could find work in a brewery, and that was Washington, D.C., in 1873.[183] More than a century would pass before another brewer would hang up a shingle in Carroll County. Until then residents relied upon the wealth of lager flowing from Baltimore and Frederick.

Frederick County

Although fightng was limited in Frederick during the Civil War, it still left an impression upon the citizens emotionally, politically, and physically. Whether choosing sides or having it thrust upon them, Frederick was in the churn that was the Civil War in Maryland. When Annapolis was occupied by Union forces and the legislature convened in Frederick, whatever belief occupants in the region had regarding the war reality was brought home with startling clarity. This was made even more visceral in July 1864 when the Battle of Monocacy was fought in their front yard. There was no escape when Lieutenant General Jubal Early made his way into Maryland with 15,000 Confederate soldiers and a plan to skirt south and take Washington, D.C. A quick warning from the Baltimore and Ohio Railroad crews who spotted the advance allowed General Lew Wallace to greet them with a force of 6,000 Union soldiers. The Union lost the battle but stalled the advance. Neutrality was not an option as the war came to Frederick, and everyone felt the burden of it.

In Frederick not only do we see the continuation of the prolific John Lipps, Dr. William Zimmerman, and Peter Baer breweries operating during and after the Civil

War but also a few new brewers planted stakes in Frederick hoping to find triumph. John Elour was a saloon owner who also opened a brewery to feed his saloon business in Emmitsburg in 1867.[184] Although the business was low in production it served the small community of Emmitsburg, which had never had a brewery before. Many in the neighborhood enjoyed the fruits of Elour's labor for nearly a decade.

Paul Hauser was a brewer who succeeded Peter Baer in the Brewer's Alley location in the heart of Frederick. Like his predecessor, Hauser was a German immigrant. He was also predisposed to penny pinching and lived above the brewery instead of shelling out additional money to support a separate residence. The plant was constructed in extremely close quarters and expansion was not a viable option for Hauser or any of the brewers occupying that location. Hauser initially brewed ale and small beer and eventually added lager beer to appeal to a wider audience influenced by the nearby breweries in Baltimore and Cumberland. At his peak, Hauser produced just under 500 barrels per annum, enough to survive but not enough to thrive; the brew was supplying his saloon but not much beyond that. He was paying out $1,000 in wages per year for four employees to work twelve-hour days in 1880. This was indicative of two things. First, there was no union forming in Frederick at the time; and second, considering the value of his brewery matched the investment, he was losing money or breaking even annually.[185] He gave up the plant when his health deteriorated.

A prominent lawyer in Frederick, Christian Eckstein, took over the plant. The Eckstein family hailed from Frankfurt, Germany. Christian had been born in Baltimore, and the family moved to Frederick seeking greater opportunity. When he was merely nineteen years old he began to study law. At twenty-one he was admitted to the bar (1866) and eventually served as a justice of the peace, police justice officer, and a lawyer in the Democratic Party.[186] Although little was spoken of his side endeavors, as they paled in comparison to his illustrious legal career, Eckstein owned the tiny brewery that had been occupied by Hauser. It was a brief stint, and the brewery was quickly turned over to another brewer in 1891.

John Kuhn was perhaps the most fruitful brewer in this procession of brewers, taking over the Eckstein plant in 1891 and calling it the Gambrinus Brewery, after the god of beer (of course). It appears he too was looking for good fortune to be bestowed upon him and he certainly found it. Kuhn lived at the brewery with his wife, Elizabeth, and their five children, much like Hauser and very unlike Eckstein, operating both brewery and saloon. Kuhn hailed from Bavaria, having emigrated in 1870, and produced strictly lager beer, as was tradition in his homeland. Despite the cramped quarters, he too housed his workers in his home with his family.[187] The brewery was quite prosperous, with many adulations for the quality of his lager. Kuhn most likely would have continued operations in Brewer's Alley until he could expand to a larger plant, but catastrophe struck in 1901. A spectacular and destructive fire destroyed the brewery and the saloon, as well as the family home. Kuhn had no choice but to abandon the brewery he had given more than a decade of his life building. He moved on to Baltimore with his family to make his living operating saloons. It was several decades before another brewery operated in Frederick after the loss of the Gambrinus Brewery.[188]

Battle of Antietam (LOC).

Washington County

There is no doubt that the Civil War impacted the brewing industry in Washington County, as it did for many Maryland counties. Washington County felt this weight more than almost any Western Maryland territory due to the Battle of Antietam in 1862 and Falling Waters in 1863, when Kilpatrick drove two Confederate cavalry brigades right through Hagerstown while Lee headed for the Potomac before facing off against Meade's Union forces. It is well known that the Battle represented the bloodiest day in the history of the war, a day that was not soon forgotten by anyone on either side of the conflict. Twenty-three thousand men died at Sharpsburg, a hair's breadth from Hagerstown, when Union forces under McClellan squared off against General Robert E. Lee. Additionally Hagerstown, and its prime location on the railroad line, proved integral to resupplying Union troops, and it was costly when Confederates were able to sever or seize track over the course of the war.[189]

The Peter Middlekauf Brewery certainly felt the economic strain from the conflict. The war was difficult for Middlekauf's business, and he chose retirement from the industry and returned to his roots as a farmer in 1864.[190] The experience was a trying one for him, as his family later testified to. The deep lagering vaults below the brewery turned out to be a blessing for the family during the war, as their home and brewery were ransacked by Confederate soldiers on numerous occasions. The vaults became a safe place for the family to take refuge and an even better place to hide valuables, sentimental items, and even prized horses (and hay) they did not want stolen. As has been said, war is hell. Despite the trouble the family had with Confederates, each and every night the daughters left pails of water out for soldiers, Union and Confederate alike.[191] This was indicative of the attitude of many people at the time, trying to survive the best they could, offering kindness whenever possible.

One brewer who chose to open in Hagerstown during the Civil War was Louis Heist, who had partnered in a brewery with Andrew Leibold in the decade prior to the hostilities. Heist located on Potomac, a main thoroughfare where he was assured of substantial business via foot traffic and word of mouth. After acquiring the property in 1854 he operated a grocery on the premises for a number of years before deciding to take up the brewing business again in 1862. Coincidentally, 1862 was the year his former partner, Leibold, died. Perhaps Heist waited out of respect for the competition—or he may have waited to pay off his mortgage prior to financing construction of a new brewery building. Once the brewery opened, he hedged his bets by operating as both a grocer and a brewer, maximizing patronage.[192] His ale was well received since he perfected it in his previous business with Leibold and was a welcome return to the city. Heist was a well-known man in town and a trusted one. Often he was called upon to act as a trustee or executor, as he was known to carry out his duties with integrity and efficiency. To the neighborhood children he was warm and kind, providing a place for them to lift weights and muck about in the rear of his grocery.[193] Heist managed his brewery for fifteen years, never selling more than a few hundred barrels of ale per year. Combined with his grocery business, that was more than enough to position his family quite well in Hagerstown. Heist was considered one of the more prominent landowners, and he engaged in numerous land transactions that supplemented his income from his grocery and brewery until his death in 1877.[194]

The brewery was sold to Justus Heimel, another German immigrant who operated a brewery just down the street from Heist. In fact, he operated the very same plant Heist shared with Leibold over two decades before (clearly Heist knew how to pick optimal brewery locations).[195] The new plant of Heimel was far superior to the former, as Heist had taken advantage of the many underground caves beneath the brewery for fermenting and storage. Heimel, however, added ice machines as they became available instead of relying upon the unpredictability of sustaining temperatures with blocks of ice, as the old methods dictated. He also converted the grocery at the front of the building into a saloon, catering to clientele in a different way. His son William trained as a brewer in Chicago and worked with him in the business. Heimel matched the output of Heist until he added the ice machine and production increased substantially. Heimel continued brewing for fifteen years, after which he became the director of the Washington County Savings Bank and his son William ran the saloon.[196]

Another brewer who bravely hung his shingle in Hagerstown near the end of the war was Robert Shuster from Baden, Germany. Shuster, along with his wife, Barbara, opened the brewery at 120 West Franklin. He established a small common beer brewery in the beginning but moved on to the brewing of lager after lagering cellars were constructed.[197] Baden being close to Bavaria, Shuster was no doubt accustomed to drinking and most likely was quite familiar with the manufacture of lager. He was quite fruitful, and his production matched that of other breweries across town. He raised nine children while operating the brewery on Franklin and Jonathan and ran the brewery until he died in 1888.[198] It was not a family legacy, however, as none of the children followed him in the industry.

William Wagner was yet one more German brewer from Hesse-Darmstadt who came to America to open a brewery. He settled in Hagerstown, as it was just large enough to operate a small brewery with limited competition, and started out working in the brewery of Katherine Leibold, the widow of Andrew Leibold, Lewis Heist's former partner. After a brief stint he was ready to open his own plant and he too chose to locate on Potomac to maximize visibility and traffic. He produced common beer, which was still a preferred style over lager in 1865 Hagerstown. Wagner found a wife and started his family in his new home just a few blocks from the brewery.[199] His wife, Catherine, was the daughter of Andrew and Katherine Leibold. As has been mentioned, this was incredibly common—intermarriage among brewing families—just as it was in Baltimore. It was not, however, restricted to large cities, often occurring in smaller locales that fostered close relationships. Together the couple had a son, Conrad, but in a cruel twist Catherine died before his tenth birthday. Wagner continued on, just father and son together, producing common beer. His method was sound, as he was turning out almost double the product compared to his Hagerstown competition.[200]

Allegany County

Allegany County served as a weigh station and a fortress of sorts during the Civil War. Many Union soldiers were placed in Allegany County, due in part to the National Road running east/west, but, more important, Cumberland housed the rail lines for the major artery of the Baltimore and Ohio Railroad between Washington and West Virginia. Additionally, Cumberland was the western terminus of the C&O Canal, another critical artery for supplies and troop movement. To say that Cumberland and Allegany County were strategically critical to the Union war efforts would be an under-statement. Union forces could not allow Cumberland to fall to Confederates without fear of losing the war. Confederate troops repeatedly raided and attacked the rail lines, roadways, and canal to try to unclench the grip of the Union fist, but to no avail. The situation became critical in 1864, after Brigadier General McCausland set his sights on Cumberland and the railroad after his Confederate troops left Chambersburg in ashes and were thwarted in Hancock. To defend Cumberland, General Kelley hastily gathered 3,000 troops, including a host of about 200 citizens from the town of Cumberland, and sent them out to meet the incoming Confederates near John Folcke's mill. Although outnumbered, with heavy artillery Kelley retained the advantage. After several hours of fighting, McCausland was forced to retreat. The town of Cumberland had saved itself, suffering only two casualties.

Despite the ravages of war tearing through western Maryland, breweries still opened and operated to serve their constituents and their comrades in battle. Some breweries even chose to open during the conflict with thoughts that the Union army needed hydration of a certain malty note. One such brewer was Peter Hinkle, who opened his establishment in Mount Savage, where only one other brewery was operational—that of James McNulty. Hinkle was a widower born in 1803 in Hesse-Kassel, Germany, and immigrated to America with his three surviving children in 1856.[201] He landed in Allegany County, where a large contingent of the Hinkle clan had settled over the previous century. His first stop was Frostburg, and within six years he relocated to Mount Savage, an event that coincided with the nuptial celebration of his eldest daughter, Sophia.[202]

Hinkle was not a young man and was pushing sixty when he opened his brewery in 1862. It was a business he knew and one he hoped to share with his son Henry, who was only fifteen at the time. His eldest son, Valentine, had already moved to Pennsylvania, where he found work as a farmer. Once the brewery opened Hinkle produced common beer for the small population of Mount Savage, which was less than two thousand, and of course the Union soldiers who frequented the area during the war. Hinkle did well for himself and was running a profitable operation within a decade, despite, or perhaps because of, the war and his location near the railroad, which engendered much business. It did not hurt that his business rival McNulty closed up operations in 1867, leaving Hinkle to supply the thirsty town on his own. Hinkle was also busy acquiring land surrounding the brewery, which was ideally located on a creek.[203] He was building the future he sought for his family, albeit a bit later than most.

Peter Hinkle ran his brewery well, teaching Henry the ins and outs of brewing operations, finances, and management. When Peter died in 1877 Henry was ready to take the reins. He also wanted to do things his way, which meant stepping up the production of lager beer at the brewery. This was not surprising, as in 1869 his father purchased an adjoining lot in Mount Savage that already possessed underground caves perfect for lagering.[204] The brewery did well, charging $1 per case of beer, and $1.75 per quarter keg, rivaling some of the prices high-end breweries in Baltimore charged.[205] Henry seemed to place quality above quantity, as his production numbers were relatively low.[206] It did not hurt that the Hinkle family never experienced any competition for the rest of the years the brewery was operational. Henry continued the brewery as his father had taught him, taking in his sister Sophia when she was widowed. Sophia taught music while Henry brewed. The siblings were entrenched in their community. It was their home, despite their choosing never to naturalize as American citizens. Henry retired in 1904. That was the last brewery to operate in Mount Savage.

Another Allegany brewer who chose to open during the war to maximize potential profits was Bartholomew Himmler. Himmler had previously owned a brewery in Cumberland before moving away with dreams of opening a distillery across state lines. Shortly after the war broke out he decided to return to Cumberland and enter the brewing industry once again. Perhaps Virginia was too dangerous or maybe he did not agree with the Southern cause. Either way, Himmler was still going to be located in the thick of it in Cumberland. Bartholomew set up the plant on North Mechanic Street, central to much of what was going on in town, in ready relation to active soldiers, and near the National Road transporting them. He employed his son George in the brewery, as well as his eldest son, John, when they were old enough to help. He also brought over a brewer from Holland, Henry Turner, to assist in brewing operations.[207] John eventually

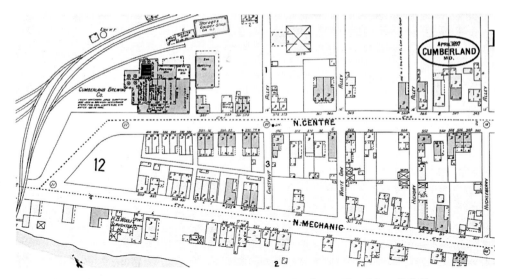

Cumberland Brewing Company, 1897 Sanborn Fire Map (LOC).

opened a saloon attached to the brewery, and the Himmler family was operating at a profit, acquiring land, and expanding their opportunities once again.[208] They survived the war intact and reestablished their brewing legacy in Cumberland.

Bartholomew was no spring chicken and his sons George and John took over the plant when he retired in 1870, calling it J. Himmler and Brother Brewing.[209] Things ran smoothly and production was strong, even after the cessation of hostilities. John, however, chose to forge his own path and opened a whiskey distillery across the street from the family brewery on Mechanic.[210] George continued alone, hitting peak production of lager and common beer even without his brother.[211] His own children helped in the brewery, just as he had with his father. The torch was being passed. Sadly, before George completed the training of his sons, he perished, leaving his wife, Mary, to operate the brewery for about a year.[212] By 1885 Mary sold her interest to her brother-in-law William Himmler, who ran a saloon on Centre Street and had learned the art of brewing from his father and brothers.[213] The plant was immense under William, as he continued building upon what George began. Ice machines were installed to coincide with an expansion of the brewery. Fortunately William Leonard's Cumberland Malt House was just a few doors down, offering copious quantities of malt for Himmler's use.[214] It was a perfect match. William continued operations, employing both his nephew and his cousin until 1891.

Himmler's cousin John H. Zink purchased the brewery in 1891.[215] John Zink (John H.'s father) was the brother-in-law of Bartholomew Himmler. John Zink purchased the Himmler family's first Cumberland brewery after they relocated. It was fitting that the young Zink take over the more recent Himmler brewery, bringing everything full circle. John H. Zink had been brewing for the Himmlers for over a decade when he purchased the brewery.[216] The families remained close despite the brief relocation. John H. Zink's sons were named George and William, after two of the Himmler brothers. It truly was the definition of an extended brewing family. Young Zink brought his sons into the business to train them and continue the legacy.[217] He had a more difficult go of it than

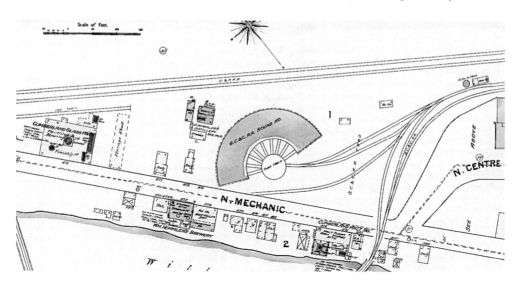

William Himmler Brewery, adjacent to Cumberland Malthouse, 1877 Sanborn Fire Map (LOC).

William, as by this time the Cumberland Malt House had burned to the ground and was not rebuilt, making acquisition of malt more challenging than before.[218] Zink and his family continued operations for fifteen years after taking over, until the competition from the remaining two Cumberland breweries knocked him out of the business. He took a position as a brewer at his former competitor's brewery to continue taking care of his family.[219]

Other Civil War era breweries in Cumberland fared well. German brewer George Schulz, who in 1863 operated the Washington Brewery on Paca Street, on the site of the former Gessner Brewery, was one. Trained as a brewer and maltster in Germany, he worked the plant for nine years before selling to perhaps the most famous small brewer in Cumberland, Paul Hugo Ritter.[220] Ritter was born in Württemberg, Germany, in 1840. He trained as a brewer and worked at several breweries across America from Ohio to the Christian Heurich Brewery in Washington, D.C. It was at Heurich's brewery that Ritter learned the exceptional art of making lager beer. This was what he crafted when he came to Cumberland in 1872 with his wife, Kate, and six children.[221] Not only did Ritter produce lager beer but he also had an adjoining watering hole for thirsty patrons.[222] For a small brewer he was manufacturing quite a bit of his Bavarian lager, on apar with what John H. Zink was turning out at his peak.[223] Ritter suffered the seemingly unimaginable twice. In 1888 his brewery burned to the ground. Fortunately he rebuilt, taking advantage of the restructuring and installing an ice machine to aid in consistency and efficiency. He also added a few new products to his Bavarian lager, including an Export, and a Budweiss. Lightning should never strike twice in the same spot, but for Ritter it did. In 1894 his brewery burned to the ground once again, ending his prolific brewing career and some of the best lager in Cumberland.[224]

A brewery that was operational in Cumberland during the Civil War was run by Gustav Stucklauser and known as the City Brewery. By 1872 Stucklauser had relocated to Mechanic Street. Although it was mere blocks away, it provided more foot traffic from the building businesses in Cumberland and greater access to necessary amenities like water coming from Wills Creek and, most important, an underground stream running beneath the brewery.[225] This is why Stuckauser named it the Blue Spring Brewery, although most people who knew Stucklauser from his former plant continued to call it the City Brewery.[226] Gustav and his son August worked together in the brewery, producing mostly common beer. Over time they ventured into the production of lager beer, which kept the plant relevant as tastes of consumers adjusted. Gustav purchased a tract of land near Wills Creek and the brewery that was perfect for lager storage, and he thus expanded the footprint of the brewery.[227] However, he did not grasp the immediate need for ice machines when they became available. The traditional method of brewing, fermenting, and storing seemed to work just fine for him and his son August. The death knell eventually sounded, as they couldn't compete with those breweries that had embraced the refrigeration technology and provided a more consistent lager beer. In 1872, after more than three decades in business serving Cumberland, Stucklauser retired from the brewery, which was then turned into a slaughterhouse.[228]

The brewery that was seizing much of the business from other Cumberland and regional breweries was that of Michael Fesenmeier. Fesenmeier started out in a small brewery in Lindnersville, on the outskirts of Cumberland, in 1877. Fesenmeier, like many of the brewers discussed in this work, was a German immigrant born in Württemberg. He settled with his wife just outside of Cumberland and worked as a farmer. As he saved and his family began to grow, Fesenmeier purchased his own property to farm.[229] By the time his family had grown to eight, he brought over laborers from Bavaria to help on the farm and he acquired more property.[230] The laborers he brought from Bavaria may have played an instrumental role in his push to brew beer. By 1870 he was listed as a brewer in the census, with substantial real estate holdings.[231] Although most give the date of the start of his brewery as 1877, there exists solid support that he had by 1870 what could be considered a farm brewery, where he was brewing common beer for sale and harvesting enough crops to feed his family while selling goods to others at the same time. Accordingly, he was generating as much as most of the brewers in and around Cumberland by 1879.[232] As his sons Michael and George began to participate in the business they became excellent students in the art of brewing, and eventually lager beer was manufactured at the plant.

George was content with the plant and the location on the edge of Cumberland. Michael was not and wanted a larger operation complete with the technological equipment of the age. Michael senior was not ready for that commitment and continued to brew at the original plant on Baltimore Pike (Valley Road) with his son George, while he sent son Andrew off to Chicago to professionally train as a brewer.[233] Michael Junior left Cumberland and brewed in St. Louis for Anheuser Busch before moving on to Dallas and Wagenhauser Brewing.[234] Fesemeier eventually added the ice machine to the primitive plant in 1888, but the family wanted more than what the small brewery was capable of.[235] The decision to relocate to a larger property where refrigeration and other technological brewing enhancements could be capitalized was made upon the return of Michael Junior to Cumberland. That coincided with the availability of an old cotton mill off of Centre Street, near the railroad and many other necessities.[236] The brewery was operational by 1890, and the sons had transcended the expertise of their father in brewing.[237] Many prominent men in the industry or related industries were involved and part of the incorporation. This was the talent pool from which the brothers drew their management. The versatility provided greater depth in areas like sales and engineering, boosting the plant's chances of success and increasing efficiency in processes. They could not have scripted a better plan for the brewery's future. In the first year the plant was producing 8,000 barrels, and it was only going to expand. By 1891 it reached 22,000 barrels of lager beer. There were a variety of brews offered including Fort Cumberland Brew, Rheingold, Old Export, and Erlanger.[238] There was no slowing down, and the family was set to produce even more when the founder, Michael Fesenmeier, passed away in 1883. Although he had resisted the expansion of the brewery and would never see it reach its full potential, it was heartening to see the immediate success reached with the persistence and determination of his sons. Fesenmeier left a legacy for his sons to embrace and build upon, carving a future for themselves and their own children.

The brothers pushed onward to create the largest brewery in Western Maryland. They added an office building, a bottling plant with state-of-the-art bottle washing equipment, and eventually a new ice plant with superior capabilities.[239] The cream on the top was not only the outstanding production but also the addition of Pflauder glass-enameled steel tanks, the same type John Wiessner installed in his plant in Baltimore. It was not surprising that other breweries in Cumberland were struggling to stay afloat. Once John H. Zink closed his brewery it was Cumberland that he went to for work. The Fesenmeier brewery was also a contributing factor to Ritter's choosing not to rebuild his plant, and the Beck family, who had been operating the Beck Brewery with various family members since 1861, eventually decided to close. Not only was the Cumberland Brewing Company one of the largest in the state, the quality of the product was unmatched in the west. The Cumberland Brewing Company established its reputation as reliable, crafting quality lager beer known throughout the state and beyond. The legend would continue to grow as the years ticked by.

Maryland brewing survived the Civil War, and thrived, becoming one of the top producing states in the industry. As breweries embraced technology, the process was refined and the quality improved. Those that did not grasp onto the advancements were left behind or put out of business. It was no longer enough to be the only brewer in an area and succeed. Now beers were crisscrossing the state by way of the railroad. Brews from Cumberland found their way to Baltimore and vice versa. Out-of-state breweries like Bartholomay's out of New York established a plant in Baltimore to keep up with East Coast distribution, further cutting into the profits of small Maryland breweries. Not every brewery was poised to compete, but some would not only keep their market share but also increase it. As the century turned, however, a dark shadow was cast, a harbinger of changes to come that would threaten the very existence of the industry and rock it to its core. Those breweries that braced for the impact of the upcoming two decades had a glimmer of hope towards survival, but the fight and the consequences would be immense. The industry would feel the rattle of the saber, and brewing families of Maryland would be torn asunder.

BREWERY LISTINGS

Allegany County

BREWERY	PROPRIETOR	LOCATION/ NEIGHBORHOOD	YEARS	PEAK PRODUCTION (IF KNOWN)
Hinkle Brewery	Peter Hinkle & Henry Hinkle	Mount Savage	1862–1877	500 bbls/yr
	Henry Hinkle	Same	1878–1904	114 bbls/yr
Himmler Brewing Company	Bartholomew Himmler & Family	836 North Mechanic Street Cumberland	1863–1870	
J. Himmler & Brother Brewing	John & George Himmler	Same	1870–1877	
Himmler Brewing	George Himmler	Same	1877–1884	591 bbls/yr
	Mrs. Mary Himmler	Same	1884–1885	
	William Himmler	Same (changed to 426 North Mechanic)	1885–1891	1,000 bbls/yr
John H. Zink Brewing	John H. Zink	Same	1891–1906	500–1,000 bbls/yr
Washington Brewery	George H. Schulz	34–44 Paca Street	1863–1872	
	Paul Hugo Ritter	Same	1872–1894	665 bbls/yr
Cruetzberg Brewing Company	Henry Cruetzberg	Barton	1867–1868	
	George Schramm	Same	1874–1877	85 bbls/yr
Kolberg & Co	Kolberg	Same	1877–1878	500 bbls/yr
Langlotz & Co	George Langlotz	Detmond Street and Main near the bridge Lonaconing	1869–1875	1,560 bbls/yr
Hohing Ale and Common Beer Brewery	Conrad & Otto Hohing	Same	1875–1890	500 bbls/yr
Benfield Brewery	Joseph Benfield	Westernport	1871	
Erpelt Brewery	Joseph Erpelt	Westernport	1871	
Knorr Brewing	Margaret Knorr	Westernport	1871–1884	65 bbls/yr
Nau Brewing	Conrad Nau	Same	1884–1894	500 bbls/yr
Blue Spring Brewing Company AKA: City Brewery	Gustav & August Stucklauser	174/176 North Mechanic Street Cumberland	1872–1892	700 bbls/yr
Eisfeller Brewing	G.H. Eisfeller	Frostburg	1874–1875	85 bbls/yr
Mayer Brewing	John Mayer	Uhls Alley Frostburg	1874–1888	300 bbls/yr
	Elizabeth Mayer	Same	1888–1893	500 bbls/yr
Biddington Brewery	M.J. Biddington	Frostburg	1875	40 bbls/yr
Davis Brewing Company	Thomas D. Davis	Frostburg	1875	40 bbls/yr
Christian Hartung & Company	Christian Hartung	Cumberland	1875	850 bbls/yr
Zink Brewing[240]	George H. Zink	Knox and Centre near Viaduct Cumberland	1875–1876	1,045 bbls/yr
Fesenmeier Brewing Company	Fesenmeier Family	56 Valley Road Lindnersville	1877–1889	500 bbls/yr
Beck Brewing	George F. Beck	Same	1889–1891	
Haneykamp Brewery	Haneykamp & Fredericks	Jackson Street	1877–1879	1,345 bbls/yr
	C.F. Fredericks	Same	1879–1880	500 bbls/yr
Leonard Malt House & Brewery[241]	William Leonard	296 Mechanic Street Cumberland	1878–1879	500 bbls/yr

BREWERY	PROPRIETOR	LOCATION/ NEIGHBORHOOD	YEARS	PEAK PRODUCTION (IF KNOWN)
Kolb Brewing	John A. Kolb	Cumberland	1880–1882	
Martin Brewery	Thomas Martin	Georges Street	1880–1882	
Beck Brewing Company	William & Henry Beck	19–21 Front Street	1886–1892	500 bbls/yr
Cumberland Brewing Company	Fesenmeier Family	397 North Centre Street	1890–1920	22,000 bbls/yr

Baltimore City and County

BREWERY	PROPRIETOR	LOCATION/ NEIGHBORHOOD	YEARS	PEAK PRODUCTION (IF KNOWN)
Albion Brewery	Jacob Mulhauser	Belvedere & Greenmount Ave (and Lanvale)	1862–1865	
	Jacob Green	Same	1865–1872	
	Sophia Green	Same	1873–1875	1,035 bbls/yr
	Frederick (Fritz) & Christian Schneider	Same	1875–1876	
Belvedere Brewery	Christian Schneider	Same	1876–1878	
Albion Brewery	Bernhard Berger & Family	Same	1878–1893	6,000 bbls/yr
John Berger Brewing Company	John B. Berger	Same	1893–1899	10,000 bbls/yr
Odenwald & Joh Brewing	Philip Odenwald & Ferdinand Joh	7 Calverton Road	1862–1873	4,000 bbls/yr
Sommerfeld Brewing	John Sommerfeld	Same	1873–1895	12,000 bbls/yr
Lion Brewing Company	Harry Biemiller	Same	1895–1901	12,000 bbls/yr
Weber Brewing	Fred Weber	Harford Road & Herring Run	1862–1889	3,254 bbls/yr
Butschky Brewing	Viet Butschky	Belair Avenue	1863–1869	
Spengler Brewing	Christopher Spengler	Same	1869–1871	
Schlaffer Brewing	Franz Schlaffer Family	Same	1872–1881	3,701 bbls/yr
Hohnberger Brewery	C. Hohnberger	210 West Lee Street	1863	
J.F. Wiessner Brewing Company	J. Frederick (Fritz) Wiessner & Family	Belair Avenue	1863–1920	110,000 bbls/yr
Bauernfind Brewing Company	John Bauernfind	70 South Wolfe Street Fell's Point	1864–1880	
	Dittman	Same	1880–1882	3,000 bbls/yr
	Stier	Same	1882–1883	
Empire Brewery	G.W. Umbach	Same	1883–1891	10,000 bbls/yr
	Mary Miller	Same	1891–1892	
Greenwood Park Brewery	George Bauernschmidt	Belair Avenue	1864–1899	300,000 bbls/yr
Schneider Brewing	(Frederick) Fritz Schneider	249 Aliceanna Fell's Point	1864–1866	
Shettle & Company	Daniel Shettle	Holliday & Franklin	1864–1866	
Maryland Brewery	Jacob Medtart	Same	1866–1872	
	Thomas Dukeheart	Same	1872–1884	8,000 bbls/yr
Spring Garden Brewery	John Bauernschmidt & Marr (1879)	1540 Ridgely Street	1864–1889	50,000 bbls/yr
Wiessner & Miller Lager Beer	George F. Wiessner & John Miller	Burke & Essex Streets	1864–1867	
Wiessner Lager Brewery	George F. Wiessner	Same	1867–1869	
Stab Canton Lager Beer Brewery	William Stab	Same	1869–1877	915 bbls/yr
	Lina Stab	Same	1877–1882	500 bbls/yr

BREWERY	PROPRIETOR	LOCATION/ NEIGHBORHOOD	YEARS	PEAK PRODUCTION (IF KNOWN)
August Beck Brewery	August Beck	44 Garrison Lane & Frederick Road	1865–1871	3,000+- bbls/yr
August Beck and Son Brewery	August Beck Senior & August Beck Junior	Same	1871–1879	8,000 bbls/yr
August Beck Brewery	August Beck Junior	Same	1880–1899	10,000 bbls/yr
John Marr Independent Brewery	John Marr	Same	1899–1900	
Nitzel Brewery	Michael Nitzel	NW Cor. Clinton & Elliott Streets Canton	1865–1867	
	Albert Wagner	Same	1867–1868	
	Samuel Nitzel	Same	1868–1870	
Von der Horst & Rupprecht Brewery	John Von der Horst & Rupprecht	Belair Avenue	1865–1866	
Von der Horst Eagle Brewery	John Von Der Horst & Family	Same	1866–1899	40,000 bbls/yr
Baier Brewery	Anna Baier & Family	390 Canton Avenue & Chester	1866–1869	10,000 bbls/yr
Wunder Brewery	Anna & Frederick Wunder	Same	1869–1872	
	Same	3rd & O'Donnell Streets Canton	1872–1885	5,899 bbls/yr
National Brewery	Joseph & William Straus	Same	1885–1899	
Bayview Brewery	Jacob Keinzle	Eastern Avenue & Ponca	1866–1876	20,000 bbls/yr
	Hect & Miller & Company	Same	1876–1887	10,000 bbls/yr
	William Miller	Same	1887–1889	40,000 bbls/yr
Bayview Baltimore United	Baltimore United Breweries Ltd.	Same	1889–1899	40,000 bbls/yr
Brehm Brewery	George Brehm	Belair, Erdman & Bowleys	1866–1899	100,000 bbls/yr
Engel Brewery	Otto Engel	Belair Ave & North Avenue	1866–1869	
	Anna Engel	Same	1869–1870	
Schreier Brewing	Joseph Schreier	Same	1870–1882	7,200 bbls/yr
	Ewald & Schuman	Same	1882–1884	
Hertlein's Brewing Company	Gottfried Hertlein	4440 Block Belair Ave	1866–1879	1,406 bbls/yr
	Otto Woerner	Same	1879–1890	
Heil Brewery	Charles Heil	494 West Pratt Street Pigtown	1867–1870	
Miller Brewing Company	Ambrose Miller	368 Light Street near Cross	1867–1877	250 bbls/yr
Mueller Brewing	Valentine Mueller	32 Burke Street Canton	1867–1878	1,080 bbls/yr
Luis Muth Brewery	Luis Muth	1800 block Belair Avenue	1867–1880	7,700 +- bbls/yr
Louis Muth & Son Brewery	Luis Muth & Son Louis Junior	Same	1880–1888	
Nagengast Brewing	John Nagengast & Family	370 Pennsylvania Avenue near Pitcher	1867–1878	925 bbls/yr
Werner & Honig Brewing	Henry Werner & Honig	Same	1878–1879	1,258 bbls/yr

Brewery	Proprietor	Location/ Neighborhood	Years	Peak Production (if known)
Phoenix Brewery	Henry Werner	Same	1879–1888	23,000 bbls/yr
	John & Franklin Manning	Same	1888–1892	
Rummelmann Brewing	John Rummelmann	326 South Bond Fell's Point	1867–1871	
Annapolis Beer Brewery	John L. Zwangswer & Family	Annapolis Road near Old Fishouse Westport	1868–1881	
	Adolph Beck	Same	1881–1882	
Baier & Altevogt Brewing Company	Paul Baier & Frederick Altevogt	Trappe Road & O'Donnell Canton		1868–1870
Baier Brewing Company	Paul Baier & Family	Same	1870–1877	
Berger & Co. Weiss Beer Brewery	John M. Berger & Andrew Dittman (1868)	22 Thames & Bond Streets	1868–1878	
Grimmer Brewery	Valentine Grimmer	Lancaster & 3rd Highlandtown	1868–1878	1,180 bbls/yr
Beh Brewery	John G. Beh	Same	1878–1880	2,300 bbls/yr
Boehn Brewery	Anton Boehn	Same	1880–1881	
Oriental Brewing Company	Franz Schlaffer & Family	Same	1881–1899	15,000 bbls/yr
Miller Brewery	George Miller	Harford Road Lauraville	1868–1872	
	Conrad Siegman	Same	1872–1873	
Darley Park Brewery	Straus Brothers & Bell	Same	1874–1889	12,950 bbls/yr
	Baltimore United	Same	1889–1899	60,000 bbls/yr
Pabst Lager Beer Brewery	John & George Pabst	Trappe Road near Clinton Canton	1868–1871	
Schneider Brewery	(Frederick) Fritz Schneider	3rd and Dillon Streets Canton	1868–1889	3,000 bbls/yr
	Straus Brothers	Same	1889–1892	
Fort Marshall Brewery	George F. Wiessner	Eastern & Highland Avenue Highlandtown	1869–1872	
	Andrew Hoenervogt	Same	1872–1876	
	Elizabeth Wiessner Hoenervogt	Same	1876–1888	3,500 bbls/yr
John F. Wiessner & Bro Brewing Company	John F. & Christopher Wiessner	Same	1888–1899	6,000 bbls/yr
Kalb Brewing	John Kalb	710 Light Street	1869–1874	
Abherhart Brewery	Frank Aberhart	Same	1874–1875	
Mueller Brewery	John Mueller	394 Pennsylvania Avenue	1869–1880	732 bbls/yr
	Catherine Mueller	Same	1880–1884	
Mueller & Handloeser Western Maryland Brewery	Catherine Mueller & Robert Handloeser	Same	1884–1890	5,000 bbls/yr
Western Maryland Brewery	Robert Handloeser	Same	1890–1897	4,000 bbls/yr
Scrans Brewery	JL Scrans	2nd & O'Donnell Streets	1869–1873	
George Miller Brewery	George Miller	Same	1873	
William Kemper Brewery	William Kemper	Same	1877–1880	2,799 bbls/yr
Mason Brewing	Joy C. Mason	136 South Sharp Street	1870–1871	
Röst Brewery	Sophia Röst & Sons	Belair & Patterson Park	1871–1881	10,000 bbls/yr

BREWERY	PROPRIETOR	LOCATION/ NEIGHBORHOOD	YEARS	PEAK PRODUCTION (IF KNOWN)
Standard Brewing Company	Henry & Levi Straus (Joseph Raiber)	Same	1888–1889	
	John & Franklin Manning	Same	1889–1894	
	Daniel Manning	Same	1895–1896	
	John Marr	Same	1896–1899	25,000 bbls/yr
	Joseph Gottschalk	Same	1899–1912	
Pabst Brewery	George Pabst & Family	O'Donnell & 3rd Streets Canton	1872–1875	
Lion Brewery	John Trost & Family	Same	1876–1883	5,000 bbls/yr
	William Miller	Same	1883	
Mount Pleasant Brewery	Straus Brothers & Johnathan Raiber	Baltimore & Garrison (Franklintown)	1871–1872	
Mount Pleasant Brewery	John Schultheis	Same	1872–1886	2,504 bbls/yr
Union Brewing Company	John Schultheis & Robert Wiesenfeld	Same	1886	
	John Schultheis & Oscar Teschner	Same	1886–1889	
Theodore Seeger Brewery	Theodore Seeger	426 Frederick Road	1872–1873	
Bauer & Buechler Brewery	Gottlieb Bauer & Frederick Buechler	Clinton & Lancaster Highlandtown	1873–1874	
Sebastian Helldoerfer's Brewery	Sebastian Helldoerfer & Sons	Same	1874–1899	20,000 bbls/yr
Joh Brewery	Ferdinand Joh	28 Wilkins	1873–1876	
Eigenbrot Brewing Company	Louisa & Henry Eigenbrot Alexander Straus (1892–1899)	Same	1876–1899	50,000 bbls/yr
Mount Brewery	John T. Bauern- schmidt	803 West Pratt & Mount Streets	1873–1889	16,000 bbls/yr
Schierlitz Weiss Beer Brewery	Jacob Schierlitz	413 West Baltimore Street	1873–1881	270 bbls/yr
Spengler Brewing	Christoph Spengler	382 Eastern Avenue	1873	
Weiss Beer Brewery	Balthazar Salzig & Louis Bitter	46 South Washington	1873	
Ferdinand Brewery	J. Ferdinand	Pratt & Exeter Streets	1874–1875	3,010 bbls/yr
Kohles Brewery	John Kohles	36 South Wolfe Street	1874–1884	300 bbls/yr
	Elizabeth Kohles	Same	1884–1888	300 bbls/yr
Weiss Beer Brewery	Salzig & Bitter	377 East Lombard	1874	
Boehn Brewery	John G. Boehn	317 South Bond	1875–1876	
Celebrated Weiss Beer Brewery	Henry Beck	153 East Fayette	1875–1884	113 bbls/yr
	Mama Ernestine Beck	Same	1884–1912	Less than 500 bbls/yr
Eichhorn Brewing	Theodore Eichhorn	360 South Caroline	1875–1877	25 bbls/yr
English & Company	William English	Hanover & Conway Streets	1875–1876	
Baltimore Brewery of Butterfield & Co	John Butterfield & Frederick Gottlieb	Same	1876–1880	1,500 bbls/yr
Gottlieb & Hobelmann	Gottlieb & Hobel- mann	Same	1880–1881	
Globe Brewing & Malting	Gottlieb Hobelmann & Wehr	Same	1888–1899	60,000 bbls/yr
Krebs Weiss Beer Brewery	Michael Krebs	16 South Frederick	1875–1876	20 bbls/yr
		216 Lexington	1876	

Brewery	Proprietor	Location/ Neighborhood	Years	Peak Production (if known)
George Streib Brewery	George F. Streib	72 Thames	1875–1876	416 bbls/yr
Striebel Brewery	Frederick Striebel	317 South Bond	1875	
Berger & Company Weiss Beer	John M. Berger & Andrew Dittman (only 1878)	Same	1875–1883	2,987 bbls/yr
Fell's Point Brewing Company	Elizabeth Berger	Same	1883–1887	
Christian Gehl Brewing	Christian Gehl	3rd & O'Donnell Streets	1876–1878	
Guenther & Gehl Brewing	George Guenther & Christian Gehl	Same	1878–1880	6,851 bbls/yr
George Guenther Brewing Company	George Guenther	Same	1880–1899	50,000 bbls/yr
Crystal Springs Brewery	Franz Thau & Paul Mulhauser	Garrison (Franklin-town) & Baltimore	1876–1881	1,000 bbls/yr
Enterprise Brewery	E.E. Adler & Paul Mulhauser	Same	1881–1883	12,000 bbls/yr
	E.E. Adler	Same	1883–1888	6,000 bbls/yr
Vogt Brewing	George W. Vogt	Eastern Ave & 3rd Highlandtown	1876–1880	
Kemper Brewery	William Kemper	Same	1880–1885	
Extel Brewery	N. Extel	360 Pennsylvania Avenue	1877–1878	174 bbls/yr
Schultheis & Brothers	Schultheis brothers	Frederick near Tollgate	1877–1878	183 bbls/yr
Joseph Claus Pioneer Lager Beer Brewery	Joseph Claus	Cross & Covington Streets Federal Hill	1878–1880	428 bbls/yr
Knecht Weiss Beer Brewery	John Knecht	Carrolltown	1878–1879	83 bbls/yr
Miller Brewery	R. Miller	373 Biddle Street	1879	36 bbls/yr
Dukeheart Brewing	Thomas Dukeheart & partners	Calverton & West Baltimore	1884–1903	10,000 bbls/yr
Sandkuhler Brewing	Frank Sandkuhler	2338 McElderry & Montford Ave.	1886–1895	
Martz Brewery	Charles Martz	521 North Conkling	1887	
Baltimore Brewing Company	Paul August Seeger, Paul Weilbacher, & Waldo Bigelow & Company	2206 West Pratt & Frederick	1888–1899	16,000 bbls/yr
Berger Brewing	John C. Berger	836 South Bond	1888–1890	
Pabst Weiss Beer Brewery	Louis Pabst	840 South Bond Street	1889–1909	500 bbls/yr
	Barbara Pabst		1909–1911	
Moller & Paul Weiss Beer Brewery	Nicholas Moller & Paul	1234 Jackson Street	1890	500 bbls/yr
Moller Weiss Beer Brewery	Nicholas Moller	Same	1891–1892	500 bbls/yr
Germania Brewing	Conrad Eurich	Frederick Avenue	1892–1899	30,000 bbls/yr
Baltimore Berliner Weiss Brewery	Herman Wilms, Andrew Gebhart, William Harke (1896), August Fenker (1904)	1715 North Spring Street	1895–1917	500 bbls/yr
Sandkuhler Brewing	Frank Sandkuhler	101 North Collington Avenue	1895–1919	1,000–1,500 bbls/yr
Columbia Brewing & Ice Company	Unkown	Bayard & Columbia Avenue	1899	

Carroll County

BREWERY	PROPRIETOR	LOCATION/ NEIGHBORHOOD	YEARS	PEAK PRODUCTION (IF KNOWN)
Westminster Brewing Company	William Leidlich	West Main Street Westminster	1869–1871	
Zeller Brewing	Valentine Zeller	Green Street Westminster	1870–1872	

Harford County

BREWERY	PROPRIETOR	LOCATION/ NEIGHBORHOOD	YEARS	PEAK PRODUCTION (IF KNOWN)
Sarick Brewing Company	John H. Sarick	Havre de Grace	1875	

Frederick City and County

BREWERY	PROPRIETOR	LOCATION/ NEIGHBORHOOD	YEARS	PEAK PRODUCTION (IF KNOWN)
Elour Brewing Company	John Elour	Emmitsburg	1867–1875	
Hauser Brewery	Paul Hauser	Brewers Alley	1875–1888	1500 bbls/yr
Eckstein Brewing	C.H. Eckstein	Same	1889–1890	
Gambrinus Brewery	John Kuhn	Same	1891–1901	500 bbls/yr

Washington County

BREWERY	PROPRIETOR	LOCATION/ NEIGHBORHOOD	YEARS	PEAK PRODUCTION (IF KNOWN)
Heist Brewing	Lewis Heist	9–11 Potomac Street Hagerstown	1862–1877	198 bbls/yr
Heimel Brewing Company	Justus Heimel	Same: Now 13–17 South Potomac	1878–1893	172 bbls/yr
Good Brewing	David M. Good	Franklin & Potomac Streets Hagerstown	1864–1867	
Shuster Brewery	Robert Shuster	120 West Franklin Hagerstown	1865–1888	150 bbls/yr
Wagner Brewing Company	William Wagner	52 South Potomac Hagerstown	1865–1882	236 bbls/yr
Fisher Brewing Company	Fisher Family	Franklin Street Hagerstown	1867–1868	
	M. Marganstern	Hagerstown	1867–1868	
Heimel Brewing	Justus Heimel & John Spiegel	112 South Potomac Street Hagerstown	1871–1877	

Stillwater & Mikkeller Rauchstar. One of the many collaboration beers of Strumke.

Gunther Beer Light Dry Lager, as advertised. It was the beginning of the trend for the light, dry, lagers and accommodated the taste preferences of soldiers returning from World War II.

DeGroen's Mug Club, prominently displaying Gambrinus (god of beer).

B

Free State Brewing coaster, ca. 1939.

Old German beer coaster, n.d.

Wild Goose Snow Goose winter ale label.

The Edgar Allan Poe Series

The Raven Special Lager

A southern German lager that is well balanced between the hops and malt. Exceptionally smooth with a long malty and clean aftertaste. *The Taste is Poetic.*

Malts: 2-row Pale, Munich, Crystal, Vienna
Hops: Bravo, Tettnanger, Mt Hood
ABV: 5.25%
IBU: 18
Bottles: 4x6x12oz. Cases
Kegs: 1/6 (5.2 gal) 1/2 (13.2 gal), Firkins

BOTTLE   6-PACK   CASE CARTON
7 83583 92088 9   7 83583 92091 9   7 83583 92092 6

Tell Tale Heart IPA

Your first experience with this IPA is the citrus bouquet from its rocky white head. The initial taste is subdued but gradually becomes intense without any harsh bitterness. Citra/Simcoe dry hopped. *It Never Skips a Beat.*

Malts: 2-row Pale, Dark Munich, Caramalt
Hops: Bravo, Chinook, Simcoe, Citra
ABV: 7.25%
IBU: 50
Bottles: 4x6x12oz. Cases
Kegs: 1/6 (5.2 gal) 1/2 (13.2 gal), Firkins

BOTTLE   6-PACK   CASE CARTON
7 83583 92089 6   7 83583 92096 4   7 83583 92095 7

Pendulum Pilsner

This clean, dry and crisp pils is very drinkable like an American domestic but has the craft aroma, body and taste that you expect. Unlike other pilsners, this is *A Cut Above the Rest.*

Malts: 2-row Pale, Munich, Crystal
Hops: Bravo, Saaz
ABV: 4.5%
IBU: 22
Bottles: 4x6x12oz. Cases
Kegs: 1/6 (5.2 gal) 1/2 (13.2 gal), Firkins

BOTTLE   6-PACK   CASE CARTON
7 83583 92090 2   7 83583 92094 0   7 83583 92093 3

The Cask

A dark, smooth, sweet full-bodied & robust beer that warms the insides from its 8% alcohol. Serve in a snifter glass. *Bricked in Double Bock.*

Malts: 2-row Pale, Dark Munich, Vienna, Crystal, Blackprinz
Hops: Hallertau Hersbrucker
ABV: 8%
IBU: 28
Bottles: 6x4-Packs x 12oz. Cases
Kegs: 1/6 (5.2 gal) 1/2 (13.2 gal), Firkins

BOTTLE   4-PACK   CASE CARTON
7 83583 92098 8   7 83583 92105 3   7 83583 92106 0

Annabel Lee White

This Belgian-style wheat beer is true to style. Light, white, effervescent and slightly hopped. This easy drinking wheat beer has a hint of orange and coriander and is truly *A Wheat Beer Angels Envy.*

Malts: 2-row Pale, Light Munich, Unmalted Wheat, Crystal
Hops: Tettnanger
ABV: 4.5%
IBU: 20
Bottles: 4x6x12oz. Cases
Kegs: 1/6 (5.2 gal) 1/2 (13.2 gal), Firkins

BOTTLE   6-PACK   CASE CARTON
7 83583 92101 5   7 83583 92100 8   7 83583 92102 2

Brewed by RavenBeer, P. O. Box 9829 Baltimore, MD, 21284-9829, 443-847-6223 ravenbeer.com, info@ravenbeer.com

The Poe Series of Beers (BWBW), The Raven Beer.

D

Fin City Brewery in the "attic" of Hooper's Crab House, Ocean City.

Watershed Moment, a lifesaving collaboration between Jailbreak Brewing Company and Flying Dog Brewery for the benefit of victims of the Ellicott City flood.

Cascade hops, Adam Frey's hop farm.

Frey's Brewing logo. A brewery on a farm!

Key Brewing logo of Mike McDonald's new brewery in Dundalk.

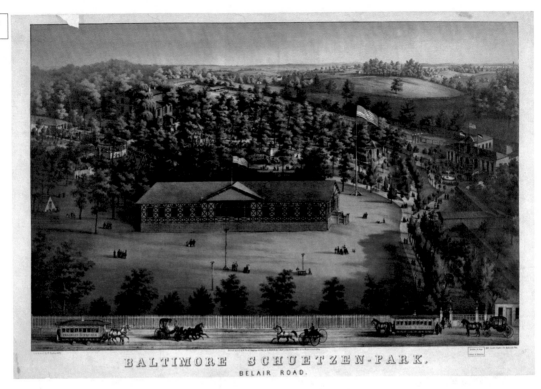

Schuetzen Park, 1867 (LOC).

National Premium advertising with the iconic Mr. Pilsener once again. Although the brew is updated, it is still a Maryland classic!

Reclaiming the Bauernschmidt family legacy, James Bauernschmidt crafts incredible varieties of mead under the family banner.

Oliver Brewing Company, Shannon Drive Baltimore.

Brewing Industry Foundation ad. Beer equated to American Freedom advertisement, reminding folks it belongs with sensible and kind Americans, and Americans have the freedom to choose beer!

Arrow Beer "The One and Only"
Calendar advertisement 1942
(courtesy Larry Handy, ECBA).

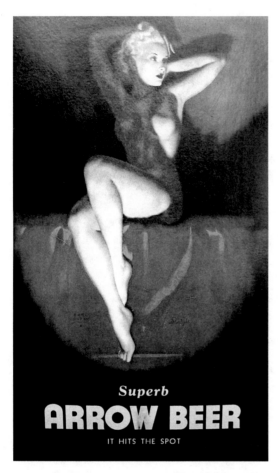

Arrow Beer "Superb" calendar advertisement,
1945 (courtesy Larry Handy, ECBA).

Arrow Beer "Naked Truth"
calendar advertisement, 1941
(courtesy Larry Handy, ECBA).

Checkerspot logo for the Checkerspot brewery opening in 2017. It is a collaboration between Judy Neff, her husband Rob, and Stephen Marsh.

Mully's Logo.

*Manor Hill Farm
Brewery logo.*

*The new Backshore logo,
replacing the Shorebilly logo
after the lawsuit began.*

L

The contentious Ozzy label that Brewer's Art was forced to replace with the Beazly label in 2014.

Full Tilt, The Bay IPA. Proceeds sponsor the Chesapeake Bay Trust. Every sip helps to save the Bay.

5

The Dawn of a New Century

As the century turned, many changes awaited the brewing industry and the people of Maryland. Technological advancements far outpaced those seen in previous decades, unions were organizing to protect workers, and ripples of change altered society and the understanding of daily life. No one stood firm in the shifting sands, as all were forced to adjust, bracing for the changes ahead. Two of the greatest technological advancements in manufacturing occurred just prior to the dawn of the 20th century that would literally propel brewing into the new age like a rocket. The first was a little invention that completely transformed not only how the breweries operated but also where they could sell their products. It was the crowning achievement of a little-known inventor from Baltimore.

William Painter was the son of a traveling medical doctor who had treated natives in the West Indies before becoming a farmer and grocer in Maryland. William was born and raised in Maryland, although he went off to school in Delaware, ending up as an apprentice in the leather working industry by the age of seventeen.[1] He moved on to work in other fields—as an editor, a grocer, and machine shop foreman—but he was best known for tinkering. His inability to be satisfied with inventions as short of perfection hindered him at times. He missed out on patents because he waited too long to apply, "perfecting" his inventions.[2] The Civil War contributed to the interruption in his career as an inventor as well. Neither Painter nor his family ever gave up on his dreams of being a well-known creator of nifty, useful, groundbreaking machines, even though success arrived late in life. With the encouragement of his wife and children, Painter continued exercising his mind around the new mechanical wonders that might benefit the manufacturing industry. Although he often encouraged his children to "tinker," none of his them went on to become inventors like their father. His youngest daughter, Ethel, once invented a mouse trap. She brought the plans to Painter and was told, "This mouse trap is too complicated and expensive to build, and you should just let the mouse go."[3] Ethel let the mouse go and worried no longer about the best way to catch them, nor did she concern herself with many inventions after that.

It was shortly after the cessation of hostilities between the North and the South that Painter finally began to hold patents for some of his incredible inventions. This was due in no small part to his work with patent attorney William C. Wood. Painter invented a wire retaining bottle stopper, known as "The Triumph," that met with great success in 1885 and a rubber "Bottle-Seal" that became the standard for bottling machines. His pivotal invention, however, came in 1891 when he invented the "Crown

Cork Closure" (forebearer of the modern bottle cap).[4] This was patented in February of 1892 and revolutionized bottling. Immediately he invented the "Crown Machine" to apply the closure to bottles. Painter always stated that it was much more difficult to invent the machine to apply the closure than to create the closure itself. Understanding the gravity of what he created, he retired from his position at the machine shop and incorporated the Crown Cork and Seal Company in 1893.[5] The name was chosen by his son Orrin, who worked for him at the new company. This revolutionary closure allowed the beer in the bottles to stay fresh and free from the oxygen that would spoil it. Beer therefore could be transported far and wide outside of Baltimore and Maryland to a thirsty and demand-

William Painter, ca. 1895, *The Jews of Baltimore.*

ing public. Sadly, shortly after the opening of the company, Painter suffered what was known at the time as a "bouts of nerves" and became fragile in health. After bringing his children and extended family into the now family business, he retired from his company in 1903 and died only three years later. The birthright he left for his family and the breweries cannot be underestimated. At the time of his death he employed more than two hundred in Baltimore.[6] The family would continue the legacy well beyond Painter's death and into the modern era.

The other fantastic technological advancement at the turn of the century did not come from Painter but it certainly came from Baltimore. The Consolidated Gas, Electric, Light, and Power Company was formed out of the remnants of the Gas Light Company of Baltimore (which was the very first gas company in the United States) and the consolidated gas companies of Baltimore in 1888. In 1906 the merged gas companies absorbed the combined electric light companies, and the Consolidated Gas, Electric,

THE CROWN CORK.

Crown Cork Seal (Courtesy BMI, CCS Collection).

Light, and Power Company was formed.[7] The merger provided relief from the rate wars raging in Baltimore in the last decade of the 19th century and prompted city legislators to prevent new competition from entering the city after the merger to avert future bouts. Consumers were still reeling from the impact of those wars and were thrilled with the outcome of the consolidation and the subsequent decrease in rates.[8] Outages and shortages were commonplace during the rate wars and the merger brought consistency in service. Eventually the state granted municipalities legislative power to regulate utilities, and regulatory commissions were put in place to forestall many of the problems that led to the rate wars.[9] Westport and Spring Garden were the earliest plants that supplied gas and electric power to manufacturing industries and residences (that could afford it) in the city. Subsequent plants were upgraded and added as more businesses moved to centralized power, changing the landscape inexorably.

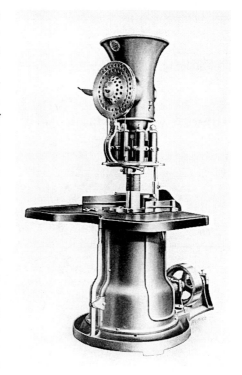

Crown Cork Seal Machine, *The Jews of Baltimore.*

Crown Cork and Seal was one of the earliest to sign on for purchased power instead of relying on steam generators on the premises. Electricity was brought to the factory from Westport and gas from Spring Garden, allowing Crown Cork to operate twenty-four hours per day without losing power or paying exorbitant fuel costs for the generator. The result was greater efficiency and production, permitting Crown Cork to expand and meet the growing national demand for their closures. Not all companies would take advantage of purchased power, as it was quite new, but one brewery, Globe Brewing Company, would sign up. They understood how tough the competition in the regional beer market was, but they wanted to saturate their own market and expand beyond the borders of Maryland. Purchased power facilitated this growth. Globe, also a vast malting facility, seized upon the new technologies as they became available to facilitate the malting process as well as brewing and bottling operations.

In addition to centralized power, the turn of the century also witnessed the construction of a sewer system in Baltimore and throughout Maryland. This was a blessing for breweries as much as it was for private residences. Winters could be brutal. When they were it was problematic for everyone, but breweries struggled mightily. Beer pumps caused copious amounts of water to flow into the alleys, and in the winter of 1903/1904 ice averaged between four and five feet high near the breweries, making alleys impassable by horse or cart.[10] In addition to the many hygienic benefits of a sewer system, Baltimore had plans for a two-stage system that created one independent storm sewer system and another independent sanitary (or unsanitary) system that would flow to a

Guggenheimer and Weil buildings on fire, 1904 Baltimore Fire (LOC).

treatment plant in Back River for filtering.[11] This was a visionary and magnificent plan and one that required great disruption in the city to implement. The entire process of building the sewer systems was interrupted by the great fire of 1904, which once again had a major impact on the breweries and Baltimore.

During that terrible, cold winter of 1904, on the Sunday morning of February 7 a fire broke out just before 11:00 a.m. at the Hurst building on German Street. The fire raged until 3:00 p.m. on Monday, February 8, 1904. Firefighters were hindered by impassable alleys and high winds. The fire finally stalled because of the Jones Falls and the bravery of the firefighters from Baltimore and others from adjacent states who came to aid them. For years prior to the fire, "fireproof" buildings were constructed in Maryland and cities across the country. None of those "fireproof" buildings in the path of the Baltimore fire survived.[12] Fortunately for Baltimore the fire occurred on a Sunday, and the buildings stood empty since most people were at church with their families instead of working. Two structures that survived the fire by just a block were Zion Church and city hall—where many fled to once the blaze broke out.

After the fire was extinguished, the city seized the opportunity to build the planned sewer system but also chose to redesign Baltimore to accommodate both firefighting and business. What became known as the Baltimore Standard became the national standard coupling for all fire hoses. This tragic lesson was learned during the fire when neighboring city and state fire engines could not couple their hoses to access water and help dispatch the fire, as the sizes were all different.[13] After the fire, all structures were equipped with the new Baltimore Standard, preventing future tragedies due to lack of accessible water. A renaissance of architecture and building in Baltimore ensued after this fire, along with a redesigned harbor equipped to fight fires and keep the city safe, and paved the way for the new sewer system.

Washington, D.C., Fire Department racing to Baltimore to help subdue the blaze (LOC).

Maryland was also witness to the brewing trust, a national trend at the turn of the century that mimicked the consolidation of the energy companies. These trusts in reality were monopolies that purchased as many breweries as they could in order to control the market and maximize profits by reducing competition. The Midwest was rife with these trusts and the conglomerate fever threatened to take hold of the eastern breweries. The first taste of the consolidation came from the British Brewing Conglomerate, known as Baltimore United Breweries, in 1889. It purchased the top four breweries in Baltimore in an attempt to repatriate profit from former colonies. In addition, the British conglomerate set up satellite offices not only in Baltimore but also throughout the United States, purchasing 79 breweries in total. The Baltimore branch of United Breweries purchased John Bauernschmidt's Mount Brewery, the Spring Garden Brewery of Bauernschmidt and Marr, and the Darley Park Brewery for $1,600,000. The endeavor was not a completely successful one, as the breweries were sold off within a decade. Competition was stiff and there was a great outlay of money to saloonkeepers to stock the conglomerate's beers. Many operational issues were also noted, and business lagged dramatically in the heavily competitive industry in Maryland.[14]

That would not spell the end of the rise of the brewing monopolies. It did, however, put an end to the Brewers Exchange, which was a protective organization operating in the interests of the breweries and those in affiliated fields. With the rise of the trust, many owners like George Bauernschmidt who sold to the monopoly realized they no longer needed the protection of the exchange if all of the breweries were under the ownership of a single corporation. That corporation would be the Maryland Brewing Company, or so it was believed. In 1899 the Maryland Brewing Company purchased the Baltimore interests of Baltimore United Breweries and thirteen other Baltimore area breweries. Not only did this change the landscape of the industry but it also, in many cases, undermined the fabric of the families that created the industry in Baltimore. The George Bauernschmidt Brewery was valued at over $1.5 million. In addition to the cash value given to George, stock in the Maryland Brewing Company was turned over totaling over $2.5 million.[15] Immediately a lawsuit was brought against the Brewers Exchange by the remaining independent breweries for dissolution of the exchange and dissemination of assets. They charged that the Brewers Exchange no longer carried out the duties of the intended purpose since its founding in 1888 because the Baltimore United Breweries, along with the thirteen other breweries, would now be owned by the Maryland Brewing Company.[16] The best interests of the remaining breweries would therefore no longer be met.[17] This was the first stand against the brewing monopolies that were forming in Baltimore (and across the nation). Unfortunately one of the main complainants in the suit, George Gunther, sold out to Maryland Brewing Company for

Brewer's Exchange, where the interests of the brewers were negotiated before the conglomerates shut it down.

staggering profits. Gunther regretted his decision fairly quickly and attempted to remedy the situation shortly after the sale of his famous brewery.

Maryland witnessed a strong push back against the building monopolies and found great support from the patrons. A true distrust existed toward monopolies from both the customers and the other breweries that fought long and hard to make quality beer and achieve a loyal, consistent consumer base. Additionally, many of the seventeen breweries purchased by Maryland Brewing Company were scrapped for parts or closed altogether so brewing operations could be moved to more productive and modernized breweries within the monopoly. The amount of money spent to acquire the breweries might perhaps have set the course, as it was far in excess of any return for the monopoly at over $7 million. The claim by the monopoly was that the brewery wars of the previous decade harmed consumers more than breweries, and with the new combine consumers would save, as prices would go down. This was based upon the closing of certain breweries and the refusal to pay saloons to carry beer, which was costing in excess of $500,000 per year.[18] Many of the brewery owners who sold to the combine were retained as part of their boards to promote the still local brews that were sold in hopes of retaining loyal patrons. There were even plans for the combine to open breweries in Tennessee and parts of the South as a strategy for nationwide expansion.[19] That never came to pass.

Within two years the Maryland Brewing Company was beset by labor strikes, infighting, unpaid debt, and lagging profits and was forced into receivership.[20] Additionally, one of the managers of the combine was a supporter of the Temperance movement, an ideal difficult to reconcile with his job and an added challenge to the credibility of the monopoly.[21] It certainly didn't help that brewers like George Guenther, who regretted his decision to sell, built a new brewery in Canton. Since his beloved plant was no longer available and he could not use the name of his former brewery, he named the new brewery George Guenther Junior Brewing Company (after his son and partner), which was located right next door to his former brewery. The Maryland Brewing Company sued Guenther, citing the noncompete clause in the sales contract, and lost. The conglomerate was folding, and Guenther, like many, took full advantage.

A new combine was quickly formed out of the vestiges of the old. GBS (Gottleib-Bauernschmidt-Strauss) purchased the viable breweries from Maryland Brewing Company, as it was in foreclosure. Two of the founders were owners of the extremely successful Globe brewery, the George Bauernschmidt Brewery; the third owner, Straus, controlled the largest malt house in the state. These men believed that with better financial planning, less investment, and lower risk the combine could be successful. In part the plan was for each brewer to operate his own brewery once again under the newly formed combine, instead of the responsibility being placed solely in the hands of the conglomerate. Resources and stock would be shared and priced favorably among the fifteen-member breweries.[22] Profits increased as operational control returned to brewers, along with consumer confidence—to some degree. Many people who missed their favorite brews found them once again with the new combine. GBS expanded bottling operations to including construction of one of the largest bottling plants in the nation, with designs to ship bottled beer to South America and the West Indies.[23] They continued operations until Prohibition, but they never achieved the prosperity they had seen before the advent of the brewing trusts.

Immigrants going to work passing George Gunther Junior Brewery ca. 1910 (LOC).

The mitigating factor to success was a distrust of brewing monopolies and the incredible patron support for the independent breweries, most notably Frederick Bauernschmidt's American Brewery. This brewery grew out of the sale of Frederick's father's brewery to the Maryland Brewing Company in 1899. The family worked together in the George Bauernschmidt Brewery prior to the sale. George's son William worked in the office handling management and administrative functions. Son John trained as a brewer in Chicago at Seibel and returned to take the helm as brewmaster. Frederick Bauernschmidt also worked as a brewmaster for a time at his father's brewery but had trained as a lawyer prior to joining the family business. Once the brewery was incorporated, Frederick was promoted to treasurer. It was after his appointment as treasurer that family relations took an unexpected turn. George Bauernschmidt was offered a sum around $2,500,000 for his brewery, between cash and stock.[24] At the time, it was the most productive brewery in the state. George decided to sell the brewery, much to the chagrin of two of his children, Frederick and William. All family members (stockholders) received $500,000 as a result the sale.[25]

Frederick was devastated that the business would no longer be in the hands of his family. He resigned as treasurer before the sale was completed and was paid $100,000 for his shares in the company.[26] His brother William followed suit. They both chose to open separate breweries and remain independent from the conglomerate that purchased the family business. Frederick was enraged, and that rage fueled his desire. He moved from the home he and his family occupied (situated a few houses from his father), and began to plan a new brewery, while his father stayed on to guide the new owners of the once beloved family brewing operation. Eventually, Fred suggested to William that they would both be better served pooling their money and resources to open a much larger brewery than either would be capable of independently. William agreed and the new brewery went into production.

By January of 1900 the brother's brewery on Hillen Street was completed and producing beer. The fireproof facility was maximized with the latest technology, including a 260 bbl brew kettle, refrigeration machines, malting operations, a bottling house, stables, storage, and all of the accoutrements to produce at least 80,000 barrels per year, which quickly turned into 130,000. Experienced brewmaster John Knecht was hired to head the brew house.[27] Frederick created an operation to put the monopoly that purchased his family's brewery out of business. By all accounts this brewery was not only extremely productive like his Uncle John Wiessner's but also revered for the quality and "independence" of the operation, earning both name recognition and consumer loyalty. Fairly quickly Frederick would increase operations to accommodate 400,000 barrels annual production, never believing the warning bells that tolled toward Prohibition.

Frederick opened his plant specifically to put the combine out of business. He succeeded against the Maryland Brewing Company and was thriving by the time GBS came to fruition. His brews were of exceptional quality, he possessed the latest technologies available to him, and he was extremely motivated. He was forced to expand his brewery on Hillen Street at a regular pace to keep up with demand.[28] The brewery operated three separate bottling lines. The bottle house was equipped with Hydro-pressure soakers, automatic washers and a pastuerizer.[29] Frederick's American Brewery was a mainstay in the region. He was incredibly successful through his two decades of brewing. A measure of success came from his treatment of his employees. Fred Bauernschmidt truly valued his workers, not only treating them as a critical component of the well-oiled plant but also providing pensions for them when they retired averaging $50.00 per week.[30] Additionally, he brought all of his employees to his summer home in Essex for crab feasts and retreats, offering rest, fun, and renewal to reinvigorate all for the hard work ahead at the brewery.[31] Despite the success, all was not rosy in the Bauernschmidt clan.

While constructing the grand new brewery, Frederick and William's father, George Bauersnschmidt, died on April 12, 1899. Accordingly, the rift between father and son had never been repaired nor could be. After the death of their father, their mother, Margaretha, placed into trust $95,000 for each of the surviving children. Additionally, she divided $4,000 in gold coins among them.[32] Margaretha also decided to place the majority of the estate with the Baltimore Realty Company, a company George had formed after selling the brewery in an effort to protect the family assets. The eldest son, John, acted as president of Baltimore Realty as well as president of the Maryland Brewing Company, the firm that purchased the family brewery.[33] William and Frederick took their mother to court, claiming that she possessed the remaining $10,000 in gold coins and that her assessments of the value of their deceased father's estate were inconsistent with the true value determined by the auditor. The two sons demanded more. In addition, they argued that John exerted undue influence upon Margaretha to act counter to her role as executrix of the estate.

The battle dragged on for a few years, straight to the appeals court. The judge agreed in part with Margaretha and mostly with Frederick and William, ordering her as executrix of her husband's estate to be supervised by the court until her death. The appeals court ruled with regards to Margaretha. First, she had distributed her late husband's assets equally among all surviving children in six separate safety deposit boxes, and second, she was not determined to know conclusively where the remaining $10,000 in gold coins were located (they once resided in the front steps) and was therefore not responsible for more than the $4,000 already accounted for. It is interesting to note here that Margaretha refused to testify under oath throughout the process. With this the court stated they believed she was acting with integrity as executrix. The remainder of the court's decision, however, supported the two brothers, and Margaretha (and consequently Baltimore Realty) was prevented from selling any of her late husband's stock or real estate holdings without consent of the court, and no further actions other than a life contract for her to remain on the estate would be granted.[34] Although both parties found support in the decision, family dinners were never quite the same for some time.

Things with the American Brewery however were not as smooth as they appeared to be. William was never a partner in the business but an employee, despite his hefty investment. Within a decade of pooling resources with his brother to help build a competitive brewery, William was out of the business after Frederick returned William's capital investment.[35] The family rift had grown and showed no signs of dissipating. William never returned to the brewing industry. John, however, left the brewing conglomerate and returned to the family business, eventually joining Frederick in the American Brewery as brewmaster once William departed.

Margaretha contracted cancer and passed away in 1912. Fortunately the fissure that pitted the sons against their mother was repaired long before her passing. William sent his children, George, Margaret, and William, to visit their grandmother every Friday night. The children were invited to order anything they wanted for dinner, no matter how complicated or expensive, and the chef would prepare it. George always ordered something relatively simple, but Margaret would order incredibly difficult concoctions like Baked Alaska. Often their cousins would be present to partake of the Friday night meals that followed the piano lessons, games, and fun. The children took the trolley home after an evening of visiting their grandmother. George was particularly fond of those evenings and loved his "oma," as he called her.[36] Margaretha was fondly remembered by all who knew her as both a shrewd business woman (as executrix of the estate she grew the remaining assets to $425,000) and a generous soul who gave to numerous charities, particularly those involving children and hospitals.[37] For those who knew her this was not a surprise, as her own daughter was a deaf/mute.

Others struggled with the loss of family brewing businesses as well much like the Bauernschmidt family. John Wiessner repurchased the Canton brewery at a discounted rate after the failure of Maryland Brewing Company in 1901, turning it into an ice manufactory. John Wiessner, unmarried and in extremely ill health, passed away from heart failure and gastrointestinal disease at the age of forty-six in 1904.[38] In his will he left the majority of his estate to be used for the construction of the John Frederick Wiessner Orphans Asylum at Eastern and Highland Avenue. The orphanage has been relocated and renamed several times through the course of its storied existence and was always operated with integrity and dedication by staff and supporters alike.[39] Most recently, in 1996, the name was changed to the Wiessner Foundation for Children. The foundation's sole mission is to provide funding to needy organizations for the purpose of helping children.[40] Additionally, Wiessner left money for an altar to be built at Zion Lutheran Church, the Brewer's Church, in honor of his family. Even without children, his legacy has endured as a brewer and philanthropist who gave back to his community, even to this very day.

John Frederick Wiessner, Sr., like his brother George, passed on and left the John F. Wiessner & Son's Brewing Company to his children. He never sold to the combine, so the legacy left for his sons entailed competing against the brewing monopolies. Upon his death, one hundred shares of stock in the brewery were equally distributed among the five Wiessner children. The three sons ran the business, and the daughters (Margaret and Elizabeth) received annual dividends on the value of the stock shares they possessed. The business was incredibly successful under the management of the sons, as they adhered to their father's rule of quality first.[41] They also had an imbedded understanding that the business was for family only, therefore it was never sold and no outsiders were ever sold shares of the company. John Jr. (known as Frederick, like his father) was an avid yachtsman who found time for recreation along with the running of the brewery. Tragically, Frederick passed away in 1906 from Bright's disease at the young age of forty-seven.[42]

It was shortly after his death that difficulties arose within the brewery and the family. The product was still exceptional, but the stock shares became problematic. Margaret Wiessner married a Dr. Wegefarth in 1901 after the death of her father. Therefore, the twenty shares from her father's estate were received prior to her marriage. When her brother perished in 1906, his twenty shares were distributed equally among the surviving siblings. It was well known throughout the family, however, that John Frederick Jr. wanted to distribute his shares to his brothers only upon his death, so they, as operators of the family business, held the majority stock. Unfortunately, he died intestate; thus the shares were evenly distributed among the siblings. This did not immediately cause problems in the family but rather upon the death of Margaret in 1912. When Maragaret died, she left $33,000 to charities in Maryland, including various children's asylums (orphanages), while the rest of her estate was left to her husband, whom she named executor.

Dr. Wegefarth straightaway gave up his medical practice after marrying Margaret and began to gamble in real estate development businesses across the city. Maragret's estate at the time of the marriage was worth over $100,000. Wegefarth used Margaret's annual dividends from her twenty-five shares of brewing company stock to keep them afloat. The gambles never paid off and by the time Margaret died, Wegefarth had used the twenty shares as collateral on over $120,000 owed to the Merchants Mechanics National Bank in Baltimore. The surviving brothers wanted to purchase those shares from Wegefarth, and after much difficulty and grappling with the bank as the arbiter the Wiessner brothers eventually bought the twenty shares for $160,000 in 1914.[43] Five years after the settlement, Wegefarth appealed, accusing the brothers of fraud. He stated that the brothers attempted to defraud him out of the true value of the shares, while strong-arming the bank in an attempt to ruin his credit and reputation. Wegefarth was represented by William Marbury, a noted attorney in the city; while the Wiessners were represented by none other than (soon-to-be governor of Maryland) Albert C. Ritchie. The presiding judge determined that Wegefarth was in a financial bind of his own creation, the brothers had acted with integrity, and the charges of fraud were completely unsubstantiated. The original settlement judgment of 1914 was upheld.[44] The brothers enjoyed successfully running the brewery, by this time operating at over 110,000 barrels per year, until Prohibition shut them down a year later.

Frank Steil's was another notable independent brewery that rose after the formation of the combine. Steil was born in Kirschberg on the Rhein, Germany, in 1865 and immigrated when he was just ten years old. Considered a gregarious, handsome, and charismatic man, he excelled in the restaurant business before entering the brewing trade.[45] He eventually married a local girl from Zion Church in Baltimore and settled down to married life and raising a beautiful daughter. Unfortunately the marriage wouldn't last, but Steil's determination to succeed took root through his brewery.[46] Steil built his brewery on the site of the former August Beck Brewery with the expectation of competing against a very unpopular brewing monopoly. He not only relied upon loyalty, he also created one of the best breweries of the time. Steil had some of the most extensive underground cellars in the city of Baltimore—460 feet in length and 28 feet deep.[47] Frank Steil advertised to his consumers not only the brewery's independence but also the purity of his Ye Old Steil Beer, harkening back to the way quality beer ought to taste instead of the new beers many were offering. This slight was directed at the new brews coming from the monopolies, no doubt.[48]

An incredibly productive independent brewer in Maryland was George Brehm. Brehm trained as a brewer in Bavaria before he immigrated to Baltimore in 1865 and began working in different German-owned breweries. Shortly after signing on with George Neisendorfer, a German brewer in business for more than a decade on Belair, Neisendorfer passed away. Brehm continued working at the plant for the widow, whom he eventually married. He raised the stepchildren along with the three more who would bless him and his wife. He continued to operate, rebuild, and expand the brewery, eventually renaming it after himself. Brehm added mechanical refrigeration and expensive bottling operations in 1895 to modernize the plant and keep pace with the Wiessner and Guenther breweries. He also added a bowling alley and beer garden to keep the patrons entertained and relaxed during a day at the brewery. He paid to have his nephew John travel from Germany to attend brewing school in Chicago at Seibel so he could join the family business.

When the opportunity presented itself for Brehm to sell the plant he jumped at the chance, earning $400,000 from his modernized operation in 1899. Quickly he regretted the move and yearned for his former plant. Since the Maryland Brewing Company was not solvent and suffering from the weight of the combine, they quickly sold the plant back to Brehm at a loss for $185,000. Brehm chose to remain independent, and renamed the plant George Brehm & Son Brewing Company, with the addition of his son Henry joining operations as a full partner. The focus of the One Grade Only brew the Brehms produced was about quality and purity, staying away from adjuncts. They set themselves apart from the conglomerate and as time passed they realized that sticking with traditional methods of placing beer in casks and lagering them in deep underground storage cellars without preservatives was the key. This was done instead of using refrigeration machines like all of the other advanced breweries. They advertised the low-alcohol content of brew through this production method. It was a successful operation until the death knell from Prohibition began to sound. Henry (succeeding in operating the brewery alone after his father's death) brought in his nephew Jospeh Kuper to aid in management of the plant. Kuper correctly realized that kegging operations needed to be diminished in favor of bottling, as saloons might not survive Prohibition but bottled beer would. They invested in Pflauder glass-enameled steel tanks, completely ending the kegging program by 1915.[49]

Many that knew the restaurant (or related) businesses attempted to dip their toes into the competitive pool of brewing in Maryland. This included German immigrant John Tjarks. Tjarks had been the owner of restaurants in Baltimore before he entered the brewing industry as an investor, first in the Darley Park Brewery, which was sold to Baltimore United Breweries, and then in the independent Monarch Brewing Company. This was one of the most modernized breweries in Maryland. Designed by noted brewery architect Otto C. Wolf, the brewery possessed the first gravity process for fermentation through shipping. No lagering cellars were constructed, and instead modern refrigeration equipment was used throughout. This was financially too much for the owners and the brewery was sold before it could be completed. The brewery was completed and became operational in 1900 as the Monumental Brewing Company. The Straus brothers, who had run the National Brewing Company before they were part of the GBS monopoly, were brought in to run operations. They flourished as an independent quality production facility, taking many accounts from GBS.[50] This in turn allowed opportunity for expansion of the facility.[51]

The Straus brothers worked diligently on developing new techniques for keeping the purity of the beer intact, from production all the way through shipping. Perhaps they worked a little too hard, as they were sued by the Wallersteins (Wallerstein Labs) for infringing on a patent for a beer chiller that kept the brew free from microorganisms. The lawsuit was successful and the brewery had to pay for the use of the device.[52] Competition aside, all brewers came together annually to celebrate the industry. Tjarks acted as toastmaster for the 18th anniversary of the Brewmaster's Association of Baltimore in 1905.[53] He continued to keep his investments in the brewing fold, where he had many close friends, from Henry Romhildt (former Darley Park brewmaster) to Frank Steil, but he decided upon expansion into the hotel business (Hotel Raleigh). This was a wise choice for a politically active investor who was naturally concerned for the rising support of the Temperance movement. He exerted his political clout through helping the German Community in Maryland and throughout the country. Tjarks became the 3rd vice president of the German American Alliance of the United States, which eventually became a symbol of suspicion due to World War I and was shut down.[54]

Julius Jackson also fought for prosperity as an independent brewer, free of the conglomerate. After a brief tenure with Monarch Brewing and then Chesapeake Brewing Company, he purchased the old Bauernschmidt and Marr Spring Garden Brewery on Ridgely Street, which was given up by the Maryland Brewing Company after insolvency. The Mount Vernon Brewery, as it was named, began production in 1906 after an extensive remodel of the Three Star Brew.[55] The massive 100,000-barrel, technologically advanced brewery, complete with a brand new bottling house, seemed like a strong

The Tjarks and Steil families. At center back is mustachioed John Tjarks; to his left is Frank Steil; and to his right with the cigar is Pastor Hoffman. Charles G.E. Stalfort is the clean-shaven young chap with the beer glass in the back row. The woman front and center at the table is the wife of Frank Steil, Bertha Steil. The names of others in the picture have been lost to time. John Tjarks was affiliated with the Darley Park Brewery, while Steil operated his own brewery independent of the conglomerates. Although the date is unknown it is clearly a vacation photo aboard a ship, as the porthole can be seen on the right (courtesy Zion Church).

contender.[56] Despite extensive experience in the Maryland brewing industry and a superior plant, the operators of Mount Vernon struggled. In the midst of the financial debacle, they were also ousted from their Ridgley Street property in the middle of the night through a questionable back-room deal between Jackson's landlord and Chesapeake Brewing Company, Jackson's former employer.[57] In both 1906 and 1908 the majority ownership changed hands.[58]

The Eurich family of brewers from Darmstadt purchased the Mount Vernon Brewery in 1908, hoping to turn the business around. Conrad Eurich operated breweries in Brooklyn, New York, and Baltimore prior to his purchase of Mount Vernon. His Brooklyn Brewery was lost to receivership.[59] In Baltimore he owned Germania Brewing Company, which was so productive during his tenure he sold it for $250,000 to the Maryland Brewing Company. Bored with retirement, he believed Mount Vernon to be the perfect opportunity to get back in the industry and prove he could turn any brewing operation to profit. Perhaps his time for triumph had come to an end, as he was forced to shutter the brewery in 1909. Sadly, it wasn't a mere closing of the brewery but imprisonment for Eurich and his sons for tax evasion for nonpayment of beer taxes. Worse yet was the family's inability to pay bail before the trial due to the immense brewery debt and the "independence" of the brewery, having no partners to help with financial concerns.[60] This is one example of independence backfiring heartily. The property was placed in receivership for nonpayment of debts and sold to yet another owner in April of that same year. The owner was another German immigrant, Gustav Bachman.[61] The brewery was never operational again, and the site was used for other business concerns. Mount Vernon Brewing Company was not a story of failure but a glimpse of how difficult it was to maintain independence from the conglomerates and succeed. The end was no better for Conrad Eurich, who died from a throat obstruction in 1911 after the loss of most of the legal suits brought against him.

The great rival of Mount Vernon, Chesapeake Brewing Company, fared somewhat better in the brewery wars in Maryland. A former Confederate veteran with the First Maryland, Josiah Polk purchased the Old Phoenix Brewery property in 1900 for $78,000.[62] After he suffered a stroke his comedic acting career was cut short and he looked to the brewing industry as his future. Polk intended to compete against the monopolies and the other independent breweries vying for patrons in Maryland. Fortunately he followed tradition and brought his brother and his family into the business with him, as they conducted the business of the brewery after his death from another stroke in 1902.[63] Like many breweries they pursued the key to wooing consumers to not only to partake of their brews but also to keep the name and beer as a staple of local conversation. The answer was duckpin bowling.

Chesapeake held regular duckpin bowling tournaments, with hefty prize money of $50 for the winning team.[64] Competition was stiff in the region and the brewery struggled at times, perhaps explaining the attempt by Chesapeake to seize the Mount Vernon site out from under them. At this time Josiah's brother Col. Lucius Polk was at the helm with son Gabriel despite an incredibly strained relationship.[65] Gabriel continued to run the company after his father's death in 1916.[66] Chesapeake sustained operations but revenues were down and debt collection efforts were fervent, often resulting in lawsuits against the debtor's estate.[67] The wartime grain rationing affected the brewery, as it did all other breweries. Worse yet was the movement of other breweries into Maryland from states that had already enacted Prohibition, driving the owners to conduct business in "wet" states.[68] Chesapeake would struggle, but they managed to stay afloat until 1920.

The demand for the beer was in place along with a desire to continue operations, but the growing malt shortage made things that much more difficult. As the United States prepared to enter World War I, grain rationing began, when malt was already in limited supply.[69] This created even greater competition among the breweries and was a windfall for the maltsters that had the goods to provide for an increased price. Growth among breweries in the country was paralleled by the growth in maltsters to meet the demand until 1917.[70] Without enough malt, maltsters were fewer and collection of outstanding debts (from breweries) was higher. Many breweries did not make it to Prohibition merely because they fell into receivership for lack of payment. In addition, breweries had already been engaged in heated competition since the turn of the century, and the

Brewer's Association recommended against sharing the output numbers, as that would only fuel an already vicious atmosphere of competition and increase tax burdens.[71]

Out west, Hagerstown Brewing Company attempted to rise independently from the monopolies claiming many Maryland breweries. In 1899 a corporation was formed to provide Washington County with a much needed beverage—beer. The investors were numerous (in part to mitigate potential loss) and included George McHenry, Martin Cesare, the Herrmann brothers, Charles Schwan, N. Hartman, A. Abbatolis, R.C. Lupton, and C.E. Ochs. The brewery was constructed at Franklin and Foundry streets, and operations were underway by the fall of 1900 to an enthusiastic gathering.[72] It established a reputation as one of the finest breweries in the state, using only the choicest hops and the best eight-day malt. It was also noted that the brewery was extremely clean and relied upon the latest science to produce the purest of beers.[73] This was not surprising, as a push was on in the early twentieth century for a return to pure beer. Many of the brewers were Germans who had been raised with *Reinheitsgebot* (the German beer purity law) as the golden rule. With stiff competition the one way to set a brewery apart from the others was to hearken to the purest of ingredients and the finest brewing traditions—the golden rule. This was another attempt to demonstrate Old World techniques and revealed an aversion to the adjuncts many brewers in the states were using.

Hagerstown Brewing Company would struggle despite the fantastic initial success, as the cost of malt and constant expansion to remain competitive (including a state-of-the-art icehouse) would prove to be too heavy a burden. In 1913 the brewery and ice plant were sold to receivers. The new owner, Walter Wilson, chose to keep the brewery operational and attempted to restructure the finances.[74] Within three years the plant was in the green and operations were running smoothly, quenching thirsty palates throughout the region by producing over 50,000 barrels per annum. The bottling line, fillers, and pasteurizer were expanded and everything seemed to be on track for a prosperous future. All would not remain bright for the brewery, however, as it almost closed in 1916. When Maryland held the vote for statewide prohibition, had it passed Hagerstown Brewing was to be converted into a flour mill. Fortunately the measure was put down and the brewery remained open.[75] The increasingly high cost of goods combined with a vote by Washington County residents just over a year later to go dry forced the brewery to close before either state or national prohibition was passed into law.[76]

Many other independent breweries formed throughout Maryland to compete with the monopolies and seize the opportunity to establish brand loyalty in various markets. The Frostburg Brewing Company was formed in 1907 by Karl Schlossstein and a small group of investors.[77] The brewery was completed in 1908 to meet the needs of the growing town of Frostburg, which no longer had an operational brewery after the closing of the Mayer brewery in 1894. Schlossstein was a brewer trained at the United States Brewer's Academy in New York and apprenticed in Bavaria. He was quite talented at producing lager and some porter and put his efforts to work for the community.[78] Almost immediately Schlossstein invested more in the brewery, recognizing the need for improvements, including bottle washers and filters.[79] Despite another round of improvements and expansion in 1915 financed by a restructured mortgage, it would not be enough to survive what many knew was inevitable—Prohibition.[80] Despite the fact that Maryland repeatedly defeated the enactment of state prohibition by a vast majority of the population, Schlossstein understood that federal regulation was next.[81] The brewery would close by 1917, a victim of the difficult circumstances.[82]

Another Allegany County brewery was the German Brewing Company erected on Market Street in Cumberland in 1901 by then acting mayor Warren C. White. This provided staunch competition to one other brewery (and arch rival) operating in the city at the time—Cumberland Brewing Company. Mayor White was a colorful figure, challenged by a mayoral contender for potential ballot box discrepancies not unlike the hanging chad debacles in the modern world.[83] White was cleared of any wrongdoing and the court of appeals affirmed his mayoral victory in December.[84] He also started a lumber business and purchased property to construct a hotel a year later to diversify his interests and plan for his post mayoral career.[85] It seems the spotlight loved Mayor White, and a judge in town (the very same Judge Boyd who ordered an investigation into the ballot box debacle) was out to bring him down. In 1904 White was indicted by a grand jury for malfeasance in office for not providing overdraft reporting to the city council for payroll deficits.[86] Fortunately for White, he was tried and cleared of all charges less than a month after his indictment with overwhelming evidence he acted with integrity.[87]

In the midst of it all, German Brewing Company got off to a quick start. From construction the latest equipment available was installed to produce a quality of beer that could compete in the market. As the brewery became successful the owners realized that just touting the purity and quality of their Old German Beer was not enough. They

Fred Bauernschmidt's (Independent) American Brewery, ca. 1905 (HSBC).

The Bauernschmidt Family in the Beer Garden: seated left to right: two unknown children (of their live-in domestic worker), Sarah, Margaretha, George, Sr., John, Frederick; standing left to right: William, unknown woman (live-in domestic worker), George, Jr., Elizabeth and Emile (Courtesy James Bauernschmidt).

Frank Steil Letterhead.

not only kept up with the changes in technological brewing advancements, like installing the 200 bbl Barry-Wehmiller pasteurizer, they also touted the health benefits of their brew with testimonials from city health officials.[88] While this advertising approach worked for almost a decade, the celebration of German heritage and beer soured on the public as World War I continued. White died in 1915, and his surviving partners decided the best way to demonstrate their patriotism in such a climate was to change the name of the brewery from "German" to "Liberty" Brewing Company in 1917.[89] Regrettably, this would not suffice to save the brewery from either grain rationing or Prohibition and like many others the operation would be forced to close, in 1918.

As the new century neared its third decade, sweeping changes came to the brewing industry in Maryland. Once pitted against one another, monopolies and independent breweries joined together in an attempt to prevent Prohibition. In 1914 Gottleib-Bauernschmidt-Straus, Frank Steil Brewing Company, George Guenther Junior Brewing Company, and George Brehm Brewing Company, despite their differences and competition, joined together in a cooperative education program to inform the public on the purity of beer. The program detailed what beer was, placed a food value on it, and demonstrated the purity, and nutritional content. This was a rare collusion, all in hopes of turning the tide away from the Temperance movement, at least for the production of beer.[90] They signed anti–Prohibition petitions, shared testimony from doctors noting the healthy benefits of beer in comparison to spirits, pointed out the rise in crime and the "ills" of society taking place in states like Kansas that had already enacted Prohibition.[91] Grain rationing forced the use of corn and other grains to finish the brews that were precipitously in decline, challenging the industry further. Some brewers, like Alexander Straus, patented a method of producing nonalcoholic beer as a way to cope with changes forced upon them. Others, like Fred Bauernschmidt, continued to expand operations, believing Prohibition would be overturned quickly if it ever was enacted.[92] Some left the brewing business and turned their future to malting, as malt was needed even if beer was no longer legal. Complicating it all was the anti–German fervor due to World War I. This conflagration spelled the end of brewing in Maryland—almost.

BREWERY LISTINGS

Allegany

Brewery	Proprietor	Location/Neighborhood	Years	Peak Production (if known)
German Brewing	Mayor Warren White, et al.	208 Market Street Cumberland	1905–1917	100,000 bbls/yr
Liberty Brewing	Same	Same	1917–1918	
Frostburg Brewing	Karl Schlossstein	Adjacent to PA & Cumberland RR Frostburg	1908–1917	

Baltimore

Brewery	Proprietor	Location/Neighborhood	Years	Peak Production (if known)
Maryland Brewing Company	Richard Sperry, Charles Jones, et al.	20 Park Avenue	1899–1901	450,000 bbls/yr
Monarch Brewing Company	Peter Schmidt	Eighth & Lombard Highlandtown	1899	NP
Monumental Brewing Company	Frank B. Cahn & William Straus	Same	1900–1920	150,000 bbls/yr
Fred Bauernschmidt's American Brewery	Fred Bauernschmidt	1108 Hillen St	1900–1923	400,000 bbls/yr

Chesapeake Brewing Company	Josiah Polk & Family	370 Pennsylvania near Pitcher	1900–1920	40,000 bbls/yr
George Guenther Junior Brewing Co	George & George Guenther Junior	3rd & Toone	1900–1920	50,000 bbls/yr
Frank Steil Independent Brewing Company	Frank Steil	44 Franklintown Road	1900–1920	40,000 bbls/yr
George Brehm & Son Brewery	George Brehm & Family	Belair, Erdman, & Bowleys	1901–1920	30,000 bbls/yr
GBS Brewing Company	Gottlied, Bauern-schmidt, Straus	Hanover & Conway	1901–1920	600,000 bbls/yr
O'Neill & Fitzgerald Brewing Company	Daniel O'Neill & John Fitzgerald	Chester & Bank Streets	1902–1903	
Mount Vernon Brewery	Julius Jackson	1540 Ridgely	1906–1908	
	Conrad Eurich	Same	1908–1909	
	Gustav Bachman	Same	1909	

Washington

BREWERY	PROPRIETOR	LOCATION/ NEIGHBORHOOD	YEARS	PEAK PRODUCTION (IF KNOWN)
Hagerstown Brewing Co.	George McHenry, Martin Cesare, et al.	344 W Franklin & Foundry Streets	1899–1913	50,000 bbls/yr
	Walter Wilson	Same	1913–1920	30,000 bbls/yr

NP: Non-production brewery

6

Prohibition

The winds of change were wending their way towards the demise of legal drink by the mid-nineteenth century. By the early twentieth century the winds reached gale force and the sad inevitability of the dry years became reality. The change was brought about by the Women's Temperance Movement, the Sons of Temperance, and eventually the powerful Anti-Saloon League, among other dry entities. The belief of these organizations was that if alcohol was illegal men would leave the bars and go to work, stop beating their wives, stop committing crimes, start to save money, and attend church regularly. The "evils" of alcohol were all-encompassing in the eyes of the dry advocates. Surprisingly, not all temperance members subscribed to the theory of total abstinence. John Anderson of Annapolis, in corresponding with his wife while traveling, mentions attending a Sons of Temperance meeting where he ran into a few associates.[1] He revealed how his friend "Wright" was a Son of Temperance who continued to drink beer and wine but refrained from libations.[2] Although a moderate approach, this was not the prevailing trend for the temperance movement, and total abstinence eventually became the goal. Frances Willard, 1879 president of the Women's Christian Temperance Union, had a progressive agenda based upon the belief that the government would act to elevate men's characters and create a sober and pure world of total abstinence.[3] Great pressure was exerted upon Washington politicians to support this change over the following four decades.

Maryland by nature was a predominantly "wet" state. The majority did not desire the passage of the Volstead Act, the law carrying out the 18th Amendment prohibiting the importation, exportation, and production of alcoholic beverages into, out of, and within the United States. There was quite a vocal minority—based predominantly on the Eastern Shore and far western regions of Maryland—that did relish the passage of the "noble experiment." The Washington Temperance Society was established in 1840 in Baltimore (the heart of the wet citizenry) by former heavy drinkers. Curiously they chose to name their society after our first President, George Washington, a known distiller of whiskey and supplier of beer rations for his troops. Eventually these temperance groups allied in the late nineteenth century in Maryland and began preaching the ills of alcohol and the benefits of a "dry society." Beginning in February of 1874 initial meetings of this Temperance Alliance were held in Cecil County, where many signed petitions promising to abstain from drinking and provide entertainment to men in coffee houses to lessen the temptation.[4] In May of that same year 400 delegates and 260 unified temperance supporters from Baltimore (male, female, black, white) attended the inaugural convention of the Temperance Alliance for Maryland.[5] Headquarters for the movement would eventually reside in Silver Spring, Maryland, where the group received a less hostile greeting than in Baltimore.

The National Prohibition Party was founded in 1869 and regularly nominated members to run for U.S. president. In 1896, Joshua Levering of Maryland was nominated and received approximately one hundred and twenty-five thousand votes. This was clearly not enough to win the office for Levering. As the century turned, other measures were taken to press the "dry" agenda, and anti–German sentiment, chiefly connected to the outbreak of World War I, suited their goals. After the United States entered the Great War in 1917, a wartime prohibition was put in place for grain conservation. Many conjectured this targeted the beer industry in America because so much of the industry was established by German immigrants.[6] A vast majority of German-Americans supported Wilheim II and the German cause prior to 1917, since their family members were still in the homeland and in the middle of the conflict. This did not win German-Americans favor in the United States. In great consequence this is evidenced by the establishment of a Judiciary Committee by Senate Resolution 307 (in 1918) to investigate the Brewer's Association, a faction of German brewery owners, and their activities with regard to buying a newspaper in the capital specifically to promote pro–German sentiment within the government and promote the liquor trade, which benefited the major breweries in the country that were German held.[7] This came on the heels of Congress's revoking the charter of the National German American Alliance in 1918 (which they had held since 1907) for funding anti–Prohibition efforts.

Effects of this anti–German sentiment were seen locally in Maryland at Zion Church. The church helped raise funds for the German and Austrian war widows and participated in other efforts to help their parishioner's families in Germany and Austria. This was looked upon with great suspicion by the surrounding community in Baltimore.[8] However, when America entered the war, Pastor Hoffman and Zion Church immediately helped the U.S. war efforts and American soldiers preparing for battle. It was a clear statement of loyalty to their adopted country that we all stood together as one. Solidarity strengthened the community and the anti–Prohibition sentiment. Despite, or perhaps because of, all of this the Anti-Saloon League in Maryland could not gain traction, since dividing the populace was ineffective, and the stance against the implementation of Prohibition crossed religious, gender, and political lines. Repeated attempts at the incorporation of prohibitory laws were defeated in Maryland by the legislature.

Another group avidly supporting the 18th Amendment was the Invisible Empire of the Ku Klux Klan. The Klan had experienced a resurgence in America after the Great War, touting Americanism and unity while excluding immigrants, Catholics, and those deemed racially unequal. This influx in membership came from a few Protestant denominations in the middle-class segment of the population that already held anti–German sentiments and distrusted the power of the papacy. A national call went up to members to support public education as a way to decrease the influence of private or religious schools, where specific American values and morality could be taught in greater proportion than grammar and math. Maryland responded.[9] The Mt. Rainier Chapter (# 51) was a most vocal chapter in the state, with approximately 80 members at its peak. During Prohibition membership in the Klan across Maryland rose to 33,000.[10] Given the anti–Catholic and anti–German rhetoric it was not surprising that the Klan on a national and state level would support Prohibition, as both Catholics and Germans stood in strong opposition to Prohibition. This was particularly true in Maryland since the law was not enforced by the state.[11] A demand for financial support to influence political candidates eventually led to a downturn in Klan membership and lack of support for the Maryland chapters, thus rendering their efforts ineffective.

The Volstead Act, HR 6810, was passed into law on October 28, 1919. The act was intended to "prohibit intoxicating beverages, and to regulate the manufacture, production, use, and sale of high-proof spirits for other than beverage purposes, and to insure an ample supply of industrial alcohol and promote its use in scientific research, and in the development of fuel, dye, and other lawful industries."[12] President Woodrow Wilson vetoed the act on both constitutional and ethical grounds, but Congress overrode his veto and passed it into law. In reality, what did this translate to? An intoxicating beverage was considered to be anything more than one-half of 1 percent of alcohol by volume according to section 29, title 2, of the act. There were exceptions to the rule, which included wine production for communion given at churches across the country, and beer and spirits production on a very limited basis explicitly for the purpose of medicinal treatments as prescribed by a physician, or wine if you produced it within your own home for personal consumption by your family and invited guest(s). You could also consume whatever alcoholic beverages you had in your possession prior to the effective date of the act, January 16, 1920.[13] As anticipated, this was extremely confusing.

Notably, many states went "dry" years before the 18th Amendment was ratified on January 16, 1919. Not only did these states provide foundational case studies of potential success or failure, they were also touted as shining examples for all to aspire to without taking into account the actual effects of the movement. As a response, and to open a legitimate dialogue, the *Anti-Prohibition Manual* was produced and distributed annually by the National Wholesale Liquor Dealers Association of America in the decade leading up to Prohibition. Within these pages, one could find federal, state, and local statistics comparing "dry" and "wet" states. Of the many comparisons made, to include murders, crime, pauperism, divorce, spousal abuse, annual savings of citizens, and the multitude of "issues" Prohibition was promised to cure, a definite trend was seen. The gist was that Prohibition wasn't solving these societal problems. Head-to- head, Kansas (one of the first states to go dry) had higher divorce rates, higher crime rates, higher rates of insanity, and less money saved per family than wet states listed.[14] What was most compelling wasn't the social aspect of crime and debauchery so much as the ominous predictions made and the statistical support behind them in reference to the massive unemployment that would ensue from Prohibition.

A major consideration in adopting Prohibition should have been job loss. The prevailing belief was that that brewers, vintners, and distillers would find jobs in other industries such as bakeries, butchers, cloth manufactories, and the like. This was not the case. In reality, over two million who were employed in the liquor industry and affiliated industries in the United States (farmers, railroaders, painters, cork manufacturers, bottle manufacturers, etc.). would lose their jobs, with no other industries to replace them or to create jobs.[15] This was the reason major labor unions opposed the

implementation of Prohibition. This also included famous union lawyer Clarence Darrow. To further the point, a tally of liquor industry revenues alone showed the impact Prohibition had on the economy.[16] Adding in affiliated industries and the lack of tax collection by state, federal, and local governments, the loss exceeded $300,000,000 annually. How was this deficit going to be recouped?[17]

Taxes were raised on employed Americans and businesses, and estate and income taxes skyrocketed. But these increased taxes couldn't cover

Above: Federal "dry" agents destroying booze during Prohibition (LOC). *Left:* Zion Church beer garden.

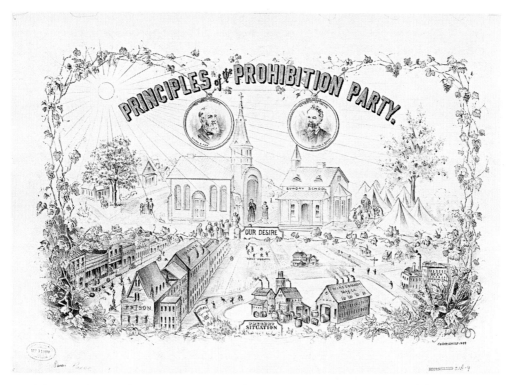

Prohibition Party Advertisement, 1888.The temperance societies touted the benefits of a "sober" life and often provided entertainment for men to lure them away from alcohol (LOC).

the loss and only slowed the economy in dry states. This was a major indicator of things to come for America. Regardless of this fact, the 18th Amendment went into effect on January 16, 1920, and was to stay for 13 years. In that time, America would have to contend with not only extreme job loss and economic hardship but also drought, and repercussions from the war debt and subsequent loans to Germany, France and England, which would not be repaid, thus plunging the intertwined economies into the worldwide Great Depression. President Coolidge convened a research panel to investigate social and economic trends through the 1920s. The findings did acknowledge major unemployment trends that were more than cyclical and more than a result of technological advancements replacing manpower. The report also condemned the 18th Amendment and its total disregard for property rights such as closing private businesses and detailed how negatively the amendment impacted job growth and the economy.[18]

The economic realities of Prohibition were not the only problems facing our "dry" nation during the thirteen years of the "noble experiment." Prohibition was not temperance. The push for total abstinence came mainly from the WCTU and certain churches, which preached morality and used it to push through their legislative agenda. The shift from moderation to complete abstinence was indeed problematic for a society that drank beer and cider through the course of the day from the earliest colonization. Alcohol was used in society in myriad ways, notably as a medicinal remedy. Although prescriptions were available for ailments requiring alcohol as a treatment, many could

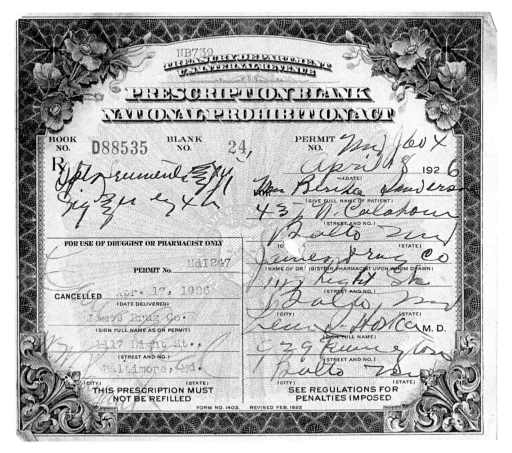

Prohibition prescription for alcohol, 1926.

neither afford the doctor nor the prescription they would write, which averaged $2 each. By 1927 several studies demonstrated that moderate drinking was beneficial, not life threatening, thus supporting the medicinal uses of alcohol.[19] Those who stockpiled their wines, beers, and spirits ran out in just a few short years and were desperately seeking a solution. Some turned to hard drugs, while others turned to bootleggers or homebrewing. Besides all this, the law was ambiguous in regards to both enforcement and verification, including regional requirements. Maryland however was the *only* state that did not pass a law enforcing Prohibition; therefore, all actions fell to Federal Dry Agents or local municipalities for enforcement and clarification in Maryland.

One famous example of this confusion came from a determined congressman from Maryland, John Philip Hill, during his "Battle of Franklin Farms." In August of 1926 Hill posed a challenge to Maryland Anti-Saloon League superintendent G.W. Crabbe and Prohibition commissioner Wayne B. Wheeler to define nonintoxicating fruit juice. One-half of 1 percent was the limit of what was allowed to be produced within city limits versus the surrounding countryside, where farms were allowed to legally ferment their own fruit juice up to 2.75 percent ABV. Why was favoritism shown to farmers, but city dwellers were more tightly controlled? This was the question Hill wanted answered. With the advent of Prohibition it was nearly impossible to find a hydrometer to measure

IRS Beer Meter, an attempt to measure alcohol content, Harris & Ewing Photographers (LOC).

gravity (used to calculate alcohol percentage). How, then, did one determine if he had reached ½ of 1 percent ABV as legally allowed for a city dweller? No clear answer was given and Hill decided to test the theory. He purchased grapes in Anne Arundel County and a press in Baltimore and proceeded to make his own wine. Calling it fermented fruit juice, he sent regular correspondence to Mr. Wheeler, with photos, and often invited the *Sun* to record his experiments. Hill repeatedly asked the superintendent how long he was to ferment his fruit juice before it became illegal. Dry agents showed up at this home on 3 West Franklin Street in Baltimore to determine the legality. They brought an ebulliometer to measure boiling point but could not convert the calculations to determine alcohol content and left. Hill continued fermenting the "fruit juice" even sending samples to the Prohibition Department for analysis. Private testing showed 6.31 percent ABV, and eventual testing came in at 12 percent ABV.[20]

As expected, the U.S. attorney convened a grand jury in October 1926, sending agents to padlock Hill's wine cellar. As a Harvard-educated lawyer and colonel in the national guard, Hill wanted to go to trial, but the government did not want the negative publicity. Hill responded by claiming to become a farmer, raising apples. This entitled him to the privilege of fermenting his fruit juice to a higher ABV. His "apple farm" consisted of apples brazenly tied to trees with string on his patio at West Franklin Street. He fermented cider and invited guests to partake. This forced the hand of the prosecutor and a trial date was finally set for November 10, 1926.[21] Hill was indicted on 2 counts: manufacturing and possessing intoxicating wine and cider and maintaining a public nuisance at his home on West Franklin Street. Due to the ambiguity and discrepancies in the law, Judge Morris Soper ruled that the ½ of 1 percent limitation was not applicable and Hill was found not guilty of all charges.[22] This certainly was a victory for the "wet" leaders in Maryland, but it was not the end of Prohibition.

On the heels of Hill's victory, Governor Albert Ritchie of Maryland announced that any places selling alcoholic beverages would not be bothered as long as they paid their taxes. Since it was illegal to sell alcohol, how could one legitimately pay taxes— perhaps through cigar storefronts? Speakeasies lined the Route 1 corridor in the guise of cigar stores, complete with glass cases filled with cheap cigars. Customers need only walk in and knock on the door while stating, "Joe sent me" to gain access to the club in the back of the store where beer, wine and spirits awaited the thirsty traveler.[23] Ritchie was Maryland's only four-term governor. He was a "wet" leader who started his first term the same year Prohibition began in 1920. He never supported Prohibition and effectively campaigned to end it, garnering support for a possible place on the Democratic presidential ticket in 1932. His popularity in part was due to his platform of repealing the 18th Amendment and in greater part to his stringent defense of states' rights.[24]

Maryland was not the only state witnessing challenges to Prohibition. Congressmen from New York were also noting the hypocrisy of the law. Notably, Fiorella LaGuardia, serving in the House of Representatives from New York State, testified in 1926 on the failures of Prohibition during the hearings before the Committee on the Judiciary, U.S. Senate. LaGuardia laid out the ineffectiveness of Prohibition, noting that alcohol was still being consumed, only at much higher ABV than the beer and wine consumed prior to the law, and no taxes were being paid (except in Maryland). He also noted the corruption in enforcement, detailing the numerous dry agents who owned liveried chauffeurs when they made only $2,000 annually. This of course was impossible without taking bribes to ignore liquor trafficking. LaGuardia also pointed out that the Treasury Department was well aware of the increase in illegal trafficking of alcohol (bootlegging) because of the rapid uptick in the production of $5,000 and $10,000 bills in the five years following the onset of Prohibition. This could only be due to the bootlegging industry and its need for large bills, as they operated on a cash-only basis when moving vast quantities of booze.[25]

Maryland had 3,190 miles of shoreline bootleggers used to smuggle alcohol. Many stories abound of smuggling from the Isle of Wight across the inland bay to points north, all coordinated via signal lights.[26] Fisherman doubled as bootleggers on Maryland's coastal shores. Even when caught by police, these fishermen were released to continue their daily jobs catching fish, crab and oysters.[27] With organized bootlegging by trusted locals and little to no oversight, violent crime was not as problematic in Maryland as it was in many places in the United States during Prohibition. It was opportunity organized by community, and community was reluctant to turn upon itself. Crime was endemic to the United States during the dry years and organized crime thrived in many cities. With "wet" Governor Ritchie in charge, Maryland saw less organized crime than cities like New York or Chicago, where mobsters like Al Capone made their fortunes in the illegal alcohol trade. Overall, there was a sharp spike in violent crimes during Prohibition across America, increasing 24 percent in just the first year of the Volstead Act, filling the prisons. From 1920 to 1933, homicides increased 40 percent, a trend that reversed after Repeal, belying the claims of Wheeler and the Temperance associations that crime would decrease due to Prohibition.[28] Many breweries and distilleries had closed down in Maryland but a few were operating with a close eye from the federal agents and fined when found to be in violation. Among those arrested and fined were Karl Schlossstein, head brewer of the Frostburg Brewing Company, and most of the brewers and owners of the Baltimore Brewing Company (formerly Brehm's Brewery, which failed in attempts to create near beer).[29] George Gunther, Jr., of the George Gunther Manufacturing Co. (formerly the George Guenther, Jr. Brewing Company) was also arrested for Prohibition violations. Maryland juries. however. were quite sympathetic and usually acquitted those brought to trial.

Some breweries, like Fred Bauernschmidt's American Brewery, attempted to stay open. Bauernschmidt paid his employees for three years believing initially that Prohibition would never pass. After the Volstead Act became reality Bauernschmidt believed it would be immediately repealed, and he wanted to be prepared with equipment and employees. Reality was an ugly mistress, and he was forced to shut down, unable to find a buyer for his brewery.[30] This devastation and eventual financial destruction was commonplace throughout Maryland and the country during the dry years.

Gunther's, however, was typical of many breweries that attempted to stay open during Prohibition by manufacturing ice and serving "near beer," which was beer that was reboiled to reduce the alcohol to the allowed ½ of 1 percent ABV. The process began with the actual brewing of normal, full-strength beer before it was reboiled. As a matter of course, several barrels of real beer were put aside that were not reboiled. This was strictly for the staff of the brewery and their invited guests. The near beer Gunther's produced was not of very good quality; in contrast, the real beer was said to be outstanding! Visitors were welcomed by appointment Monday through Friday each week at 4:00 p.m. The office clerk at the time was a young local named Mike Lardner. It was Lardner's responsibility to procure the food for these "gatherings" where real beer was supplied. He took great pleasure in obtaining a standard of five barrels of Chincoteague Oysters, two dozen live Diamond Back Terrapin, deer, bear, cheese, celery, pretzels, and onions. "Mommy Schlee," grandmother to Chip Winterling of the famous Winterling's Restaurant and Bar in Highlandtown, was the cook and most noted for her sour beef and dumplings and her terrapin soup.[31] Gunther charitably covered the expense of all foods. A generous man to a fault, he took exceptional care of his Belgian horses, having them visited by a veterinarian daily. He even paid for night school for employees like Lardner to move up within the company.[32] This compassion was a character trait Gunther would exhibit throughout his life, mentoring those employees who held promise, like Lardner, and generously helping in his community, which was struggling in the throes of the depression. In 1919 he even opened the Hebrew Home for Incurables, which also served as a humanitarian center. Gunther was a successful businessman and knew to keep influential folks happy and close to help survive the dry years.

These nightly "Gunther gatherings" entertained such notable guests as Governor Ritchie, Baltimore Mayor Broening, H.L. Mencken (then still known as Henry) and a contingent of department heads from Johns Hopkins. Mencken was a regular visitor to the brewery, usually accompanied by a band of his friends and family. According to Lardner, Mencken would always lead his group in a songfest and regale them with stories from his past as a reporter with the *Herald*. He held debates on where the largest nickel beer was sold; all agreed it was a saloon that was demolished to build Healy's bank on the corner of Carrolton and Baltimore, the First Carrollton Bank.[33] The conversations knew no limits and often lasted into the wee hours of the morning. Sometimes they would discuss such topics as the benefits of breastfeeding over bottle feeding. Everyone was warned to take taxis, so there were no cars visible from the exterior and few people knew what was transpiring inside the brewery.[34] However, despite Gunther's best efforts, late night gatherings were not enough to keep the brewery open, particularly when combined with his incredible generosity. Despite the availability of real beer, many would continue to brew within their homes during Prohibition, particularly after the Gunther brewery entered receivership in 1931.

Mencken was an avid home brewer, acquiring his yeast from the Lowenbrau brewery in Germany whenever he could and resorting to Fleischmann's baker's yeast when he could not.[35] He kept extensive journals on his home brewing, detailing the precise amounts of Chattalanee water from Greenspring Valley, corn sugar, hops, and malt. His copious notes also mentioned the cobweb-like fungus that was often found growing on his vat and his curious solution to stop it—milk of magnesia.[36] Most likely this was wild yeast, and the milk of magnesia seemed to neutralize it. Clearly baker's yeast was not optimal, but it was most often used by home brewers who could not acquire brewer's yeast. Mencken told of his sometimes explosive results when home brewing, noting in letters to friends that his *methodistbrau* was exploding in the bottles—but what was left was quite tasty.[37] Mencken, as much as he enjoyed imbibing, did have self-imposed restrictions, including not drinking during daylight or while working. For centuries doctors touted the merits of alcohol, but one night Mencken heard something quite different and this had a great impact on his drinking habits. In the winter of 1899 he was in a saloon and overheard a fire department surgeon stating that alcohol was a depressant (not a stimulant), and cooled you down, promoting pneumonia, something Mencken was loathe to contract.[38]

By contrast, the famous Globe Brewery was also open and producing "near beer," Arrow Special, during Prohibition. This beer was considered the best of the near beers in Maryland. The Globe Brewery operated quite differently from Gunther's, principally due to brewmaster John Fitzgerald. Fitzgerald was quite an interesting man. Born in 1868 in County Cork, Ireland, he immigrated to the United States, earning his citizenship in 1892.[39] He worked by day and at night earned his brewmaster's certification. It was a natural occupation, as Fitzgerald had worked at the Guinness Factory in Dublin before emigrating from Ireland for greater opportunities in America. He also worked for a brewery in Scranton, Pennsylvania, called Fountain Spring before relocating to Baltimore to open a brewery with a partner, Daniel O'Neill, on South Chester Street. This venture failed and he returned to Scranton and opened a porter and stout brewery called Fitzgerald and Sullivan. His business partner Sullivan cheated him out of the earnings and his patent for a submarine (Fitzgerald had a calling as an engineer) and disappeared. Fitzgerald paid off all brewery debts over the course of ten years.[40] He relocated to Baltimore to be near his sister, worked as a brewer, and found love. On September 19, 1904, John married Bridget Delia McCormick in Baltimore.[41]

Fitzgerald can only be described as an extremely devoted family man. Upon marrying his love, he gave her a China set valued at $300 (in 1904), which was worth more than the house he would buy her. They had seven children together before Delia succumbed to tuberculosis in 1916 at the age of 35. Not only did John raise his seven children but he also raised his widowed sister Jennie's two children after her death from TB. He never remarried, as he was "married for life" to Delia, often bringing the children to visit her at the cemetery. He walked to work every day from their home on the 300 block of East Biddle Street to save money, as all of the children went to Catholic school, an expensive undertaking. Accordingly, Fitzgerald and the nine children never missed a Sunday mass. He was a strict father but a warm and loving man by all accounts. Financially things were difficult, but Fitzgerald managed, and the children helped out. His daughter Eileen did the cooking, while Mary acted as a seamstress, sewing clothes for others. Every child had a job and the family survived with John as the only parent. John never stopped his own education and vowed to learn ten new words each night, which he did. He taught his children and grandchildren to read as well as securing their formal educations.[42]

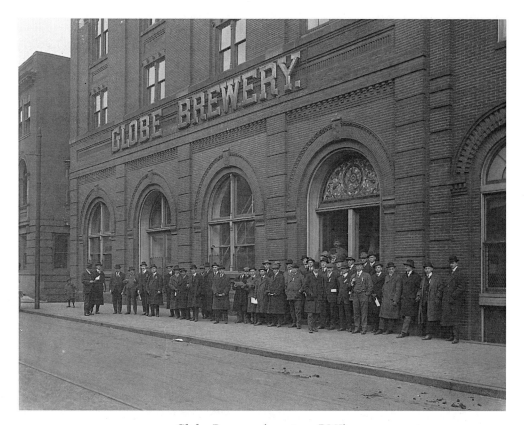

Globe Brewery (courtesy BMI).

John Fitzgerald, brewmaster of Globe Brewery, shown with daughters Margaret, Mary, and Eileen, 1936 (courtesy Ann Lansinger).

Fitzgerald was just as devoted to his job as to his family. He started work at 6:00 a.m. and ended at 6:00 p.m. six days per week. He brought the children to work periodically at the Globe Brewery for family picnic days. They enjoyed the interaction with their father's crew and noted the pride he took in his work. Unlike the Gunther Brewery, Fitzgerald would not stand for the production of anything but "near" beer at the Globe. He refused to break the law, even if he did not entirely agree with it. This is one of the reasons the Globe was never cited for Prohibition violations. Moreover, Fitzgerald adhered strictly to the law at home. He did make his own wine at home that met Prohibition mandates. This wine was consumed only in his home by invited guests over the age of 21. Many tried to bribe him to sell it or to make real beer, but Fitzgerald always refused. He was an upstanding man who would not entertain any hint of lawlessness.

There was plenty of lawlessness continuing throughout the state in spite of Fitzgerald's efforts, and it surpassed the manufacture of homemade wine and beer. Beer, cider, and wine (as in the case of John Hill) were definitely the safest methods of producing your own alcohol. If something went wrong the worst problem one would develop was usually a stomach ailment. Distilling, however was a far more dangerous pastime, the results of which could end in blindness or death, which occurred because of the methanol produced during distillation. That is why the first batch (steam) in the distillation process has to be discarded, as it contains methanol that metabolizes in the liver and retina causing blindness and liver failure. The second and third batches (steam) are far safer. Unfortunately, those who attempted home distilling (bathtub gin, white lightning, and other spirits) did not always understand this necessity of process and drank whatever they produced. Bootleggers were not always the safer option and sometimes bottled industrial alcohol in various forms, without appropriate practice to remove the poison (methanol), demonstrating a rather callous lack of concern for the results.[43] The United States government even added methyl alcohol into denaturing solutions for the creation of industrial alcohol. This caused death, paralysis, and blindness, among other severe medical issues. The government knew about this possibility and chose not to label the bottles as poison (which had been a requirement since 1906) due to pressure from Wayne Wheeler and the Anti-Saloon League. Wheeler stated that the government was under no obligation to provide people with drinkable alcohol when it was constitutionally prohibited. Partaking of industrial alcohol was deliberate suicide.[44] Outraged public opinion at the monstrous arrogance of those responsible for the unnecessary deaths of tens of thousands of people marked one of the turning points towards Repeal.

Baltimore and its "wet" leaders became the home for the Association for the Repeal of the 18th Amendment. This was not surprising considering the state never officially adhered to the amendment in the first place. Mike Lardner would be the association's youngest member. By that time he had worked his way up to bookkeeper for the Gunther brewery (he continued his education and eventually became a writer for the *Sun*).[45] As predicted, there was great support for repeal in Maryland, and many families and organizations operated to garner local support that would translate on a national level. The Women's Organization for National Prohibition Reform (WONPR) was established by Pauline Sabin, who was angered after hearing the WCTU president's statement that they spoke for all American women and all American women were in favor of Prohibition. The St. Valentine's Day Massacre in Chicago in 1929, where rival bootleggers unleashed a bloodbath in the fight over control of illegal booze and territories, also influenced Sabin greatly toward Repeal.[46] WONPR established a Maryland chapter, headquartered in Baltimore, which quickly grew to over 1,000 members by 1930. Mrs. C. Baker Clotworthy was chairman and Louise Este Bruce (wife of Senator William Cabell Bruce) was vice chairman.[47] Membership was statewide, covering every county, and included some of the most prominent women in the state, from wives of rabbis and ministers to the wife of the president of Johns Hopkins University. This provided a strong foundation for membership that was quickly spreading across the nation. Women supporting Prohibition reform were unexpected by the WCTU, but the damage caused to society by Prohibition was more than WONPR could stand. They also did not desire a return to the conditions that brought Prohibition (the saloon) but it was clear to WONPR that prior to the 18th Amendment, underage drinking and binge drinking were not common, nor was death from impure drink. None of these conditions was conducive to the growth of a family and the raising of healthy children. Politically, Prohibition pitted citizen against government and usurped states' rights.[48]

From 1929 to 1932 the wheels of Repeal picked up speed. National organizations like WONPR, the Women's Moderation Union, the Voluntary Committee of Lawyers, and the Crusaders gained incredible support. The Crusaders, founded by Fred G. Clark, avoided the grind of political machinery, promising to support candidates of all party affiliations that were "wet" and to fight all "dry" candidates. The name itself was a slap to the WCTU and their early "crusades" for temperance. Walter Chrysler, the automotive giant, called Prohibition a "doomed, utter failure" and donated financial support to the Crusaders. Many other notable men joined in supporting them, like E.F. Hutton, Harry Ford Sinclair, and the Edgar Allen Poe family.[49] The WONPR, however, was the only organization to actively support a presidential candidate, choosing Franklin Delano Roosevelt (FDR), despite reservations, stemming from his previous show of support for Prohibition. Our esteemed Governor Ritchie also made a bid for president in 1932,

A member of the Crusaders, rallying to bring about Repeal (LOC).

although it was not enough to garner the necessary votes. Roosevelt actually requested that Ritchie be on his ticket as vice president but Ritchie refused and continued to serve Maryland, guiding them out of the "dry" years he had fought so long to end.

By 1933 Roosevelt was president and America was changing. On March 22, 1933, Roosevelt signed the Beer and Wine Revenue Act into law, levying federal taxes on the legalized sale of beer and wine, with an option for states to choose legalization or not. Many states began to adopt changes to the 18th Amendment in anticipation of repeal. The first of these was legalizing beer, hoping to steer people away from the hard spirits they had been drinking in such large quantities over the past thirteen years. Governor Ritchie imme-

diately legalized the selling (with a license) and consumption of beer at 3.2 percent in Maryland. This took effect on April 7, 1933.[50] Eighteen other states followed suit that day with the legalization of beer. Just after midnight on April 7, 1933, H.L. Mencken was at the Rennert Hotel in Baltimore drinking the first legalized beer—a Globe Brewing Company Arrow Beer. It is no great surprise that Mencken was invited to partake of the first beer available in Baltimore at the Rennert, as he was not only a regular guest but also an avid proponent of the Rennert and its culinary expertise in all Maryland cuisine, of which he was particularly fond.[51] Years earlier, Globe had held a contest to determine the slogan of the near beer they would make to replace the "real" beer made prior to 1920. Walter Samuel of Baltimore won the contest with this: "Arrow Beer, It Hits the Spot."[52] The Arrow advertising slogan of Walter Samuel would remain in use for years, even subtitling the scandalous Arrow Beer nude posters over subsequent decades.[53]

President Roosevelt signing the Beer and Wine Revenue Act into law on March 22, 1933 (LOC).

The taps were flowing once again, but that wasn't enough for Maryland or the nation. Between March and December of 1933, thirty-six states (the necessary number for ratification) voted to adopt the 21st Amendment. This was the only amendment in United States history created to nullify a previous amendment to the Constitution. On December 5, 1933, the 18th Amendment to the Constitution of the United States of America was repealed, making it once again legal to manufacture, sell, and consume alcoholic beverages in America.[54] This was in no small part due to the efforts of Governor Ritchie and the wet leaders in Maryland. The difficulty came in implementation of the new

Walter Samuel, winner of the Globe Brewing Company contest to name the near beer. His slogan, "Arrow Beer, It Hits the Spot," won.

laws within the state. Governor Ritchie decided on a rather bold plan of action that would appease both dry and wet territories within the state. In his message to the Extraordinary Session of the General Assembly of Maryland, Ritchie laid out his plans for liquor control for the first time in thirteen years. He detailed an approach that was not state-wide but local. This allowed for each county and incorporated city to determine what would be prohibited or allowed in their territory in Maryland. What Ritchie stipulated (as well as defining beer, wine, and spirits) were the licensing fees and organization for manufacturers, distributors and retail sellers of alcohol, thus creating the three-tier system in Maryland. This "Liquor Control Act" was adopted in 1933 by special session.[55]

Some difficulties of this new approach to liquor control transcended the time and survive into our modern era. One notable aspect of the law made it impossible to fully own an industrial brewery in Maryland while having full ownership of another brewing facility.[56] This hearkened to the pre–Prohibition days when many breweries operated saloons as a way of controlling what was served. Unfortunately, this also brought blame and responsibility for the problems occurring in the saloons (the same problems the Anti-saloon League was railing against) to the brewery owners. In Ritchie's quest to "leave it in the hands of the locals" to determine alcohol consumption, many dry regions like the Eastern Shore were quite happy with the changes. Others have complained to this day about the incongruity from territory to territory when it comes to licensing and distribution, as it is not uniform (like it was in most states). This was a demonstration of the old adage, "You certainly cannot please all of the people all of the time."

Maryland found her way through the failed "noble experiment," the Great Depression, and extreme job loss, but the road ahead would require great patience to navigate the ever-changing landscape of the brewing industry.

BREWERY LISTINGS

Allegany

BREWERY	PROPRIETOR	LOCATION/ NEIGHBORHOOD	YEARS	PEAK PRODUCTION (IF KNOWN)
Queeno Company	Blaine White, William Rizer, et al.	208 Market Street Cumberland	1920–1922	Near Beer

Baltimore

BREWERY	PROPRIETOR	LOCATION/ NEIGHBORHOOD	YEARS	PEAK PRODUCTION (IF KNOWN)
Brehm Beverage Company	Henry Brehm	3501 Brehm's Lane	1920–1923	Near Beer
Baltimore Brewing Company	William Stoffel, Harry Karnofsky, Nathan Karnofsky	Same	1927–1933	Near Beer

George Gunther Manufacturing Company	George Gunther, Jr.	1211 South Conkling	1920–1931	Near Beer
Gunther Brews, Inc	Abraham Krieger	Same	1931–1935	Near Beer

BREWERY	PROPRIETOR	LOCATION/ NEIGHBORHOOD	YEARS	PEAK PRODUCTION (IF KNOWN)
Globe Brewing & Manufacturing Company	Same	313 South Hanover	1920–1935	Near Beer
Theodore Reichhart Brewing	Theodore Reichhart	2208 Harford Road	1930–1931	

7

Recovery

The 21st Amendment repealed Prohibition, but recovery was something that would happen at a much slower pace than most people counted on. Certainly jobs were created, and the economy was thirsty as the country attempted to pull out of the Great Depression. Unfortunately there were conflicting concerns over what road to take for the much-maligned liquor industry. The heyday of the late 1800s were gone, never to be retrieved, but the stunned, punch-drunk citizenry of Maryland were ready to begin anew. What direction would they take? Governor Ritchie's plan to ease the transition by leaving liquor decisions in the hands of the local municipalities may have seemed brilliant at the time, but it also laid the groundwork for a firestorm of controversy for future decades. The immediate concern was getting breweries back up and running. This was no small feat considering the changes that had taken place in the preceding fifteen years—namely electricity from a central station, changes in water and sewage, and building fire and safety codes. It was quite a tangled web of permits and bureaucracy to navigate through.

What began as the first gaslight franchise in America, the Gas Light Company of Baltimore, in 1816, would metamorphose into Consolidated Gas Electric Light and Power Company of Baltimore in 1906, forever changing Baltimore and the state of Maryland at their core. Globe Brewing Company was the first brewery to use electricity from a central station prior to Prohibition and went through further upgrades in 1935 to operate new cooling towers and mash tuns.[1] Gunther Brewing would be the last to convert from steam power to central station electricity, in 1934.[2] The distinct advantage of continuous electricity was that it enabled the operation of vast numbers of machines 24 hours a day, 7 days per week, a necessity to compete in Maryland. The older breweries that were reopening, as well as brand new plants, were switching over to central power as part of their standard operations. National Brewing Company reopened in its former plant in 1933 using central power. They installed all new brewing and fermentation equipment. Free State Brewing Company, opened by the Bauernschmidt family in 1933, would completely rebuild the former Fred Bauersnchmidt American Brewery on Hillen Street to accommodate central power, making this the largest brewery in Baltimore. American Brewing Company opened in the old John F. Wiessner brewery on North Gay Street (formerly Belair). During Prohibition it was called the American Malting Company. They manufactured ice and malt syrup but quickly converted to brewing as well as malting immediately after Repeal. The average cost of these renovations, converting from steam to electric power, ran between $500,000 and $1,000,000, no small investment. Although they signed on for purchased power prior to Prohibition, Crown Cork and Seal also took advantage of post repeal electric upgrades to facilitate the needs of the breweries reopening. Crown Cork needed to operate twenty-four hours per day to accommodate the regional and nationwide demand.[3]

Fortunately for many of the breweries trying to come up to code and begin operations, there was help, both financial and technical. The Master Brewer's Association of the Americas, which had been in operation since the height of brewing in America in 1887, planned technical programs for brewers to reenter the industry, learning the new equipment, best practices, and techniques.[4] Seibel Institute, founded in 1868, which had taken to teaching the arts of baking and milling during Prohibition, cancelled all non-brewing courses to prepare brewers for a return to the industry. Educational programs were instituted for beer distributors and tavern owners, with tutorial films made on everything from pipes to cellar runs to storage temperature of beers to promote good quality.[5] In addition, loans were made available from the federal government for the modernization of distribution warehouses and taverns. This included loans specifically for air conditioned structures to house beer and patrons alike.[6] Advice was freely offered for small breweries through trade magazines. Some industry suggestions included combining with other small breweries to market as a single brand, thus mitigating advertising costs. It was also suggested to restrict territory to limit advertising dollars spent, and of course the idea was pushed that it was best for small brewers to modify their recipes to achieve "similar profiles" to the top-selling beers in the country, like Anheuser Busch and Pabst.[7]

Despite the intensive and expensive operational upgrades, not all of the breweries survived the return to "wet." Experts from across the industry weighed in on what caused the failure of post–Repeal breweries, noting management was the main issue. Egotistical managers who refused to ask for help moving forward with new marketing plans and making critical operational adjustments (or in some cases not making them) were often listed as the cause of local brewery failures.[8] It was quite a bit to contend with. All breweries were aided by the many physicians emphasizing myriad health benefits of beer to the public.[9] This had been the case prior to Prohibition but it fell upon deaf ears. By 1933 people were so very eager for legal beer that the health benefits were less of a concern but still touted to assuage the temperance societies.

A shift in focus to American grains and hops instead of imports from Europe also resulted. In part this was a celebration of Repeal and a return to American-grown grains that were the norm before the Volstead Act. It was also a necessity. European maltsters like Briess (Czechoslovakia) were moving operations to America for opportunity and to escape a growing political power shift that might not be favorable for international business. Additionally, scientific investigations were carried out regarding the characteristics of America hops versus their European counterparts and the results were promising; some were even considered superior.[10] As a result, barley and hop production increased substantially. By 1938 Maryland was producing more than forty-eight million bushels of malt and over 855,000 of hops.[11] The Old Line State found its way back to her crop rotation of winter barley planted in September just after the potato crop. Within a year barley acreage was up across the United States by more than 16 percent.[12] Another aspect to the grain-bill induced changes in America included a very small percentage of grain (notably corn and rice) grown specifically for use in brewing (as adjuncts). This was something the brewers in America participated in out of necessity in the colonial era (like using spruce or birch instead of hops or Indian corn for malt) and again prior to World War I when grain rationing went into effect. After Repeal, Seibel Institute and other scientific labs like Wallerstein spent considerable time and energy not only researching the use of adjuncts but also plugging the quality of the corn and rice adjuncts available in the late 1930s, comparing them favorably to the crude adjuncts used in the pre–Prohibition years.[13] This would indeed be foreshadowing of what was to come in a mere two years.

Another change that Maryland breweries faced was the canning of beer. All efforts to can beer prior to Prohibition were abject failures. After Repeal, the American Can Company developed a "keglined" can with an enamel liner which prevented the "metallic taste" (problematic in previous attempts) when the CO_2 chemically interacted with the tin plate. The process also became more sanitary with the use of rubber gaskets and a shift to pressurized canning technology, preventing the other pre–Prohibition problem of contamination.[14] Despite all of these positive changes, not a brewery in Maryland was willing to risk its reputation and revenue to can beer in an unproven experiment.

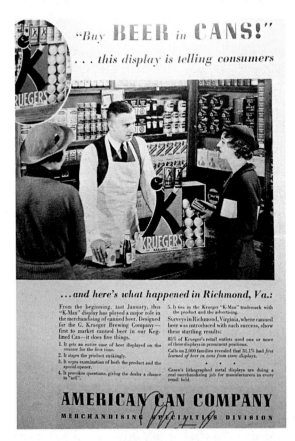

American Can Company placing the first beer (Kruegers) in cans, a selling point in *Beer Distributor* of 1936.

Krueger's Brewing Company out of New Jersey was willing to be the guinea pig for the canned beer test as long as it was run in a limited market: Richmond, Virginia.[15] The test was a huge success and the demand for canned beer became a nationwide phenomenon, with over two hundred million canned beers sold by the end of 1935.

As quickly as they were re-opening, Maryland breweries had adjustments to make to compete on a national level as well as the local level, from central power to canning machinery. Crown Cork and Seal was forced to adjust once American Can began canning beers across the nation. To compete Crown developed its own patented, double-coated, aluminum-lined can with the conventional Crown Cork Seal cap.[16] They were now just as relevant in canning as they were in bottling. Another difficulty in operations, and perhaps a contributing factor to the eagerness for breweries to enter into canning, was the decided lack of coopers left after Repeal. Baltimore alone boasted not only in-brewery cooperages but several throughout the city in the early 20th century.[17] Many were now purchasing barrels out of state due to the dearth of coopers. Things had definitely changed, and the breweries were attempting to adjust.

As breweries in Maryland were finally getting back on their feet, turmoil was beginning in Europe. German efforts at recovering from World War I and the economic devastation of accepting the terms of the Treaty of Versailles and the $33 billion dollar debt they agreed to repay had failed, and the Weimar Republic no longer existed. A former artist with a vision for economic recovery became chancellor in 1933. His name was Adolf Hitler, and he delivered the throngs suffering in Germany and Austria from the stranglehold of the depression that choked them while promising to restore Germany to greatness. For Europe, Hitler was a concern, but it was a concern Europe would appease to avoid another war. In America, the country followed Roosevelt's plan for recovery with the New Deal and waited to see how things in Europe evolved.

As America was slowly drawn toward the war in Europe, supplies were funneled to Britain and other allies to aid their war efforts. American pilots (male and female) also headed to Britain to help with transport, reconnaissance, and bombing missions. On December 7, 1941, the Japanese attacked Pearl Harbor and America was officially at war. This shifted manufacturing operations drastically. Crown Cork and Seal still produced closures for beer and soda, but the majority of production was turned to military needs. The factory produced tripod mounts for .50-caliber machine guns, bushings for airplane propeller blades, turret parts for patrol boats, and gears for Liberty ships. Crown Cork also established two brand new divisions for wartime production: first an aircraft wing assembly division with 800 employees; second, a metallic link division with 5,600 employees, half of which were women.[18] American Can Company, in addition to producing cans for beer and food, added over 350 new employees to produce bomb fuses for the military.[19] Free State was not yet canning beer at the start of the war and could not send their brews overseas, but they delivered 5 percent of their total production to military bases in the Mid-Atlantic and southern regions of the eastern United States.[20]

Agriculture was also realigned due to the war. Grain rations were instituted (as in World War I) to shuttle wheat and corn to U.S. citizens and to the U.S. military abroad. Part of the problem America faced was the loss of farm laborers to the war effort. The government, taking note of Britain's use of women during wartime, instituted the Women's Land Army from 1942 to 1945 in an effort to replace the significant shortage of agricultural workers and produce the lifeline of grain for the United States and its military. More than 27 percent of the agricultural labor force in America was made up of women, roughly three million strong.[21] The average farm laborer was paid $25-$50 per month, a far cry from the $120 monthly salary women in the factories earned. Many American women worked alongside POWs, but even so, agricultural labor fell far short. The gasoline rationing equated to a reduced number of functional tractors and lower production.[22] This meant a drastic reduction in the percentage of barley planted, requiring a new approach to producing the beer America loved. This is when we really see adjuncts take hold of the beer crafted in America. Corn and rice were used as fillers to make up for the lower percentage of malted barley used in production. Seibel was at the forefront of preparing for this now absolutely necessary trend in brewing with limited malt. This contributed in part to the loss of the full malted barley flavor that had once again become the custom since Repeal. There was no restriction on the quantity of beer produced at this time as there was during World War I, just the availability of the grains to manufacture it.

The U.S. military would also note the loss of flavor due to the shipping of beer across the Atlantic and Pacific despite the canning technology. To be honest, the "beer drops" instituted days after the invasion of Normandy certainly didn't help things. As the Allies hit the beaches of Normandy, drinking water was at a premium, as many of the wells were contaminated. A solution was for RAF and USAAF pilots to load beer into the drop tanks (instead of extra fuel) and fly them into Normandy for the men. Although the tanks were steam cleaned prior to filling them with beer, the taste of fuel lingered a bit. By the time our soldiers and sailors returned home they were accustomed to a beer that was lighter than what they had been drinking before they shipped out, or in some cases a little heavy with petrol. As their taste changed so did the production of beer in order to meet that consumer preference for the lighter and dryer beer, though definitely not the fuel-tinged brew!

In Baltimore we see Gunther Brewing attempting to meet that demand rather quickly. The brewery introduced a series of dry beers beginning in the late 1930s. The Krieger family that ran the brewing plant knew how to make excellent quality beer and continually tested new products for the loyal consumers. One of the most popular was the "dry beery beer," a light, very dry lager of really great flavor and quality.[23] The ABV was low, at 3.2 percent, which was a bonus for the still dry-tinged society. Gunther was the first to produce this and many breweries tried to follow suit. They even created a sugar-free beer in the 1950s to target housewives concerned about their figures, and they still managed to keep the ABV around 4 percent.[24] The brewery also understood that not everyone wanted to drink lager, and they continued producing ale in the "English" tradition. They wasted

Brewing Industry Foundation advertisement for beer and for boosting the morale of soldiers, 1944.

no opportunity for promoting the Gunther brand. Gunther sponsored a series of mysteries in 1934 known as the *Black Moon Mystery*, which aired on local radio. The show aired on Thursday nights on WFBR in Baltimore and also in Washington, D.C., on WRC.[25] Although intriguing and a distraction from societal concerns, the series ended in April of 1935.

Rather quickly, Gunther found a new radio promotion that not only kept consumers interested but also invested, and even provided an opportunity for them to win money competing against their rival city. The premise had contestants from Baltimore challenge contestants from Washington, D.C., in a game of intellect. It was called *A Quiz of Two Cities*. The winner not only received the monetary prize but also bragging rights for his city. It was a brilliant idea that caught fire in 1938 when it aired on WFBR in Baltimore and WTOP in Washington on Tuesday nights.[26] The program quickly garnered a large following, not to mention increased beer sales! By 1940 the shows were standing room only, and other venues had to be secured to house the excited crowds. Often auditoriums like the Wardman Park Theatre or television stations were used to accommodate the throngs.[27] The "quiz" spread across the country between rival cities in New York and Chicago. Listeners and contestants enjoyed the opportunity to drink a great beer and test their knowledge. By 1950 Gunther had other plans for their advertising dollars, however, and withdrew sponsorship. It was a surprise, but many marketing experts today would call it perceptive, as it allowed Gunther to move on to the next big thing before the audience grew bored.

Gunther sponsored the Washington Senators in the late 1940s while simultaneously sponsoring the quiz show. They produced collectable "beer cards" of the players with the Gunther logo on the back.[28] Gunther eventually ceded sponsorship to the Christian Huerich Brewery out of Washington, D.C., in a bid to find another sports franchise, which they found in the Baltimore Bullets, an American League basketball team. Unfortunately, the team folded in 1954 and Gunther was looking yet again for a team to sponsor. Baseball and beer have always married well, and the new brewery leadership under LeRoy S. Cohen (Krieger's son-in-law) saw the opportunity to increase sales revenues. When the Baltimore Orioles (formerly the St. Louis Browns) started playing in Baltimore in 1954 it was a rough start, but it began a love affair with the community that endured any weather. Gunther quickly seized the sponsorship and broadcast rights to the team. This was a dream advertising opportunity for the brewery locally, with a loyal consumer base and the chance to appeal to a larger audience with the national broadcasts. Gunther invested in the Orioles and at Memorial Stadium erected the largest all-electric scoreboard in the world at the time.[29] The whole country knew about Gunther Beer and the Orioles.

In 1957 Gunther acquired Fort Pitt Brewing Company of Pittsburgh and showed no signs of slowing expansion.[30] Business was booming and expansion was necessary to meet demand. In 1955 Gunther underwent a multimillion-dollar renovation of the entire plant and offices. The new facility was of steel construction and took everything into consideration, including air conditioning and areas designed specifically for the female employees to rest, work, and congregate. The brewery employed six hundred and was capable of producing one million barrels per year, although production never topped 800,000 barrels. Paul V. Glomp was installed as the new brewmaster after renovations were completed in 1956, and the building was topped with the "golden brew" tower representing Gunther's Premium beer offering. Gunther continued to lead the way by tapping into consumer preference without losing loyalty. Gunther was considered one of the best, if not the *best*, quality beer in the state. Despite all of the success, they were still producing about 100,000 barrels less per year than National Brewing Company, which was positioned right next door.

National Brewing Company began producing beer fairly quickly in the completely modernized plant in 1934, with National Bohemian lager the first beer off the line. Owned by the Hoffberger family, this new plant embraced the legacy of the former Baltimore pre–Prohibition brewing giant along with the name of the former beer, although not the recipe. Saul Hoffberger hired the former Ballantine brewmaster Karl Kreitler to concoct the recipes Baltimore would come to love. Shortly after the welcomed response of consumers to Bohemian, National released its National Premium pilsener. Demand for the beer was so strong the plant was forced to increase capacity within six months. This was the story of the National Brewing Company throughout the 1940s. Everyone in Baltimore came to recognize "Mr. Boh," the one-eyed, mustached icon of National Brewing introduced in 1936.[31] Mr. Boh was introduced by the marketing genius of Arthur Deute, who had a family history of brewing in Oregon and a firm grasp on innovative marketing campaigns and strong labor relations to guide National into the future.[32]

National canned beer like many other Baltimore breweries did, and much of it was

National Brewing Company, 1949 (courtesy BMI, BGE Collection).

shipped overseas during the war, forcing yet another increase in production capacity. The demand showed no signs of dissipating. The Hoffbergers (son Jerry was at the helm postwar) kept up with the latest technological innovations and continued investing in the upgrades of equipment and space to meet expanded volume. They were in a competition with Gunther for the palates of the regional consumers and in reaching for the taste buds of the broader national market. Seeking name recognition and increased sales, National Brewing endorsed sports teams much like Gunther did with the Senators, Orioles, and eventually the Colts. National was part owner of the Orioles when the team arrived in Baltimore but diverted sponsorship to the Washington Senators when Gunther won the Orioles broadcasting rights and invested in the scoreboard. National eventually controlled both by the early 1960s.[33]

It was the advertising that really seemed to capture the region and eventually the nation. Mr. Boh was doing his part, but a new campaign slogan created in the 1950s seemed to secure the foothold for exceptional growth beyond any other brewery in the state. "The Land of Pleasant Living" was the most recognizable slogan affiliated with National Brewing. The catch phrase was spoken by Jerry Hoffberger during a plane ride over Maryland while he gazed at the beauty of the shoreline. There was no turning back from that, and many rather catchy jingles heralding National's production on the shores of the Chesapeake Bay would eventually accompany it. National had seized upon what made Maryland great and what made National Beer great as well. National Beer, Mr. Boh and the Land of Pleasant Living would become iconic and synonymous with Maryland. National opened a plant in Detroit to meet the increasing demand out west. Production in Baltimore topped 1,000,000 barrels per year, making National the largest brewery in the state and the region and ranking in the top 20 in the country.

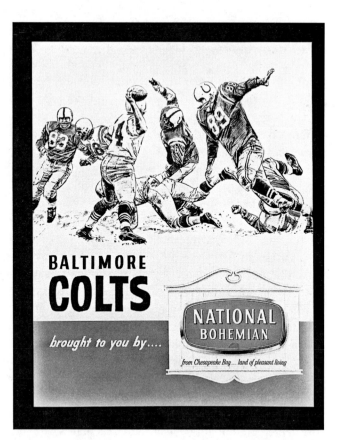

National Bohemian (National Brewing Company) sponsoring the Baltimore Colts after Gunther sold to Theo Hamm's Brewing.

Competitor American Brewing Company was owned by John Fitzsimmons while it was the American Malting Company (during

American Brewing Company "cereal cooker," 1956 (courtesy BMI, BGE collection).

Prohibition). After legalization they produced American Pilsener. They continued malting their own barley for use not only in their own brews, but they also supplied some of the largest breweries on the East Coast after Repeal. Within a year American also offered the Old Baron (a special dark) and the Nut Brown Ale to thirsty consumers. American became a staple brew in the state, and in part this was due to the stringent quality control put in place by brewmaster (and eventual president) Raymond Klussman, a Siebel graduate who demanded only the best. If any beer was "off-taste" it was dumped and a new batch was brewed. It was never recombined with new batches but was destroyed so every consumer knew the product they paid for was manufactured and delivered without compromise.

Although American did not sponsor local sports teams, they did create a few slogans that resonated in the region including, "Greatest Beer in American History!" The interesting note here is that many local consumers thought American beer was a good, local, inexpensive beer but not the best in the state. American was producing around 350,000 barrels per annum and was in no way competing with Gunther and National, but it still managed to hold its corner of the market. The difficulty for American came with the changes in grain rationing during the war (1942) and the subsequent price ceilings placed on barley. The company altered the price charged for its barley malt syrup (sold to other breweries) based upon the cost of the barley (prior to malting). This seemed like standard practice, but not with a price fixe in place. American thought the ceiling did not apply because it was malt syrup, not strictly grain. They were fined $32,117 for the overcharges in 1942 and 1943, plus three times that amount in "damages." American paid the nearly $100,000 without admitting wrongdoing, appealed the ruling and won (finally, in 1955), but the ordeal forced them to discontinue malt production after 1944.[34] This hit the profit margin hard but ended the copious financial penalties from the U.S. government that also compromised the bottom line.

Globe Brewing Company, having produced the first real beer in Maryland after Prohibition, continued on its quest to seize consumer loyalty and build support throughout the region. Globe began offering a premium beer by 1936 with catchy slogans to match. The slogans weren't just used in ads but were also printed on gilt-edged playing cards consumers received in exchange for Arrow beer crowns. This was a viable alternative to get customers invested when you had no sponsorship of a local sports team, or a radio show: "Better because it costs more to brew!," "Drink Arrow Beer for three weeks, and you'll drink for life!"[35] Globe also canned beer relatively quickly after Krueger, and they were able to ship beer overseas for the U.S. military during the war. Unfortunately Globe was limited in capacity to 300,000 barrels per year and found it difficult to compete with behemoths Gunther and National as they expanded.

Globe introduced new styles in addition to Arrow beer and Shamrock pale ale to address the competition. In 1952 it introduced Hal's and in 1947 offered an Arrow Imperial lager. Both brews were a creation of the new brewmaster, Karl Hennige, who replaced Fitzgerald after the latter died. This marked a return to lager, which Globe had been known for prior to Prohibition instead of the ales it became known for after Prohibition. Arrow Imperial was made at a time when adjuncts were necessary due to wartime grain rationing, Hal's was produced when barley acreage was on the rise once again and the use of corn grits and rice fillers was limited. Hennige not only tweaked Fitzgerald's triple-hopped Arrow beer recipe (less hop, more light malty notes) but he also introduced a virtually adjunct free pilsener known as Arrow 77 in 1955. Both received acclaim, but the Arrow 77, a pilsener with "zing," was by far the more popular.

Although Frederick Bauernschmidt was initially part of the new Free State Brewery, he was an advisor who lent name recognition to the operations. Sadly, he passed away before the first beer was sold in March of 1933. Free State Brewing, despite having the largest brewery in the state at the time, was under pressure from the moment it opened. The strain was due in part to competition, and in part due to the fact that the cost of modernizing the brewery exceeded $1 million.[36] Quickly, capacity was surpassed by Gunther and National, both having decided to begin canning their beers, while Free State continued bottling. The expense of a canning line was not justifiable in light of the financial weight the brewery was already under. Free State engaged in many activities in the state to gain name recognition, including hockey matches against other local businesses representing every company from Cheverolet dealers to bars.[37] This had a limited impact on sales.

By 1939 Free State was struggling and had introduced a new brewmaster, Eugene Schwoerer (former brewer at Baltimore Brewing), and a new chairman, Harry Wolfe.[38] The hope to revitalize the brewery and bring in new customers was behind the reorganization. Free State began offering regular patrons gifts of playing cards, bath towels, and silk hosiery for turning in bottle caps.[39] The brewery targeted advertising towards women, a tactic that became more commonplace as Free State recognized the need to include them as a growing percentage of sales. The war years aided Free State's survival when they branched into military industrial manufacturing. After the war they reached

Globe Brewery, Arrow Beer truck in distribution just after Repeal (ATHS).

Arrow Beer truck, ca. 1940 (ATHS).

Arrow Beer "Perfection" calendar advertisement, 1947 (courtesy Larry Handy, ECBA).

an annual output of about 75,000 barrels per year. It was still not enough to keep up with the competition in Maryland. The brewery did not last for long once the war ended, and it fell into receivership in 1950. It was not the end of brewing operations, as the plant was purchased by a new brewing company with an old familiar name: Wiessner.

The Wiessner family attempted to open another brewery after Prohibition in 1934 on North Chester Street, but all efforts failed and the plan was abandoned.[40] In 1950 Morton Sarubin and W.H. Ruppert incorporated under the (now defunct) Wiessner Brewing Company, Inc. The plan mirrored that of National Brewing, strictly name recognition, as no Wiessner family members participated in the new venture of taking over the failed Free State Brewery. The brewmaster, however, was linked to the brewing family. Fred Nuemiester was the son of a former Wiessner brewmaster.[41] Sarubin thought he understood how to compete in the tight beer market in Maryland. A new canning line was installed along

An American Beer truck from the late 1940s. It was not uncommon for folks across the state to see American trucks like this one making deliveries in the 1940s and 1950s (ATHS).

with updates to the bottling equipment to maximize distribution. In addition to more than doubling output, Sarubin hoped the brewer's lineage would tie into the name recognition and break through the staunch grip of competition. It never did. Within two years the brewery was placed in the hands of receivers and auctioned off piece-meal.[42] This was just one of the many indicators of the difficulty of profitability in the brewing industry after Repeal.

The Baltimore Brewing Company, located in the old Brehm's brewery, struggled during Prohibition. They held the distinction of logging eight arrests for violating Pro-hibition laws.[43] The state forced the sale of the brewery, and a newly formed entity con-tinued with the name Baltimore Brewing Company. This new Baltimore Brewing Company employed some of the former workers and capitalized on a financial influx from New Jersey brewery owners to secure operations. However, new blood and new money would not be enough for the brewery to succeed. The new ownership hired Eugene Schwoerer (former maltster with American Malting) as brewmaster. He created the first brew, BB Perfectly Brewed, which hit the market in October of 1933. Although the beer was well made, the cost of updating the plant and the limited production (40,000 barrels per annum) were not enough to provide an advantage in the tough Maryland market. By 1935 a new brewing concern had purchased the failing brewery.[44] The majority owner, L.M. Burton, was a hay and grain dealer. After taking possession of the brewery Burton retained Schwoerer and many of the employees but brought in (former) sales managers from Globe and other successful local breweries to help run it. By 1936 Bruton Brewing Company was not only running smoothly but was also expanding bottling operations to meet demand. The brewery reached a capacity of just over 150,000 barrels per year in 1939, which was just enough production to compete in the market.[45] It was producing Brewmaster's Special and Duke's Ale that were well received and also produced a seasonal bock beer that was considered exceptional.[46] Bruton attempted to tap into the local market with contests and ad campaigns to capture consumer interest.[47] Predictably the brewery did not can beer, only offering bottles and kegs, which was a hindrance to profit. This was accompanied by mounting uncollected debts and a hefty mortgage that was almost impossible to pay.[48] Unfortunately, the brewery ended up in receivership by 1940 and was sold off piece by piece to cover the mortgage and acquired debts.[49]

Many other Baltimore breweries met the same fate as Baltimore/Bruton. Theodore Reichert had opened his brewery on Harford Avenue by 1934.[50] By 1939 Reichert had changed the name to Chesapeake and was out of business.[51] Bismarck Brewery opened in 1934 to produce Bismarck beer.[52] Success was elusive, and the brewery changed hands, eventually becoming Imperial Brewing Corporation by 1939 and almost merging with Bruton to survive. Neither plan worked to save the plant, and the brewery forfeited its charter by 1940.[53] Brooklyn Brewing Company on Bolton Street had a federal permit (much like the modern TTB) to begin brewing in 1934, but by that summer it was placed in the hands of the receivers and the brewery was closed and sold for parts.[54] This was also the case with Liberty Brewing Company, situated on the corner of Boston and Ponca. The owners hired experienced brewmaster Charles Brohmeyer, added a bottling line, and estimated capacity at well over 150,000 barrels per year, certainly enough to compete. They were sued within six months of opening and the operation was placed in the hands of receivers to sell off and distribute assets to creditors.[55] Charles Brohmeyer attempted to open his own brewery on the same premises and was also bankrupted and was forced to sell by 1937.[56]

Other breweries across Maryland met this same tragic fate. Shore Brewery, part of the Shore Beverage Company of Salisbury, opened in 1934 with a state-of-the-art, advanced technology plant employing fifteen workers. The brewing operations were headed by renowned chemical engineer Gilbert Wilkes, who adhered to *Reinheitsgebot* (German beer purity law) and planned to produce quality beer with the exceptional Salisbury water.[57] Within a year of opening brewing operations were discontinued. Other breweries never got past the planning stage. The Prince Georges Brewing Company registered in both Prince Georges County and Howard County but never opened its doors. The oddly named Peoples Service Company in Frederick was a planned brewery but never opened either.

Hagerstown Brewing Company attempted renewed operations beginning in 1934 on Franklin and Foundry streets in Hagerstown. David Hammond of Pittsburg secured a mortgage on the former pre–Prohibition plant in 1933 and named it the Hagerstown Ice Company. He foresaw the end of Prohibition, as did many other people, and wanted to prepare the plant for production legitimately, thus offering ice until beer was once again legal.[58] Hammond set about updating the plant to operate beyond its 50,000-barrel former output. He increased capacity to 100,000 barrels per annum.[59] As the only brewery in Washington County prior to and after Prohibition, it seemed like a guaranteed success as long as the beer was as good as everyone remembered. Hammond hired an experienced German brewmaster by the name of Adolph Molitor. The product was a lager, oddly called Holland Beer. By 1936 the brewery filed for 77b bankruptcy and underwent reorganization.[60] Hammond was forced out, and a new president, C.D. Walton, was installed. Reorganization wasn't enough, as the brewery could not make its mortgage payments and was foreclosed upon in 1937.[61] This is an interesting case, as the lack of regional competition and ideal location, in a former brewery, should have spelled success. Secretary Betty Winn noted severe financial mismanagement on the part of Hammond before his departure.[62] A look at the write-ups on the brewery in newspapers of the time sheds light on the problem that most likely cascaded into financial hardship. One paper noted in 1935 that Hammond worked to update the plant to turn out Holland Beer as fast as possible, even altering the structure of each floor of the brewery. Perhaps too much money was spent in that endeavor and not enough on quality.[63] Even with the updates, the new plant never eclipsed the production of the old, a telling detail indeed. The brewery was sold in 1938 to a frozen foods company.

Fortunately, Cumberland would see the successful renewal of its former brewing glory, much like the handful of Baltimore breweries that tasted victory. Both Cumberland Brewing Company and German Brewing Company would immediately begin to produce real beer. Both produced near beer during Prohibition and that product kept them alive, operational, and with name recognition in place. Shockingly, Cumberland's near beer was so good it was long a target of thieves who couldn't afford it and were forced to steal it.[64] Both breweries quickly converted to 3.2 percent ABV after Repeal. Cumberland Brewing Company was still run by the Fesenmeier family, which had founded the brewery in the nineteenth century.[65] The brewery was right back to producing their full-strength Old Export (bock and winter brew) and the new Fort Cumberland Ale while reaching maximum capacity of around 100,000 barrels per year. Plans for continued update and expansion were stalled when Michael Fesenmeier passed away in 1934. Control of the brewery would change hands repeatedly after his passing.[66] Eventually George Bibby took the helm and kept them on an even keel for the remainder of the brewery's existence. Bibby was formerly with Gunther and Globe in Baltimore and had a strong track record of success. Bibby led the brewery into the canning of beer and controlled expansion, guiding it through the pressures of a competitive market in a small region. The ageing brewery was challenged as much by the century-old infrastructure of the building as it was by its nemesis, German Brewing.

German Brewing Company (which had renamed itself "Liberty" during World War I) was back in business as a fully operational plant producing real beer in 1933. During the "noble experiment" the brewery not only produced the near beer Queeno but also ice, soda, and malt syrup in order to stay (barely) profitable. After Repeal they chose to embrace the genesis of the plant built by Warren White and their quality product by returning to its original trade name of German. Regionally their beer was well remembered, with Old German the favorite and therefore the first produced in 1933. This was not a difficult task, as Henry Nuemann was still brewmaster, as he had been prior to Prohibition. Making near beer vexed him so much he was elated to swiftly engage in the production of real Old German once again. That was not going to meet demand, and the brewery immediately invested in the expansion of the facility. They added a new bottling house, expanded the brew house, and increased storage capacity. Despite almost losing the brewery to the devastating flood of Wills Creek and the North Potomac River in 1936, the brewery prospered.[67] By 1939 German was producing more than 200,000 barrels per year, more than almost any other brewery in the state (other than the few in Baltimore).[68]

German Brewing soon found itself in a déjà vu scenario as 1940 arrived—a war in Europe where once again the Germans were the aggressors. The board was determined not to lose business and took decisive action prior to America's involvement by changing their name once again. This time the name would stick: Queen City Brewing. They would also suspend the Old German and instead substitute Queen City so as to generate no ill will from consumers. The brewery invested in the canning of beer, which was good for the war but also the standard for consumers here at home. After the war, the name Queen City Brewing remained, but the original brands returned and Old German was back. In addition, the brewery added a bock and a winter brew. This was familiar and certainly generated staunch competition with the brewery's greatest rival, Cumberland Brewing Company.[69] The advantage for Queen City was outpacing Cumberland in production, sales, and modernization. Like many Baltimore breweries they began marketing specifically towards women. The Whiting family, at the helm of the brewery since Repeal, understood not only loyalty to the brand but also how to reach their target audience, in part because they were able to actually identify who that was, where many others missed the opportunity for sales growth. This allowed the brewery to weather the subsequent storms of a coal shortage and a sugar crisis.[70] Queen City Brewing was the superior brewery in the Cumberland, West Virginia, and Pennsylvania markets, exceeding Cumberland Brewing in every facet. By 1958 the latter was struggling and stockholders were itching to sell. That year Queen City Brewing purchased controlling interest in Cumberland Brewing.[71] Executives from Queen City were placed in the top positions at Cumberland and the brewery remained operational. Queen City (for the time being) completely controlled the regional market.

What was once a mecca for brewing in the United States was still one of the top thirteen states, selling 87 percent of the beer nationwide.[72] This achievement was met by only a handful of post–Prohibition Maryland breweries, however. The future prognosis was not promising even for those that thrived in the new world of legal drink.

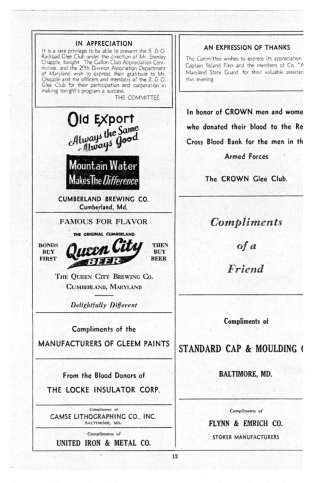

Queen City advertisement, among others, including Cumberland Brewing advertisement touting the mountain water quality in their Old Export beer, World War II.

BREWERY LISTINGS

Allegany

Brewery	Proprietor	Location/ Neighborhood	Years	Peak Production (if known)
Cumberland Brewing Company	M.L. Fesenmeier, Tasker Lowndes, George Bibby	711 N. Centre Street	1934–1968	200,000 bbls/yr
German Brewing Company	F. Brooke Whiting	208 Market Street	1933–1939	200,000 bbls/yr
Queen City Brewing	Same	Same	1940–1974	325,000 bbls/yr

Baltimore

BREWERY	PROPRIETOR	LOCATION/ NEIGHBORHOOD	YEARS	PEAK PRODUCTION (IF KNOWN)
American Brewing Company	John Fitzsimmons	1701 North Gay Street	1933–1972	350,000 bbls/yr
Baltimore Brewing Company	New Jersey Trust	3501 Brehm's Lane	1933–1934	40,000 bbls/yr
Bruton Brewing Company	Leonard Bruton	Same	1934–1940	150,000 bbls/yr
Bismarck Brewery	Bischoff	1808 N. Patterson Park Ave.	1933–1934	
Bismarck Brewing Company		Same	1934–1938	
Imperial Brewing		Same	1938–1940	
Free State Brewery	Frederick Bauern- schmidt & John Merzbacher	1108 Hillen Street	1933–1949	75,000 bbls/yr
Weissner Brewing Company	Morton Sarubin & W.H Ruppert	Same	1949–1952	150,000 bbls/yr
Gunther Brewing Company	Abraham Krieger	1211 South Conkling Street	1933–1959	800,000 bbls/yr
Liberty Brewing Company		Boston & Ponca Streets	1933–1934	
Brohmeyer Brewing	Charles Brohmeyer	Same	1934	
National Brewing Company	Hoffberger Family	O'Donnell & Conkling Streets	1933–1975	1,650,000 bbls/yr
Theodore Reichart, Inc.	Theo Reichart	2208 Harford Road	1933–1936	
Chesapeake Brewing	Same	Same	1936–1938	
Brooklyn Brewing	P. Martin	2000 Bolton Street	1934	
Eigenbrot Brewing		Lombard & Eton Street	1934	
Globe Brewing Company	Morris Schapiro	313 S. Hanover Street	1935–1963	300,000 bbls/yr
J.F. Weissner & Sons Brewing	Wiessner Family	1732 North Chester	1934	

Frederick

BREWERY	PROPRIETOR	LOCATION/ NEIGHBORHOOD	YEARS	PEAK PRODUCTION (IF KNOWN)
Peoples Service Company	Unknown	809 East Frederick	1934	NP

Prince Georges County

BREWERY	PROPRIETOR	LOCATION/ NEIGHBORHOOD	YEARS	PEAK PRODUCTION (IF KNOWN)
Prince Georges Brewing Company	Unknown	Laurel	1934	NP
Same	Same	Hyattsville	1934	NP

Washington County

BREWERY	PROPRIETOR	LOCATION/ NEIGHBORHOOD	YEARS	PEAK PRODUCTION (IF KNOWN)
Hagerstown Brewing	David Hammond/ C.D. Walton (1936)	344 West Franklin	1934–1937	50,000 bbls/yr

Wicomico

BREWERY	PROPRIETOR	LOCATION/ NEIGHBORHOOD	YEARS	PEAK PRODUCTION (IF KNOWN)
The Shore Beverage Company	Gilbert Wilkes	Salisbury	1934–1935	10,000 bbls/yr

8

The Decline and Fall
of Brewing in Maryland

The breweries in Maryland that were able to recover from the dry years met with looming uncertainty as they entered the 1960s. The landscape had changed drastically after the war. As 1960 dawned, there were only a handful of breweries left operating in the state. What happened to this once thriving industry that was one of the top producing states in the nation? The easy answer stops at competition. The real answer requires a longer examination of the industry and the hard-wrought changes forced upon them. There was no doubt that beer was in demand, but tastes had changed. The grain rationing of the war years coupled with the now acquired taste for lighter beers limited what a brewery could offer to patrons and remain profitable. Adjuncts were now a standard ingredient of American beer. Quality was still the key to success but required a higher price point for breweries, particularly those operating on a smaller scale. This came to be a major issue in the region and one of the contributing factors toward decline.

Another aspect of the brewing industry that Maryland seemed to grasp, and many other breweries in the nation had to learn, were new marketing techniques. Certainly women were a prime target for brewery advertising, just as they were in the 1940s and 1950s. Women were a rising consumer medium who needed marketing campaigns specifically targeted to them. However, there was another group of consumers targeted by breweries—blacks. The civil rights movement was in full swing and Lyndon B. Johnson passed the Civil Rights Acts in 1964. Maryland had always fared more favorably when it came to race relations than many of her southern neighbors. Immediately after the Civil War, breweries in Maryland began to hire blacks. There were many free blacks in Maryland who owned property and enjoyed freedoms not seen in southern states in the early centuries. Until the Civil War many travelers from slave holding states commented on Baltimore and Maryland's lack of oversight of slaves because they were able to do whatever they desired once they finished their work, until they needed to return to their duties the next day. It is not surprising that we see a more forward-thinking approach from Maryland breweries in the 1960s. It was the rest of the country that had to catch up. This was most notable in the 1967 *Beer Distributor*, which dedicated several pages on the specifics of marketing to "Negroes."[1] This was a relatively unexploited market that demonstrated great potential, not only for profit but also for employment. Maryland breweries already knew this and stood as stellar examples of how to market to this untapped group. More important, Maryland breweries were not only marketing to this group, they were also employing workers from this group in every capacity from laborers to managers, based purely on merit, regardless of race.[2] Maryland was leading the way in many respects; unfortunately, it wasn't enough to sustain brewing operations in the state long term.

Gunther was one of the breweries in Maryland that seemed to have gotten everything right. This success went well beyond name recognition, sponsorship, and radio programs. Gunther produced a high-quality beer. It was light and dry but lingered with a pleasant body that made it a favorite beyond the region. The brewery also experimented with other styles and beers that might be considered more appealing to certain segments of the market, like sugar free and extra dry beers. Consumers preferred the extra dry (lager) and the Old English Ale as the staple brews from Gunther. The board of the brewery also engendered community good will through their support of charitable organizations, much like the pre–Prohibition Gunther Brewing Company. Sinai Hospital and the Jewish Medical Center, along with several social welfare agencies, benefitted from the success of the brewery through both donations and service. Despite all of the community outreach, Gunther never lost sight of the competition and made an intriguing and ultimately brilliant decision to sell the brewery and walk away while at the top of the market. As of December 31, 1959, Gunther Brewing Company had been sold to Theodore Hamm Brewing Company for an undisclosed sum just north of $14,000,000.

Theodore Hamm Brewing Company was founded in St. Paul, Minnesota, in 1865. They had a series of plants in St. Paul, San Francisco, and Los Angeles to meet demand, and wanted to open an east coast plant. With updates to the Gunther Brewery complete, and a willing seller with a large distribution market, Hamm's seized the opportunity to open a brewery in Baltimore. The plan was to spend $10,000,000 to renovate the plant to accommodate the Hamm's brewing process and ultimately providing an exact duplicate to the western plants. The mission was to have no discernable difference in the taste of the beer, as the methods were identical in every plant.[3] In addition to the purchase, the caveat was to continue sponsorship of the Orioles, as Gunther had done for years on both radio and television.[4] This, however, would not be enough for the midwestern brewery to meet with any measure of success. Although Hamm's owned the Gunther label and recipe, they refused to make it—upsetting a very loyal consumer base. Locals called Hamm's Beer "green" because they said once it was consumed, illness soon followed.[5] The more modern connotation of green beer describes beer that has not been conditioned before packaging, as the yeast still needs time to work. This was most commonly seen in pilseners that require several weeks prior to packaging, after primary fermentation.[6] For Maryland consumers it was just plain awful.

In addition to quality issues with the beer, other major miscalculations set Hamm's off on the wrong foot. Hamm's shipped their beer from the Midwest until renovations on the Maryland plant were complete, again compromising the taste of the product. The regionally tone deaf decision to retain the Midwestern-themed marketing campaign of Hamm's was confusing to locals in the Mid-Atlantic region: "From the land of sky blue waters (waters), From the land of pines, lofty balsam, Comes the beer refreshing, Hamm's the Beer Refreshing." The product did not meet sales expectations at all and an attempt was made to engender some good will among locals. The reintroduction of Gunther beer to turn profits around was a sound idea, but was implemented too late.

Hamm's $10,000,000 renovation of the former Gunther plant, ca. 1961 (courtesy BMI, BGE Collection).

The wary market was fed up with Hamm's and no longer trusted what they produced. When Gunther beer returned, some believed it was really Hamm's beer in a Gunther label.[7] By 1963, a mere four years after acquisition, Hamm's sold the Baltimore plant to F & M Schaefer Brewing Company out of New York.[8] Schaefer had been established in 1842 and was one of the first lager breweries in America. They were ranked in the top ten for breweries nationally when the purchase went through.

Schaefer continued to sell both Hamm's and Gunther in addition to their own products as long as demand existed. There was not much demand, at least not for Hamm's. By 1964, after yet another million dollar remodel of the plant to accommodate the Schaefer process, Schaefer was fully producing their own beers out of the Baltimore facility. Hamm's discontinued sales in the East and sold the Gunther label to Schaefer.[9] Hamm's was bought out by a larger brewery within a year. Schaefer used the Baltimore plant for Schaefer products and shifted distribution of Gunther products to Globe Brewing. Globe struggled to remain competitive in Maryland and eventually moved brewing operations to Queen City Brewing in Cumberland in 1963, using Baltimore strictly as a distribution hub.[10] Surprisingly, this move facilitated distribution of Gunther beer, not Globe. This lasted only for a short time, as Globe Brewing completely closed the Baltimore plant in 1966. The property was sold and the building razed to construct a parking lot. Gunther would not be sold again by Schaefer until 1973, when demand

Cumberland Brewing Company, which was absorbed by Queen City Brewing in 1958.

became too great to ignore. Curiously, they produced Gunther in New York and distributed it in and around New York, Baltimore and Washington, D.C.[11] Gunther was no longer purely a Baltimore institution. This was the fate of many Maryland breweries. American Brewing Company also began contract brewing its beer through Fort Pitt Brewing Company and closed the Baltimore plant in 1973, the same year it was recognized on the National Register of Historic Places. It could not be torn down but neither was it maintained, and it was left vacant to decay and indifference, a sad sign of the once great but flagging industry.

Queen City Brewing Company, which absorbed Cumberland Brewing in 1958, rode the wave of success for years until major changes in the industry began to take hold. An extremely potent descriptor to assist understanding of what was happening at the time comes from Bob Leasure, a sales manager at Queen City until 1968. Mr. Leasure moved up through the ranks of Queen City, starting as a salesman and known throughout the region as the "silver dollar kid." He made a habit of giving silver dollars to the bartenders for their children, thus earning the moniker. It was a smart marketing technique that each bartender in every establishment in western Maryland, West Virginia, and Pennsylvania looked forward to. Sales were easy in the 1950s and into the early 1960s, as regional beers were preferred to national beers 100 percent of the time. Brand loyalty was as important as locality and everyone wanted the Old German beers. Leasure also worked harder than other salesman in his plant and other competing plants to get his product to market. He brilliantly targeted out-of-region consumers through the process of setting up sampling programs at job sites where many out-of-state workers were known. Leasure would show up on Friday evenings at 5:00 p.m., when the shift ended, with cold Old German, cheese, and sausages. This instilled a desire for Queen City beers and sales doubled, creating a demand for the beers in new markets, which in turn helped earn Leasure a promotion to sales manager.[12]

For Leasure, the view from management was quite different. He was responsible for more than just selling and often solved many of the problems associated with the industry at large. A major concern was the theft of brewery kegs from bars and pubs. On more than a few occasions Leasure ended up talking his way into rival breweries in Ohio and other states in an attempt to determine where his stolen stainless steel kegs ended up. This is a common problem today, but the cost in the 1960s was enormous compared to the modern aluminum kegs, which were much preferred by wholesalers and breweries alike. Two-thirds of the beer Leasure sold was draught, not packaged, and the kegs were the cornerstone. Bottled and canned beer was also sold and most of those sales were predominately in (returnable) bottles. When cans were sold to retailers, can openers had to be used, as no tab top can openers existed at the time. Retail was the first place Leasure noticed devastating changes in the market. He felt a deep sense of foreboding due to the shifts in the market and the encroachment of big beer. He decided it was time for a career change, and many others were in the same predicament.[13]

As the mid–1960s arrived, so did national competition, with brute force. Retail shops were the first to succumb, a place where the regional beer once reigned supreme. The big breweries like Schaefer, Anheuser-Busch, and Budweiser were setting up displays several times the size of those of regional breweries. To make matters worse, the beer was also sold at cut-rate prices to attract local consumers. Little did the customers notice that the "cheaper" beer was actually in 10-ounce cans, not 12-ounce cans like their regional favorite. They were indeed paying less, but they were also getting less— unbeknownst to the unthinking consumer. For the tight economic times of the 1960s this (misperception) was an incentive to try national brands. For a while, the bars were still the haven and profit center of regional beers. At 35¢ a pint, everyone was happy to pony up for 16 ounces of tasty local brew. This, however, began to change. In part it was caused by the establishment of the national brands displayed prominently in the retail shops; more ominously it was a product of technology. That technology was television and advertising.

During Leasure's tenure with Queen City, television sets were few and far between in his market, a true rarity. As the 1960s reached the midpoint, TVs became more commonplace, and with them came advertising campaigns by the likes of Budweiser, Miller, and Schlitz. The death knell for regional breweries that could not afford expensive television advertising began to sound. Retailers and bars were provided with incredible incentives to switch to the national brands. Soon there was no room at the tap for the regional brews, and the demise was felt throughout the culture. Leasure left Queen City in 1968 to work for a Lowenbrau importer. One of the vivid recollections he shared included the brewery (his brewery) that once produced the most prominent beer in the region. By 1968 it was no longer profitable and was only kept open to provide jobs for the many workers at the plant.[14]

What Leasure described eventually came to pass for all breweries in Maryland. This was not only predicted but was an inevitable result of allowing national breweries to operate within the state, and one that regional breweries fought doggedly to prevent. In 1956, five chief Maryland breweries joined forces to attempt to block legislation allowing national breweries to set up operations within the state. They argued before then Governor McKeldin that allowing Carling, a subsidiary of Canadian Breweries, Ltd., to construct a multimillion dollar brewery near Baltimore would be "predatory, destructive, and drive them out of business."[15] They requested a "Beer Bill" (SB38) that would protect them from predatory breweries opening operations within the state. Many people testified from all sides. The State Department sent letters denying the judiciousness of the "Beer Bill" and demanded favorable international relations be maintained with Canada. Duquesne Brewing Company executives also testified regarding Carling and their predatory tactics that wiped out large segments of their Pittsburgh market by undercutting all pricing in the area and flooding the market through their distributors and ostentatious displays, thus putting Duquesne out of business. Concern for the workers in the state breweries was discussed, as once Carling entered the state and cut prices to lure consumers they would raise prices as soon as local breweries folded, leaving a devastated economy and no job prospects for workers. This, Duquesne testified, was the pattern of Canadian Breweries, Ltd., in Canada and America as they opened new plants location by location.[16] The arguments fell upon deaf ears. SB38 was never passed and Carling began construction on the $16 million plant immediately in 1959. It was completed and operational in 1960, capable of churning out 800,000 barrels per year of stiff competition. As foretold by the Maryland brewers and witnessed by Leasure, Carling behaved exactly as predicted. One by one the breweries closed, and hundreds of people were left without employment.

National Brewing Company in Baltimore seemed to weather the storm, at least for

Carling Brewery Halethorpe Plant, ca. 1975 (courtesy BMI, BGE Collection).

a time. Jerry Hoffberger managed to make National synonymous with Baltimore sports through his sponsorship of the Colts and Orioles once Gunther sold out to Hamm. Their charitable accomplishments outshined all other interests. The family created Hoffberger Family Philanthropies to support children's development, health, and education in Baltimore. These consolidated foundations fulfilled that mission for more than 70 years and continues to do so today. Hoffberger called this "*tzedakah*," a Hebrew word for kindness and sharing, a concern for others that he inherited from his father and uncles.[17] This sense of community and charity aided the Hoffberger family in not only maintaining loyalty and recognition of the brewery but also in opening plants in the West (Detroit/Phoenix) and South (Miami) to accommodate demand.[18] Hoffberger also engaged in a planned expansion of the Baltimore location to meet demand, including a state-of-the-art canning system capable of filling 1,000 cans per minute. National was the largest producing state brewery at over 1,400,000 barrels per year and the numbers just continued to climb.[19]

Hoffberger hired the best to keep National on top in the region. As noted, Maryland set the tone in the brewing industry for equal opportunity employment regardless of race. National received an Emphasis Award for hiring beyond racial boundaries in 1966.The Washington branch manager of National was a black gentleman, Carl D. Anderson. Anderson's role in management was considered unprecedented, but there was no mistake that it was based purely upon merit. He earned his way into the position through hard work and unwavering commitment to his job.[20] The family and the brewery were well regarded in the community, for the sports sponsorships, for the equal treatment of employees and growth opportunities available to them, and of course for their philanthropic works. National also understood the need for television advertising as well as print media and had enough room in the budget to fund it. They studied the market and the target audience they needed to stay relevant and profitable. They spent more than $22 million to advertise toward a younger, educated, audience, placing commercials only during shows the target demographic watched.[21] The catchy jingles certainly helped keep the regional market engaged, and the dashing yet unaffected star of the ads (always surrounded by chaos) was quite worthy of national commentary.[22] Guest spots held by Redd Foxx and others also drew in a younger, wider audience, along with advertising during football games. National seemed to have everything they needed to carry on long into the future. This was not to be.

By 1975 the Detroit and Miami plants were closed, and other signs of trouble began to emerge. The Baltimore plant engaged in layoffs to reduce costs in 1974. An agreement was entered into with a British plant to brew their iconic Colt 45 for England. All of this was done to maximize the Baltimore plant, which began operating 24 hours a day, six days per week and included the expansion of the railcar bay to ship beer to military bases across the world while still meeting demand in the United States.[23] The expansion of the facility now accommodated twelve railcars (instead of four), allowing the plant to rehire many of the laid-off workers and meet production goals. Unfortunately National was competing with Carling and Schaefer within the same city and did not have either the capacity or the distribution, although it had been ranked in the top 20 of national breweries a few short years before. By 1975 the impact of three major national breweries in one location was felt by all. Carling and National merged into Carling

National and all operations were moved to the Carling plant in Halethorpe.[24] Hoffberger remained with Carling National as the head of the U.S. branch, overseeing four plants. This merger was not enough to save them, as they still faced stiff competition across the country and in their own backyard. By 1978, Carling National closed the O'Donnell Street plant, and Hoffberger stepped down. By 1979 Carling National would see another merger, this time with up and coming G. Heilman.[25] Heilman continued operations at the Baltimore facility into the 1990s.

By the end of the 1970s much of Maryland's brewing legacy had been gutted. No breweries were left within the city limits of Baltimore, as Schaefer had also closed their Baltimore facility along with Carling National. Vacant breweries across the state stood as ghostly reminders of a once vibrant past that was now hollow. Nothing was left to fill the void but job loss, uncertainty, and longing for the return of the prolific industrial past that drove Maryland's economy and built her communities.

BREWERY LISTINGS

Baltimore

BREWERY	PROPRIETOR	LOCATION/ NEIGHBORHOOD	YEARS	PEAK PRODUCTION (IF KNOWN)
Theodore Hamm Brewing Company	William Hamm, Jr.	1211 South Conkling Street	1959–1963	800,000 bbls/yr capacity
F & M Schaefer Brewing Company	Rudolph Schaefer	Same	1963–1978	Same
Carling	Canadien Breweries LTD/IR Dowie	Washington Blvd. Halethorpe	1960–1975	800,000 bbls/yr capacity
Carling National	Jerry Hoffberger/ Canadien Breweries, LTD	O'Donnell & Conkling Baltimore/ Washington Blvd. Halethorpe	1975–1996	2,000,000 bbls/yr capacity

9

A Change in the Mash Tun

As the 1970s were drawing to a close the fate of brewing in Maryland seemed perilous at best. There were only a few breweries operating in the state, and they were on life support. Fortuitously for the brewing industry of the United States of America, James Earl "Jimmy" Carter, Jr., was elected to the presidency in 1976, beginning his term of office in 1977. The following year President Carter signed HR 1337 into law. That was a watershed moment for the country and brewing in Maryland. What was HR 1337? It legalized home brewing once again at the federal level for the first time since Prohibition. Curiously wine was legal to create within one's home after Repeal but not beer. Was it something overlooked or something intentional? Regardless of the reason, now those who chose to participate in the creation of their own fermented beverage could do so at will.

At the time the legislation was signed, beer drinkers in America were limited in their choice of malted beverages to the standard light lagers like Coors, Bud, etc., or paying for imported brews. The unfortunate truth with imported beers then, as today, was the fact that they did not travel well. The term most often used, "skunked," described the photochemical reaction that takes place when ultraviolet light compromises the acids of hops in the beer by breaking them down so they mix with the sulfurous proteins, creating molecules producing that "skunked" smell. Green bottles have always been a culprit of skunking—think Heineken—and brown bottles also succumb to the process, just not as quickly. In other words, options were limited and Americans wanted more flavor choices. In addition, imports were expensive. With the new legislation Americans turned to home brewing.

Attempting to brew at home in the late 1970s and early 1980s was like preparing for a science experiment with no instruments. Many had no idea what to expect nor any expectation of the equipment they needed. There was no Internet on which one could quickly look up the "how to home brew" guide or seek advice from experienced bloggers. Many crafted their own equipment out of lobster pots and propane tanks hooked to Bunsen burners or some such derivation. It was an excruciating process for many. To make matters more difficult there were no "home brew" stores at which to pick up an easy supply of hops and malt. To say it was an adventure would be an understatement, yet determined people found their way to failure and then to flavor. The demand for more variety in American beer equated to a larger flavor profile, and home brewers were getting in touch with that. In Maryland this was the impetus for change. Change in federal legislation helped, but things at the state level were decidedly dicey.

The foray into brewing at a micro level would come from a restaurant wanting to add to their offerings and address the needs of thirsty, flavor-conscious beer drinkers.

The name "Sisson" is immediately recognizable in Baltimore and Maryland. There is a Sisson Street in Baltimore named after the original Hugh Sisson from Baltimore. He was a great man who helped build that city. A shining light in nineteenth century Baltimore, Sisson was hard working and dedicated to his family and his adoptive city. Born in 1820, he was the son of Martin Sisson of Virginia and Mary Beard of Ireland. He became an apprentice mason at the age of sixteen, specializing in marble. By the age of twenty-three, in 1843, he was a master mason and opened his own shop in Baltimore.[1] His work was exquisite and immediately in demand. Sisson quickly had to expand to fill the orders, which meant relocating his central office and opening a sales room. Much of his marble came from Italy, including the famed Carrera and Sienna marbles. Eventually, as his business grew, Sisson purchased Beaver Dam Marble Company, with quarries in Cockeysville. He quickly realized that the outstanding quality of the marble right there in Maryland rivaled many imports. As his sons Hugh and John B. were brought into the business, it was renamed Hugh Sisson & Sons.[2] This family business grew to employ more than 1,015 people and became one of the most renowned marble works in the country. Sisson's craftsmanship can be seen throughout Baltimore and the country, in the Washington Monument in Baltimore, the U.S. Capitol Building, the South Carolina State House, city hall, many churches, cemeteries, and homes, and of course the Guenther Brewery.[3]

Hard work was something Sisson never shied away from, and he instilled it in his children. The desire to create change and improve the community around him did not stop with his business acumen and craftsmanship. Sisson wanted to help in more profound ways than employment and economics; he wanted to help reform criminals and set them on a healthy, successful path. Sisson operated as director of the Maryland Penitentiary for years, living his life and teaching by a Latin proverb, "Palma non sine pulvere" (The palm is not gained without the dust of labor).[4] In other words, there can be no reward without effort. This was the birthright passed down through generations of Sisson children and the multitude of people he aided in his community. This was what helped build Hugh Sisson (the fifth generation) and foment his drive to change Maryland and its brewing legacy.

The modern Hugh Sisson, reminiscent of the nineteenth century stonemason, has always been a character. That was perhaps why he pursued a PhD in theatre, and more appropriately that was his foundation for becoming the suc-

Hugh Sisson sketch, ca. 1870, Thomas J. Sharf.

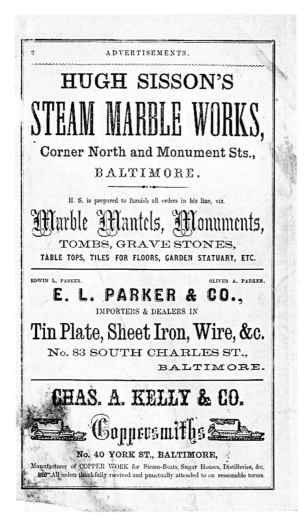

Advertisement for Hugh Sisson Steam Marble Works, ca. 1867.

cessful entrepreneur he is today. No longer in the marble business, the Sisson family owned a restaurant in Federal Hill beginning in 1979. Hugh Sisson was handed the keys to his family's establishment when he returned from graduate school in the summer of 1980. He quickly figured out the business and realized the niche they could fulfill in a market thirsty for craft and imported beers. He built his own home brewing equipment out of stockpots and experimented with recipes and processes to supplement the beer tastings and food pairings he was offering at the restaurant. For Sisson, this took all the fun out of brewing because he was constantly reengineering.[5] At this time there were no home-brew stores in the Baltimore region, as President Carter had signed the law into effect only in 1978 and people were still catching up and figuring out what it all meant. Sisson was far ahead of most and thought the addition of a pub brewery in the restaurant would be a perfect fit. The only problem was the legislation to do so didn't exist yet in Maryland. Never one to give up on an idea, Sisson got together with Senator George Della to reformulate the law and legally open his brewpub. It was with a bit of shock that the bill was signed into law in 1988 and Sisson was able to brew his own beer on the premises beginning in 1989.[6]

There were a few industrial brewery equipment manufacturers and Sisson was able to acquire a pub system appropriate for the size of his restaurant. After the home-brewing shenanigans, the lessons were learned and the process proved to be much easier on the industrial pub equipment. This was aided by Sisson's additional training at UC Davis, along with a number of beer books. The brewpub was the first in Maryland after Repeal and was a major success. Space, however, was limited, and although the pub produced 1,000 barrels per year, Sisson yearned to expand. He had no room to increase the system in Federal Hill, which thus limited his options. He wanted to open an industrial manufacturing plant but the antiquated and somewhat disjointed law would not permit one majority owner of two separate brewing facilities within the state. It was time for Sisson to move on from the family business and into his own industrial brewing plant. He divested his share of the family brewpub in 1994 and used that money in conjunction with $1,000,000 of private equity raised from December 1994 to March 17, 1995, to open the Clipper City facility in Halethorpe. Over the next nine months, the equipment was placed. By December 1995 the first batch was finished.[7]

The difference between brewing on pub equipment and brewing on the industrial-size brew house was substantial. Sisson noted that there was a grand learning curve to overcome in order to achieve consistency and sustained quality. This process took about six months. He also underestimated the demand for the product, and he and his three employees (including Tom Flores, currently brewmaster at Monocacy) were clobbered with orders in January of 1996. They were still trying to figure out distribution and shelf life at this time. Sisson was acting in every role at the brewery from accounting to sales to operations. One hundred-hour weeks defined his first year in business. Another issue also arose for Sisson and his fledgling brewery, a flat craft-beer market in 1996 and 1997. This was when he realized he was overbuilt and undercapitalized. The key to survival was contract brewing to increase volume. In mid–1996 Clipper City began brewing beers for the Weeping Radish in North Carolina, Ipswich Ales in Massachusetts, Blue Point Brewing in Long Island, New York, and DuClaw in Maryland. Contract brewing equated to survival for the first five years, even though 75 percent of the beers going out the door were not Clipper City brews.[8] Eventually they would acquire a second brand, Oxford Brewing Company, in 1997. This company, based in Maryland, produced English-style ales. It was decided to sell the brand since they too suffered from the flat craft-beer market and were no longer profitable. Ironically, one of their best sellers was the Oxford Raspberry Wheat. This was called Nuptuale and was a beer Sisson produced at the pub for a wedding and continued to produce after the wedding due to its popularity. Sisson gave the recipe to Stuart-Paul, of Oxford Brewing at that time, and they began producing it on an industrial scale. Through a twist of fate, or kismet perhaps, the recipe was his for production once again.[9]

Hugh Sisson kicked off a movement in Maryland when he turned Sisson's into a brewpub—a craft beer movement. The state was ready and embraced local brews with open arms. The opening of a home-brew shop a few years later absolutely helped. Martin Johnson (U.S. Navy retired) opened the Brew 'n Kettle, the first home-brew supply shop in Baltimore. This excited the curiosity of many people and in its own way started a movement to home brew. Now however, Johnson provided the tools for the craft. Instead of needing to moonlight as a welder to brew your own, all you needed was to head to Federal Hill! Johnson retired from the navy not only to train at Seibel in Chicago but also to open his own brewery. He was inspired, as were many home brewers. Johnson raised most of the almost $1 million in capital needed to open McHenry Brewing Company in 1994, even hiring experienced micro-brewmaster Mike Fisher out of California.[10] Despite the best-laid plans, McHenry Brewing was not to be. But many other breweries would make their mark in Baltimore and Maryland.

Within months of the Maryland law change and Sisson opening his brewpub, other brewpubs followed suit. In April 1989 Theodorus DeGroen acquired the site of George Brown's former Star Spangled Banner Brewery with plans to open a brewpub.[11] The

DeGroens (Theo and his wife, Irmtraud) were from the Netherlands and brewed in the German tradition crafting lagers, maibocks, pilseners, weissbier, and the like. It was named the Baltimore Brewing Company, and presented German fare to wed with the beers. It was the second brewpub in Baltimore after Sisson's and offered a different choice of brew for consumers. DeGroen's was located on Albermarle and Lombard streets in Jonestown at the edge of Little Italy. At the time, it was a neighborhood in the early stages of rejuvenation. In many ways it was ideal, as the brewpub lured more folks to the area and more investors along with them. It was quite the success, and the German food pairings with the sumptuous liquid offerings married well on the palates of Baltimoreans and tourists alike. The quaint beer garden harkened back to the days before Prohibition when families spent the afternoon at the brewery enjoying the weather and the fine malted beverages of their host.

DeGroen's reached about 6,500 barrels in 1996 and needed to eclipse that to stay relevant in the growing market. By 1997 DeGroen was updating the equipment to accommodate the demand, and breaching 10,000 barrels per year.[12] Unfortunately, the law that was supposed to allow a 50,000 barrel limit for the brewpubs was reduced to 10,000 barrels and no one was going to exceed it legally.[13] Word had spread and DeGroen's became a hot travel destination in the region.[14] It was a happy hour destination as much as it was gathering place for family dinners. It was the place to be when Oktoberfest rolled around, as DeGroen presented a special menu along with his Märzen. He offered the very first growler fills in the city from his brewpub. DeGroen also branched out into bottling to accommodate those who wanted a purchase to last a bit longer than a growler fill and provided greater visibility to his German style locally crafted beers.[15] The brewpub seemed to be firing on all cylinders for a lengthy and bright future. It was primed for success—until it wasn't. DeGroen's began to struggle after a decade in business. DeGroen turned over the reins of the company to James Fineran III, his sales and marketing director, in February of 2003 and moved his family to Germany to pursue new dreams.[16] Within two years the brewpub was closed. Many blamed the dropoff in craft beer in the late 1990s and early 2000s; others blamed the fateful decision for DeGroen's relocation to Germany in 2003 and the subsequent downturn in the food and beer; many pointed the finger at the monetary value of the lots the brewery was situated on over the profit the brewpub could generate; and others blamed Maryland's legislature for the end of the Baltimore Brewing Company. It was also probable that the brewery never fully recovered from a yeast contamination that plagued them in the latter years. Perhaps it was a bit of everything and the resulting conflagration ushered in the closing of what had become a Baltimore tradition.

Like DeGroen, William "Bill" Oliver and his wife, Carol, also heeded the call to open a brewpub in Baltimore with the change in legislation. Oliver was an avid home brewer who knew food. The Olivers already owned a pub in Fells' Point—the Wharf Rat—on South Ann Street. In business since 1987, the pub was thriving.[17] The goal was to acquire another property that was conducive to adding a brewing system while supplying both locations with English style ales. The Olivers purchased a property on Pratt Street across from Camden Yards, leveraging profits from the Wharf Rat to help finance the $1.3 million venture on Pratt Street.[18] It was ideal in that they would see heavy foot traffic from the Orioles games as Memorial Stadium was closed and the team had relocated to Camden Yards. The games would be played literally across the street from the brewpub. They installed a Peter Austin system (open fermentation) and got to work. It was a cramped space, to say the least, and days were long. Wisely, and to meet the demand for both facilities, Bill Oliver hired a degreed historian, Jason Oliver (no relation), of Devil's Backbone fame, who branched into home brewing and studied his way into the UC Davis brewing program.[19] In addition, they brought in another brewer, Barett Lauer (currently with District Chophouse), to split shifts, thus keeping the brewery operating more than twelve hours a day to meet demand. It was an insane schedule, but it provided a wealth of experience for both men to eventually move on to less constricting and equally revered positions.[20] This is also where British transplant Stephen Jones would take his first brewing position in America in 1999, working alongside Lauer for free until his INS status was secured and his visa came through. It would not be long before Jones was the head brewer, and as the new millennium dawned many changes were afoot for the Wharf Rat and Oliver's Brewing.

Another brewery opening in Baltimore in the midst of the craft beer resurgence was founded by a very young entrepreneur, Marc Tewey. Tewey began brewing in college, at Loyola, in Baltimore, and knew he had found his passion. He developed a plethora of recipes but had neither the resources nor the investors to finance a brewery. After exhaustive research he chose contract brewing his Brimstone brand to get his beer to market in 1993 and develop a following. He contracted through Frankenmuth Brewery in Michigan and then Lion in Wilkes-Barre, Pennsylvania, to get the ball rolling while he attended Siebel Institute to hone his craft.[21] Tewey took every penny of profit from contract brewing and hoarded it toward the opening of his own brewery. Eventually he would find an investor in his father, a prominent Connecticut businessman, and loans funded the rest of the venture. The next question was the location. Tewey found that the former National Brewery complex was offering incredibly cheap rentals of the industrial space, and he jumped at the chance to open his brewery on Brewer's Hill, thus embracing the rich history coursing through its asphalt and concrete veins and resting atop the former lagering cellars that once held Baltimore's liquid gold.

Tewey set up a 15-barrel system, with three 30-barrel fermenters and one bright tank. In addition to this he supplemented needed equipment with used dairy tanks and fire sale items from bankrupt breweries. He also added a makeshift bottling line in 1996 to obviate the need for contract brewing. It was a mash-up of parts concocted by a local machinist formerly of National Brewery, George Kalwa, who was more than happy to help out in exchange for free rent in the facility.[22] This was how Tewey worked it with almost no capital, exchanging free rental space in the oversized plant for free labor. Everything from plumbing to the bottling line was taken care of in this manner, and Tewey discontinued contract brewing in 1995. He was also not afraid to take chances. He created the first Steinbier in Baltimore since Prohibition. Steinbier (stone beer) is made by heating stones in wood-fire coals until the stones glow from the intensity of the heat. The stones are then added to the wort to boil it. When well made, and depending on the recipe, it produces a clean and complex yet inviting beer that almost always demands a second glass. Tewey also ventured into barleywine, along with his more standard ales. These were the things that helped put Brimstone on the map. Tewey still had difficulties, however, as he was underfunded and had an advertising budget that was almost nonexistent. This coincided with leveling off of the craft beer market in the late 1990s. Tewey's response was to sell in 1998.[23] Although it was for only for a few short years, Tewey and Brimstone brought life and brewing back to Brewer's Hill, and everyone rejoiced!

Brewer's Art was another brewpub that opened within the city limits of Baltimore, in the resonant Mount Vernon area. The genesis of Brewer's Art came about like many great ideas—from a few friends sitting in a bar. One of these was historian Volker Stewart. What began as a barroom conversation quickly turned into planning a brewpub. The idea of seeing the beer being made while drinking the beer paired with great food was the appeal that started the conversation. The historic Mount Vernon neighborhood in Baltimore was a perfect fit for foot traffic, logistics, and the welcome from the Belvedere Association that wanted them to set up shop. Additionally, the road was paved by Sisson's for a brewpub in Baltimore, and demand was strong. In 1994 planning began for this brewpub. Things progressed smoothly in almost every aspect from the TTB to the state of Maryland. The 10 hectolitre brew house installation in the dining area proved to be quite the challenge, however. The brew house was far too large to fit within the antechamber of the dining area without removing the antique glass, spelling its doom. That would compromise the historic integrity of the structure and take away one of the most aesthetically pleasing aspects of the main floor. The brew house had to be broken down and rewelded once inside of the room. Quite a feat! Happily they placed the fermentation vessels in more easily accessed area—the basement.[24]

Volker Stewart, founder of the Brewer's Art, standing in front of the brew house.

In September of 1996 Brewer's Art opened its doors to the cost of $525,000. The first batch of beer was brewed in December of that year. The first year went well, and brewery production ran at around 500 barrels year. There was a learning curve moving from home brewing to industrial production that was quickly sorted out. During that first year (1997) Stewart lost two partners. The first chose to leave the business and the other moved to France (and became a silent partner). Despite these changes, Stewart weathered the storm and did so quite successfully.[25] Helping him keep the brewery on track was his brewmaster Steve Frazier, a physicist by training, a brewmaster at heart. Frazier directed all facets of brewery operations, from the carbon filtration of the water to the annual hop contracts to the hectic schedule of brewing approximately twenty beers annually. Assistant brewers were well trained by Frazier to create the consistent-quality slate of flagship beers. The seasonal brews were a bit different, as they were not always brewed the same way since there was constant tinkering with the recipe. This training was extended to the staff as well in order to steer diners in a proper direction for food pairings or to help educate those consumers less experienced with craft beer through—*suggestion* not *dictation*. This helped tremendously with both loyalty and demand. Frazier doesn't always plan new beers to specifically pair with menu offerings, but he ensures a variety that would be well served with most menu items. He has also encouraged his brewers to bring in recipes they developed at home as they provide the next great seasonal brews, or at the very least they receive constructive feedback to

Dining area looking toward the antique glass gently concealing the brew house yet remaining visible for patrons to spy at Brewer's Art.

hone their skills.[26] It truly has engendered a collaborative environment, one everyone enjoys being a part of.

Another Baltimore brewpub opened in the northern reaches of the county, White Marsh. The location was in a newly redeveloped area built to attract large crowds not only for shopping but also dining and entertainment, with a family friendly vibe that was immediately embraced. Bill Blocher seized the location to create a brewpub in this new retail center. All he needed was a brew system and a brewer. Mike McDonald began his brewing career as many Maryland brewers, with a home-brew kit. He had traveled to Germany in the 1980s and loved the beer. Sadly, when he returned the American beers did not live up to the taste. After years of home brewing, McDonald eventually landed a job at Hope Brewing (the former Narragansett Brewery). He learned the craft well from Bill Anderson, the former brewmaster for Narragansett Brewery. Eventually he took his skill and moved on to the Old Nutfield Brewery in New Hampshire. There McDonald was head brewer, working with a Peter Austin brew system. After two years he was ready to move on.[27]

McDonald hoped to move to Colorado, where the craft beer movement had caught on much more quickly than in the East. He was interviewed by New Belgium and offered a job by H.C. Berger in Colorado. He was ready to move when he received a phone call from Bill Blocher at Red Brick Station. Blocher had decided to build a brewpub after he and his partner Tony Meoli traveled the East Coast, heading from one brewpub to another to taste the craft brews. Consistently the beers they enjoyed were all produced by the same equipment that provided consistency and quality beers, the Peter Austin system.[28] The Red Brick Station property was purchased and a consultant, Alan Pugsley, ordered the equipment. All that was left was the brewmaster who would create these craft beers. That was where McDonald came in. He was known in the Northeast for his mastery of the Peter Austin system and his demand for quality control implementation (one of the reasons he left Old Nutfield). Blocher thought McDonald was a perfect fit. Although McDonald was hesitant about any restaurant business, due to the extreme failure rate, he signed on and moved his family to Maryland.[29]

McDonald's first priority was to clean and sanitize equipment, as that was the only way to make quality beer. This was critical because the Austin system incorporates open fermentation, which can be easily compromised by wild yeast strains and other "things" floating in the air. The Austin system was an addition after the site was chosen. This created great difficulty for McDonald, as the 14-barrel system was separated into various segments across the restaurant. It was neither efficient nor ideal. Nonetheless, McDonald produced a variety of English ales, among other seasonal and one-off styles that totaled around 1,600 barrels per annum.[30] The secret to his success rested within the 200-year-old yeast McDonald used as the base for all of his ales—Ringwood. It was a difficult strain to work with for those unaccustomed to it but a champion yeast for McDonald. He chose wisely, as Blocher's vision for incredible food paired perfectly with the demand for McDonald's beer. Blocher's philosophy held that anything that didn't sell well was taken off the menu, keeping the offerings fresh. He also focused on using local, high-quality ingredients that the customers approved of and was very vocal about letting the customers "own" the business and provide feedback on what they did and did not want. Curiously, they have not demanded the appearance of macro brews

The Peter Austin open fermentation system at Red Brick Station.

in the bar (which Blocher never offered) to complement the in-house and craft beer offerings. Red Brick Station has made many converts. One hundred and fifty employees and no debt stands as proof of quality and good business![31]

Baltimore also bore witness to another local brew without a home. The Raven Special lager was the creation of Stephen Demczuk, a Dundalk boy born and bred. He graduated from the University of Maryland before heading off to Europe for postgraduate studies in molecular biology. This was where he fell in love with beer. He was researching in Geneva and traveled to Sweden, Luxemborg, and Germany, among other countries. Drinking German lagers and Czechoslovakian pilseners where they were first produced often provides one with an appreciation for authenticity and quality. Demczuk quickly began writing about beer and running a beer of the month club. Of course, brewing was not far behind. Soon he was partnering with a German brewer (Wolfgang Stark) to produce a stand-out lager. He availed himself of the opportunity to serve it to the American ambassador, who wanted more. It was called the Raven Special Lager. Since Demczuk hailed from Baltimore and was a huge fan of Edgar Allan Poe, it all seemed to make perfect sense. With Stark the Raven went into production in Germany, and the company Baltimore Washington Beer Works was formed. Europeans who drank the lager would know where (in part) this malty pint hailed from. Demczuk wasn't satisfied with Europe as his only market and wanted to make his beer available in his inspirational home state.[32]

It was a difficult journey for Demczuk, from labeling to finding a brewery to contracting out until demand increased enough to open his own facility. In 1998 he began contract brewing out of Clipper City with Hugh Sisson and secured placement in M&T Bank Stadium for the Ravens games. This of course was a happy coincidence—that the newest professional sports team chose the name of Demczuk's beer! It certainly increased sales during football season and was easy enough to remember. This was the foot in the door Baltimore Washington Beer Works needed in Maryland and the region while the U.S. branch got off the ground. The German half of the business was carrying the American side of the company while it got underway and developed a following.[33] Eventually the Raven was able to stand on its own and look toward the future. The future held not only increased sales but also a brewery to call home. A few feathers were going to fly along the journey, but the dream was to become a reality.

Anne Arundel

Coinciding with Sisson's fight in 1988 to open the first brewpub since Prohibition were a pair of English gentlemen, businessman Craig Stuart-Paul and certified brewmaster Steve Parkes, who opened the British Brewing Company in Glen Burnie, Maryland, crafting Oxford Ales.[34] Unlike Sisson's small brewpub, this was an industrial brewery with far greater capacity and distribution. They specialized (not surprisingly) in English-style ales. This was the first microbrewery in Maryland since the Repeal of Prohibition, a sister to Sisson's first brewpub. Parkes was an import from Britain, and much of his financing came from his partner and a British "real ale" pub chain owner. The equipment was shipped from England and reassembled in the brewery in America. They used open fermentation, as was expected from a traditional English brewery.[35] Unlike the Baltimore United Breweries from 1889, they were creating their own brewery in the traditional English style instead of purchasing operational, thriving plants. The ales were given the very English, and appropriate, name "Oxford." They were extremely well crafted and were served (as they should be) in a cask on the bar, another first since Prohibition. They were a hit, and the beers were well regarded, being written up far and wide including a nod from the Beer Hunter himself, Michael Jackson.[36] One after another, restaurants and bars began to serve the cask ales to patrons.

The idea to add a bottling line was not a bad one but one that brought great difficulty. Due to the exorbitant expense, the purchased line was refurbished and then malfunctioned with great regularity, compromising quality and production schedules. Bottling was abandoned in favor of kegging, but financial recovery was questionable. In 1992 Parkes left the brewery, and Stuart-Paul soon followed. New ownership comprised the O'Briens, a husband and wife team, and Jim Stotsky. The immediate action was to begin contract brewing for other brewers. This was standard procedure for industrial-capacity breweries that were short on profits. In a bid to increase sales they eventually rebranded as Oxford, which was the name of many of their beers and one Maryland knew to ask for. The other highlight was the aforementioned Oxford Raspberry Wheat, which was rapidly becoming their best seller. Based upon those sales and the number of beers they were contract brewing, a decision was made to expand into a new facility. The English system was ousted in favor of closed fermentation and increased capacity. The raspberry wheat was sent out for bottling at another brewery for greater distribution.[37]

Things within the brewery were shifting along with the process. Long-time brewery manager Tom Cizauskas chose to part ways with Oxford, along with brewmaster Drew Schmidt. It was an ominous foreshadowing of what was to come. What Oxford didn't fully comprehend was the downtrend that was coming for craft beer. Competition in Maryland and the nation picked up as more breweries were being constructed, and consequently sales dropped off. Many Americans were embracing craft beer but more were not quite ready to take the leap away from the macro brands, which would take several years. Word of mouth was not enough to generate sales, and money had to be spent on advertising to reach a greater constituency. Brewery after brewery began to close.[38] In addition they brought in a new general manager, formerly of Schlitz, Mike Jaeger, who began adjusting the formulas of some of the better selling Oxford brews. Placing one's own mark on beer was understandable but extremely risky. Instead of increasing sales and reaching a larger audience through the recipe tweaking, demand declined.[39] Try as they might they could not recover. They arrived at the gut-wrenching decision to sell, and this was consequently how Clipper City ended up with the Oxford brand. Despite the ending, the brewery spawned many fantastic brewers who went on to brew for other breweries across the country, much like the Germans founding the breweries in Baltimore who learned the trade in one brewery and moved on to open their own. Oxford certainly left a legacy.

The idea of a brewpub struck Bill Muehlhauser about a decade after he opened his Ram's Head Bar in the basement of a historic building on West Street in Annapolis. A beer aficionado, he wanted to take his bar to the next level. As he expanded the venue, he applied for licensing to operate a brew house within the tavern. At a cost of $1 million, the fully automated Beraplan German brew house was purchased and installed. The first brewmaster, Allen Young, trained on the equipment in Austria in preparation for the position.[40] The brews produced were going to honor the first brewer in the state of Maryland, Benjamin Fordham. Fordham Brewing was reborn in brewpub fashion. Young got to work brewing a Helles lager, a Kölsch, and a variety of German styles, eventually mixing in ales, stouts, and seasonals. The brewery, combined with the musical venue, drew in scores of locals and tourists visiting midshipmen at the U.S. Naval Academy, which was a stone's throw from the brewery, bringing in absurd amounts of foot traffic. Based upon the positive response, Muehlhauser expanded, opening another location in historic Savage Mill. Three more would follow suit as the demand increased, and eventually a Ram's Head brewpub was opened in Virginia. The original location was supplying all of the Fordham beer to the Maryland taverns, however, and that was not enough.

Muehlhauser realized he needed to open an industrial brewery to keep pace with demand, bottle his beer for retail sale, and supply it to other bar venues beyond his own. By 1997 he was seeking to open an industrial brewery in Delaware. That did not immediately materialize, and instead he began bottling his beer for distribution across Maryland, in addition to supplying kegs. This was aided by the change in legislation allowing the increase in production capacity for Maryland brewpubs, up to 22,500 barrels annually.[41] Muehlhauser wanted to take full advantage of the new law. But he still could not produce nearly that capacity in the small on-premises brew house and sought new horizons. Those horizons were coastal, just not in Maryland. Muehlhauser eventually opened his new brewing facility in Delaware, where he teamed up with distributor Southern Beverages to afford the space and corner distribution. Since the acquisition in 2003, Fordham has expanded, participating in a joint venture and buying Old Dominion Brewing (out of Virginia). Fordham eventually began contract brewing out of the facility to increase profits, and the plan worked. The "local" brews aren't quite so local anymore, but Maryland consumers still seek out Fordham brands.

Carroll County

Johansson's Dining House wasn't always a brewery. In 1998 Dave Johansson decided it would be appropriate to expand the structure built in 1913 to accommodate a brew house in the area adjacent to the eastern portion of the dining room. He thought Carroll County needed a brewery and he was willing to oblige, even if it meant locating the brewery a mere four feet from the railroad tracks. This landed them in the Guinness Book of World Records as the brewery operating the closest to active railroad tracks. The government in Carroll County was supportive, very pro-business, and never hindered Johansson's growth at all. The only problem existed in both designing the brewery and finding a brewer. The guidance came from an extremely experienced brewer, Jason Kennedy, who had witnessed success in multiple venues prior to his arrival in Carroll County. Kennedy, acting as a brewery consultant, was more than willing to help guide the brewery operation along the right path, as he was a former brewer with Wild Goose Brewery in Cambridge, Maryland, and had become head brewer for Dogfish Head Brewery in Delaware in 1996.[42] He was instrumental in directing the equipment purchases and planning. The seven-barrel brew house was purchased from Canada, coupled with four fermenting tanks. This $300,000 brewery (and expansion) was enough to get things started. The first brewer Johansson contracted was Jeff Warthen. Warthen not only saw to the initial start of the brewery but also an immediate expansion in 1999 to distribute the brews beyond the restaurant.[43] This secured Johansson's future and set the bar high for breweries in the county. The brewpub also served as a sign Carroll County was ready for more local breweries, as the population was fully supportive.

Eastern Shore

One motivated brewer decided to open the first Eastern Shore brewery after Prohibition. Allen Pugsley, a British transplant, chose to open Wild Goose in November of 1989 in Cambridge, Maryland. He found the old Phillips Packing Company facility on Washington Street, installed a Peter Austin system, and got to work brewing his very traditional English ales. The local community was pleased with the product, which was so good, in fact, that it came to the notice of Jim Lutz, who happened to be in town on business. He was immediately invested in Wild Goose Beers. Quickly he got together a group of investors and purchased the brewery, although Pugsley was still consulting brewmaster. Lutz was a brewer by trade and legacy. His uncle was a brewmaster for Schlitz, while he himself had been employed at Pabst, G. Heilman (who bought out National Brewing Company in 1979), Coors, and Miller prior to owning his own facility.[44] In 1992, when taking over the brewery, he introduced seasonal ales into the rotation that were very well received. By 1995, he doubled production, and was employing twenty workers to process the brews.

Before it became the standard symbiotic procedure, Lutz sent spent grain to the farmers for their cows.[45] Most breweries adhere to this currently but at the time in Maryland it was not so common. Lutz was a pioneer—there was no question. He kept it local, from the naming of the brews to the brewers he hired to help him. Tom Flores (who later worked for Hugh Sisson at Clipper City and then moved to Frederick) signed on in 1991 while Pugsley was still in control. Pugsley and Lutz clearly knew talent when they spotted it, as Flores would become legendary in Maryland and the nation for his brewing acumen and biochemistry expertise. The reviews were excellent and Wild Goose went the route of expansion in 1995, with an eye to increasing the market share.[46] The goal was 40,000 barrels a year, almost doubling the 1995 production numbers. Distribution was primarily in the Mid-Atlantic region but went as far as Colorado and Massachusetts. Unfortunately the timing was off, as it was for many in the industry. The market started to feel the weight of the initial craft beer boom, and things were levelling off. Lutz expanded too far and too fast to sustain it and he was struggling to stay afloat. It was a tough lesson many breweries would learn in the late 1990s. Fairly quickly Lutz was looking for a way out of the financial hole, and that meant selling his prized possession. Frederick Brewing Company bought Wild Goose, happy to take over a competing label in 1998, to the sorrow and relief of Lutz.[47] There was a distinct concentration on doing justice to the label, so much so, in fact, that by 1998 Wild Goose had reached number nine in world.[48]

Frederick

Frederick Brewing Company was founded in 1993. Carroll Creek LLC was technically the body that owned it, but CEO Kevin Brannon and his wife, Marjorie McGinnis, were credited by most as the founders.[49] The first brewery was located in the heart of town just a few blocks from Carroll Creek in a small three-and-a-half story brick building near All Saints Street. Production capacity (and thus expansion potential) was limited in the center of town, but what they sacrificed in capacity they made up for in foot traffic. They were concerned with sticking to the local appeal and wisely celebrated the picturesque geography surrounding them by choosing to brand their beers Blue Ridge. They took care in the beers produced to include a golden ale, an ESB, a rye stout, a porter, and an amber. Eventually they offered seasonal releases to complement the flagship lineup. The beers were well regarded, and the local public was on board. Within three years, demand outstripped capacity and Brannon and McGinnis decided it was time for expansion beyond the structure they occupied. In 1996 they made the decision to go public on the stock exchange as Blue II LLC, in hopes of raising enough capital to build a brand new brewery on the outskirts of town in the Wedgewood Business

Park. Frederick Brewing Company 2.0 was underway in late 1996 with a goal to raise nearly $4 million on a facility that ended up costing nearly $10 million.[50]

The new facility sat on just over an acre where a 57,000 square-foot building housed the new brewery. It was curious timing, expanding during a downturn in the market, but they thought the demand was strong enough. Within a year of moving into the new plant, they also purchased the Wild Goose and Brimstone labels. The plan was to reach consumers from one end of the state to the other by offering local brands in each region, while expanding their sales further outside of the Mid-Atlantic area and overseas. The new Hempen line created in 1997 included different styles of ale made with hemp seeds beginning with the Hempen ale. This made for sticky business in customs and delays in trying to move product in Canada's provinces. Other deals for hitting Chinese markets were also on the table to turn the tide toward profit, but the losses kept coming. The more they produced the smaller the profit margin became, which was the opposite of what was expected.[51] The three labels combined brought in more than forty awards, including four from the Great American Beer Fest. But it wasn't the quality of the beer that was the problem. While downsizing and forcing upper management to take pay cuts slowed the bleeding, it did not staunch the flow. Frederick Brewing was in desperate trouble by 1998. By 1999 they restructured but were still flailing.

In 1999 Snyder International Brewing Groups out of Cleveland (owners of Crooked River Brewing) purchased a majority share in the brewery to try to turn it around, as they had accomplished with other breweries.[52] The appeal for Snyder to acquire vulnerable but advanced breweries literally mimicked the Maryland Brewing Company's purchase of the Baltimore breweries exactly a century earlier. Snyder was after the largest brewing facility in the region with the most technologically advanced equipment. A little restructuring of the debt and shifts in production and he thought he could turn it around. Despite his best efforts, the plant never ran near capacity; capable of producing 100,000 barrels, it was topping at 35,000. Within two years Snyder was seeking another investor to bring more brands into production and reach that capacity.[53] He ended up consolidating all of his breweries into the Frederick plant to meet production goals. By 2002 Snyder International was being sued for nonpayment of debts, infringement, and noncompliance with court orders. Things had gone from bad to worse. By 2004 new trustees were appointed, as the brewery was in receivership.[54] It was a hard lesson learned in a competitive market—eerily similar to the collapse of Maryland Brewing Company in 1901.

Another Frederick-based brewery that opened during Frederick Brewing Company's tenure was Brewer's Alley. Philip Bowers wanted to restore the reputation of great brewing that had existed in Brewer's Alley long before Prohibition reared its ugly and very dry head. The change in legislation in the 1990s provided a perfect opportunity, and the historic location in Frederick was ideal. After securing the property on Market Street, Bowers filed for a Class 7 brewpub license and installed necessary equipment to start brewing.[55] What he needed was an experienced brewer. To get things started, Bowers brewed the beer on the seven-barrel system. His first brewer was Matt Hahn, an experienced brewer from Ipswich Ale Brewing in Massachusetts who had relocated to Maryland in 1995 to work for Oxford Brewing. In 1995 Hahn placed an advertisement seeking a job as a line brewer, and Oxford Brewing in Maryland responded. After an interview Hahn was hired and then relocated to Maryland. He began working under brewmaster Drew Schmidt and general manager Tom Cizauskas. Hahn's tenure at Oxford lasted only a year. A shake-up in the team led Cizauskas and Schmidt to leave the brewery and find employment elsewhere within months of one another. Hahn decided it was time to depart as well. Things had been on a downward trend and were not looking as if they would improve at Oxford. Hahn saw an opportunity in the new brewpub in Frederick, Brewer's Alley.[56]

Almost immediately after being hired Hahn began tweaking the five regular beer offerings, introducing an imperial stout that he originally created on the pilot system at Oxford. Hahn's experience paid off and capacity was increased 66 percent within a few months. Hahn loved the environment, the people who enjoyed the beer, and the proximity to the brewing process. The most exciting part for him was that Bowers was as completely invested in the brewery as he was in the food. He did not cut corners or skimp on either the ingredients or the process. According to Hahn it was the best place he ever worked, and he wished he had stayed. That was not meant to be, however, as fate dealt him a different card in the form of old friends and coworkers offering him a position at an Ohio brewery. Hahn chose to take the new opportunity, leaving Bowers to find a replacement brewer.[57] The replacement was perhaps more than one could hope for in a brewer. Bowers lucked into Tom Flores.

Tom Flores was just a high school student when he first sampled home brew. He was working as an appliance delivery person and one of the homes had a carboy full of barley wine. Flores was offered a sip and was impressed with the flavor. The following summer, a friend (Ashton) whose father had home brewed in the past gave Flores and Ashton his brewing equipment and they began experimenting. When Tom shipped off to college at the University of Maryland at College Park for his biochemistry degree he immediately noticed the parallels between the plants used for brewing and the human biochemical process. As graduation drew near, Tom's friend Ashton came across literature about the UC Davis graduate program in food science, with courses on brewing. Both Flores and Ashton applied and were accepted into the program. Over the summer of 1991, when Flores returned to Maryland, he convinced Alan Pugsley of Wild Goose to hire him at the brewery. This was Flores's first experience in an industrial brewery.[58]

As fall arrived, Flores returned to California to pursue his studies. As part of the curriculum, he lectured on some of the brewing topics at brewery functions. A few years into his coursework, he happened to be lecturing at a conference in Oregon. After the lecture he ran into Hugh Sisson, founder of Sisson's brewpub. Flores knew Sisson from a tour of the brewpub given by Hugh a few years earlier. They chatted for a bit about brewing and good beer and, of course, Maryland and the men went their separate ways. As the second day of the conference approached, Sisson sought out Flores and offered him the job as head brewmaster at the soon to open Clipper City brewery in Halethorpe, Maryland. Flores accepted. He helped start Clipper City with Sisson. From the site to the equipment to the recipes it was all a collaboration. Flores found himself working eighty to one hundred hours a week to get the brewery up and running and then navigating the learning curve of the recipes and equipment. He continued this pace for three years.[59]

In 1997 he heard through a friend about a brewing opportunity in Frederick, Maryland, with a brewpub called Brewer's Alley. The owner, Phil Bowers, could not manage all of the brewing on his own while running the restaurant. Flores met with Bowers and found the position was actually as assistant brewer, not head brewer. Flores thanked him and said he would consider only a head brewer position. A few days after the interview Bowers called him back and offered him the brewmaster position. Flores transitioned into the position fairly easily, slowly tweaking some of the recipes and introducing seasonal beers. The first seasonal creation was the Trinity stout. As far as Bowers' original recipes, Flores tweaked those not to change the flavor profile but to use ingredients that were more consistent with the beers' ancestry and hop availability.[60] This was well accepted by the customers and owner alike carrying Brewer's Alley into the new millennium with a more advanced industrial setup and an entirely new venture in agriculture.

The last brewpub to open in the 20th century was Barley and Hops off of Urbana Pike in Frederick. The Cluster Spires Brewing Group opened the brewpub in October 1999 in a location more industrial, retail, and traveled. A 15-barrel Czechoslovakian system was purchased and installed within the brewpub as a show piece in addition to the fantastic beer it was capable of churning out. The copper system wrapped around the pub like a lover's caress, reminding each patron of the reason for the visit: to partake of the luscious malted beverage brewed on the premises. It was reminiscent of an Old World pub, with both brews and food hinting at bygone decades. Many of the styles

Barley & Hops Brewpub, with Silo.

harkened back to traditional pilseners and other Old World styles. The response was more than appreciation for a novelty; consumers were enthusiastic about another brewpub offering tasty vittles with quality in-house brews. Although the brewpub continued operations into the next decade, changes were on the horizon in both ownership and brewing. Barley and Hops was more than willing to make those changes.

Prior to any brewery opening in Frederick County, a new home-brew shop was added on South Carroll Street to get things rolling for palates and hobbyists. Flying Barrel was opened in 1980 by Bob Frank to celebrate the change in federal legislation. It was one of the first in the region and helped pave the way toward a reignited passion for craft and flavor. The shop offered not only guidance but also a place to brew, as many people had neither the understanding of the process nor the equipment or space to experiment. Flying Barrel became an institution in Frederick and a safe place to master the home brew learning curve with a guiding and gentle hand. It has become a staple of the craft community and a beacon for craft beer enthusiasts.

Harford

Dave Benfield hails from the Benfield family—as in Benfield Electric. The family business was not going to be Dave's chosen path, however. His calling came while he was studying at Loyola University in Baltimore. During his junior year Dave and his roommate, Marc Tewey (of Brimstone fame), began brewing beer, which was far cheaper than purchasing it. They were quite good at it and had friends lined up on Saturdays to pick up their six packs. After finishing their studies in 1992, both men knew they wanted to enter the brewing industry. They traveled for two years from the West Coast to the East Coast, training in the brewing business at Anchor Steam and other locales, and Tewey went to Seibel. That was where they parted ways in the industry. Tewey had no desire to engage in the food industry; he wanted to keep it simple and focus on craft beer. Benfield thought the ideal would be a brewpub, where he could focus on the craft beer and a general manager could run the restaurant. That is not quite how it worked out for either man.

In 1996, at the tender age of twenty-four, Benfield opened DuClaw in Bel Air, Maryland. So where did the name come from? Benfield thought all the regional or historic names were a bit boring and he really wanted something a tad more enigmatic. The answer was to invent a word. It rolled off the tongue with a mixture of the traditional (du) and the edgy (claw). Despite what many perpetuate, it was not the "dew claw" on a dog's paw, nor was it derived from any other canine incarnation. It became the enigma Benfield hoped for and kept DuClaw in the conversation, along with the beers he produced. Benfield quickly realized that he couldn't just hand off the restaurant as he had hoped and that it was more "hands on" than anticipated. As the beer and food got underway and business picked up, he needed a brewer.[61]

In 1990 a young Jim Wagner and friend began home brewing "beer in a bag" (add warm water and hang the bag for two weeks). It was as horrific as one could imagine. Despite the outcome, Wagner wanted to brew, really brew. So he did what any enterprising young man would do: he built his own equipment, promising beer to those who

Left: **Dave Benfield, founder, DuClaw Brewing Company, appropriately positioned in front of the taps!** *Right:* **Jim Wagner brewmaster, DuClaw Brewing Company.**

aided him along the way (welding, etc.). While improving his process and equipment Wagner worked in the medical field, specifically hemodialysis. He took note of the similarities between the processes at his job and his hobby, particularly water profiles. He even had a mini reverse osmosis unit in his basement that he used for water filtration for brewing. As he improved his process he also took a brewing course from the Brewer's Guild to refine his technique.[62]

As Wagner's brews improved he entered his home brews into competitions in each state that sponsored them. Enter Tewey once again. In 1998 he entered a contest at Brimstone Brewing Company in Baltimore (after winning medals in seventeen other states) and was victorious with his highly hopped brown ale. He brewed with Marc Tewey (as his prize) and marketed the product with Brimstone. Shortly after this success Tewey offered him a professional brewing job with Benfield over at DuClaw. Wagner brought a few beers (including Devil's Milk) and Benfield put it into production, with Wagner as his new head brewer and one assistant. Devil's Milk has become one of DuClaw's best known beers and a "must order" beer for the regulars.

Like many early craft breweries in Maryland, DuClaw saw its role as both brewers and educators of consumers and the distributors that sold them. The starting assumption was always that the consumer had never tried the DuClaw beer before. That was why the brewery designed the packaging to be as informative as possible, with enough description to provide an informed choice. Wagner specifically had a very different opinion on session beers. He never saw them as "transition" beers (from macro to craft) but a beer packed with flavor that is not impaired or impeded by malts. Therein resides the great challenge, to make an extremely complex beer with abundant flavor that is low in alcohol so that consumers may enjoy more than one. Of course, as with any brewery there were triumphs and failures. DuClaw perceived failures as opportunities, whether a session beer mishap or a hop error. At times, it was kismet, where a mistake was made but that blunder turned out fabulously. The Bad Moon porter was just one example, created when the wrong tank was hopped. Even when a glorious result wasn't the byproduct, the lesson was to never give up just because it didn't turn out right the first time. Persistence has paid off for DuClaw.

DuClaw saw expansion into two additional markets, Baltimore and Hanover. The Hanover location thrived situated in a megamall complex a short distance from the airport. The Fell's Point location struggled, however, in close proximity to Max's Taphouse and a few other up and coming restaurants. Max's Taphouse was, and remains, the premier destination for craft beer in the Mid-Atlantic region, due not only to its expansive taps but also the availability of all local craft beers as well the obtainability of unique and rare imports. Every Maryland craft beer created was carried at Max's. The closure of the Fell's Point DuClaw operation may have been a blessing, as getting rid of the "dead wood" allowed for the resources to be focused on a new path, the path of large industry. The new millennium would see this burgeoning dream become a reality and Duclaw become a household name.

Howard

The very first brewpub in Howard County was located off of Route 40, the main east/west corridor that cut right through Ellicott City, buttressed by Baltimore to the east and Carroll County to the west. The strip mall where Bare Bones brewpub was located was heavily traversed from commuter traffic, locals, and many seeking a good local beer. Joseph Reese thought the addition of a brewpub to a restaurant was the key to lure in all of that traffic and, it was hoped, profits. The brewpub opened in 1996.[63] The idea was to pair a variety of house-made beers with excellent ribs and a distinctly American barbeque menu. For the first few years the brewpub was able to meet the demands of the consumers with fairly decent reviews. It offered only its own brews on tap in addition to wine, spirits and nonalcoholic options. This received mixed reviews, as folks often wanted guest taps. Eventually Bare Bones stopped producing its own beers, contracting them out to Clipper City and other local breweries. What remained was the excellent quality of the ribs and barbeque offerings, keeping the appeal and the ability to have Bare Bones in other counties across the state.

In Columbia, the idea of a brewpub was quite appealing to restaurateurs, prompting the opening of an unusual, themed restaurant called Rocky Run Tap and Grill in early 1996. The Donnelleys were a father and son team with absolutely no brewing experience but a desire to capitalize on the opportunity to fill a niche in the community—a brewpub. They secured a location off of Dobbin Road in the former Bob's Big Boy. While awaiting the decision of the liquor board to approve the brewery, they had an established plan to draw consumers just in case the brewery in planning did not pass the board. Each room of the restaurant was to have a different theme, like the Jimmy Buffet Room, or the Elvis Room. The Donnelleys already had one Rocky Run opened in Glen Burnie, although it was not a brewpub, and knew an effective formula to bring in crowds.[64] Once the brewery was approved the Donnelley's installed a small three-and-a-half barrel

BOP system. The lack of experience in brewing led them to questionable decisions like using dry yeast, something many current beer consumers would reject.[65] At the time, however, it was a novelty, and the draw was immense for curious patrons who had never seen a brewery before. The Columbia Rocky Run was designed in such a way that the brewery was visible to customers through walls of glass that were the only barrier between the customers and the brew kettle as soon as they entered the restaurant. It was thrilling.

The brewpub succeeded in a location where all previous restaurants on that same plot of ground had failed. The food and themed rooms certainly helped draw patrons, along with the myriad hot sauces that lined the walls, with descriptive names such as Butt Twister and Endorphin Rush, adding to the intrigue and chatter. The brewpub soon developed a crowd of "regulars" from nearby businesses and a neighborhood crowd excited for a family restaurant with comfort food. Patrons included a group of hard-core trivia buffs who wandered in each night looking for a colorful brew and intense competition. These were the consumers who allowed Rocky Run Tap and Grille to thrive where others had failed. Soon the Columbia location was supplying beer to Glen Burnie as well. This carried the Donnellys into the new millennium and the opening of the third Rocky Run in Baltimore. To continue the success and supply three restaurants from one small brewpub, changes had to be made in the brewing process and the staff as the new century dawned.

A third Howard County brewpub that opened just after Rocky Run was the Ellicott Mills Brewing Company. Located in historic Ellicott City, this brewpub was unique and carried a much different appeal than Rocky Run. It was a German restaurant, and it produced German-style beers. That, of course, required the open fermentation system to be imported from Germany; the brew house was Czechoslovakian. Decoction was the method used by the traditional German brewers, and it was standard at Ellicott Mills. The adherence to authenticity of the process of traditional styles was what set Ellicott Mills apart from the others in the county. This was also what made it so incredibly expensive and difficult to open. The brewpub was the brain child of Martin Vigra, who brought in partners to make it into a reality. It was all part of an investment in the rejuvenation of the critically important historic district of Ellicott City's famous Main Street, the lifeblood of the community for locals and tourists alike for over a century. This was the cause of many delays and the reason startup costs skyrocketed to $2 million. A large part of that was the fact that adhering to the requirements of construction on a historic structure within a historic district is incredibly specific and can slow down renovations. This of course retained the authenticity of the time, the building, and the neighborhood.

By the end of 1996 the brewpub opened, with authentic German fare paired with the German beer offerings. This expanded to include Australian beer styles with head brewer and Australian transplant Justin Robertson at the helm.[66] This combination of authentic beer complementing the German and sometimes wild-game offerings of meats like alligator drew curious crowds. This helped foment the development of the lovely historic town as a tourist destination, as much as a local hangout in the Rathskellar— the basement bar and cigar area. It propelled the brewpub into the next decade as both a training ground for new brewers interested in traditional German brewing and a destination for consumers to enjoy a meal while observing brewers toiling laboriously just on the other side of a glass pane. The brewery, along with all of the businesses in the small historic town, would face unprecedented challenges in the new millennium. These trials would cripple the town and deliver unparalleled devastation (more on this in the next chapter).

Montgomery

Montgomery County also felt the pull towards establishing brewpubs once the legislation changed. Olde Towne Tavern was founded in a historic building off of East Diamond Avenue in Gaithersburg. The building housed everything from an auto showroom to a post office over the years. In 1994 it finally housed a brewpub. The partnership begun by Charles Covell II and brewer Joe Kalish, among other partners, comprised the ownership that took out a loan of $651,000 to get the brewpub up and running, equipped with a seven-barrel pub brewing system.[67] Partner Joe Kalish was a brewer with decades of experience under his belt at places like Schlitz. It seemed to be the perfect marriage, honoring the historic space while introducing this (seemingly) modern concept of a brewery within a restaurant that appealed to people traversing the bustling heart of Gaithersburg. As the name implied, there was always the small-town, close-knit vibe to the brewpub, and the food alone was quite inviting. Kalish brought much more to the table than a complement to a delicious menu; he also brought soul to the brews. Any trace of the standard-fare, macro-brewed beers had no place in Olde Towne—quite the contrary, as the beers had depth, complexity, and individuality. Each beer offered a divergent experience to the consumer. This is what drew a local following and pulled in others across Montgomery County and neighboring counties. Unfortunately as these things sometimes go, the startup costs were not made up and the partnership was always operating from a deficit. They placed the brewpub for sale and filed for Chapter 7 bankruptcy and the liquidation of assets.[68]

The brewpub was purchased by Bowers Brewing, the very same founder of the Brewer's Alley brewpub in Frederick, Maryland. Bowers assumed the balance of the loan in April of 1994, taking possession of the brewpub, the loan, and the brewer (Kalish) who made it great.[69] The new name of the local favorite was Summit Station. Kalish was left to brew as he saw fit, not reengineering the brews to match what was happening at Brewer's Alley with Flores. Brewer's Alley beers were on tap whenever possible in Gaithersburg. What Bowers discovered upon taking over the new location was the excruciating tangle that was the Montgomery County archaic liquor legislation. All alcohol had to be distributed via Montgomery County. In a nutshell, alcohol either produced in or sent into Montgomery County had to be placed in the hands of Montgomery County liquor control officials who would then hand it over to distributors. This process substantially raised the cost of the alcoholic beverages since the county charged a hefty fee for this handling "service" and it prolonged the distribution process. Worse still, the product while with liquor control was neither refrigerated nor controlled in a manner conducive to placing the best product on the market, particularly when it came to craft beer that prefers temperature-controlled environments. Therefore, even though

Bowers owned Brewer's Alley he could not just bring a keg of beer across county lines to Summit Station and sell it. It had to go through Montgomery County's liquor control. This racket that the county had set up after Repeal is still in place and nets around $22 million annually![70] This in large part was why very few breweries attempted to set up shop in Montgomery County. Bowers made a go of it and tried to his best to operate under the strict and deleterious regulations set forth in a bygone era. He lasted until 2006; four years after restructuring his loan, he found a buyer.[71] The timing was quite good, as Gaithersburg was on the upswing and drawing in more businesses and residents occupying the historic town and its suburbs. In 2006 Bowers bid farewell to the brewpub for $1,500,000 so that he could concentrate on Brewer's Alley and his next steps that led toward industrial capabilities.[72]

As the 1990s drew to a close, the resurgence in craft brewing in Maryland crested and receded. It was not a dead market by any means, and it was going to witness an even stronger resurgence in the coming millennium. Chain brewpubs like Rock Bottom and Capital City came and went along with the sea swells, but the nation was starting to turn its eyes towards craft brewing and to Maryland. In 1998 the Great American Beer Fest was held in Maryland for the first time. This event was normally scheduled only in Colorado but Baltimore was placed in the spotlight for its growing malt beverage industry, and the nation took notice. Home brew clubs like the Cross Street Irregulars and the Society for the Promotion of Beers from the Wood were established, along with many others across the state. Even those breweries that did not survive the decade inspired people to brew their own or just to begin to appreciate beer on a more profound level. Much like the brewers of Maryland one hundred years before, the modern breweries of Maryland realized they too needed to protect and promote themselves, and the Brewer's Association of Maryland was resurrected. The new foundations of brewing had been laid and it was a good thing, as the tidal wave of craft beer was about to wash over everyone in Maryland, presenting a cornucopia of flavors for each and every palate.

BREWERY LISTINGS

(Chain brewpubs originating out of state not included)

Allegany County

BREWERY	PROPRIETOR	LOCATION/ NEIGHBORHOOD	YEARS	PEAK PRODUCTION (IF KNOWN)
Uncle Tuckers Wood Fired Pizza and Brewhaus	Ed Mason	12901 Ali Gahn Road Cumberland	1999–2005	

Anne Arundel County

BREWERY	PROPRIETOR	LOCATION/ NEIGHBORHOOD	YEARS	PEAK PRODUCTION (IF KNOWN)
British Brewing Company	Craig Stuart-Paul & Steve Parkes	6759 Bay Meadow Drive Glen Burnie	1989–1992	
Oxford Ales	The O'Briens & Jim Stotsky	Same	1992–1993	
	Same	611 G Hammonds Ferry Road Linthicum	1993–1998	7,500 bbls/yr
Rams Head Tavern & Brewpub	William Mulhauser	32 West Street Annapolis	1995–2007	1,800 bbls/yr
Castlebay Irish Pub & Brewery[73]	Vincent Quinlan	193 Main Street Annapolis	1999–2011	

Baltimore

BREWERY	PROPRIETOR	LOCATION/ NEIGHBORHOOD	YEARS	PEAK PRODUCTION (IF KNOWN)
Sisson's Brewpub	Hugh Sisson & Family	36 Cross Street Baltimore	1989–2000	1,000 bbls/yr
Baltimore Brewing Company (DeGroens)	Theodorus (Theo) DeGroen	104 Albermarle Street Baltimore	1989–2005	10,000+/- bbls/yr
Oliver Breweries LTD (Wharf Rat)	William & Carol Oliver	204 West Pratt Street Camden Yards	1992–2008	
Brimstone Brewing Company	Marc Tewey	O'Donnell & Conkling Street Canton	1993–1998	3,000 bbls/yr
McHenry Brewing	Martin Johnson	Baltimore	1994	NP
Clipper City Brewing	Hugh Sisson et al.	4615 Hollins Ferry Road Halethorpe	1995– present	50,000+ bbls/yr
BREWERY	PROPRIETOR	LOCATION/ NEIGHBORHOOD	YEARS	PEAK PRODUCTION (IF KNOWN)
Old Line Brewery (The Brewer's Art)	Volker Stewart	1106 North Charles Street Mount Vernon	1996– present	4,636 bbls/yr (includes contract brewing)
Globe Brewing Company LLC[74]	Charles Bowman, Louis D'Alesandro, Harold Saircloth	1321 Key Highway Baltimore	1996–1998	
Capital City Brewpub	David von Storch (chain pub from DC)	93 Light Street Inner Harbor	1997–2007	730 bbls/yr
White Marsh Brewing (Red Brick Station)	Bill Blocher	8149 Honeygo Blvd White Marsh	1997– present	1,600 bbls/yr

Carroll County

BREWERY	PROPRIETOR	LOCATION/ NEIGHBORHOOD	YEARS	PEAK PRODUCTION (IF KNOWN)
Johansson's Dining House & Brewery	Dave Johansson	4 West Main Street Westminster	1998–present	300 bbls/yr

Dorchester County

BREWERY	PROPRIETOR	LOCATION/ NEIGHBORHOOD	YEARS	PEAK PRODUCTION (IF KNOWN)
Wild Goose	Allen Puglsey & Jim Lutz (1992)	20 Washington Street Cambridge	1989–1997	25,000 bbls/yr

Frederick County

BREWERY	PROPRIETOR	LOCATION/ NEIGHBORHOOD	YEARS	PEAK PRODUCTION (IF KNOWN)
Frederick Brewing Company	Kevin Brannon et al.	103 South Carroll Street Frederick	1993–1997	
	Blue II LLC	4607 Wedgewood Blvd Frederick	1997–1999	
	Snyder International Brewing Group	Same	1999–2004	35,000 bbls/yr
Bowers Brewing Company (Brewer's Alley)	Phillip Bowers	124 North Market Street Frederick	1996–present	
Barley & Hops Microbrewery	Cluster Spires Brewing Group	5473 Urbana Pike Frederick	1999–2014	1,300 bbls/yr

Garrett County

BREWERY	PROPRIETOR	LOCATION/ NEIGHBORHOOD	YEARS	PEAK PRODUCTION (IF KNOWN)
Deep Creek Beer Works	Gregory & Sheri Mortimer	318 Spring Glade Road Oakland	1996–1999	

BREWERY	PROPRIETOR	LOCATION/ NEIGHBORHOOD	YEARS	PEAK PRODUCTION (IF KNOWN)
Deep Creek Brewing Company[75]	Same	75 Visitor Center Drive McHenry	1999–2004	

Harford County

BREWERY	PROPRIETOR	LOCATION/ NEIGHBORHOOD	YEARS	PEAK PRODUCTION (IF KNOWN)
DuClaw	Dave Benfield	Bel Air	1996– present	6,000 bbls/yr

Howard County

BREWERY	PROPRIETOR	LOCATION/ NEIGHBORHOOD	YEARS	PEAK PRODUCTION (IF KNOWN)
Bare Bones	Joseph Reese	9150 Baltimore National Pike Ellicott City	1995–2003	
Rocky Run	Bert & Mike Donnelly	6480 Dobbin Road Columbia	1996–2006	400 bbls/yr

Ellicott Mills Brewing Company	Martin Vigra, William Pastino, Richard Winter, Timothy Kendzirski	8308 Main Street Ellicott City	1997– present	2,000 bbls/yr

Montgomery County

Brewery	Proprietor	Location/ Neighborhood	Years	Peak Production (if known)
Olde Towne Tavern & Brewery	Charles Covell III, Joe Kalish et al.	227 East Diamond Avenue Gaithersburg	1994–1999	
Summit Station	Bowers Brewing	Same	1999–2006	
Tuppers Hop Pocket Brewing Company[76]	Bob & Ellie Tupper	Bethesda (contract brewing Old Dominion, VA)	1994–2007	

Worcester County

Brewery	Proprietor	Location/ Neighborhood	Years	Peak Production (if known)
Olde Towne Ocean City Beer[77]	F.J. Townsend III & John Townsend	1701 N Baltimore Ave Ocean City (contract brewed through Jones Brewing, PA)	1989–1990?	
Worcester Street Brewing	John R. Newcomb	102 Worcester St. Ocean City	1994	
Mermaid Brewpub DBA Brewmasters Brewpub	Chris DiForte	403 South Baltimore Street Ocean City	1998–2005?	

10

The Rise of the Modern
Craft Brewer, Part 1

As the new millennium unfolded shake-ups were visible throughout the industry, and many breweries closed. This was by no means a deterrent to opening a brewery; quite the contrary, it was incentive to do it right if it was going to be done. By the time the new wave of breweries hit Maryland consumers were much more receptive, eager even. Many were willing converts, happy to be a part of something exciting, shifting away from what was the norm in beer drinking to find their way to something new. The breweries that survived and thrived provided a testament to quality beer, becoming part of what was considered reliable craft beer. New breweries and brewpubs needed to contend with the established craft breweries in Maryland that knew loyalty alone would not keep business profitable, but superior beer would.

By 2002 Clipper City began to see the craft beer market open up once again and beer sales increase. Perhaps this was brand recognition, combined with a general easing of the market in favor of craft beers. Sisson grabbed the opportunity and stepped up production and distribution. The year 2003 also saw change for the brewery as they began selling the Heavy Seas line of beers starting with Winter Storm. This complemented the expanded distribution footprint of eighteen states. Slowly the Heavy Seas line grew, sometimes incorporating, sometimes replacing Clipper City beers. Sisson realized the split focus between Clipper City, Oxford, and Heavy Seas was not healthy for sustained growth and shifted his focus to one brand, Heavy Seas. Clipper City labels had run their course, but Heavy Seas was booming. The first year they were using one brand designation was 2010, and the increase in production of 35 percent was distributed across twenty states. Sisson also demonstrated wisdom by pulling out of low-demand states like Vermont in favor of higher-demand states like Alabama. It was always a juggling act but a manageable one and sound business practice. That growth was a testament to Sisson's strategy of introducing a new brand at the height of the recession and fomenting it.[1]

This of course was not where Sisson thought he would be in 1994 when he dared surmise what the future held, but that never mattered to him. He demonstrated great flexibility in adjusting his business plan to suit the market. Rebranding was a smart choice, but Sisson noted, much like his namesake, that there was always more to learn and no time to rest. Reinvention held the key to staying relevant and profitable through the introduction of new beers and expansion into new territories while delving more deeply into the regional craft beer scene.[2] This was the path to success, but it came with a price. Demand outstripped production and expansion of the facility was necessary to keep Heavy Seas in the market. Sisson was forced to embark upon a multiyear expansion plan. The plan included eleven new fermentation vessels (two 240-barrel fermenters and a 300-bbl bright tank), a new bottling line, a Newlands 60-bbl brew house (replacing the former 50-bbl brew house), a new 96,000-cubic–foot refrigeration room, and a brand new tasting room.[3] Sisson also spent quite a sum on quality control; $25,000 was paid for equipment to measure dissolved oxygen content.[4] This expansion constricted production at times, making for some difficulties with distribution, and forced a necessary scaling back of territorial growth. Ultimately it was worth the price. Capacity increased 250 percent.[5] Technically this allows Heavy Seas to produce 120,000 barrels per year. In 2014 they were slated to produce around 45,000 barrels, and target projections for 2015 were 48–52,000 barrels.[6] The beauty of the new brew house is the two brew kettles, which can manage 8–10 brews per day. The system is also so automated that process improvements have shown tremendous efficiency increases, such as no longer needing to shovel out the mash. The increased production will in-fill the existing footprint that Heavy Seas established in the market and grow into new or former customer states like South Carolina.[7]

Hugh Sisson, at the Heavy Seas/ Clipper City 20th anniversary party in 2015 enjoying the results of twenty years of hard work!

Heavy Seas has witnessed a dramatic uptick in demand for cask ales, which Sisson has unfailingly met. This falls under his need for constant reinvention, as every cask ale is an opportunity to showcase myriad flavor nuances or entirely new profiles of flagship beers. Sisson also expanded his staff and necessarily relinquished some of his countless duties to others, including sales to sales manager Joe Gold and general manager Patrick Helsel. Sisson offers his brew staff the freedom to create new recipes that of course extends to his latest brewmaster, Chris Leonard. Leonard replaced Joe Marunowski (formerly of Oxford Brewing Company), who backfilled the position left by Ernie Igot when he became brewmaster for Peabody Heights.[8] Two of the more recent additions to the brew staff include Courtney Lacey and Megan Schwartz, both female brewers from divergent backgrounds who join a growing number of women in the industry. Sisson merely provides the flavor requirements to his brew staff, but he does tweak the recipes some to produce a final product worthy of the reputation he worked so hard to achieve.[9]

New 60-bbl five-vessel Newlands Brewhouse, Heavy Seas, 2014 expansion.

Some people have challenged the rebranding Heavy Seas has undergone since they began operating under only that banner. The Märzen, once named MarzHon (while under the Clipper City banner) is now called the Cutlass, presenting a more nautical name for the brews. Will this lead to confusion or unification of the brand and its pirate theme? The cult-like following that Heavy Seas has accumulated since flying solo is a testament to the quality of the pirate-themed beers Clipper City crafts. In the long run will the thirsty consumer concern themselves with a name change? As long as they find the same award-winning product when they open the bottle, the seas should remain calm. Heavy Seas continues to introduce new year-round beers and seasonal brews to continue building the brand. Crossbones session IPA, Double Cannon double IPA, Deep 6 English porter, and Smooth Sail summer ale are the new brews on the schedule.[10]

The future for Heavy Seas is wide open. In 2014 Sisson orchestrated a collaboration with the Baltimore breweries of Brewer's Art, Union Craft, DuClaw, Oliver's and Red Brick Station. This creative brew, Stoop Sitter, benefited the Jake's Law Charity, which fights for tougher penalties for vehicular accidents caused by texting and driving. This is not unusual for Sisson, as he has partnered with many charities in the past ranging from the Oyster Recovery Patnership to college funds. Clearly the apple has not fallen far from the ancestral, entrepreneurial, and philanthropic tree. Heavy Seas has also picked up a number of medals at both the Great American Beer Festival and the Maryland Comptroller's Cup (formerly the Governor's Cup).[11] Undeniably, they helped put Maryland on the list of quality craft beer states. The sustained growth of Heavy Seas

(Clipper City) has been a defining part of that. Will Heavy Seas continue to grow? According to Sisson they will, in a controlled manner with painstaking attention paid to the building of the infrastructure to minimize surprises of the most unpleasant kind. This is his legacy, one passed on for over 175 years from the very first Hugh Sisson in Maryland.

You might say that brewing runs in the family for Stephen Demczuk. He recalls tales of his grandfather brewing beer in the bathtub during Prohibition when the family lived in Turner Station. Demczuk found his passion for beer a bit later in life, after he embarked upon the training to become a molecular biologist. He went back to his roots when he fell in love with beer and brewing in Germany, inexorably altering the course of his life. Peabody Heights was Demczuk's third attempt to build a brewery. Fortunately it should be his last, as success is almost certain. He was operating Raven Beer from Germany while contract brewing in Baltimore through Heavy Seas Brewery. Germany exceeded his expectations, and at the halfway mark of 2012 he had already topped total sales from 2010. It was time to operate his own plant in America. Finally with the new

brewery he is able to produce his beer in his own facility in Baltimore. The new brewery is currently capable of 40,000 barrels per year but can be easily expanded to produce 80,000. This is the largest brewery within the city limits of Baltimore since National left Brewers Hill for Halethorpe.[12]

The brewery is located on the site of the old Oriole ballpark, where the minor league Orioles played from 1916 to 1944, until it was destroyed by a fire. It was the fifth Oriole Park and situated just across the street from the earlier Oriole ballpark where Babe Ruth once played. The décor is very much Oriole themed, with baseball memorabilia found throughout. This is local. This is Baltimore. The brewery reaches into Baltimore's history and reminds us of the interconnectedness between sports and brewing. A recent survey of the property uncovered the fact that the pitcher's mound stood exactly where the south-facing wall of Peabody Heights Brewery stands today.[13] Workers are literally walking among the ghosts of players

Stephen Demczuk, Raven Beer founder celebrating Clipper City's 20th anniversary with Hugh Sisson, 2015. It truly was a celebration, not only of Hugh Sisson and Clipper City but also of the entire brewing community.

past as they brew and bottle. An honor? Indeed! It is also an inspiration to produce great beer worthy of such a hallowed location.

Peabody Heights started out as a

cooperative brewery that Demczuk owned with Hollis Albert and Patrick Beille. Both produced their own line of beers out of the facility in addition to contract brewing. The brewery employed eight to ten part-timers and five full-timers. The site in Waverly was an old Capital Beverage facility. This 50,000-square-foot space (with an additional 21,000 square feet of land) was perfect for a brewery. The infrastructure was sound, with plenty of drainage and well-insulated rooms that converted perfectly into cold storage. All of this was done on a shoestring budget of under $2 million. In addition to the necessary upgrades (plumbing and electrical), with the 30-barrel Newlands brew house and fermenting tanks purchased from Canada (sight unseen), Demczuk has plans to convert the entire facility into a "green" brewery within 5 years. This goal is within reach, as the equipment and upgrades he made are conducive to such an undertaking.[14]

Consumers demanded quality and Demczuk and his partners were prepared to provide it. In addition to the Raven beer that has been the staple of Demzcuk's company in Maryland, he introduced the Tell Tale Heart IPA, The Pendulum Pilsener, Cask of Amontillado, and two more seasonal beers in 2013 that fit neatly into Demczuk's Edgar Allan Poe theme. To aid in the creation of these promising brews, Demczuk hired head brewer Ernie Igot away from Heavy Seas. Igot trained as a brewer in the Bitburger Brewery in Germany, which perfectly complements Demczuk's German-style brewery. The plan was to use all local sources whenever possible, and they are following through. Demczuk hired all Baltimore or Maryland companies for everything from packaging to products to water to (it's hoped) hops.[15] Even the tap handles are made by local artisan Mark Supik, a well-known name in Baltimore.[16]

Considering the size of the facility, the owners of Peabody Heights saw fabulous opportunities for festivals, tours, and a massive tasting room. Not surprisingly, the taps were flowing before renovations were even underway to improve the tasting room. Collaboration with other Baltimore breweries was also a goal the cooperative had in sight, but not all partnerships were meant for longevity. A fracture in the relationship of the cooperative's owners forced a change of plans for Demczuk and Baltimore Washington Beerworks. Demczuk decided to move forward with the initial plan of opening his own brewery and separating from the cooperative. He was scouting a few sites in Woodlawn as of the fall of 2014 with hopes of opening in 2015.[17] Once again plans changed unexpectedly when in October 2014 the cooperative of Peabody Heights was completely bought out by Richard O'Keefe.

The new ownership placed the majority of the focus on Raven beer, with plans to increase Demczuk's brand, expanding output from the 2014 total of 12,000 barrels per year. New fermentation and bright tanks were ordered to accommodate the increase in production. O'Keefe gained ownership of, and will continue to produce, the namesake brand Peabody Heights (offering Old Oriole Park Bohemian Lager and other brews owned by former partner Hollis Albert), while Beille's Public Works brand was discontinued. Contract brewers like Full Tilt, Fin City, and Monument City will continue operations out of Peabody Heights, despite the primary focus on Raven beer brands. Another positive note includes the completion of taproom renovations and a more consumer friendly environment at the brewery for tours, tastings, and events. This obviated the need for Demczuk's plans to purchase his own brewery.[18] Today things are better than could be expected under the new governance, as Peabody Heights took home the highest honor, winning the 2015 Comptroller's Cup. Demczuk's beers can be found everywhere in the region and as far west as California. To say his footfalls are a bit lighter these days would be an understatement. It has been a turning point for Demczuk, a realization of a dream, as his beers are becoming as synonymous with Baltimore as Edgar Allan Poe: "Those who dream by day are cognizant of many things which escape those who dream only by night."[19]

Much like Demczuk, Dave Benfield and Jim Wagner were looking to change the trajectory of their DuClaw brewing operation. The future included a new industrial capacity brewery where DuClaw could focus on the beer instead of the complications of a restaurant. The Harford County facility clearly couldn't keep up with the orders. The owners attempted to meet distributor (and consumer) requirements by adding a bottling line in March 2011. By July 2011 they understood they could no longer meet consumer demand for their brews and planned for an industrial-capacity brewery. In less than two years DuClaw found a 54,000-square-foot brewing facility (with 8,000 square feet of additional office space) in Baltimore County that could house their brewery. They opened in March of 2013 at a startup cost of $5,000,000 and reached capacity by April 2013. That was entirely unexpected, but plans to expand were already underway, as four more fermenting tanks were on order from Wisconsin. With the automated touch screen, 60-barrel Rahmensudhaus brew house, operations are possible 24 hours per day, while two separate batches can be brewed at one time. This mitigates errors and increases consistency and efficiency. The maximum capacity of the new facility is 150,000 barrels per annum (with future additions of fermenting tanks of course). Benfield has not reached that yet but also cannot imagine having to consider expansion beyond that.[20] They have a bottling line which fills 100 bottles per minute and can accept 12-ounce, 22-ounce or 750-ml bottles. The new equipment was a challenge after operating on the same system for seventeen years, one that was a pleasure to overcome. DuClaw has had over twenty-five full-time employees since opening, which is ever more necessary, as distribution has expanded well beyond the Mid-Atlantic region and they continue to increase their national footprint.[21]

What element does DuClaw have that no one else does to make their brews a success? "Cool" is a philosophy. This is how every idea for a new beer originates: "Let's make it cool."[22] How does one define cool" and what does this entail? According to Benfield, it is part of forming an attachment: "Beer is intimate. You drink what defines you. People form an emotional connection to a specific beer."[23] The question then becomes how to make a beer people will form an attachment to. That starts with a few simple questions: Why make this beer? Why should it exist? What makes it worthy? This, according to Benfield, is how craft beer should be looked at. Produce interesting beers with imagery that represents feeling and demonstrates quality.[24] From the point that Benfield or one of his brewers comes up with a flavor concept, the beer is handed off to Wagner and the brewers, who all possess exceptional palates. This is always where creativity takes center stage before technique.[25] This is where DuClaw embraces their slogan, "Craft Be Cherished, Rules Be Damned!" Creativity over technique leaves room for quirks and flaws, but at the end of the day it is still going to be a flavorful beer people are drawn to. This is how DuClaw operates whether producing flagship beers or seasonal brews or one-offs that sometimes turn into something unexpected.

DuClaw barrel ageing program. Like many of the breweries in Maryland this has become an important selling point for DuClaw, both as a competitive tool and for the expanded flavor profiles brought out in the barrel ageing.

This has paid off with a silver medal at the 2012 Great American Beer Festival for the X-1.[26]

One notable DuClaw beer to mention is Sweet Baby Jesus. The genesis of this beer was the merging of a home brewing competition recipe winner, with some industrial-level tweaking by Wagner. This beer hit a sweet spot, so to speak, with consumers and has been produced year-round since its inception, cutting back production of two seasonals and Mysterium. This may sound like the goal of any brewery but not DuClaw. Benfield states that the goal is to kill off Sweet Baby Jesus. Why? Both to prevent the nixing of seasonal brews and create exciting new flavors to keep people interested and never bored! Constant evolution holds the key to success for DuClaw.[27] This philosophy leads them to corner the market on new and exciting hop strains. Although contracting hop orders four years out, they experiment with new strains and local hops. While there are not enough hops produced locally for long-term use, they do purchase hops from nearby Black Locust, feeding the local economy and fomenting the growth of hop farming in Maryland. Perhaps in ten to fifteen years hop growth in the state will be sufficient to sustain a commercial brewery. Like limited local grain availability, only time will provide an answer.

What helped facilitate the expansion and excitement over the craft beer produced is social media. This marketing forum provides feedback via Twitter, Instagram, Facebook, and other platforms. DuClaw gets input on what consumers want and consequently what they don't want. The difference in using social media instead of TV or radio is the back-and-forth communication with patrons about the actual product—not just placing an ad (like Ab-InBev) and moving on to the next ad campaign. DuClaw also has short films introducing their new beers. Although they are not nationally or regionally advertised, the films can be found on the DuClaw Web site and social media, helping consumers make emotional connections while having fun discovering the new brew. Social media provides the forum to make those new connections and give people something to talk about every time a new beer is introduced.

What does the future hold for DuClaw? Continued growth in craft beer, meeting distribution goals, remaining cool and relevant, while maintaining economic feasibility is the plan for the next ten years. By 2016 DuClaw had divested itself of the brewpubs to focus solely upon industrial production. When asked about the amazing growth in craft beer in the United States and how the industry can survive, Benfield and Wagner offered some insight. Experience is the key to lasting in a bustling market. Young people are the ones demanding the craft beer, which is an indicator that breweries will continue to thrive if they offer a unique, quality product.[28] Duclaw seemed to fit that criterion. Additionally, when it comes to the David versus Goliath competition with the mass producers like AB-InBev they see the continued trend of mass market producers losing ground against the true craft beer producers. Why? Benfield credits the lack of macro beer executives' foresight to corner the market on quality ingredients in favor of moving product.[29] Wagner notes increasing missteps by mass producers that facilitate the growth of independent breweries.[30] Craft beer focuses upon the individual, where the mass producers overlook them. Additionally, Benfield and Wagner both credit the employees that come onboard DuClaw with making it a better operation. Morgan Schell is a perfect example. Starting out as a server, she moved to marketing, and then became director of sales and marketing. Brandon Miller started out home brewing and then joined DuClaw in 2012 as an up-and-coming brewer. In 2016 he turned that industrial experience into a head brewing position at 3 Stars in Washington, D.C., where his beloved Capitals play hockey. Kurt Krol, resident artist, was another incredible young brewer with DuClaw. He put not only his brewing expertise to work but also his incredible talent at illustrations and animation. Whether DuClaw becomes a permanent home for their employees or a stepping-stone in the brewing world, all believe in the philosophy of keeping it cool and exploring the future of brewing no matter what happens next.

An extremely talented brewer in Baltimore just happens to be a transplant from across the pond. Steve Jones never dreamed of brewing beer at all. After earning his bachelor's degree in biochemistry at Warwick University in Coventry, England, he continued his studies in hopes of earning a PhD. His true inspiration came from music and that won out over a degree he no longer desired. He spent a few years on the road with bands he loved, soaking in the music and the cities he traveled to. By the time he was thirty the reality of life without a steady paycheck began to weigh upon his thoughts. It was time for a full-time job. Locally the firkin brewery (Allied Domecq) in Coventry was hiring a brewer, and Jones knew the science of fermentation technology from his university studies and thought he would give it a try. The roundtable interview of all potential candidates turned to experience, and Jones mentioned his education. He was immediately shut down and told that wasn't relevant to brewing. Jones assumed he would not get a call back, but surprisingly he did. The second interview was a success and his brewing career began in April of 1994.

The mentality of the boss was sink or swim. Jones received one week of training at the Hotlz plant in Wolverhampton, taking copious notes and filling casks. He was given only one day of training on the actual pub brewery system before being left to his own devices. The first batch of ale wasn't quite what it was supposed to be but was good enough to be a "seasonal" ale that everyone came to love. Jones became obsessed with brewing and often found himself on his days off wandering into the brewery to check on his ales. By 1996 he called himself a "brewer," as he made it past the learning curve and had the confidence of experience and a firm grasp on the balance between art and science, loving every second all the while. Awards honoring his craft ales began to accumulate just as the industry in England began to change. By the late 1990s brewpubs were being bought up or shuttered. In October of 1999 Jones was called to a meeting in Leeds and told to sell off the dry goods, as all the Allied Domecq pubs were being rebranded and the breweries closed.

Fortunately for Jones his girlfriend had just taken a job in Baltimore, a town he knew from his band years, and he relocated. After a brief marriage ceremony at city hall Jones was shopping his resume to all the local brewpubs, from DeGroen's to the

Steve Jones, Oliver Brewing Company brewmaster, pouring a beautifully crafted English ale at the new Shannon Drive location.

Wharf Rat. The Wharf Rat, a brewpub founded by Bill Oliver, was a perfect fit for Jones's cask ale experience and he was hired pending approval of his work visa. For a few weeks he worked for free, both to learn the system and to keep in practice while the visa was acquired. In 1999 he started brewing in the basement of the Pratt Street Wharf Rat and became affectionately known as the "hunchback of Pratt Street" due to extremely limited space where the seven-barrel system was located. He was forced into a "hunched" position most of his workday.

When Justin Dvorkin and his partners took over ownership of Pratt Street and the humble brewery in 2008, the need for change was palpable. Investment in the brewery became a priority and a gold mine. Baltimore loved locally made beer, so stepping up production to distribute to local bars and restaurants was in order. Meeting demand became crucial,

The Sword, Sea of Spears logo, Oliver Brewing Company. The Sword provides great inspiration to Jones in the creation of his brews, as witnessed in Sea of Spears.

even more so when the sister restaurants Ale House Columbia and Severna Park Tavern opened. Jones found himself brewing at maximum capacity, ten hours per day, five days per week. An industrial-capacity brewery was desperately needed to support the massive exoskeleton of what was once just a brewpub. In 2013 a 12,000-square-foot Clifton Park property was leased by Oliver Brewing. The former icehouse provided the perfect framework within which to construct the new brewery. The great difficulty in meeting demand would soon be eclipsed by the planning and construction of a new system. Craftwerk Brewing Systems was the chosen brew house manufacturer, as they offered an American product made to spec based upon the types of beer brewed and the projected needs. The new system is less labor intensive than the basement system but still requires the "hands-on" approach preferred by Jones. It also allows for both open and closed fermentation. This permits Jones to continue the true tradition of English cask ales while improving the quality of the American IPAs and nontraditional ales in the closed fermenters, where wild yeast finds no home.

The space was well designed by Dvorkin to accommodate growth, with each facet of the process spatially separated from the other, preventing both delays and accidents like cross-contamination. The brewery became operational in 2015, and two more 40-bbl fermenters were eventually ordered to meet demand. With the design, nothing has to be shifted or repositioned to accommodate expansion, smart planning for growth that will certainly be met and most likely exceeded. All that is missing from the brewery is a pilot system. This will come eventually, but for now the annual production of fifty-three different beers will be limited to the year-round offerings and staple seasonal beers that will sell out. The brewery owners are also investing in a barrel ageing program to meet both creative and consumer demand.

Jones loves the opportunity to be a brewer in America. It was an adjustment at first but one he embraced. Traditional brewing culture in England was regimented and did not adopt innovation like the "no boundaries" approach American brewers have always taken. An outrageously high ABV in England was 5 percent; most ales began around 5 percent in America. Predictably, Jones operated with restraint when it came to "out of the box" concepts in brewing, while Americans threw caution to the wind. That has never been his style, but he has embraced innovation and some divergent thinking, including some of those "bold" flavors Americans are so fond of. When his daughter Eva was born, he produced an ale with rose petals and raspberries to commemorate her birth, ingredients he would have balked at in 1996. There is a limit to breaching traditions, however, and he doesn't mind being called a "curmudgeon" when it comes to cask ale, because he won't add anything crazy and the Brit in him treads lightly. After his son Jacob was born, Jones took to the mash tun once again and created a very special ale reflective of his son and his heritage. Not only did his son's birth weight (8 lbs. 8 oz.) reflect the hop bill and the ABV, but the hops were half British and half American, with the inclusion of Liberty hops to celebrate the birth on the 4th of July! Jones's eldest, William, also has a brew in his honor, William's Winter Warmer, a traditional malty and smooth English dark ale one would expect in Jones's native land but one that has become synonymous with Oliver Brewing. His children are most certainly his muses, and he celebrates them through his craft.

Jones still finds inspiration in music, particularly when it comes to brewing. His favorite band, The Sword, has inspired many brews, including 3 Lions Ale, Sea of Spears, and Winter's Wolves, to name a few. Jones listens to the music and immediately calculates a recipe based upon the emotion and the artistry that speaks to both his creativity and his scientific ability. It is also a bit American. Jones has noted that American craft brewing is emotional and makes for some of the best craft beer in the world. England, Jones states, is just starting to think about craft beer in this light. One of the best parts of brewing for Jones—his favorite thing, in fact—is the creative freedom to express himself through brewing, a trait that has permeated the brewery since he began. The brewery reflects his personality— creative, methodical, inspired, and balanced—a place where quality is priority. This is also reflected in the artwork for the labels. David Paul Seymour created the rock and roll-inspired labels for the Sword Series that reflect Jones's love of the band and the unique merging of the music and ale.

Another facet of brewing in Maryland that Jones treasures is collaborating with other brewers. In part, it is the kinship that drives him, a brotherhood of brewers working together despite competition. Another aspect of collaboration that he cherishes is learning: "Brewing is one of those industries where you are always learning something.

That is why comradery among local brewers is so important, because everybody brings a different facet to the process."[31] In this there is always an opportunity to learn, to innovate, to experiment. There are a few brewers he would like to collaborate with outside of Maryland including James Watt from Brew Dog. Perhaps Jones will have an opportunity in the future. Perhaps together he and Watt will brew a historical Welsh ale (with peas instead of hops) that Jones has yearned to re-create for some time. That would be a step outside of the box for both.

At the end of the day, Jones's priority is to produce the best quality beer he possibly can in Maryland and in the country. With the advent of the canning line in early 2016, Oliver Brewing is beginning to get that recognition, as retail stores have clamored for their beers. The recognizable logo has certainly helped. Drexler, who created the original artwork for the brewery, has continued to design for the cans, and they are easy to spot for thirsty consumers. The names of the ales are just as important, particularly Jacob's Summer and Jacob's Winter Celebration (named after his youngest son), which resulted in in an infringement case with Sierra Nevada since they trademark "celebration." Now only Jacob's Summer Celebration is produced, based upon an agreement with Sierra Nevada. Jones noted that with the industrial brewery, a trademark attorney was now a necessity to maintain control of the names so personally crafted. That is the heart of Oliver Brewing—Steven Jones and his personality. A little bit of his soul is found in every beer he crafts. It is extremely personal.

Brewer's Art rode into the twenty first century with a goal of expanding to meet the masses thirsting after their anarchic Belgian beers. Volker Stewart wasted no time increasing capacity. The brewery expanded as much as it possibly could, averaging around 1,900 barrels annually, which was one-tenth the allowable annual production of 22,500 barrels for a class seven license. There are now two double- and seven single-fermentation vessels (they started with four) helping them achieve this capacity. The vessels were installed during the $200,000 expansion in 2001–2002 when Tom Creegan came in as the third partner. No space is left on the block to move into, and the brew house is not going anywhere, considering the difficult installation. Therefore, with demand for best sellers like Resurrection, Stewart and Creegan sought another avenue for distribution—contract brewing. The decision was to go with Sly Fox out of Pennsylvania in 2007. This provided the option of either canning or bottling, along with draft production.[32] All they needed was a sound distribution plan.

The key to successful distribution was recipe adjustment for the industrial brewer's system and selecting the best distributor to get it to market. Stewart went with Bond, as they were beginning to focus on craft beers by that time and understood the market. Stewart and Frazier worked through the intricacies with Brian O'Reilly (Sly Fox brewmaster) to bottle the very first Brewer's Art—Green Peppercorn Triple. This was a seasonal beer but the most popular at the time, making it a logical choice. Canard, Resurrection, and Ozzy would eventually follow.[33] The decision to contract brew allowed Stewart's beers to reach a wider audience of craft beer consumers, increasing demand substantially. In addition to the local chatter, their reputation has spread along the delivery routes. This is exactly what Stewart was hoping for, word of mouth, not print or TV spots, as the best form of advertising. Like many craft breweries today, Brewer's Art does engage in social media to help advertise. This helps to provide controlled,

Coup de Boule Brewer's Art with cardamom, cinnamon, and saffron. Proceeds benefit Baltimore City youth soccer, one of the many charities Volker Stewart and crew support.

sustainable growth. A Brewer's Art in every fridge in Baltimore? That is Stewart's plan!

Just as at many other Maryland breweries, collaborations are often in the works. Brewer's Art has collaborated with Stephen Jones of Oliver Brewing as well as Brian Strumke of Stillwater. Although these partnerships can be distracting, they always seem to be well received and patrons want more. And like many other Maryland breweries they purchase their tap handles from Mark Supik. Buying from and using "local" is important to Stewart. Problems exist, however, in using local ingredients on a regular basis. Most local hops are already spoken for, and Brewer's Art does not normally use whole leaf hops but pelletized hops. Stewart would like to use locally malted rye, which provides a greater likelihood due to its availability coupled with the growth of maltsters in Maryland. As with hops, demand far outstrips local supply. While pushing for an increase in locally grown ingredients, Stewart and Creegan conduct community outreach. Brewer's Art supports local home brew organizations like the Society for the Preservation of Beers from the Wood (SPBW) by hosting their annual meeting at the brewpub and creating a special brew each year. A contest is held among the home brewers, the winner receiving a complimentary dinner for two at Brewer's Art. This engenders that sense of community as well as supports local brewing efforts. Brewer's Art has also supported many charitable causes in Baltimore to help those in need. The Coup de Boule benefits youth soccer programs in Baltimore City, and many of the collaborations are for worthy charities. It is just one of the ways Brewer's Art has strengthened their city.

Where will Stewart and Brewer's Art go from here? With no expansion room, the only option would be an external industrial brewing facility of their own. There is no rush for that since relations have always been very good with Sly Fox. Brewer's Art has also been named the number one bar in America by *Esquire* magazine in 2008 and has received many similar accolades since then. For Volker Stewart that has been wonderful recognition, but he is focused on still being viable in the community by making quality beer that is demanded in Baltimore and across the region. He also has the honor of watching those alumni of Brewer's Art going off to do their own thing, whether opening a brewery or giving an art show (since many of his staff are artists). This is a legacy to be proud of and one that inspires many to dream.

One such dreamer was Brian Strumke. Strumke grew up a Baltimore guy, with an eye to the wider world that called out to him. A restless soul, with quite a lot of creative energy, he turned that vitality toward music, more specifically electronica. Strumke became a disc jockey, traveling the world from one gig to another. Eventually he returned to Baltimore looking for something more soul satisfying. He found beer. Conincidentally, it runs in the family, as his grandaparents worked at the iconic Gunther Brewery in Baltimore.[34] Strumke discovered beer as an adult at the Brewer's Art. It was there he developed an appreciation for the amber liquid, specifically Belgian styles, and he wanted to try it on his own. He found his artistic calling and has never once looked back.

The name Stillwater comes from his pseudonym as a professional DJ. He began producing his artisanal ales for mass production in 2010, not in his own brewery but contract brewing through DOG Brewing in Westminster. The ales were a take on the Belgian farmhouse style—but not exactly. Strumke doesn't like to force his beers into a category. He views farmhouse ale as a fluid entity, with lots of room to maneuver. More appropriately he borrows nuances from different styles, but he has one constant— his use of saison yeast. Saison yeast was a necessity when he was home brewing, as the summer months in Baltimore were oppressively hot and he needed a yeast that could stand up to that. Saison was the answer.[35] He pulls from a variety of unique and fresh ingredients to craft his brews, like the distinctive white sage he found in a farmer's market that became the basis for the flavor profile of his Cellar Door. Strumke allows his inspiration to come from a variety of places, keeping him in touch with his creative side. This would be the format of his future, defying labels and permanence. He began traveling, collaborating with breweries across the globe, making use of their facilities as he does in Maryland with DOG. The term "gypsy brewer" has often been applied to Strumke for his wanderlust when it comes to brewing and his lack of concern at having one set location to operate from. This is yet another label he shrugs off, as he is not one to be constrained by such things, but it is perhaps apropos. His brewing partnerships have taken him to five continents, and there are no signs of his slowing down. He has two headquarters, one in Baltimore and the other in New York, although with his travel schedule he rarely appears at either.

Briam Strumke, founder of Stillwater Artisanal.

Since his entrance into the world of industrial brewing, Strumke has been embraced. In 2011, after only a year in business, he made Rate Beer's list of top 100 brewers in the world, as well as being heralded as one of the best new brewers in the world.[36] Since then the accolades have continued, as have the beers. Most recently Strumke stuck true to form (or lack thereof) and changed his label design. The first five years of his labels were created by a childhood friend, Lee Verzosa, who was also a tattoo artist. They were distinguished by mystical, dreamlike, Victorian images that drove the imagination. Since Strumke introduced a new line of contemporary brews in 2015, including Mono, Stereo, and Yacht, he has departed from the mystical for cans of a decidedly contemporary label. He changed artists, much like he changes breweries, to keep things fresh, different, and interesting. It will no doubt be an adventure to see what the next five years bring from the wandering brewer.

In 2012, a brand new brewery was built in the city of Baltimore, becoming the first industrial brewery within the city limits since Prohibition was repealed. Union Craft was a joint venture between Jon Zerivitz and Kevin Blodger. Blodger was the brewer with the industrial experience. His brewmaster credits include Frederick Brewing Company, Capital City, and Gordon Biersch. Zerivitz was a home brewer who dreamed of starting his own brewery. The two were introduced at a mutual friend's wedding and decided to go into business together in 2011. Shortly after initial plans were underway, another partner with extensive accounting and financial management experience, Adam Benesch, was brought on board.

The brewery was to open in Baltimore, where there was tremendous support for craft beer. Union Mills fit perfectly. It was near the heart of a growing, changing community in Hampden and Woodberry and the idea of a neighborhood brewery was extremely well received. Additionally at the time, Maryland was only ranked 37th among breweries per capita, meaning there was room for another brewery in Maryland, specifically in Baltimore.[37] Their vision provided insight into the community support: "Craft Beer creates community, a union of the community and the brewery, a union of Kevin and Jon."[38] Their philosophy and beer were so well received the men had to turn investors away, a very good problem to have during a recession. After Blodger job swapped to relocate to Maryland, they began the grueling process of building the brewery. They faced many obstacles along the way, mainly due to the age of the building. Their lack of knowledge of the building process was one of the largest hurdles. Everything in the building had to be retrofitted, from the electrical to the plumbing to the gas lines. Although this increased expenditures Blodger, Zerivitz, and Benesch made it happen for less than $1 million.[39] That was easier said than done but they had a sound plan for growth to attain the markets they were penetrating. They started with a brand new Muir 20-barrel brew house. This system accommodates easy expansion as growth demands.

The first year they expected to brew 1,000 barrels. Beyond that, as demand picked up so did production. One hundred-hour work weeks were not uncommon. Union produced Duckpin pale ale and Balt Alt beer. Both were quite tasty and appealed to different palates. Union continued to produce these staple beers along with one-offs like the Gueze and the Schwartz beer. The theory was that if you did not like the first one you tried you would always like one of the others.[40] Thus far this has proven to be true, as crowds packed their grand opening and continue to demand Union Craft at Baltimore area bars, restaurants, and retail shops. Blodger added the Schwartz beer and the Blackwing lager to the regular lineup in 2013. By 2014 they had added the Anthem (to commemorate "The Star Spangled Banner" anniversary) and a host of others.

Blodger's German brewing experience has served him well. He wanted to fill the German beer gap in the modern Baltimore craft brewing community. He also wanted to offer what many craft beer drinkers prefer: a beer low in alcohol, with no wild ingredients, not overly hoppy, but a flavorful high quality brew. This is something Union has been

Top: **Union Craft Brewing Duckpin pale ale. This was in homage to Baltimore as the founder of duckpin bowling, which has always been synonymous with Baltimore beer.** *Bottom:* **Jon Zervitz, cofounder of Union Craft, in the taproom just before the grand opening in 2012.**

Kevin Blodger, cofounder of Union Craft, inspecting kegs before the grand opening in 2012.

extremely successful with during their short history. Eventually they added a canning line, as it was far preferable to bottling for retaining both the quality and the flavor of the beer.[41] By 2017 (the five-year plan) they plan to be a part of the fabric of Baltimore, with expansion regionally throughout Maryland. By 2022 their blueprint is for wider distribution through Maryland, Washington, D.C., Virginia, Delaware, and Pennsylvania.[42] They are well ahead of their plan; as of 2014 their brews were available in Maryland and D.C. In 2015 they were already distributing to Northern Virginia.

Their kegs have been available in all of the Baltimore craft beer bars from Max's to Alewife. The growler fills on brewery premises to thirsty customers in the previously untapped markets of Woodbury and Hampden have brought in quite a lot of foot traffic as well as external traffic via the MARC line that stops next to the brewery. Each weekend, tours and tastings are offered with food trucks, summer movies, and music, which continue to draw eager crowds. This has helped the local economy, the plan from the brewery's inception. In addition Union has been represented well at the Maryland craft beer events, and they have taken home several medals, from the Comptroller's Cup to the GABF (2012, 2014). Collaboration with other Baltimore craft brewers has been another successful avenue they traveled. All of this provides name recognition and throngs of craft beer lovers thirsting for the next tasty concoction—all of it reminding the community that *beer unites*.

Throughout the process to date, they have never lost their connection to the neighborhood, creating jobs, and giving back to those that have supported them. They have created what they set out to. By 2014 they had expanded into the adjacent space to increase production to more than 5,400 barrels annually.[43] They also brought on the first female brewer in Baltimore City since Prohibition, Lynn Pronobis. Pronobis began as an intern and quickly proved her value as a brewer. Aside from the historical implications, she provides another great face for Union Craft and a positive element at the brewery with customers and staff alike. This was intentional in part, as Blodger is one of the few African American craft brewmasters. Union set out to be inclusive of everyone in the community, to reach minorities and women as much as the main craft beer crowd (white males in their 20s and 30s).[44] They have begun to bridge that gap with both consumers and employees. Union has gotten off to a fantastic beginning, and Maryland is supportive of the direction they are headed.

Union has also received some additional fame from a request by M&T Bank to appear in a television spot promoting local businesses that are a part of the M&T Bank family. This has proven a bit more exciting than originally anticipated. Once the ad was filmed it was quite the hit and Maryland craft beer fans were happy to see one of their favorite breweries on television. It aired for only about 48 hours before being yanked from the airwaves. The commercial was edited and re-aired with seemingly innocuous words removed. As "they" say, "You don't know what you don't know." One could say the lesson in not checking phrases in the "Urban Dictionary" before airing a spot was certainly a conversation starter! No publicity is bad publicity? In this case it was absolutely true, as their many new fans will testify. Despite any hiccups they encounter, Union manages to come out of it all with great beer, a focus on the community, and a strong vision of the future where people unite through beer.

Another brewery opened within spitting distance of Union Craft on the Jones Falls in 2015. Homebrewer Roy Fisher fell in love with craft beer and yearned for the atmosphere and sense of community surrounding the trade. His friend, and local tattoo ink mogul, Bill Stevenson loved Fisher's beers and knew Fisher needed to get them on the market. Waverly Brewing Company was the genesis of this. The brewery is tucked away in a tiny industrial park, just close enough to the falls to hear the roar after a hard rain, but safely out of the flood zone. In addition to the regular lineup of stellar offerings, Waverly also produces not only seasonal brews but also joyous collaborations with expert homebrewers and craft beer clubs eager for a taste of industrial production experience. There certainly is artistry, but Fisher knows better than to assume everyone wants craft beer. In response he created the most unique yet wonderful Americana taproom, known as the "Shed." A departure from the typical brewery taproom, Fisher serves spirits and wine to cater to the non-beer crowd. Waverly also offers a beer garden that comprises the entire frontage of the property, inviting guests to enjoy fine weather, celebrate birthdays, and sample the newest offerings on tap. The brewery has endeared itself to the small community and demonstrated the craft extremely well.

Full Tilt was the genesis of Nick Fertig and Dan Baumiller, lifelong friends and family who followed divergent paths that eventually routed back to one another. Fertig joined the U.S. Navy and became a nuclear submariner, and Baumiller earned his degree in business and worked for the Department of Defense. Once reunited after Nick's service, they began home brewing together. The future merged with the recipes as the flavors developed. The realization came that a future in the craft brewing industry was a must. Full Tilt Brewing opened in 2012 in conjunction with the Peabody Heights facility. The two contract brew out of the plant. This offered the very best option for the new brewers to break into the industry. Although a great starting point, there were difficulties they had to work around and through. The first lesson: get more money on the loan, as it runs out quickly. Fertig and Baumiller appreciated the contract with Peabody Heights, which saved startup costs, and brewmaster Ernie Igot makes an extremely clean beer. That is the easy part. Scheduling and planning for future demand is the difficult part of contract brewing. The brew schedule is created three to four months in advance for all breweries contracted out of Peabody Heights. In reality this translates into needing to know what beers you will have a full season ahead, anticipating demand since it cannot be adjusted during production, based on the scheduling of fermentation tanks already in use. For a new craft beer company in a burgeoning industry, gauging these numbers can be extremely difficult. Additionally, the men were dissuaded from using Belgian yeast strains in favor of the same yeast strain that all beers brewed in the facility used.[45] Logically, this left less concern for cross contamination and more consistency in production but limited Full Tilt's options. Another element Fertig and Baumiller could not take advantage of was the opportunity for one-offs—a small-batch production of a special beer. This could not happen due to limited availability of fermenters and the need to fill them during scheduled production time. This of course would draw from the production of their flagship beers, with no guarantee they could sell the same quantity of their limited-release beers.

Despite the challenges, Full Tilt creates some very fine beers, with plans to expand their offerings as they gauge the market. In 2013 there were 2,400 barrels of Full Tilt produced, and numbers have steadily climbed since then. When asked about other lessons learned in the process of achieving success Fertig had a few interesting comments. Second lesson: they did not seek advice from any industrial craft brewers about the process beforehand to gather guidance on their journey. Since then they have cultivated relationships in the brewing community of Maryland and taken in the lessons of those who have preceded them. Another tutorial for the burgeoning business was importing kegs from China to save money. This backfired terribly, as the kegs were delayed en route due to hurricane Sandy and the brewers almost had no kegs of beer for their grand opening. All worked out, fortunately, and now they buy all American. None of these lessons were detrimental to success but have given perspective and a model for the future of their company.

Full Tilt has seen propitious moments of genius generated from their wellspring. The Berger Cookie stout is one such idea. Berger Cookie has been a Baltimore institution since 1835. Every Baltimore native knows a Berger Cookie and where to find it. This golden shortbread cookie with the chocolate fudge topping may not be everyone's favorite, but everyone in Baltimore has tried it at least once.[46] At a time when the FDA was attempting to ban all trans fats from the country, Berger Cookie was in danger of closing its doors.[47] Fortuitously, Full Tilt approached Berger Cookie with an idea to make the famous cookie into a delightfully scrumptious stout just in the nick of time, forever linking a historic Baltimore icon with a brewery trying to become one. Berger Cookie agreed, and the Berger Cookie stout was born. This provides just one example of how Baumiller and Fertig operate their business, with a mind towards Baltimore and what makes it unique. They are negotiating their place in history with hopes of becoming synonymous with Baltimore.

Like many breweries of the twenty-first century, marketing relies upon social media more than any other venue as the key to reaching consumers. Distributors still provide their share of marketing in the form of displays, tastings, and outreach, but as a craft brewer the burden is on the brewery to reach the target audience. The distributor is responsible for getting it to the right venue on time, in a drinkable fashion. Refrigeration trucks carry chilled beer to each venue, ready to tap or pour from the bottle. Like many breweries, occasional problems have surfaced with distributors. The transition of FP Winner Distribution into Chesapeake Beverages created fallout.

Nick Fertig, Full Tilt Brewing, former USNA submariner proudly displaying his Fully Tilted pale.

Delivery to Full Tilt accounts was inconsistent and sometimes nonexistent during the transition. For a new brewery, this could mean the difference between success and failure due to lost accounts. Full Tilt had accounts with Phillips Seafood (Inner Harbor location), all Green Turtle locations, all Buffalo Wild Wings restaurants, Alewife, and World of Beer Baltimore, in addition to other venues and liquor store contracts they wanted to maintain. Unfortunately, delivery fell short or failed in many instances, forcing Full Tilt to scramble to save accounts.[48]

What does the future hold for the owners of Full Tilt? Owning their own brewery is the next step, while no longer having to split their time between their day jobs and their brewing business. The idea is to locate within the city limits of Baltimore, like Union Craft. The year 2014 marked the launch of Fully Tilted—a unique line of their flagship beers that are jazzed up with more additives and sometimes higher ABV content. The Fully Tilted Pale Ale with Oak was the first. It was absolutely outstanding, offering a promise of what was to come. There are plans to expand this line. In addition to the "adjusted" regular lineup, they are looking at more seasonal specials and perhaps sours. Hops the Cat is an IPA named after Fertig's own cat—and, yes, he has a dog named Barley! Perhaps that will be the title of the next seasonal beer. The special small-batch brews are definitely a part of their future, something that became possible with new ownership of Peabody Heights and the massive expansion of the brewery.

Always near and dear to their hearts is the support of veterans. Profitability will bring with it an opportunity to support the veterans in Maryland through charitable events and, they hope, employment. For all that Baltimore and Maryland has offered to Full Tilt, they want to give back to the community that has embraced them. "Baltimore is the best driven community for causes."[49] This is something Full Tilt exemplifies. There is no better illustration than their Memorial Day 2015 release of In Memory Of. This beer was created as a tribute to honor veterans who lost their lives, a reminder that their sacrifice will never be forgotten. Proceeds from the pilsener were donated to the Military Family Relief Fund, which aids surviving family members and honors the fallen.

As of October of 2016, the cofounders decided to open their own brewpub. The new site is located in Towson, where an affordable lease and an expansive location went hand in hand. They are still securing financing, and working out the added complications of a restaurant, while creating new beers that fully express their personality. So far, they have met with great success from their Fully Tilted line of beers and plan to expand brands in the new facility, offering more on an annual, rather than seasonal, basis.[50] To quote Fertig, "Why do anything half assed when you can do it Full Tilt?"[51]

Another fixture of the industry in Baltimore, White Marsh Brewing (Red Brick Station), gained strength in the new century with increased patronage even during the depressed economic times. In part this comes from the "ownership" consumers have in the brewpub. It is also due to the quality and the support of the buy local/shop local mentality. This feeds the economy. McDonald and Blocher strive to emulate breweries that buy most of the grains locally. It will take some time to reestablish the strong growth of hops and malts in Maryland, but White Marsh Brewing is eager to engage in the use of local ingredients. Plans are in the works to open a second Red Brick Station in Bel Air. The first $2 million investment is presently paid off. The current purchasing model has saved the two tens of thousands of dollars annually, primarily because they have storage facilities to accommodate bulk purchases well in advance of their needs. They are purchasing 10,000 pounds of grain at once, all while negotiating free shipping. It is a well-oiled machine that Blocher hopes to continue with a second location. The advantage would involve designing the pub around the Peter Austin system for maximum efficiency.

Red Brick Station does not envision fitting into the Baltimore craft beer events as you might expect. This is predominantly due to their location in northeast Baltimore County, coupled with their lack of retail sales. They don't worry about getting into the retail market. The brewpub is averaging three hundred diners per hour during dinner. People throughout Baltimore know about the beer at Red Brick Station, and many are happy to travel for the great food and beer pairings. If customers so desire they can purchase a growler and fill it up to go. This business model has worked quite well thus far. In 2015 the owners added "crowlers" to their available line up of "to go" beer. Crowlers are 32-ounce cans that are filled and sealed on premises, safe for travel home or to the beach. These are a real draw that also happen to be unique in the local market, as Red Brick Station is the first brewery in the region to offer them.

McDonald always had plans to open his own brewery someday, not a brewpub but an industrial brewery. He wanted to return to his first love and produce German-style lagers and work with a variety of different yeasts. This is something prohibitive in the confines of the brewpub system at Red Brick Station. There is definitely room for another brewery in Baltimore, and as of 2014 McDonald lived his dream and opened his own brewery in Dundalk. Key Brewing Company is a partnership between McDonald and Spike Owen and opened in early 2015 with McDonald as brewmaster. The location is an old warehouse on 2500 Gray's Road near Sparrow's Point. The brand will be named Chesapeake Craft Brewers. McDonald hopes to produce packaged beers for White Marsh Brewing (Red Brick Station) once the facility is up and running. The 20,000-square-foot facility should allow for growth and accomodate a taproom and tours. The equipment Mcdonald and Owen started operations with is the former

Red Brick Station aptly named after the Peter Austin System it uses to brew.

Duclaw 40-bbl DME brew house from the closed Abingdon plant. McDonald also continues working as a part-time consultant with Red Brick Station, overseeing his former assistant brewers in the process. Key Brewing was named after Francis Scott Key and the brewery's proximity to Fort McHenry. The real joy for McDonald comes from the opportunity to get back to making the beers he truly loves, the beers of Munich. Every beer is homage to the styles that drove him to make a career out of that precious malty liquid.

One local Baltimorean also honors the deep traditions of Maryland brewing without producing a single drop of beer. Mark Supik never imagined he would play a critical role in the resurgence of craft beer in Baltimore, much less the nation. Supik was a sculptor who trained at Maryland Institute (MICA) in the 1970s. He eventually opened a woodturning company in Baltimore off of Haven that specializes in furniture, bannisters, and the repair and re-creation of historic properties (interiors, floors, tables, columns, and the like). His craftsmanship can be seen across the city. Supik was always a lover of craft beer, even more so after a visit to Prague in 2000. He toyed a bit with home brewing in college and was a home vintner as well. He was delighted to be called on in the 1990s to create tap handles for a brewpub called DeGroen's. It was his first tap handle and the start of something he never could have foreseen.[52]

One after another, brewers in Maryland called upon Supik to create unique tap handles. Heavy Seas, White Marsh Brewing, Raven Beer, the now defunct Globe Brewing, and a host of other breweries across the state have ordered their tap handles from Supik as a way to not only support a local business but also to have the exceptional craftsmanship displayed in each and every handle. Currently Supik produces tap handles for breweries across the country from Weyerbacher to Grey Sail, an enterprise that now makes up 50 percent of his business. This is the buy-local mentality at its finest, and everyone benefits. Supik has even begun regular tap handle making classes (along with his woodworking classes) for home brewers with kegerators. He doesn't want the trade to vanish and although it is a family business the increase (due in part to the tap handle surge) allowed him to hire more

Mark Supik, the creative carpentry genius behind the tap handles in most Maryland breweries over the past two decades.

employees to meet demand. One such employee, Danielle, is a finisher who works specifically on Edgar Allan Poe handles for Raven Beer.[53] Supik's wife and business partner, Nancy, is one of two females at the shop, a parallel to the brewing industry of just a few years ago—the first in the woodturning trade but certainly not the last. As more breweries open in Maryland, more tap handle requests come Supik & Company's way, fomenting the business and affirming the legacy.

Eastern Shore

Adrian "Ace" Moritz of Eastern Shore Brewing in St. Michaels, Maryland, took a different approach than many brewers starting out in the industry. His was one of community. Moritz, his wife, Lori, and daughter, Josselyn, packed up their bags after the economy took a downturn (when layoffs were visited upon his family) and moved to St. Michaels, where Moritz's parents had retired. A home brewer for years, Moritz decided to open a brewery. Fortunately for him, many in the community offered their help. Ted Dupont, the owner of the property adjacent to St. Michaels Winery, was so enthusiastic he offered free rent until the first beer was served. This was a blessing and a curse of sorts. Moritz found that he would need to rewire the entire facility as well as upgrade and install new plumbing before he could hook up the first piece of equipment. Moritz and Lori did all of the construction work. Other members of the community offered to help in various ways. St. Michaels is a town that absolutely supports use local/ buy local and this mentality aided Moritz in his opening. His spent grain goes to Dogwood Farms for the cows, and in return Moritz gets his pick of the garden. Other barter relationships have occurred as well. One included the Wildebeest head that hangs above the bar, and another brought in an old Martini-Henry rifle now mounted upon the entrance beam. The tasting room exudes the charm of a local establishment with the comfort of being a bit worn and weathered.[54]

Many challenges arose in this undertaking, from federal licensing delays to production issues. Moritz found a way through them all. He started

Eastern Shore Brewing Company, St. Michaels, Maryland.

with the purchase of an eight-barrel brew house at a cost of $6,000 to begin operations. Unfortunately, operating a home brewery does not always translate well to a larger industrial brewing operation. In addition, there were issues with water quality. When the recipes had been nailed down the consistency was compromised by the water's quality and fluctuating mineral content. Moritz was hoping for a spring opening in 2008 but was pushed back to September of that year. It was an opening well received by the community, but the inconsistency of the product threatened his success. After 18 months in business, Moritz shut down operations for four months to try to regroup and fix the production problems plaguing him. Part of the fix included hiring his first head brewer, Randall "Randy" Marquis, a UC Davis brewing program graduate. Randy immediately addressed the issue of water quality. The first thing he did was install a water treatment system to correct the pH and improve water quality. Additionally, he amended the process and finally tweaked the recipes to adjust for water and process changes. Wisely, he used different water profiles for each beer produced at Eastern Shore. Since operations have reopened, the brewery has done well. Beer sales have increased 33 percent in the tasting room with 40 percent less traffic. Moritz has also seen a 10 percent increase in draught beer sales.[55]

Many smaller adjustments have been made to the brewery including growlers and a return to stainless steel kegs from plastic kegs (which were an attempt to mitigate cost as they had no scrap value and therefore were not stolen). Additionally Moritz has added two seven-barrel fermenting tanks and two seven-barrel bright tanks to increase production. Despite all of the positive changes at Eastern Shore, Moritz still has some difficulties ahead. Distribution is a large problem. If you run out of kegs (which he has in the past) the bar is less inclined to purchase your beer again, as they want consistent availability. Currently with Kelly Distribution, Moritz can distribute only on the Eastern Shore from Cecil County to Worchester County. He is working on a contract with a distributor that handles the Western Shore of Maryland.[56]

Another problem not easily solved was the bottling line. The machine purchased had been discontinued and it operated at extremely low capacity. Marquis and crew had to rig it to operate at around five bottles per minute. This was faster than the original creator of the machine ever achieved. In fact, the creator often called Eastern Shore crew for technical support. Sadly, the quality of the beer was compromised if it sat too long in the bottle. This is why Eastern Shore focused on keg and growler sales. The easy fix for a bottling problem is to purchase a new bottling machine, but that is not possible in this case as it costs around $50,000. Moritz's brewery was completely 100 percent self-financed, as he has run his operation without an outside investor. To maintain this, he will have to wait on the new bottling line and concentrate his focus on keg and growler sales.[57]

Eastern Shore has produced a fine variety of craft beers, predominantly ales. This is supported by the silver medal won at the Governor's Cup in 2010 for the Duck Duck Goose porter, a silver medal for the St. Michaels amber ale, and a bronze medal for the Lighthouse golden ale.[58] Moritz and his brewery are a staple in the community. The brewery is considered a family location, as parents are welcome to bring their children along for a soda or to play some of the many children's games available in the taproom. Locals and tourists alike take advantage of this family friendly tasting room. Beer dinners at the brewery or at a local restaurant in St. Michaels often showcase the wonderful local cuisine and how well it pairs with the ales from Eastern Shore. Despite all the neighborhood support, the majority of Moritz's business does not come from locals, as St. Michaels is a small community. The bulk of the sales arrive in the form of tourists from April through October. Winters are fairly slow for Moritz, with a 60 percent decrease in sales. It is winter when the brewery caters to the locals, also using the down-time for process improvement or brewery expansion.[59] Eventually sales across the Chesapeake Bay to Baltimore and points west will see a growth in revenues that will foment brewery expansion and fund a new bottling machine. This also promises to make a household name out of Eastern Shore Brewing, the Moritz family, and their brewmaster.

In 2013 Eastern Shore had a new brewmaster, Zach Milash. Marquis resigned from the brewery to open his own brewing plant in New York with his father. Milash, Marquis's former assistant brewer, has taken things in a positive direction for Eastern Shore. He has tweaked some recipes and created a passel of new brews receiving critical acclaim, particularly from the Belgian styles he produced (as well as the ales), taking awards at the 2013, 2014, 2015, and 2016 Comptroller's Cups.[60] Milash is a native of the Eastern Shore of Maryland and isn't planning to go anywhere just yet. The future is promising for Mortitz and Eastern Shore, with recent expansion into Delaware, where many more craft beer consumers have the opportunity to sample Milash's creations, keeping the brewery on the map and in the growler.

The brewery now has company, with both St. Michaels Winery and Lyon Distilling sharing the same block and proving to be a real treat for locals and travelers alike. Together the three have helped one another increase awareness of great beverages produced in St. Michaels and increased tourism to not only the brewery but also the local shops, hotels, and restaurants. This is what Moritz hoped for when he started this venture—to become not only an important fixture in the community but to give back. Don't forget to bring your dog, as Moritz doesn't stop at welcoming humans. Quadrupeds are always invited!

Due east from St. Michaels on the path to Ocean City resides another unique Maryland brewery, Burley Oak. Bryan Brushmiller started like many brewers, home brewing out of his garage. His family was a part of the brewing tradition in Baltimore. His aunt worked for National Brewing Company, and she often brought Natty Boh home. His grandfather was a loyal National drinker until the Hoffbergers sold the Orioles. Beer and Baltimore were part of Bryan's DNA, so it therefore came as no surprise he wanted to open a brewery. He had lost his job in 2008 prior to Christmas and realized it was time to do something for himself. He did what was necessary to the pay the bills while he developed a business plan to open his brewery. At this time it was not easy to garner support, as the craft brewery boom had not fully reached the Eastern Shore.

Bryan and Nicole Brushmiller, founders of Burley Oak Brewing Company

Burley Oak Brewhouse.

Brushmiller wanted to retain full control of his company, but as banks said "no" to business loans, investors lined up—for a price. Bryan turned them down, as he wanted funding without sacrificing control or ownership.

By 2011 Brushmiller had altered his business plan from a "Cadillac" plan to a downgraded "Chevy" plan. What did this mean for startup? Bank loans were taken out with his house as collateral. He was able to obtain economic development loans with a little help from Bill Turner, vice president of development at Farmer's Bank. Working in conjunction with Lois Hagerty, who specialized in small business development in Maryland, a business plan was formed to help the brewery open. Brushmiller calls this a "community-built brewery," since every pint supports jobs in Berlin. Berlin residents support the brewery, and the economic cycle is triggered. It really doesn't stop at the pint, however, as Burley Oak uses local hops (1,200 hop vines grown locally for his brewing) and local grain (40,000 pounds of two-row barley, now expanded to wheat and rye whenever available). This puts money into the local economy and also realizes in large part Bryan's vision—a small brewery supporting Maryland. Local goods help keep prices down and the economy moving. Bryan has done his part and will continue to do so.

The name of the brewery was chosen due to the historical roots of the town. Burley Oak was a plantation from the seventeenth century that served as a stop for travelers, a boardinghouse, and an inn (the Burley Inn was shortened to "Berlin"). The "oak" came from the cooperage that once operated in the building that houses Brushmiller's brewery. Kismet? Perhaps, but he has a strong reliance upon history and historical lessons.

This is one of the reasons he malts his own barley—avoiding indebtedness to the maltsters, historically the downfall of many Maryland breweries. Brushmiller noted there are three maltsters in the United States that control about 97 percent of the malt. That is something he wants to separate from, and consequently he began working with the University of Maryland to design a malting facility that would accommodate the needs of his small brewery. Trained as a biologist, Brushmiller has a full understanding of the needs of germination and the malting process for brewing. His scientific mind is certainly stimulated by the process, and that translates into excitement, dedication to process, and ultimately quality.

Another lesson learned from brewing history is to never sacrifice quality for quantity. Burley Oak has grown since its opening in 2011 and production has more than doubled. The taproom has fifteen different Burley Oak brews on tap at any given time. The brewery has distribution on the Eastern Shore with Carey Distributing and in the rest of Maryland with Legends, but Brushmiller does not feel the need to expand beyond Maryland anytime soon. Growth at Burley Oak is allowed only if quality can be maintained and the local economy supported. This is about community as well as quality. Cost effectiveness never entered the equation if it sacrificed quality and Brushmiller found a way to make it work. Old surfboards were turned into chalkboards, fermenting tanks came from Craigslist in Iowa, dairy tanks from Wisconsin, and the walk-in freezer from a Bonanza steakhouse. This is where the budget was tightened, but the premise to never sacrifice the final product was honored.

Caring for his community through responsible business ownership demonstrates the philosophy he espouses and lives by. In an effort to produce quality beer, build communities that can sustain the economy, and support families, Brushmiller has also aided other local breweries in their efforts as he was helped with his. When he was getting started, Sam Calgione from Dogfish Head and Tom Knorr from Evolution Craft Brewery were very supportive, answering questions and giving suggestions and guidance along the way. In turn he has done the same for Fin City and Shorebilly (now Backshore Brewing). To Brushmiller, the responsibility is more than a "pay it forward" attitude; it is about creating businesses that manufacture quality goods that sustain the local economy, "If Tom produces a great beer, that only helps me because the more he sells, the more I sell."[61] Berlin is on the way to and from Salisbury and Ocean City. There is extensive traffic filtering through town. The breweries all benefit from one another as long as they are turning quality brews. This also provides a greater source of income to the local economy, not just from the brewery but from the other local establishments as well.

Burley Oak has eight full-time employees, four of which are bartenders. That is a truly shocking statistic for a brewery producing around 2,000 barrels per year. It becomes obvious that Brushmiller not only has a handle on successful brewing operations but the business side as well. He claims to struggle as a businessman because he is an artist. All indications are to the contrary, however; based upon his success, he has mastered both. With such a small operation, the majority of his income (80 percent) is derived from pint sales in his taproom. Initially, he was not allowed to sell pints. This should have spelled disaster for Burley Oak. Undaunted, and with the help of the local politicians who saw the economic potential, Brushmiller was able to get the laws

Top: Evolution Craft Brewing, Salisbury, Maryland, taproom. *Bottom:* Tom Knorr and Geoff DeBisschop of Evolution Craft Brewing, 2013.

changed to allow pint sales. This was no small feat, but it also demonstrates the changing attitude of politics and policies toward breweries since Prohibition. They are a source for positive growth within a family community. To emphasize the family, Brushmiller offers child-friendly options like homemade root beer and strives to make families welcome. The children and adults can watch see the panoramic window the 10-hectolitre brew house and several of the fermenting tanks, capturing a small glimpse into the operations allowing imagination to take flight. All are invited to observe how his philosophy translates into hand-crafted beer that he considers a step beyond craft. Brushmiller defines handcrafted as "a made by hand, artisanal, quality product, with somewhat less consistency than craft beer."[62]

He defines craft beer as, "distinctive, striving for quality and consistency, which as a consequence lacks the artistry he pursues."[63] This is also advocated by his employees like Zach, his beerologist. Zach spearheads consumer education, introducing people to this craft beer world or igniting passion for those familiar with hand crafted beers by exhibiting patience, knowledge, and a true love for the process and the final product. A prime example is noted in Mike Spalding, a lifelong Budweiser drinker who now arrives daily to sample his next handcrafted brew. Since Burley Oak's opening Spalding has sampled over 800 craft beers! This is a true testament to the quality and the education provided by Burley Oak and a reminder that David can defeat Goliath.

What does the future hold for Brushmiller and his brewery? No substantial changes are anticipated other than barrel ageing on a larger scale, a sour program, and perhaps a dedicated lager tank. Large-scale growth is not in the cards, as that would be deleterious to hand crafted beers, and that is what Burley Oak will never stray from. Although they plan to stay in Maryland, word is quickly spreading beyond those borders and they are gaining national recognition.[64] All of this attention only urges Brushmiller to continue on the path he has forged: local quality. This has been manifested in his partnerships with local farmers like Brooks Clayville to plant acreage of hops and malting grains, which he plants responsibly and sustainably. Although Brushmiller does not always malt his own grains (they are usually shipped to Massachusetts for malting) they are local, as are a large percentage of his hops. With a new malting plant under construction in Delaware, Brushmiller will truly be keeping it all local![65]

A short ride on Route 50 takes a parched traveler from Berlin to Salisbury. This is where Tom Knorr can be found. Knorr fell in love with craft beer while in college out West. In the 1990s when he returned to the East Coast there wasn't much craft beer available. By 1996 he had opened his first restaurant, Red Roost, and served only craft draught beer (Sierra Nevada, Dogfish Head). Tom and his brother John own Southern Boyz Concepts, creating restaurants with unique local food and wine/craft beer pairings in the Delmarva area. Craft beer was always a part of the future for the Knorrs. A decade after the first restaurant Knorr wanted to make a change and build a brewery. He purchased the train station in Salisbury in 2007 with hopes of turning it into a brewpub. Unfortunately, the city at that time wasn't so cooperative and wanted a colossal impact fee. Knorr had no intention of losing money before he even opened his doors and chose to move operations to a more welcoming Delaware. In December of 2008 they began construction on the production facility at a startup cost of $800,000 and installed a 10-barrel brew house system with several moving parts. It was a bit difficult to operate and there were a few hurdles. Licensing was the greatest challenge, as with many starting breweries the TTB process did not occur in a timely manner.[66] The head brewer they chose to hire was a recommendation by a friend (Larry Horowitz). Geoff DeBisschop was a Seibel-educated, experienced head brewer out of New England who would deftly guide them through the obstacles.[67]

The creation of beer recipes was fairly easy with an experienced brewer like DeBisschop. The limitations came with the food pairings. Those involved never wanted a beer to overpower but to remain complex, approachable, and always excellent. Geoff DeBisschop was able to craft this vision exceptionally well as evidenced by the rapid growth Evolution experienced. The Delaware facility had a capacity of 4,000 barrels annually, which was reached within the first two years of operation, sparking the need to move to a larger facility. There was literally no walking space at the Delmar brewery, and they required four shipping containers just to hold support stuff due to the lack of space. Expansion at the Delaware facility was far too expensive, but the Knorrs still had Salisbury in mind. They found a building that got around the impact fee because it was in an ice building with thirty-foot ceilings, loading docks, and a six-inch well pipe. It was perfect for a restaurant and brewery.[68]

In autumn of 2011 the Knorrs began the build out of the structure to house the brewery and restaurant, anticipating opening for business in 2012. A 40-bbl Newlands brew house was installed, along with a bottling line. Additionally, they have a filler space (the equivalent of a clean room), which prevents contaminants and should turn out an even better beer. The maximum capacity of the new space can reached 60,000 barrels annually if operated 24/7. There are no immediate plans for around the clock operations just yet. Knorr is happy with the distribution in Maryland, Washington, D.C., Northern Virginia, Delaware, and Pennsylvania. Perhaps expansion into Southern New Jersey will come in the future, but that would be the extent of it. Knorr has no desire to go beyond those boundaries, as he wants to be a big brewery but not too big. He wants (and has) quality beer with controlled expansion, after the local market has been penetrated, much like New Glarus of Wisconsin.[69] This is definitely not the easy route, but it is the designated course for Evolution. They are also limited by the brewpub license, which limits production to 22,500 barrels annually. This is a number Knorr is pushing up against as of 2016.

DeBisschop had a similar vision to Knorr. He possesses great passion for beer and quality, but the focus shifted once he began brewing. It is a laser focus on process improvement; making things more efficient improves quality. A relationship is developed with each beer created and perfected. This is not surprising for a brewer with a master of arts degree in business who is always striving for more. This also defines his view of the future of craft beer, which brewery by brewery depends upon their business plan and the quality created to distinguish it from others. This determines success or failure and whether there is enough market share.[70] DeBisschop always viewed the beer as the priority, and if there comes a time when a marketing campaign or shareholders become the first priority it is no longer considered craft beer. A brewer must be emotionally invested and have touched the beer for it to be considered crafted.[71] As far as David versus Goliath for DeBisschop, that is not a concern. He notes that brewers from AB-InBev teach at Seibel and are quality, talented brewers. The competition is really only at the retail level from the sales representatives, not on the part of the breweries.[72] Some people might say it comes down to sales and shelf space, but not DeBisschop.

This is how DeBisschop has created his artistry, relying upon those who understand crafting in each part of the process. He notes that as a judge at the Great American Beer Festival he is often inspired to raise his level of craft due to the incredible beers he encounters. He notes that true maltsters are really good brewers (craftsmen) in order to obtain the quality and consistency for large-scale operations without error. He is smitten with the grain coming from the maltsters. He mentioned that Sierra Nevada and Rogue are malting their own, which is not something Evolution will adopt but is appreciated. Grain agreements are integral to the creation of quality beer and each brewer is responsible for keeping them in place. Evolution also has hop contracts out three years to guarantee the hop supply necessary for both regular and seasonal brews. Under the guidance of DeBisschop, they steer away from what are considered "trouble" hops that may not be consistently available due to limited production. Amarillo is just one proprietary hop in limited resource they stay away from. The yeast strains are fortuitously well planned and used for six to eight generations. Local grains or hops are not dismissed, but large quantities of either are prohibitively expensive and often unavailable. When they are available in smaller numbers, they are used for special, limited-release beers, of which Evolution produces around fourteen or fifteen annually.[73]

The brewery operates efficiently and in conjunction with the restaurant and taproom. There are many pairings offered with the exquisite menu selections. This is what keeps people coming in the door and back again in an industry where the success rate is so low. For many people, the beer is what gets them through the door to the food, thus building a strong clientele both locally and transiently. The events like beer week or pint nights keep them interested. What is it that Knorr hopes to create? To have a generational legacy of craft beer drinkers who knew about Evolution when they were children and to create great memories with Evolution when those people are adults. They hope to extend this beyond Delmarva and perhaps open a tasting room in Baltimore, to begin building the legacy on the western shore. Like the name they chose, they wanted to take tradition and evolve to the next level, leaving a legacy of no gimmicks, just true quality.

DeBisschop has since moved on to open a brewery in Sanford, Florida, but has left behind a very well-trained staff capable of continuing the exceptional process he put in place, leaving a trail of incredibly well-crafted quality beer. Tom Knorr has always had the mentality that Evolution is a team, and although a key member of that team has gone everyone knows what to do and will press forward. Additionally in 2016, Tom Knorr's outstanding leadership was called upon by the Brewer's Association of Maryland, and he was tapped as vice president. He is also leading the charge in Annapolis to change the brewpub license barrel limits to 60,000 annually. The brewpub community across the state eagerly awaits the results.

One such brewpub, Shorebilly, also opened its doors in 2012. Danny Robinson grew up on the boardwalk in Ocean City, Maryland, where his uncle owned a hotel. Robinson and his family would stay with his uncle most summers, grabbing Italian ice and pizzas, watching the people walk by. All this was imprinted on Robinson. Although born and raised in the Bronx, New York, as his accent reveals, it was Ocean City summers he longed for. One might suggest that this life was in his blood; the urge to care for people (food and shelter) and watch them go about their business meshed with his New York roots where the whole family would get together and make wine. Robinson never realized this was what he wanted to do for the rest of his life, but the past he yearned for became his reality.[74]

Robinson, a self-described serial entrepreneur, owns six restaurants and two nightclubs in Ocean City under Southbound One, Inc. He had owned Hammerheads on the boardwalk for ten years by the time he opened Shorebilly Brewing in the space next door. It wasn't a winery (as he thought) but a brewery. Robinson has operated under the guise that what is good for his brand must be good for Ocean City or it will not progress. Therefore, Robinson saw a need not being met in Ocean City—an actual brewery in Ocean City. This, he noted, goes back to the European model of the local baker, the local butcher, the local brewer, etc., which has become part of the regional mentality to buy local. Robinson not only wanted to meet the demand for a local brewery but he also wanted to leave things better than how he found them. In this case, he wanted to improve the economy, job opportunities, and tourist access in Ocean City. He also envisioned this as family friendly and not a deterrent.[75]

With $100,000 of his own money Robinson opened the brewery in the old ice

Shorebilly Brewing Company on the Boardwalk in Ocean City, a step from the ocean. This was prior to the name change to Backshore.

Danny Robinson, the owner of Shorebilly, now Backshore Brewing Company.

cream shop adjacent to his restaurant on Tenth Street and the Boardwalk in 2013. He purchased a two-barrel brew system, four two-barrel fermenters, and two two-barrel bright tanks to get started, which could produce about four barrels per day. Water minerality required the installation of a carbon filter. Licensing was relatively straightforward, and Worcester County was very accommodating. Always the businessman, Robinson realized he needed greater production to meet demand for his restaurants, so he contract brewed 2,000 gallons of his three flagship beers (Kolsch—his "gateway beer," a brown ale, and an IPA) through Tall Tales Brewery to get started. Shorebilly plans to use local hops from Whaleville when there is enough quantity for large production and local barley (probably malted by Burley Oak) as it becomes available in order to honor the buy-local mentality. All the food in his brewpub is also locally fished or harvested as well. The wood in the brewery was taken from a local two hundred-year-old barn (Snow Hill) that was going to be destroyed. The barstools were made of recycled kegs.[76] Robinson also kept it local with the brewer he hired, Robb Dunne. Dunne was a local home brewer with fifteen years of experience.[77] All of this became the backdrop for about 400 barrels annually of fresh, local brew on the boardwalk in Ocean City.

For a town that has three million tourists on the boardwalk, profits happen in a limited one hundred-day season, forcing Robinson to focus both his efforts and his product. Marketing beer had changed from the days of large-breasted women in bikinis selling beer to a concentrated word of mouth and social media campaign to build brand loyalty. The locals supported the opening and the beer, encouraging Robinson to go forth with creating seasonal recipes in addition to the flagship offerings.[78] The community has also been part of the journey, through participation in naming campaigns and tasting the development. Tourists enjoy the opportunity for local as well and are equally attracted by a freshly brewed product on the beach. The deck seating provides both. Another local piece of Robinson's brewery was the name: Shorebilly. This local Maryland term was initially a derogatory term for people living on the east side of the Chesapeake Bay. The implication was they were unconcerned with education and work, desiring only to spend their days at the beach. This has even translated into a regular Ocean City blog offering by Syd Nichols.[79] The derogatory term has clearly been turned into a badge of honor denoting geography and pride instead of a lack of education or work ethic. This is what Robinson wanted his brewing company to embrace—its heritage—and what brought him back to his summer home.[80]

Unfortunately this was not to last, at least not the name. A trademark infringement lawsuit was filed in 2013 against Robinson and Southbend One, Inc., for violation of the "Shorebilly" name, which was trademarked by a T-shirt retailer, Teal Bay Alliances.[81] Robinson noted that the term is common usage and not subject to trademark, but he acquiesced nonetheless and renamed Shorebilly "Backshore Brewing Company" (with a little help from the locals).[82] Unfortunately, Teal Bay Alliances demanded all profits made while using the name "Shorebilly Brewing Company" and pressed on to federal court. This was quite unusual, as most startup breweries do not show a profit in their first year of business and Robinson stated openly that he would not draw a salary for the first five years the brewing company was open in an attempt to keep it (closer to) the profitable margin.[83] The trial was set for summer of 2014, with Southbend One alleging that Teal Bay fraudulently acquired the trademark from the United States Patent Trademark office.[84] Regardless of the suit, the locals still have a stake in the brewery with the new name and the variety of offerings. The tourists also seem to enjoy the new name and the same flavors they remember from 2013. The question was whether or not Robinson would financially survive the lawsuit and the exorbitant legal fees.

What does the future hold for Robinson and Backshore? Robinson foresees expansion throughout Maryland and into nearby states over the next five years, one account at a time. His priority is to make sure every account is happy and satisfied with quality beer, building trust and brand loyalty. He notes that ciders, shandies, and potentially distillation (Worcester County has given a potential green light already) are possible within that time frame as well. The long-term future includes an industrial-capacity brewery on the peninsula, using the brewpub for pilot batches, and keeping the boardwalk location operational and relevant. He also sees Backshore not as part of competition on the Eastern Shore but part of the brotherhood, where success is good for everyone.[85] The year 2014 brought many changes to Backshore and Robinson. When the name Shorebilly was changed to Backshore, a new brewmaster (Adam Davis, formerly assistant brewer at Growler's of Gaithersburg) was hired. Shortly thereafter Robinson reached the end of the lawsuit. The judge agreed that the lawsuit was frivolous and without merit and ruled in favor of Robinson, requiring the complainant, Teal Bay, to pay $30,000 in legal fees to Southbound.[86] Despite all the upheaval, Backshore is clearly a success and has made its mark on Ocean City both in and out of season. Backshore wears the personality of its owner and consumers proudly, and everyone who tries a beer gets a welcome taste of the sweet life on the boardwalk!

Another brewery operating within walking distance of the Ocean City beach is Fin City. Vince Wright was spawned from a family of brewers. His maternal grandfather brewed beer during Prohibition. Wright's grandmother planted the seed of brewing in his ear in 2004 when she began to describe the beers his grandfather used to create. This only heightened Wright's interest. His father was a chef and a first-class beer drinker, and this family heritage seemed to merge. Wright began touring breweries from Dogfish Head to Sam Adams to find out more about the industrial brewing process. He purchased his first home-brew kit at Xtreme Brewing in Delaware. It didn't take much for him to decide that he wanted to brew for a living. He knew there was a distinct difference between brewing in his garage and brewing in an industrial facility. He also knew he wanted to remain in Ocean City, with the sun, sand, surf, and fishing. This is where the name and the logo comes from, a picture of a swordfish skeleton he discovered at the Smithsonian. It was an image he couldn't shake, an image that felt like home.[87]

Along with producing his own beer, Wright started entering contests—and winning. One notable example was his pumpkin ale entry in the Punkin Chunkin 25th anniversary contest in 2010 in Delaware. Sam Calagione, Dogfish Head founder, encouraged him to enter since it was Calagione's Punkin ale that won it in 1994 before he ever opened his own brewery.[88] People lined up by the hundreds to look at Wright's label, even though he could offer them no samples. Discovery Channel filmed the Fin City label and it appeared on the *Brew Masters* television show episode with the distinction of his ale winning the contest! Wright attended a microbrew contest at Hooper's Crab House the following week. This was kismet. Wright looked up to the loft above the bar and said, "This is a great place for a brewery!"[89] He chatted for a while with Patrick Brady and the owners, Mr. and Mrs. Shepard. Wright came back later with his home-brew samples and they all agreed to start a brewery.

Fin City began brewing operations in 2012 at Hooper's Crab House. It took over a year to acquire the TTB permit. Maryland and specifically Lou Berman of the state comptroller's office were integral to obtaining the permit.[90] They had no issues getting things through the county government at all.[91] The greatest challenge they faced after the permit process was adjusting from home brewing to industrial brewing. Wright and the staff were guided by Doug Griffith of Xtreme Brewing, the same person responsible for guiding Calagione in his Dogfish Head setup.[92] They started with a custom-built, five-barrel brew house assembled in the home of a friend. This system was completely manual, with no automation whatsoever. Next they installed three fermenting tanks, which fortunately had a small degree of automation for controlling temperature. The water in Ocean City is decidedly hard, with a high mineral content. This required the installation of a Culligan inline carbon filter, which took care of the problem. Regular testing is scheduled to make needed adjustments.[93] Startup costs hovered at $60,000, a steal compared to most new brewery costs.

With everything in place, brewing began in earnest. Wright continued his full-time job as a defense contractor, while his wife, Michele, ran an at-home day care. They both brew in the unair-conditioned loft above the bar in the dark of night when it is definitely cooler. Unfortunately, that offers little comfort as the Wrights haul twenty-gallon buckets of ice up the attic-like stairs more than fifteen times a night to cool off the beer coming out of the brew kettle before it enters the fermentation tanks. Fortunately, grain is hoisted on a palette with a winch/pulley system so no humans are responsible for hauling it by hand. All new beers have been tested on a pilot system in Wright's garage before anyone engages in the toil of brewing them in the loft.[94]

The success of the brewery was immediate and palpable. The extremely creative fishing pole tap handles allowed them recognizable space at many bars and liquor stores, which triggered consumer recognition. Within a year, the brewery added a new fermenting tank, bright tank, and made plans to replace the brew house with an upgraded seven-barrel unit.[95] This demand stems from a sound business plan and quality beers. Wright was committed to quality first and everything else (including growth) second. Hooper's knew the target audience and guided the beer in that direction. Old Bay and crabs require a lower alcohol beer, and Wright accommodated. He uses all local products for the beers. When it's possible, and if available in large enough quantities, he prefers local grains and hops. Currently he has annual grain contracts, but hops are acquired without a contract. The Wrights educate the staff on the beers and the possible pairings, allowing bartenders and servers to suggest choices and perhaps turn a Budweiser drinker on to a Fin City light.[96] With five flagship beers and two seasonal beers, growth was inevitable. Fin City was supplying kegs to nearby bars and restaurants along with Hooper's. They were also bottling bombers and six packs of special beers for sale. This left little time for creating new beers during the busy season (June through August).

Winter was slower and was the time Wright got creative to plan for the next season. To keep in touch with the community and heighten name recognition, Fin City sponsored homebrewing contests. The winner was rewarded with industrial production of the beer at the brewery and seeing it consumed by thirsty tourists and locals at Hooper's. This, combined with a strong business plan aimed at slow sustainable growth, has allowed Fin City to pay off the startup cost already and look to the future.[97] What does the future hold? Contract brewing through Peabody Heights in 2014 to keep up with the increasing demand was the first step. Canning is the second step, for the convenience of beachgoers and stadiums. The future goal is to open an industrial brewery capable of producing enough for the entire state and beyond. Wright has never been shy about advice, whether from the consumers or from brewers. He intentionally sought out critics and gurus to find out what he should do next and the guidance has been instrumental in his success. Mentors to Wright include Calagione, Brushmiller, Noda Brewing, and Stone Brewing, to name just a few. Even though Wright acknowledged they are all competing for shelf space, he also recognizes they are all in it together, craft brewers versus the macro brewers.[98]

Wright's plan for growth does not include national distribution but a strong focus on the Mid-Atlantic, and East Coast. He foresees a potential franchise of a Fin City brewpub in a coastal town like Annapolis or Baltimore following the construction of the industrial brewery. Wright does envisage some fun collaborations with Calagione and others who have aided and inspired him. Currently, he just wants to keep producing quality craft beers. So how does he define craft? "Brewers taking the freshest local ingredients to make unique beers that are not always consistent but consistently creative."[99] Wright has earned his place in the craft brewing scene the hard way, which makes success twice as sweet. There is always more competition to come, forcing him to keep working just as hard.

A competitor to Wright's operation resides inland from Hooper's Crab House in a most unsuspecting location. Jason Hearne was a landscape architect and owner of Blue Heron Landscaping. He decided to take a risk in a struggling recession and use half of his Parsonsburg landscape building to open a brewery, thinking it woud be "recession proof."[100] He brought in investors (Paul Sens and T.J. Schiff) he had worked with in the landscaping business to help fund the operation.[101] Together they consulted experts like Bryan Brushmiller of Burley Oak and Tom Knorr at Evolution.[102] With no restaurant or brewery experience this was a smart decision, along with the hiring of experienced experts like Natalie Matthews to run the bar and restaurant, head chef Bill Wainright, and brewer Mike Kolankowski, who hailed from a family tradition of industrial brewing.[103] Together they opened Tall Tales Brewing Company in 2011. The theme of Tall Tales can clearly be spotted in lore, legend, and myth with names like "Red Headed Step Child" and "Calamity Jane." The names also hint at the style, or at least some of the ingredients. These beers are perfectly paired with small food offerings like brick-oven pizza and wings. Kolankowski has worked not only to make award-winning beer (Good Beer Festival Taster's Choice Award Winner 2013) but also to condense the beer for the chef to create unique beer-infused offerings.[104]

Response was strong enough for the product that Tall Tales began contract brewing out of Peabody Heights Brewery in Baltimore for their popular beers to be bottled. Tall Tales does have a pilot system to test recipes but lacks the in house bottling line. Distribution is slated for Northern Virginia, Maryland, Delaware and Pennsylvania.[105] Distribution seemed to have increased sales as Tall Tales brought on another brewer in 2014. Jimmie Sharp was a Wicomico native who went to Dogfish Head Brewery with his wife after graduating from UNC Wilmington in 2005. The taste of the beer was enough to change him from a "Bud" drinker into a craft beer guy on the spot. With a little push from his wife, he began

Tall Tales Brewing Company sculpture, independent brewery—contract brewing for Backshore.

home brewing in 2006.[106] Even as he worked as an environmental planner with Wicomico County, Sharp continued to brew, perfecting his recipes and his craft.[107] Recognized for his talents, he was offered the head brewer position at Tall Tales in March of 2014, replacing Kolankowski. Since opening in 2011, Tall Tales has expanded into most of the space that once held the Blue Heron offices. Office operations have subsequently relocated to the upper level of the structure. Perhaps the continued growth will require expansion beyond the current structure and a bottling line of their own. In the meantime the brewpub attracts quite a following in season and out with their events, entertainment, and pub fare.

In August of 2013, Reale Revival (RaR) opened its doors to a Cambridge, Maryland, population interested in discovering what a craft brewery would mean for the small Eastern Shore town. The idea for this brewing operation was hatched by two lifelong friends, Chris Browhan and J.T. Merryweather. They loved craft beer and decided to try home brewing with a Mr. Beer kit in 2009. By Chris's thirtieth birthday party at Victoria Gastro Pub they were drinking home brew and craft beer and began to discuss more commercial brewing opportunities. Five of the friends, including Browhan and Merryweather, got together and each chipped in $3,000 for a professional all-grain brew system, which was placed in the back of the Ocean Odyssey Restaurant. They all tried their hand at brewing but only Browhan and Merryweather were successful. The two credit innovative recipes and meticulous recordkeeping. This spawned the idea to go into the craft brewing business in their hometown of Cambridge, Maryland.[108]

Browhan and Merryweather spoke with Brushmiller from Burley Oak, Knorr from Evolution, and Moritz from Eastern Shore Brewing to garner insight into the industry in the tight-knit community on Maryland's eastern shore. All provided invaluable information that coincided with Browhan and Merrweather's research. That was enough to convince them, all they needed was equity. Browhan and Merryweather courted three equity investors to supplement the University of Maryland Eastern Shore Rural Development Center loan acquired with the help of Keasha Haythe.[109] After Browhan and Merryweather purchased the building with their own funds, the investors and loans provided the rest of the $600,000 startup costs. This allowed them to acquire a 10-barrel brew system and six fermenters (two 20-bbl, four 10-bbl). It supplied the cost of contract brewing with DOG Brewing until the plant in Cambridge was operational.[110] They also brought in head brewer Randy Mills, formerly of Evolution Craft Brewing, to spearhead some recipe creation and refinement.

Browhan, an electrician by trade, and the creator of the logo, and Merryweather, a marketing guy, set up a fairly sound business plan. They create beer sourced with as many local ingredients as possible from local hops provided by friends Toby Todd and Larry Johnson (Cascade hops). Occasionally they even use a wild-yeast strain for seasonal brews. The business model included no central distribution but saturation first in the local market, keeping the money in the taproom, much like Burley Oak. They planned to use every possible conduit in Dorchester County to capture loyalty and have locals take pride of ownership in the brewery.[111] They chose to target through social media campaigns and strategic word of mouth promotions to reach their target audience of 21–35-year-olds, which make up 28 percent of the craft beer consumers in the United States.[112] They are also counting on the effects of the recession and consumers' distrust of big business to spur their commerce. Generationally passing this down will aid in the loyalty of the local consumer toward craft beer and RaR.[113]

Although they will not rely upon distributors for too much business or education (they will educate consumers) they are using Legends as their wholesaler and will continue relations with them since they distribute statewide. Merryweather will visit each account personally to educate servers and put a face to the name. They plan to attract crowds year round with nightly promotions, local food offerings, and entertainment. Additionally they are setting their sights on making historical re-creations (pre-Prohibition style beers) as specials, along with a full series of cask ales. They want to connect with the local home brewing community, holding contests to win the opportunity for RaR to manufacture their home brews. All of these tactics seem to add up to a successful beginning.[114] By 2015 RaR was not only distributing through Baltimore, Annapolis, and the Eastern Shore, they also reached Washington, D.C. This forced the need to package the beer on premises to meet demand. RaR purchased an adjacent building for the housing of a canning line to do just that.[115]

Browhan and Merryweather believe the future of craft brewing in Maryland is sustainable because Maryland is behind the curve in production and things are on an economic upswing. Merryweather sees the market as wide open and RaR has carved its place in sustainable future growth beyond the next decade. This can be achieved (according to Merryweather) only by not growing before debts are paid and keeping it

J.T. Merryweather and Chris Browhan of RaR Brewing inside of the taproom at the brewery while finishing construction in 2013.

local. The founders do not foresee the future of RaR as one where they become a vast brewery producing 100,000 barrels. It is all about remaining local, earning the loyalty region by region, and crafting one new beer at a time, relying on local ingredients and local businesses working together.[116]

A fixture on the Eastern Shore, Tim Miller is an affable man. He comes from a family well known in the region both in personality and the family business, McMahon Oil. This was a company his grandfather started in the 1940s. Being a part of the Miller family meant being a part of something larger, the family industry, a business the Millers learned working from the ground up. No one was immune from performing menial tasks in order to get the job done, which grounded the children and gave them an appreciation for hard work.[117] A greater sense of community was also imprinted upon the Miller family.

Thus begins the story of National Premium's return to Maryland, a circuitous route most certainly but one destined to land on the shores of the Chesapeake Bay once again. Tim Miller grew up like many on the Eastern Shore of Maryland, working in the family business, playing lacrosse, and noting the beers his father and family drank. National Premium Beer was on the list. Tim went off to college and like most college kids enjoyed the cool repast of a beer or two.

After college he returned to his hometown and eventually got into a career in real estate, as the family oil business had been sold. His father had ownership ventures in a local tavern and Miller started a family of his own. Real estate paid the bills of a growing family but it was not the only endeavor he was interested in. For years Miller had researched the possibility of branching out into something more—but what? He was very tied to community and family and possessed a deep sense of nostalgia. Shopping in old antique stores and seeing the beer glasses, tap handles, and trays of past icons led to a desire to bring back one of Maryland's favorite hometown beers.

In November 2010 fate showed her hand when Miller noticed an auction in New York City where Mesiterbrau and National Premium trademarks

Tim Miller, owner of National Premium Beer in Easton, a short drive from the McMahon Oil property that will serve as his waterfront tasting room.

were available. Technically it was the logo letters and domain name that were available for National Premium, and Miller signed up for the auction and walked away with the rights to National Premium for $1,200. The next step was to figure out the recipe and a marketing campaign.[118] The advantage for Miller was loyalty. Maryland remembered National Premium, the connection to the Orioles, the Baltimore Colts, and crab feasts.

Once Miller had the trademark the question became how to create the recipe. Kismet is a word too often used and rarely appropriately. But in this case there is no better description of the events that transpired for Miller and his quest to bring National Premium back to life. Several years prior to his acquisition of National Premium, he was introduced to the founder of Wild Goose, Jim Lutz, at a beer tasting. He asked Lutz what he thought of bringing back one of Maryland's old beers. Lutz advised him that whatever path he chose he should resurrect only one beer and do it well. This was sage advice. Miller was introduced to Joe Gold (Heavy Seas) through a coworker. Gold happened to know the very charming and very Irish Timothy Kelly, a former employee of Carling in Halethorpe. Once Kelly established Miller's level of commitment to bring back National Premium, he introduced him to a former Carling brewmaster. Tim Kelly collaborated with other brewers, from Milwaukee to Tampa, and within a few weeks a statement of process was constructed based upon an adapted recipe with new brewing equipment. The only problem Miller had left to solve was where to brew the beer. The

The view from McMahon Oil, owned by National Premium's Tim Miller and soon to be the location of an amazing boat-accessible taproom for National Premium and Wild Goose.

facility he had in mind was a future remodel of the McMahon Oil property, which was ideal but several years from production. An old lacrosse friend of Miller's happened to know the owner of Fordham (Rams Head) Brewing in Delaware. Coincidentally Fordham was operating at half capacity and looking for contract brewing opportunities. In addition, Jim Lutz was now president and CEO of Fordham Brewing in Dover.[119]

A 20-gallon test batch was brewed in November 2011 with Jack Ehmann, former brewmaster with Pabst and Schlitz. Further adaptations needed to occur to bring the recipe current, including a work around of the (former) corn component. By March 2012, another test batch (50 barrels) was produced. The April tasting revealed a pasteurizing issue that cooked the beer accidentally. The process was corrected and by May 2012 a 100-barrel batch was produced and sent to market.[120] Some tweaking has occurred since that first batch hit the market, but Miller has now achieved the consistency of a quality brew that people will recognize both for the history and the taste.

The beer has been well received in the state where it has been marketed. There is, of course, a list of residents with long memories. Some say the taste is different than what they recall drinking in National Premium's heyday. Others experience it for the first time and enjoy the new (to them) beer with the historic Maryland roots. Curiously those who enjoyed Mr. Boh over Mr. Pilsener still argue over which is preferable. This was a sign of the trouble brewing beneath the happy return of a Baltimore legacy beer. Unfortunately for Mr. Miller, the owners of National Bohemian (G. Heileman, now Pabst) filed a cease and desist order against Miller and National Premium. The grounds seem to be based upon the confusion between Mr. Boh and Mr. Pilsener. Although the trademarks are held separately by different entities the argument was that consumers will purchase National Premium thinking they are purchasing National Bohemian. Well, a look at the packaging is fairly clear even to uneducated consumers as to what product they are purchasing. Decide for yourself, but Miller claimed the likeness has harmed his sales more than Pabst. Regardless of that, in a settlement agreement with Pabst he had to agree to stop using Mr. Pilsener.[121] Consequently he has tweaked the label and the tap handles to comply and to get a fresh start beyond the legal turmoil.

National Premium is a reestablished Maryland legacy beer that has long been identified with the Chesapeake Bay. Miller is adjusting to changes in contract head brewers while continuing to receive guidance from the Hoffberger family, who were thrilled at the return of National Premium. The next move for Miller is to garner placement in Camden Yards (home of the Baltimore Orioles) and then look to expand throughout Maryland. National Premium is now available in cans, which facilitates transport to multiple venues, from stadiums to beaches. The end goal is to open his own brewing facility and tasting room in Easton on the water in the old McMahon Oil building his family has owned for generations. The site holds great promise and Miller has many ideas. The hurdle is water and sewer accessibility, which is expensive and desperately needed for brewery operations. Growth, however, is essential to this vision and is being met in part by social media, the up and coming method of reaching consumers without expensive television ads. It also is helpful that Miller sees himself as competing with the macro brews, since National Premium was a macro brew. He clearly understands his target audience and how to reach them to compete with Heineken, Stella Artois, and Molsen. He also notes that all he really needs is a marketing machine to push him over the top. To begin, he has hired a full-time salesperson to reach his target Washington, D.C., consumer. Eventually he will reach into Pennsylvania and Virginia; it is only a matter of time.[122]

In December of 2015 Miller added the now defunct Wild Goose brand to his repertoire, which went into production in October 2016 with Snow Goose. He has not ruled out other styles to add to his brand, including a seasonal dark National Premium based on the former recipe, and potentially re-creating historic Gunther beer. Regardless of style expansion, Miller has a solid game plan and is known by locals throughout the Eastern Shore and increasingly throughout Maryland. His charisma, patronage, and earnest desire to rekindle the love of a Maryland beer legend has won the hearts of beer drinkers throughout the region, craft or macro drinker alike, solidifying his place in the beer industry for years to come.

Howard

Rocky Run continued producing beer at the Dobbin Road location for the three restaurants they owned, but the competition was increasing in Howard County and the quality of the beer around them was forcing a change. In 2001 they brought in Matt Hahn, formerly of Oxford and Brewer's Alley, who had been bouncing around Ohio as a brewer since leaving Frederick. There was much he needed to accomplish as far as process improvement. The Donnelleys, being unfamiliar with the brewing trade, made understandable mistakes like using dry yeast, buying two years' worth of specialty malt stored in direct sunlight warmed glass (thus rotting the malt), and taking all of the hops out of their sealed packages and placing them in less than airtight bins. Other problems included a leaking brew kettle and pipes and myriad electrical problems, but Hahn got it straightened out, taking a twelve-hour brew day down to an efficient eight hours.[123]

Hahn loved the brewpub once the system was revamped to his specifications. He very much liked interacting with the customers, giving tours, and teaching people about the craft. The team environment that was created with the bartenders and serving staff was a highlight, and eventually an assistant was hired to help Hahn in supplying the three restaurants, fomenting an atmosphere of comradery. Business, however, was slowly and steadily falling off, despite correcting the brewing problems. A change was needed, with a stronger focus on the beer, on the Web site and in marketing, but that did not happen. Once the smoking ban was in place in Howard County, according to Hahn, people were drinking less. This was coupled with the general drop-off after September 11 that many restaurants noticed. Profitability was decreasing and by 2008 things were dire.[124] In February of 2008, Hahn and his assistant were laid off. House beers were no longer served in any of the restaurants, and the Columbia Rocky Run closed its doors in September 2008 to the shock and dismay of the many loyal followers. Baltimore followed the next year and Glen Burnie in 2010. The competition in Howard County was meeting with mixed results. Bare Bones also ceased brewing operations, but Ellicott Mills was faring far better. Ellicott Mills Brewery continued operations into the new millennium, matching the award-winning cuisine created by Rick Winter with the consistent lagers and ales produced in the brewhaus according to the Bavarian purity law (Reinheitsgebot) established in 1516. They claimed to produce more Bock-style beers than any brew house in America. The awards won by Ellicott Mills for their beers over the years seem to support not only the variety of beers but also the quality.

Ray Andreassen joined the brewery as head brewer in 2005, the third in the line of successful brewers at Ellicott Mills. Beau Baden and Jason Oliver preceded him at the position and moved on after securing brewing positions at large industrial breweries in Pennsylvania and Virginia respectively. Growing up, Andreassen always knew he wanted to work in a brewery. When the opportunity became available, he seized it. He began as an assistant brewer to two different head brewers, learning the intricacies of the brewing trade, and quickly learned the equipment was the biggest concern. The brewery has a three-tank system. There is the mash tun, which is steam fired, a decoction brewing Lauter tun, and a whirlpool that allows solids to come to the middle and draw off the cold wort. Hot clarified wort runs through the heat exchanger and then downstairs to the open fermentation vessel. This is where the yeast ferments the sugars into alcohol. Open fermentation requires a very sterile environment, as anything in the room can compromise the quality of the beer, particularly wild yeast. Additionally there are bright tanks for the beers with carbonation (instead of still beers). Ales sit for two weeks and lagers condition for at least a month. One week of lagering is required for every degree of plato. The grinding of grain into grist is critical. When milled, too fine of a grain is not desirable, as husks are needed as filters. The base malt is most important, followed by the barley. The hops change from year to year and the brewer is reliant upon sensory analysis to determine if the hop is stronger or weaker than the previous year so the recipes can be adjusted for consistency.[125] Andreassen is a true technician, loving every component of the process.

Ellicott Mills is predominantly a German and Australian beer brewery. The brew house is Czechoslovakian and the rest of the brewing equipment is German, an interesting combination of language requirements, to be certain, but Andreassen knows the piece-

Ray Andreassen, brewmaster, Ellicott Mills Brewing Company, and consultant brewer at Frisco's Taphouse (Push American Brewing).

meal system well and is aided by assistant brewer Matt Hobbs. It is a labor-intensive job that requires a strong back and willingness to abuse it. Each full keg is 130 pounds, and each bag of grain weighs 55 pounds. Some of the brews, like the Kolsch, require ten bags of grain, ground into grist and then added to the mash tun. Others, like the Bock, are higher in alcohol and require twenty bags of grain. Despite some of these physical drawbacks Andreassen looks at home in the brewery. He loves the nuts and bolts of brewing, as well as recipe formulation. This is why he is able to put out a consistent product. The consistency of the beer was put to the test after the devastating flood of 2016. Ellicott Mills Brewing Company was underwater after the town received six inches of rain in

Matt Hobbs, assistant brewer, Ellicott Mills Brewing Company.

just over thirty minutes, causing a devastating flash flood that killed two and destroyed most of the businesses. The town was closed for several weeks while the structural integrity of the buildings was assessed and washed-away segments of the roads replaced. The brewery reopened along with just a handful of businesses in October 2016. Andreassen was able to get back to being the technician once again. As far as the future is concerned, he is quite happy to stay where he is, loving the production of bock beers. His skill as a brewer has also led to his assisting other breweries in the area like Frisco's Brewery and the Tap House.[126]

Adam Carton opened Frisco's Grille and Cantina in 2008 in Columbia. He grasped the need for quality craft beer and offered nineteen rotating taps. The Mexican food he paired with fabulous craft beers was a hit, along with the pint nights and specials. The growth was rapid and Frisco's was ready to expand beyond the occupancy restrictions. In December 2010 they moved to a new location in Columbia and rebranded as Frisco's Taphouse and Brewery. The intent was to begin brewing their own beer, beer good enough to serve alongside the fifty-six craft beers they already offered on tap. The space was more than twice as large as the previous location and provided a show spot for brewing operations through panoramic front windows. A planned enticement perhaps, for the craft curious. The difficulty would be permits and financing.

The permit process alone took six months. The entire process, including financing, extended beyond eighteen months. Eventually the Premier Stainless seven-barrel system, valued at almost $150,000, was installed. Alex Taylor, the director of operations of Frisco's Taphouse and Brewery, noted the help they received from the Maryland brewing community, from Evolution Brewing to Ellicott Mills. Not only did these brewers provide guidance to navigate the choppy waters of opening a brewery, they also provided a brewer to get things started. Ray Andreassen moonlighted for Push American Brewing to get it rolling and has continued to be an advisor since the brewery opened. Other brewers have come to work at Push during this time, including former home brewer Chris Meyers. This was a critical component, mitigating risk by hiring a brewer experienced with industrial equipment to train incoming brewers. There was still a learning curve with the system and the recipes that they quickly overcame. The recipe adjustments centered on the IPA and the need to dry hop.[127] This was swiftly corrected, much to the delight of consumers.

By August of 2012 the brewery was operational and serving Push beer on tap. According to *BeerAdvocate* ratings, Push has done what it set out to do, with an average rating of 93 percent out of 100 percent since they opened.[128] This was no small challenge. Like other Maryland breweries, Taylor also saw the role of Frisco's as one of educating the consumer about craft beer while offering a menu that runs the range of safe and expected to experimental and exotic. Taylor believed that craft beer drinkers are adventurous at heart and more willing to explore rare and untried foods. As far as education, he noted that he has turned 95 percent of the macro beer drinkers who come to Frisco's into craft beer drinkers, through education not intimidation. He grasped how scared new craft beer drinkers are and worked diligently to make it as painless as possible for them to explore new beers based upon what their own taste preferences are. This is where his extremely educated bar staff closes the gap and introduces novice beer drinkers to a new and wonderful world of diverse flavors and aromas.[129] A quick read of the *BeerAdvocate* reviews verify this "education" and "conversion" to craft beer by many Frisco patrons.

What comes next for Frisco and Push? The long-term plan is for expansion into an industrial facility once demand reaches the point the 1,000-barrel–capacity system can no longer meet requirements. In the meantime, Frisco's has begun distributing Push to other bars and restaurants and will continue to educate patrons with the host and guest beers, sponsoring beer dinners, and collaborating both locally and nationally. They have engaged in fruitful collaborations with Heavy Seas, Troegs, Yards, Flying Dog, Terrapin, Brewdog, and Boulevard thus far with positive results. Push will continue to let the creativity of its brewers guide the direction of the beers in conjunction with the tasteful demands of the consumers. Ben Little, brewmaster in 2014, did a remarkable job improving the Reckless Ascension IPA, accepting praise for his efforts. Although he has since moved on to Manor Hill Brewing, the care of the brews and the creativity of the brewers has continued. The success has already generated a need for expansion, not of the brewing facility just yet but of the tap house. In 2014 Frisco's opened a second tap house in Crofton, Maryland. The new location relies upon the same seven-barrel system at the Columbia Frisco's, with hopes to eventually expand into an industrial brewery in the future. The growth is only part of the future for Taylor, as he wants to see craft beer in Maryland become synonymous with Push.

The first industrial brewery in Howard County was Jailbreak Brewing, which opened in April 2014. Oddly enough, the idea was inspired by plans to own a vineyard on the part of wine connoisseur Justin Bonner. The reality of owning a profitable vineyard outside of California was unlikely at best and Bonner shifted gears. He and cofounder Kasey Turner had known one another for years. Like many brewers in Maryland they purchased a beer-making kit on the Internet and experimented with it. As expected, their brew was not a "tasty" concoction. They tried again. They also began to tour breweries across the country to glean insight and information. When they toured Flying Dog in Frederick, Maryland, they noticed how happy everyone was; even the laborers were joyful at their jobs. Neither Bonner nor Turner were happy with their occupations. Congenial Bonner was CEO of a defense contracting company and missed interacting with people like he did as a salesperson. He also longed to have more of a say in the product he was responsible for marketing. Turner was also in the defense contracting business as an electrical engineer and was greatly lacking any job satisfaction. Both helped to build incredibly successful companies, demonstrated by huge growth and investor buyouts. But there was no joy at all.[130]

Bonner decided they needed to open a brewery, something they both believed in. This was the path to bliss for both. They attended the Craft Brewers Conference in Washington, D.C., in 2013. Afterwards, they drew up a business plan from their experience running companies and the knowledge garnered from the brewers at the conference. Bonner quit his job and told Turner to do the same. Turner still needed to stash reserves and continued working while they hunted for a venue for the brewery. Eventually they found a brewing consultant to guide them. One thing was clear: they would not bring in investors but would fund the entire operation themselves.[131]

There was great familial support for the venture. Turner's wife, Erica, also an engineer by trade, was scheduled to go to Seibel to learn the art of craft brewing while Julia, Justin's wife, would help in graphic design. In searching for a consultant, a friend mentioned a relative who was a head brewer at some place called "fish head" brewing. When they called him, it was an Alaska telephone number. Not knowing what to expect, they chatted with Ryan Harvey, who happened to be the head brewer at "Dogfish Head" Brewing in Delaware. Harvey had graduated from the Master Brewer Program at UC Davis and had previously brewed for Alaskan, Keegan, and Empire before heading to Delaware. He was excited to be a consultant for Jailbreak. With a leap of faith, Harvey eventually agreed to leave Dogfish Head in August 2013 to become brewmaster at Jailbreak. Erica took online classes from Seibel to become Harvey's assistant brewer and they began recipe formulation on a pilot system in Turner's backyard.[132]

Bonner and Turner honed in on a facility in Laurel, Maryland, at the same time Harvey agreed to move to Maryland. Merrit was most willing to work with them for heavy industrial zoning in Howard County. This was a wait-and-see operation, however, as Turner was concerned with the potential legislative and zoning changes required and waited to sign the lease. Howard County had limited manufacturing, low vacancy rates, and mostly catered to the defense services industry; therefore a brewery was not at all standard. The backup plan if things did not go forward in Howard County was Baltimore, a county possessing vast experience with zoning of industrial breweries. Howard County executive Ken Ulman reached out to help with the zoning and legislative side of things if Turner and Bonner would work with him to open the brewery.[133] Peter Franchot's office also offered aid to get them started on the tedious and somewhat painstaking process.

The lease was signed, the equipment ordered, and the brewery was in process. The estimated expense was $1,000,000. The actual expense was double that. This was a surprise considering the research and experience of Jailbreak's founders. Where was the miscalculation? There really wasn't one. The problems came with the contractors. Most had limited or NO experience working on a brewery, so there was a learning curve—at the owners' expense. The architectural drawings alone totaled $50,000. Additionally, the permits and zoning requirements produced many legal hurdles to jump over, despite help from the state and county. Again this came at the owner's expense, along with the five attorneys they regularly consult with to make sure everything is in order, from taxes to trademarks to human resources. The last budgetary issue was perhaps avoidable but would have detracted greatly from the finished product: the tap room. The tap room was inspired by Stone Brewing and Greenflash Brewing out of California.[134] This culminated in a beautiful mix of stone, industrial lighting, piping, and décor, with flat-screen TVs, a shuffleboard, and a warmth that flows through the incredible picture window into the brewery for all to see. Jailbreak by many is considered to have one of the most beautiful tap rooms in the state. Money well spent!

Like every new business there were a few glitches that hindered the start, but for-

The Jailbreak bar, with beautiful stonework surrounding the picture window into the brew house.

The Jailbreak brew house with argolith tile floors to mitigate chemical damage.

tunately there was nothing major. The more-than-anticipated expense for the lawyers almost tops the list, with patent attorneys alone averaging just under $800 an hour. For the brewery it was a little challenging as well. The gylcol system was oversized for its current usage, the hope being that it would not be necessary to replace it as they expanded. It began to leak shortly after the brewery opened. There had been a solenoid failure and the tank cracked at 39 degrees. Reflecting back, Turner thinks he should have gone with cool fit instead of copper pipes, but it is done now. These were very small issues on the scale of what typically happens with a brand-new brewing operation. Despite the hiccups, Harvey and Erica began brewing at the new facility in March of 2014. Turner quit his job a month later. Operations have run smoothly, and perhaps that is due to the design of the brewery. The boiler is kept in a separate room from the 20-barrel brew house, which has a "Big Ass Fan" to keep things cool for the brewers. The brewery floor is made of argolith tile, which is resistant to chemicals (and damage). This mitigates any repair or resurfacing long-term, a wise investment that demonstrates the plan for a strong future.[135] This future is already knocking on their door, necessitating the acquisition of the 5,000-square-foot space next door to them for immediate expansion that will include a quality control lab and offices. This facilitated the moving of some materials to make room for more fermenters, which were desperately needed. Jailbreak opened in April 2014 and the demand since has been quite high, enough so that they needed to produce more beer. The maximum capacity of this brew system was 4,000 barrels per year, and they breached that capacity. As expectations were exceeded, Jailbreak doubled capacity by obtaining the industrial spaces on either side of them in 2015.[136] They also brought in five additional fermenters. It was more than Turner could have hoped for. In addition to the fermenters, as Jailbreak never chooses quantity over quality, they installed a new canning line and with that a DO (dissolved oxygen content) seam checker to quality check the beer in the cans. They are only the third brewery in the state to invest in a seam checker, along with Heavy Seas and Flying Dog. Jailbreak also added a grain silo, which has cut costs while providing increased output.[137]

With this great demand also comes great responsibility. Turner and Bonner wanted to build a company where the product was of great quality and always fresh. They brew on the days the yeast is delivered. They have hop contracts going out seven years, but the grain is ordered as needed and delivered regularly. Any beers that do not turn out as planned are dumped instead of being added to other tanks. What is most important to them is to build their company from within and provide for the employees. Beginning August 1, 2014, Jailbreak provided health benefits to all full-time employees. Including the owners, there are more than a dozen full-time employees and expanding. Jailbreak wants the employees to become invested in the company, to be a part of the success and benefit from it. Harvey made the move to Jailbreak not only because he had control over the brewing process and the products he was creating, but he was also offered ownership potential with his position. This is something remarkable. It builds a legacy for those employees who choose to stay with the company as potential shareholders in the future.

With every new beer produced at Jailbreak there is a story as to why the beer exists and what it represents. The espresso stout Dusk till Dawn uses espresso beans roasted in Annapolis: they wake you up at dawn and renew you at dusk. The Decider, their apple cider-based ale, comes from McKutchins and is pressed the day it is delivered to Jailbreak, with honey from Lancaster, Pennsylvania. Jailbreak has two hundred fifty-one Beta testers trying every new formulation before it gets to the public. A very honest lot, they offer stark criticism that has helped to hone the beers into quality craft brews. Theses testers were also counted on to judge the quality of the brews in cans when the canning line was added. Whether draught or can, the taste must always be the same. That is quality, which demands consistency. They have also heard the consumers when they demand better than the food trucks as an accompaniment to the brews. Jailbreak is considering changing their industrial license to a brewpub license now that they have the space to add a restaurant.[138] This could bring in more patrons but also more bureau-cratic headaches.

Turner and crew also desire greatly to give back to the community that supports them. Charitable events are commonplace at Jailbreak. Barely a month goes by that Jailbreak hasn't hosted a fundraiser for a worthy cause, whether fighting multiple scle-rosis or helping homeless quadrupeds. Jailbreak is prepared to help by hosting and donating. Recently, Jailbreak stepped up to help when it counted the most. The horrific and devastating flood in Ellicott City in July of 2016 destroyed the town and left many people without jobs, homes, and businesses. The brewery not only held a fundraiser and raised thousands for the victims but also collaborated with Flying Dog Brewery in creating an IPA, Watershed Moment, immortalizing the instantly recognizable town clock that was swept away in the flood waters. All of the proceeds were donated to the victims of the flood. There is a clear understanding of community, and Jailbreak serves those in need.

The name Jailbreak springs from a desire to escape from those things that pull you down. Turner and Bonner escaped the corporate nine to five that was depleting and drowning them. They offer an opportunity to escape from whatever ails you, whether a rough day at work or bad traffic. Jailbreak wants you to smile and relax and enjoy really good beer. With more than a dozen different beers to choose from there should be something to make anyone smile. That, however, is not the only legacy they hope to leave. Forty years from now Jailbreak wants the employees to buy the company from them as part of their 401(k) package. This will be the last job Bonner or Turner will ever have, but the brewery will live on in the possibility of escape from the everyday.

11

The Rise of the Modern Craft Brewer, Part 2

The resurrection of the Maryland brewing industry was not limited to the Baltimore region and the Eastern Shore. The rejuvenation touched every corner of the state, from the deepest southern territory to the farthest western reaches, leaving no palate unquenched.

Calvert County

Carlos Ynez had a dream and the availability of land through his father-in-law. He also had a strong partnership with Michael Kelley, a restaurateur behind such places as Tavern on the Green in New York City who helped make that dream a reality. The curious name was chosen by a focus group of 10 friends who were given a list of names. All of the friends chose "Ruddy Duck," a name which was misrepresented to Ynez the first time he was told of it. A friend jokingly told Ynez the "Ruddy Duck" was a duck that migrated from South America to Southern Maryland annually, much as Ynez had migrated to Southern Maryland from Argentina. This was not true, of course, but the name stuck, as did the plans to use the duck theme not only to denote the brewpub as a Southern Maryland original but also a child friendly, family friendly location. The artwork alone is inviting, not only for the wee ones but also the accompanying adults. This is a focal point of the restaurant and a platform for the brews and the conversation.[1]

Ruddy Duck opened its doors in June 2009. It was quite a process, as the journey was weighed down in the mire of compliance regulations for this first brewpub in Southern Maryland, which was also, unfortunately, coupled with a flagging economy. In addition, the 10-hectolitre brewing system ordered from China sat in the parking lot for almost two years and the brew kettle never reached a boil once it was filled. A copper coil (with steam) was added, all electrical components were replaced, and brewing finally commenced. Other difficulties existed outside of the equipment, as the pH content of the water needed to be adjusted and a softener was added for the occasional appearance of gypsum or calcium chloride. This was finally solved and by 2010 Ruddy Duck was producing award-winning brews in Maryland.

Ynez, an engineer by trade, was also an accomplished home brewer and distiller who landed in Maryland after living in London, Holland, Belgium, and Argentina. To

Top: Ruddy Duck brew house highlighting the award-winning brews with the several medals prominently displayed. *Bottom:* Carlos Ynez, cofounder, and Matt Glass, brewmaster, Ruddy Duck, 2013.

say that he brought his experienced palate and passion for outstanding beer and food into this brewpub would be an understatement. The beer is crafted by hand on a manual system (except for the regulation of tank temperatures in the fermenters). One expects nothing less from someone who demands so much of himself and is so attentive to every detail, ensuring his customers receive the very best.[2] Despite all of this, Ynez chose not to brew his own beer. Jonathan Reeves was the first brewer for Ruddy Duck, in 2010. Matt Glass, another Ruddy Duck brewer hired in August 2010, took over primary brewing responsibilities when Jonathan left for a larger brewery. Glass brought with him twenty years of brewing experience, from Florida to North Carolina to Maryland. He helped to create award-winning beers, where quality and consistency were not lost in the transition. It is here where the term "craft" must be emphasized. Glass defines craft beer as one "crafted by hand, where the brewer is physically touching the ingredients to craft this artisanal product."[3] This is also why Ruddy Duck sponsors local home brew events at the brewery, to foster the growth and education of craft beer in the community.

Ruddy Duck uses local ingredients as often as possible in everything they can. The Blueberry Witte contains 80 pounds of locally grown blueberries. Crabs, oysters, and fish are all locally grown and sourced for the pub. One thing Ynez and company would like to see is more locally grown hops and grains. A local farmer was working on fifteen acres of hop fields at the time of the interview. This will take a few years to reach peak, but it is still not enough volume for production at the brewery. This won't hinder the buy local–use local mentality. Ynez has planned for a future where local hops become the mainstay of his brews. Like many breweries in Maryland, Ruddy Duck gives back to the community that supported it through several charitable endeavors.[4]

The community response to the brewpub has remained quite positive. After just two years in business, Ruddy Duck has grown at a rate of 50 percent per year, a feat in the poor economy and given the limited consumer population in Ruddy Duck's community. Business has stabilized, and the name has grown. The future for Ruddy Duck appears quite bright. The awards keep coming from the annual Comptroller's Cup, racking up medals for Maibock, Americana, and Fest. Ynez is in talks with Peabody Heights to contract brew for retail sale, as he would like to access that side of the brewing industry and bottle, or preferably can, his beer for sale. Also, Ynez never rules out a future distilling operation, either on premises or linked with the brewpub. That remains a matter of legislation.[5] Ruddy Duck opened another location on Saint George Island in Piney Point. Expansion is a good thing. Ruddy Duck certainly knows how to manage growth and is looking forward to an extremely bright future, having cornered the brewpub market in Calvert County.

Mully's is the first industrial production brewery in Calvert County. The brewery was founded by Jason and Cindy Mullikin, a husband and wife team. Jason started home brewing with a "Mr. Beer" kit and quickly moved to a five-gallon extract system in his garage. From there he switched to an all-grain ten-gallon system created to emulate a commercial system. He realized rather quickly that brewing was his calling in life, particularly since the beer was so well received. This is where his story begins to diverge just a bit into the unexpected.

One of Mullikin's longtime friends was Marc Moore. Moore and Mullikin played

Marc Moore and Jason Mullikin in front of the fermenters at Mully's Brewery, January 2013.

volleyball together for years. After a bit of time pursuing life in different directions, Marc and Jason once again found themselves back on the court together. At tournaments in places like Virginia Beach, Mullikin would bring along a variety of his home brew for Moore and other players to sample. A following for the beer developed. By 2010 players were not only familiar with Mullikin's beer but also were thrilled when he offered to sponsor a USAV volleyball team as "Mully's Brewery," for which he provided the shirts and a great design. The one team quickly grew to three, and by 2013 there were16 teams, all sponsored by "Mully's Brewery." Mully's was still operating out of Mullikin's garage.[6]

As of January 2013, Mullikin had several life- and career-changing events take place. At the close of 2011, he received a buy-out from his job at Verizon. His wife, Cindy, was in real estate, which was suffering along with the rest of the economy at the time. Mullilkin took a leap of faith down the "rabbit hole," as he said, and chose to open his own brewery. He headed to Seibel Institute to train in preparation for opening a production brewery. One of the most rewarding courses included brewers sharing their stories, including the mishaps and pitfalls of opening and operating a craft brewery. This aided him in creating an incredibly efficient business plan, with provisions for disasters and the unexpected. One of the decisions the Mullikins came to was where to locate the brewery. They wanted it near their home in Southern Maryland. Calvert County turned out to be the ideal location for many reasons. The county was incredibly supportive of a local brewery since none existed at the time. The zoning was exactly what Mullikin needed for opening a brewery and expanding operations as they grew. Water and sewage agreements were easily created at reasonable prices. This self-same agreement has often broken a brewery operation, yet Mullikin was able to work out a manageable fee schedule with the county. The industrial park where the brewery is located was also perfect for a new brewery. The price was reasonable, and the owners were flexible with growth. Once the agreements were in place Mullikin needed equipment.[7]

By another stroke of fate perhaps, the Lazy Magnolia brewery out of Mississippi had equipment to sell. The Hendersons were willing to sell their 15-barrel brew house and four fermenters to accommodate their growth to a 60-barrel system; they were also willing to ship. Mullikin decided to use the fourth fermenter as a bright tank until they could acquire one. As fate would have it this was the same system the Hendersons used to create a GABF medal winner. All the pieces were quickly falling into place at the start of 2013. With a budget of $250,000, the Mullikins were 30 percent under budget and close to operational. Mullikin lined up distributors with a planned distribution of kegs in the tri-county area and slow, controlled outward growth. Moore, as expected, became a large part of the brewery. With his background in finance and gift for public relations and organization he was a perfect partner to help grow the business.[8]

The opening was March 2013, with all of the Mully's Brewery volleyball teams there. The brewery includes a tasting room, tours, events with food trucks and music, and bombers available for purchase. Contests are held for home brewer's to demonstrate their talents as well—perhaps homage to how Mullikin got his start? Eventually a canning line will be added to the brewery as part of the planned growth. Capacity at opening was 1,200 barrels. It appears as if Mully's opening goals have been achieved. Distribution has reached Baltimore and continues to expand every year. Was it destiny? Perhaps, but sustainable quality production and consumer demand will be the key to the success of Mully's. Considering the dearth of breweries in Southern Maryland and the growth of craft beer in the state and the nation, Mully's got started at just the right time. In addition to their fine beginnings, they have also begun collecting medals supporting the quality of beer produced. The Shucker stout and Carmelite Wheat beers won silver medals, and the Jack Straw IPA won bronze at the Dublin Cup in Ireland in 2014. The Shucker stout also won gold at the Kentucky Commonwealth the same year.[9] This is all in addition to the large volume of Comptroller's Cup wins Mully's has taken since opening. Opening match to Mully's!

Carroll

Johansson's whirled into the new century with a firm following and a cornered market in Westminster. New brewer Jay Lampart came on board at Johansson's as a part-time assistant brewer in 2005. By that time things were well established, and Carroll County was celebrating the addition of the brewery to one of their favorite dining establishments. Jeff Warthen, former head brewer, left in summer 2005, and his replacement, Joe McMonagle, moved on to Stoudt's Brewery in Pennsylvania just a few months later.[10] Lampart, an engineer by training, at the time was newly married, with his first child and a healthy love for home brewing in his blood. Lampart's grandfather had worked at Schaefer Brewing Company in the Brooklyn plant. That facility is currently operated by Brooklyn Brewery. There was more to it, as Lampart's combination of engineering, brewing, and pastry chef skills culminated well in his new job and positioned him to take over brewmaster duties.

Since taking over, Lampart turns out about 350 barrels per year (28 barrels per month). He maintains three flagship beers, at least six seasonals, and occasional specials, one such special brew this author had the privilege of brewing with both Lampart and Humbert (from DOG Brewing). It was a re-creation of a historic ale made with shed spruce, heather, and maple syrup. Over more than nine years of head brewing Lampart has only dumped four batches of beer. This was no small feat for a brewery without a pilot system—a true testament to Lampart's ability to brew, repair any problem in the brewery, and quickly assess quality control issues (like needing to replace the lines) affecting his brews. Another factor he contends with is hops. Johansson's has hop contracts for single-year increments. This often leaves a shortage of hops for both flagship brews and seasonal brews. Lampart has learned to adjust, getting creative with hops, and yeast when necessary, based upon availability.

Lampart would like to see more locally grown grains and hops, but availability and consistency are at issue. The brewery, however, has contributed locally to farmers. The spent grain is picked up regularly by a local farmer from Damascus for his livestock to feed on. Eventually, Lampart believes there will be enough demand for more farmers in Maryland to grow hops and produce malting barley. Johansson is also a believer and may even be a purveyor, as he has his sights set on venturing into the farming industry specifically for hops and grains to supply the brewery, along with farm fresh ingredients for the restaurants.[11] This, like everything Johansson operates, would be a family business. His wife and all four children work in the family

Lampart emptying the spent grain at Johansson's. The grain is sent to a farmer that uses the grain as feed.

Jay Lampart and George Humbert collaborating, as they often do, this time at Johansson's.

businesses. Currently his wife, Wendy, handles much of the day-to-day operations and the entire catering end of the business. The children work in various capacities among the assorted restaurants. A farming venture would operate in a similar manner.

What does the future hold for Lampart and Johanssons? Johansson sees further expansion of brewing operations if Lampart moves to Carroll County (he currently resides in Baltimore). The well-traveled corridor between Gettysburg, Baltimore, and Frederick is limited in the number of breweries that are operational (DOG, and Ruhlman's making up the other two). There is much growth potential, as many come from outside of Westminster to partake of freshly brewed ales by Lampart. In addition, the collaborations that Lampart engages in with DOG Brewing also bring more attention to the brewpub. This is a positive for recognition and growth. Additionally the restaurant offers special brewer's sessions to engage the public the second and fourth Saturdays of each month, drawing even more interest.

Lampart, however, has a different idea. As a family man, his focus is always on what is happening in his household and the gift he has been given of a loving wife and beautiful children. With that said, would Lampart desire to open his own brewery? The first concern he revealed includes the growing number of craft breweries in the country. How many is too many? Lampart doesn't know but quotes Papzian: "Something has to give." Too many breweries in the industry is not a formula to make money or support your family, which is always his first priority. Lampart continually self-assesses to find the niche that he fits into. Working several jobs, as he does to support his family, he is sure burn-out is near and something will have to give, at least for him. One thing he is certain of is that God has a plan; he hasn't been informed of the plan just yet, but that has always been fine.[12] However, little did Lampart know the plan was to be quickly be revealed. He opened his own home brew shop right across the street from the brewery, partnered with Johansson once again. Westminster House of Brews saw its debut in 2015 in a county filled with eager home brewers beyond pleased to have a local resource and experts to answer any questions about brewing. The business has fared well and has met with great reviews from many local home brew clubs like Midnight Home-brewers League. The future is looking bright indeed for Lampart and Johansson's. "There is a beauty that we never know what the future holds."[13]

Greg Norris was not native to the Carrol County area but was an exceptionally knowledgeable brewer. He spent years in the industry in a variety of positions, most critically installing new brewing equipment and creating recipes to accompany those systems. His experience spanned the likes of Anhauser Busch, Coors, and the Guinness Brewery in Dublin. He finally decided to settle down and open his own brewery when he was informed by his employer, brewery engineering firm Tuchenagen, they would be shutting down operations in Maryland. He rented a 4,000-square-foot space in an industrial park in Westminster, a city that seemed eager for another local brewery. Nor-ris invested just over $500,000 in the space and equipment to get the brewery off the ground,[14] and Clay Pipe Brewing was born. His extensive practice in recipe creation coupled with his brewery system engineering background equipped him well for the 15-barrel system he created and the recipes that followed. His notable best seller, Backfin pale ale, was a supple ride not overpowered by the hops and aptly named as a perfect beer to partner with Maryland blue crabs. Norris came up with a host of other styles that also garnered many accolades. The Hop-Ocalypse was the counter to Backfin and drew the hop heads like a bunny to carrots. He welcomed visitors to the brewery and even produced YouTube videos to spread brand recognition.

After a few years in business, Norris had reached half of the brewery's capacity. He wanted to add a bottling line to get his beer to market for consumers to take home. In addition to the beers he was producing under his own brand, he was taking in con-tract brews from other brewers for production. In 2006 he shifted to contract brewing with Flying Dog, which had an advanced bottling line he longed to take advantage of. Norris maintained an office on Carroll Street for the purpose of marketing his beer. To be as profitable as he needed to be, the brewery needed to expand beyond what he was willing to invest in time, resources, and sacrifice. It was named after his children, and family time was a precious commodity he was unwilling to compromise with. By 2010 Norris called it a day for Clay Pipe Brewing.

The brewery in Westminster did not remain dormant, however, as another brewer was ready to take the reins. George Humbert is a kind-hearted, unassuming man, low-key and contemplative, yet extremely determined and dedicated to his family, his craft, and his community. He worked at Olde Towne Tavern in Gaithersburg prior to its changing hands. There he learned the business and used that knowledge to springboard his venture into the pub business. Thirsty Dog Pub was opened on Cross Street in Fed-eral Hill in Baltimore in 2001. Gourmet pizza was the attraction, along with the excellent beer selection. It was the best of both worlds for most pub goers. When Humbert found out that Norris was selling the brewery, he was ready to invest in more reasonable hours to accommodate his growing family. Thus DOG Brewing was created.

Humbert embraced the new role and flourished. He developed a host of DOG beers to match his gourmet pizzas at his Cross Street pub, now renamed Pub Dog Pizza and Drafthouse. Not only did Humbert produce his own line, he also accepted contract brews from talented brewers like Brian Strumke who were looking for opportunities to get their products to market. Within a year another Pub Dog location was added, in Columbia, Maryland, to serve the suburban community. Humbert eventually added a bottling line to the brewery as well, allowing the DOG line greater consumer reach. He takes part in all the local events, including the Union Mills microbrewery festivals, where many people get to sample his beers, and he also judges the home brew contest creating the victor's beer at DOG Brewing with distribution in Buffalo Wild Wings.[15] This was absolutely about recognition for his beers, but it was also about community. Humbert, like neighboring brewers Jay Lampart and Henry Ruhlman, always makes himself available for regional events, whether a charity or the local historical society. Humbert is also a man who enjoys delving into history, re-creating pre–Prohibition recipes as he did for the Hops in History event in 2014. He has always been willing not only to collaborate with other breweries, as he has done many times, but he also has a knack for taking in displaced quality brewers (like Eric Gleason) when they are between brewing jobs. He is often mentioned as the brewer many other brewers in the state want to collaborate with. This is not surprising, as he is willing to take risks, like his decoction cereal mash using Hopi blue corn for his Belgian Blue Corn Tripel. Perhaps it is his easy nature or his calm demeanor or merely the fact that he consistently brews quality beer. He is a technician, as is often proven when the Comptroller's Cup rolls around each year and DOG Brewing brings home the medals. Blond Dog, and Hoppy Dog are just two regular award winners that continue to mark Humbert's territory in craft beer.

Frederick

As the years have passed since its inception, Brewer's Alley has become known well beyond the Frederick city limits. Many people in Baltimore and Washington will travel there for a great meal and an even better brew. With the resurgence of craft beer, Brewer's Alley could not keep up with demand. The seven-barrel system was not enough. Bowers and Flores have since opened Monocacy Brewing. Most of the brewing operations for Brewer's Alley have been moved to Monocacy, and Brewer's Alley has shrunk to a three-barrel system fit for special firkins. Currently the yield at Monocacy is 3,000 barrels per year. The brewery facility itself can be expanded as needed since there is room for more growth.[16] The first priority is crafting quality beer in the new facility to supply Brewer's Alley and the surrounding markets.

Flores would love to use predominantly locally grown hops and malting grains for brewing. Both climate and investment are factors in the limited availability, but that is expanding with more hop growers over 2012–2016, and projected growth in hop farming is on the rise. Amber Fields is a collaboration between Flores and Greg Clabaugh, a dairy farmer. This was a planned grain farm and malting operation specifically for beer production at Brewer's Alley and Monocacy. The operation began in 2000, with the hope of being the first malt house in Maryland since Prohibition to use its own Maryland grain for malting purposes. The plan is eventually is to open a farm brewery on premises. Thus far the operation has been a success, and malting operations have provided enough grain for special and seasonal brews since 2011.[17] Monocacy truly has represented Maryland from hop to malt in a manner not witnessed since Prohibition shut down the breweries of old. Monocacy and Brewer's Alley have continued expanding distribution and collecting medals. They are a Maryland brewery born and bred

Tom Flores proudly displaying the new Monocacy Brewing logo glass.

Brewer's Alley, Frederick, Maryland.

and will continue for the forseeable future. As Flores stated, Monocacy isn't about gimmicks, it is about the beer from harvest to bottle.[18] This is evidenced in every sip. Flores has also stepped up his presence by becoming a Board Member representing Brewpubs with the Brewer's Association of America, allowing every brewpub in the nation to receive the benefit of his tutelage and expertise.[19] Flores certainly is a shining star for Maryland breweries. Monocacy however is not the only industrial brewery in Frederick.

Jim Caruso tasted his first beer at the age of five. There is no need for shock at that young age, as Caruso hailed from a family of Old World tradition of mixed Italian and Russian descent. This is where his love of true craft beer began, although the route to operating a brewery was a circuitous one. Jim graduated with a master's degree in economics, which led him to a variety of different positions. He was president of large restaurant chains, and he even operated a wine store, but his passion remained in beer. While in Denver in 1988 he was offered an opportunity to partner with John Hickenlooper (later governor of Colorado), who wanted to create a brewery and save historic buildings in Denver. The solution for one historic structure was to convert it into a brewpub (Wynkoop). This worked extremely well and was Colorado's first brewpub in Lower Downton (LoDo) Denver. Eventually this became the blueprint for Caruso and Hickenlooper—building breweries in historic buildings and selling them.

This is also how Caruso met George Stranahan, brewer and owner of Flying Dog brewpub in Aspen, Colorado. Hunter S. Thompson was a tenant of Stranahan in one of the many properties he purchased to prevent developers from destroying the mountain scenery. A joint venture was formed between Flying Dog and Wynkoop in 1994 to merge as Broadway Brewing Company in the historic Silver State Laundry building on Broadway and Market. Brewing and bottling were completed for both breweries in the facility. Unfortunately, although they had rights to the Rocky Mountain acquifer, they did not use the resource due to the lack of access to the water in the historic building. By 2000 Flying Dog (and Caruso) had bought out Hickenlooper's interest in the brewery and it was renamed Flying Dog. Caruso and Hickenlooper parted ways, the latter heading into politics. Caruso closed the Aspen brewpub as it was not profitable. Flying Dog moved out of the historic building into a brand new structure across the street (Blake Street), where production quickly reached 38,000 barrels annually and water access was no longer a factor. By this time they were shipping to forty states. Things were profitable and the quality of the beer always consistent. The Great American Beer Festival medals were all the proof he needed. Caruso had exactly what he longed for in beer and in business and a trusted brewmaster to see it through.

Matt Brophy started home brewing as a teenager after hearing an NPR interview with Charlie Papazian regarding the *Complete Joy of Homebrewing*. This captured his imagination and he read the book in one day. He has been home brewing ever since. He augmented his knowledge of brewing with other books and much practice until he was twenty years old. By that time he knew he wanted to brew professionally. In 1997 Brophy wrote a letter to Joe Petriccini, the head brewer at Flying Fish in New Jersey, asking for a job. He was hired as a brewery helper and was able to learn from start to finish each part of the industrial brewing process, including the intricate installation aspects like glycol lines and malt conveyance equipment. Flying Fish was a great place for young, aspiring brewers to work. It was a collaborative environment, with great mentors willing to teach and allow for creativity to blossom.

By the spring of 1998, Brophy headed off to the Seibel Institute in Chicago to expand his brewing education. He enrolled in a variety of classes including "Microbrewers Preparation Course" and "Quality Control, Microbiology, Engineering," and myriad others. Later that year Joe Petriccini left Flying Fish and Brophy was offered the assistant brewer position. Culturally at that time New Jersey was a challenging market and he was interested in living in a more "craft centric" culture. He took a road trip through the South and then headed to the West. Somewhere between Pueblo and Boulder he decided to move to Colorado. He drove home, told his girlfriend they needed to move to Colorado and left with $3,000 and no job.

After two weeks of living in Col-

Matt Brophy, chief operating officer (former brewmaster) of Flying Dog Brewery.

Flying Dog lab, where everything is tested to assure quality, and the utmost QC measures are taken including measuring dissolved oxygen content for the cans.

orado at a campsite and with no job, Brophy finally found an apartment in Denver. He was also offered a position at Great Divide Brewery in filtration and packaging. In late 1999 he became a brewer and was eventually promoted to head brewer by 2001. At the time, and still today, Colorado was a close-knit group of brewers that comingled extensively. In 2003 the manager at Flying Dog was seeking a new brewer and hired Brophy away from Great Divide. Brophy was ready to make the move. Unlike Flying Fish, Great Divide was not a collaborative environment that welcomed creativity, but Flying Dog most certainly was. Flying Dog embraced change and collaboration at every step. It was just the environment a brilliant young brewer could thrive in. One of the earliest, and perhaps bravest, changes for Brophy was the suggestion to Eric Warner that the Snake Dog IPA was not assertive. The original recipe was an English ale made from Goldings hops. Brophy suggested using Columbus hops, which since has become the current recipe for Snake Dog.

As blissful as the work at Flying Dog was, change was on the horizon. By 2005 Flying Dog had reached capacity and was looking to grow into another facility. Flying Dog was distributed in 48 states, with the majority of sales east of the Mississippi. The concern revolved around shipping the beer east more efficiently while keeping it fresh. The opportunity to open a second Flying Dog Brewery presented itself in the form of the bankruptcy of the Frederick Brewing Company in 2005. Caruso decided to buy the facility and open Flying Dog Brewery, the East Coast edition, in 2006. The brewery was purchased for $1.6 million dollars and was large enough to produce 100,000 barrels per year with room for expansion. This was no easy undertaking and a difficult decision for Brophy, who had moved himself to Colorado years before with only change in his pockets and hopes of a brewery job. As with many difficult decisions, it came down to family. By now a father of two, having grandparents in the vicinity of his new location was all the push Brophy needed to pack up his family and head back East.

Running two breweries two thousand miles apart was not easy. From 2006 to 2008 reciprocal tastings had to be done from each brewery to verify the taste was exactly the same regardless of the brewery the beer originated from. Luckily for Brophy, the water profiles in Frederick and Denver were quite similar, causing fewer problems in the duplication process. As for the labels that came with the purchase of the Frederick Brewing Company, some were quickly sold (Crooked River, Little Kings, Hempen, and Brimstone). Flying Dog retained the Blue Ridge label and continued to produce Wild Goose for the first four years in business in Frederick. Eventually the decision came, in 2008, to close the Denver brewery completely. This allowed for greater efficiency in production and distribution. Coupled with the size of the Colorado brewery (maximum capacity of 60,000 barrels per year) and the untapped market in the East for craft beer, it was the most economically feasible decision to make. Slowly equipment was moved from Denver to Frederick to increase capacity. On January 15, 2008, the last bottle of Flying Dog came off the production line in Denver, Colorado. Denver, however, still has a tasting room for Flying Dog beers, and the public in Colorado still demands their Raging Bitch IPA, among others.

As of 2012 Flying Dog was being distributed in thirty-two states. In 2013, the brewery began operations twenty-four hours per day at about 20 percent below full capacity. By 2015, they breached 97,000 barrels annual output. They have plans for expansion that will take them to 500,000 barrels annual capacity. Currently Flying Dog is producing between 38 and 43 different beers annually. They continue to engage in the management styles and collaborative efforts that have made them successful. Each year they have an all-hands production meeting held at the State Park Tea Room and host what is called "Brew House Rarities." Every person (even those who do not know how to brew) is allowed to present an idea for a new beer. Each person gets three minutes to pitch the idea. In 2012 nineteen concepts were pitched. The selection committee chose twelve. One is produced each month of the following year. The winners were involved in each step of the process, from federal and state approval, recipe creation, marketing, and on to production. Jim Caruso was responsible for the creation of Underdog Atlantic lager. This was a pre-Prohibition style lager demonstrating the true hop characteristics indicative of the time. This became a regular Flying Dog offering. It is a very collaborative process that teaches as well as produces fine craft beers.

Flying Dog also gives back to the state that welcomed them in unconventional and amazing ways. They produce a Pearl Necklace oyster stout that not only aids in the oyster recovery program for the Chesapeake Bay, but they also donate a percentage of the profits of every Pearl Necklace sold to the Oyster Recovery Partnership. In 2014 Flying Dog created Dead Rise, an Old Bay ale in conjunction with McCormick Spice. This very Maryland ale is also philanthropic. A percentage of the proceeds are donated to True Blue, the Chesapeake Bay Watermen's Advocacy group. Flying Dog also challenges themselves to keep the public apprised of what they are producing and how it is produced. They offer tours every Saturday to the public. They have altered their tour planning and strategy to insure that each person understands the process, can ask questions, and can taste everything, from the grains to the yeast to the final product. Videos have been created for portions of the process that may not be visible at the time of the tour. In addition, every member of the staff is trained on the process and the beers. This creates a staff that can interact with the public with strong knowledge of the process and the styles of beer produced. This also provides education, which Brophy and Caruso agree is the key to reaching more consumers: take away the fear, make them comfortable, and they are more likely to give the "craft beer" a try. The most important aspect to employment at Flying Dog is a passion for beer.

This has fomented the growth of the brewery, which has more than doubled in volume including an increase in sales of over 600 percent since 2008. Flying Dog is also one of a handful of American breweries exporting to Europe. It can be found in Italy, the United Kingdom, the Netherlands, and Sweden. There is potential for European growth but never at the expense of the United States market. Caruso will never allow a shortage here at home. This model served them well and continues to do so today. There have been a few hiccups along the way, most recently in 2013 concerning the label dispute with AB-InBev. There is no question that Flying Dog labels are iconic and unique, even a little outrageous. There is also no mistaking the work of Ralph Steadman, a friend of Hunter S. Thompson and the artist responsible for the creation of all the Flying Dog labels since 1995. It was surprising in this age of litigation that the macro producer would approve the use of a label so closely resembled the Flying Dog graphics, but that is exactly what transpired when AB-InBev came out with their Wild Blue and Wild Red beers. These were so incredibly similar in design to Flying Dog packaging labels that consumers purchased them on a quick glance, believing them to be Flying Dog. This cut into Flying Dog sales. AB- InBev denied that it was intentional and remarked that there was no similarity in the packaging. Reports from liquor stores around the country, however, noted that AB-InBev sales reps requested that the Wild Blue, Wild Red, and Wild Black be placed next to Flying Dog on the shelves. Caruso is realistic in responding that Flying Dog would be crushed in legal fees alone if they sued due to the size of the monolithic producer. This may speak more to the attempt of the macro brewers to compete in the craft market and reduce loss of market share, apparently even resorting to infringement and obfuscation.

Despite the impertinence of the macro brewers' attempted intrusion, Flying Dog is succeeding. Future plans include reaching their maximum capacity (500,000 bbls) while still maintaining quality (and GABF and world medals). In the meantime, Flying Dog can be found in local sports complexes like Orioles Park and National Stadium. Frederick will always be home to Flying Dog, even if growth requires the opening of another facility to meet demand. Innovation and community relationships are key, as Flying Dog will never dumb down recipes or damage partnerships to sell beer. Their latest community outreach involves Flying Dog University, which offers a series of "classes" for patrons interested in beer education. The topics range from beer and cheese making to advanced brewing techniques and everything in between. It is a unique and novel idea and the first of its kind from a Maryland brewery.

Montgomery

Growlers has deep roots in the Gaithersburg community. The building was constructed in 1889 and operated as everything from a post office to an auto showroom to town hall.[20] For more than two decades the building served the community as a brewpub. First it was the Olde Town Tavern and then Summit Station. Joe Kalish was the brewmaster for both before taking a brewery position with Williamsburg Alewerks in Virginia. In 2006 Summit Station was purchased by a partnership including chef Alex Zeppos, with plans to completely remodel the menu and the beers. Eventually Zeppos reopened the brewing side of the restaurant and brought in a head brewer. Growlers' new brewmaster, Brett Kimbrough, introduced a pilot system made out of kegs and a new brand of brews. He wasn't shy about coming up with some out of the box ideas like a stein beer, brewed outside in the German tradition of dropping boiling hot stones (granite) into the kettle.[21] Kimbrough definitely brought character to the beer at Growlers along with imagination based on tradition. This brought people back into the brewery.[22]

Eric Gleason became the next brewmaster of Growlers Brewpub. Like many brewers discussed in this book, Gleason started as a home brewer. After his very first batch of extract, he switched immediately to all grain and has done nothing but perfect his craft since then. What was his inspiration for brewing? It can be found in Sam Calagione's book *Brewing Up a Business*. This work by the Dogfish Head founder not only changed Gleason's life, it also motivated him. Originally from Pennsylvania, he earned his degree from American University and was an environmental consultant for fifteen

Eric Gleason, brewmaster with Adam Davis, and Thomas Vaudin, the fabulous brew crew of Growlers, 2013.

years until the housing bubble burst. By that time he was ready to move on to brewing. In 2011 he walked into Growlers and told Kimbrough that he would work for free for one month as a brewer's assistant. If it did not work out Kimbrough could let him go, or if he did work out Kimbrough could start paying him. Not only did Kimbrough pay him, but also, after Kimbrough left in November of 2012 to become head brewer at Vintage 50 in Leesburg, Virginia, Gleason became brewmaster (and accounts payable manager—to make enough to feed his family).

There were many challenges Gleason faced as brewmaster, and he was more than willing to tackle them. He had an eight-barrel brew house with two eight-barrel fermenting tanks, two 16-barrel fermenting tanks, and six keg-only lines. Capacity is 1,200 barrels annually, but Growlers was only producing 800 barrels per year. This was due to a few systemic issues that Gleason sought to correct. First, he needed process improvement to gain efficiency and consistency. The only way to achieve this was to eliminate variables that cause inconsistency, which included replacing draft lines; cleaning the boil kettle after every brew; standardizing the cleaning process; standardizing CIP and cellar work; replacing parts BEFORE they broke, and the like. Along with the aforementioned, Gleason was the first brewer at Growlers to keep an inventory log, a production log, and a maintenance log, and to set up a preventive maintenance plan. Perhaps in what was a critical move, Gleason also signed a hop contract into 2014. Without the guarantee of certain hops, recipes that many consumers loved were forced to alter based upon hop availability. This was a gamble Gleason was no longer willing to take.

These changes were only the beginning. As consistency increased, Gleason's philosophy of brewing began to shine through, and that was the concept of simplicity. He started with the Beer Judge Certification Program (BJCP) guidelines as his base and tweaked slightly from there. He believes great flavors are achieved without twenty ingredients. A base malt, a color malt, and one or two hops as your foundation can create a fantastic beer, using a consistent, clean process and just a few additions beyond that. Furthermore, Gleason has not treated the water. The city of Gaithersburg has great water with a good mineral profile, and Gleason adjusted the recipes to the water profile when necessary. He also acquired a pilot system to test recipes before they occupied valuable time by the brew house. This approach to brewing worked. Demand was so high for the renovated beer menu that the conference room was turned into cold storage to accommodate the growth and the need. His reward was clearly visible in his 2013 Governor's Cup gold medal win that was a culmination of his revamping of the brewery and the process improvements.

Gleason's assistants were not only trained in making great beer through his process, but they also had input. This was a collaborative effort. Just for the opportunity to learn, Thomas Vaudin, assistant brewer, worked for Gleason for a year before he was paid. By 2015 he was drawing a salary. Adam Davis was a volunteer who had logged three months of unpaid service before he was added to the payroll as funds permitted. Both assistant brewers offered their personal recipes for potential production and had a say in what seasonal or special brew was made. This coincided with his regular education of the staff. All of Growlers' staff were trained on the beers, both style and flavor profiles, to help inform and sell the beer to consumers. Gleason always spoke to the customers; whether receiving good feedback or bad, he never snubbed a customer. This was where he has gleaned critical information on the beers and enabled the brewpub to make necessary changes to the offerings. He has never forgotten his home brewing roots, and dreams. Growlers has allowed the home-brew contest winner from the county fair to help in the industrial production of their beer at the brewpub. This process has not always been easy, however, and has produced some of his toughest critics. There is a vast difference between brewing on a small home brew system and brewing on a professional system. The recipes are adjusted for this difference, but not all home brewers are pleased with the necessary alterations. As with most things, it is a learning process for all.

What does the future hold for Gleason? He would like to own a brewery. He went to the Seibel Institute in Chicago for their "Starting Your Own Brewery" course. It was an eye-opening experience from those in the industry who have been through the journey. A realization that he had no experience with packaging was something he would need to learn to make his dream a reality. One thing he does have is a foundation of strong roots from which everything is possible. When asked what kind of brewery he would like to open, Gleason most likely say he would open a farm brewery as opposed to a brewpub or industrial brewing facility. He is not fond of the complications of food, yet he does not want the separation from the public. A farm brewery accomplishes both. This would also provide an opportunity to delve further into the "local ingredients" trend that he began at Growler's, perhaps by growing his own. As often as possible he used local hops in his brews. There has been limited availability in Maryland with three suppliers to Growlers: Bill Hendry of Granby Farms, Tom Barse at Stillpoint, and Dell Hayes. Additionally he would like to use local grains. Copper Fox in Sperryville malts their own grain but it is an unmilled grain more suitable to smoked beers, which are made only periodically at Growlers. Other brewery options include opening in Annapolis or Washington, D.C., viable, underserved markets. Beyond a solid, in-demand brewery Gleason would like to open a distillery. Whatever the future holds, he is clear on one thing. When asked what legacy he wanted to leave behind he replied, "Wow! That guy had a solid approach, a good foundation, and believed in the right things: a good product, and a good service."[23]

In September of 2013, Gleason demonstrated his prowess to the state with his Yorkshire porter. This iconic Gleason creation won gold for best in category (porter) and overall best in show in the Comptroller's Cup. In addition, he took home gold in the Specialty/Fruit category for his Freaky Kreiky, and a bronze in the stout category for his Broken Shovel.[24] Gleason continued on this path of making a really great beer until nature intervened. In May 2014, Growlers was forced to undergo remodeling due to the catastrophic flooding that struck the building. This forced the closure of the brewery until August 2014, when renovations were complete, forcing brewers to find employment elsewhere in the interim. This was also when a new brewmaster was brought in to get the beer rolling once again. Kevin Lesniewski was hired as Growlers' new brewmaster. A charismatic fellow known as "Dude," Lesniewski continued Gleason's award-winning recipes and has added a few of his own, along with the home brewer's contest. Gleason moved on to work for DOG Brewing but has kept working toward opening his own brewery.[25]

Over the course of the brewpub's history, many employees and customers noted strange events occurring in the building, ranging from things moving unexpectedly without explanation to doors opening without human assistance. Most striking was the bar stool that went from the floor to the top of a table with no humans in the room when it happened. All of this led to a paranormal investigation, the results of which were unknown to the staff. There is no doubt that renovations may have stirred supernatural talk once again. Whatever may reside in this historic structure, hopefully the spirits are happy with progress and enjoy great beer. Before Gleason got a chance to open his own brewery, he was offered the head brewer position at Barley and Hops brewpub in Frederick. He has of course knocked it out of the park, winning gold in the 2016 Comptroller's Cup in his very first year in the position. There is a bright future in store for him—and for the present in an already-established brewery.

Others dreamed of opening a brewery in Montgomery County to reach an underrepresented market, more specifically within the city limits of Rockville. To describe this Dane as a jack-of-all-trades, a Renaissance man, or a dabbler in just about everything is an untruth, as he is so much more. The Dane, Paul Rinehart, came from a family (on the paternal side) of brewers. His family settled in the United States in the eighteenth century in New Market, Maryland. During Prohibition his great-grandfather (a member of the board of directors of Carlsburg Brewing) made moonshine and his great-grandmother delivered it to thirsty consumers. His grandparents live in Denmark next

Paul Rinehart, owner of Baying Hound Aleworks.

to the Turborg Brewery. It was no surprise that Rinehart began home brewing at the age of fourteen and started distilling by the age of sixteen. From his teenage years it was a curious path he took to owning and operating his own brewery in 2010.

Rinehart embarked upon many career paths that eventually led him to his brewery. He began at culinary school in 1992, has held many jobs from apprentice shoemaker, street corner barista, Web developer, chef, ordained minister and finally brewmaster/owner of Baying Hound Aleworks. Rinehart believed every step led him to that point. Working with Montgomery County and the city of Rockville to become the only manufacturing and distribution brewery was at times difficult and at times painless. One of the primary issues he faced was changing (or making up) the laws as they went along to allow for zoning. Once zoning was completed for his nano brewery, Baying Hound Aleworks was off and running in Rockville in a small industrial strip off of East Gude Drive.

Why Baying Hound as a name? Rinehart absolutely loved dogs. He and his wife helped with animal rescue (dogs) when in New York and the name was a natural byproduct. One hound caught their hearts, a bloodhound named Marmelade. She was the inspiration for almost everything in their lives. The name was run before his focus group along with his home-brew samples, and Baying Hound was the unanimous winner. This also explained the artwork—all dogs in various states of repose and action. The name of each beer produced had an equally involved backstory surrounding a beloved canine. Sometimes those were memorials to past quadrupeds, and other times they were flights of fancy. Regardless of the source, they captured the attention and hearts of even those who never had a four-legged friend.

Rinehart operated a one-barrel brew house. It was not much to start with but he produced over 200 barrels per year in 2013. For a nano brewery, this was to be expected. Startup costs hovered around $40,000. Rinehart footed the bill alone to prevent investors and loss of control of the brewery. This also meant he was averaging over 100-hour workweeks. Rinehart was initially responsible for everything from brewing to paperwork to distribution. Within three years he had quite a bit of help. Distribution eventually was handled by Chesapeake Beverage and Dionysos Distribution once Rinehart ceased self-distribution. He also received help from Leigh Anne Alexander. Alexander, a trained chemist, came in with a home-brew sample one day and became a fixture at the brewery, teaching home-brew classes, aiding in quality control and handling some administrative angles. Alexander operated in a strictly volunteer capacity. Rinehart welcomed the home brewing community into his brewery in a variety of functions. Some wanted feedback on their brews; others want to help brew. This was where Rinehart gave back to those who helped him. Instead of payment for their services, Rinehart held contests to allow the winner to brew at the brewery and get distribution through the Baying Hound brand. In addition to the winners, every "employee" got to produce their own pilot beer. Quite the incentive!

Notable brewers have been spawned from this process, including Eric Gleason of Growlers fame and 2013 Comptroller's Cup gold medal winner.[26] Gleason was responsible for the Black IPA that became a regular seasonal offering from Baying Hounds. His former assistant also started at Baying Hounds and moved on to Growlers with Gleason when Gleason became brewmaster there.[27] Lindsey Miller was a brewer at Baying Hound in 2011 and has been active spreading the knowledge of brewing among the female population in the community, bringing more women into beer through brewing and tasting classes.[28] Rinehart took pride in fomenting the careers of those volunteers. The last brewer to gain recognition was Chris Kuhn, recognized by *Scoutology* as one of the head brewers to watch in the Mid-Atlantic.[29]

Some of the challenges Rinehart and his volunteer crew faced included standard brewery operations. The water used was Rockville city water, which was generally very good water. Occasionally the pH had to be adjusted. In addition, the heat was a major problem for Baying Hound, and one that did not have resolution, particularly in the warm Maryland summers. Rinehart had an air conditioning unit, but it was not large enough for the facility. He located the a/c unit in a segmented area and placed the fermenter in with it to operate as a chiller. This was critical to Baying Hound operations, as the beer was unfiltered and unpasteurized, becoming even more susceptible to the heat and possible compromise. Additionally, Rinehart had no control over his twenty-two-ounce bombers once they left the plant unless he returned to self-distribution. He acknowledged the mistakes he had made since planning began but felt certain any mistake could be overcome with a quality product. He saw craft beer consumers as numerous and forgiving, willing to try (again) any beer that was handcrafted and thoughtful. He also imagined Maryland as the next Portland Oregon, as the new craft beer mecca.

Rinehart's beers were unique. He and his crew loved to experiment. They brewed a S'more stout (yes, they hand-roasted marshmallows to place in the wort, and graham crackers were added to the mash), Old Bay ale (they wanted to use steamed crabs in the beer but shellfish allergies prohibited this) before Flying Dog, and they discussed a possible cicada beer (specifically for the unique "nutty flavor") but did not put that into production! In addition to the experiments, there were classic styles that many loved including the Black IPA, the Lord Wimsey pale ale, and a brilliant collaboration with George Humbert of DOG Brewing on the Scratch and Sniff red rye IPA. Clearly Rinehart was unconcerned with sticking to Rheinheisgebot, and that was just fine.

Baying Hound received promotional help from the City of Rockville and hosted beer trucks and festivals to introduce the crowds to his brewery. This brought in tourists from Denmark and France to sample his beers, and his beer traveled to Kiev and Seattle via satisfied customers. As word spread, demand increased and Rinehart had to plan for the future. His ideal included a seven-barrel brew house and 15-barrel fermenters, with a bottling line for twelve-ounce bottles. He acknowledged that investors would be a requirement to expand operations, but he wanted to retain controlling interest. He would have liked to have paid his employees, who were often as devoted to the brewery's success as Rinehart was himself. He even considered stepping away from brewmaster duties in the future, providing an opportunity for his protégés without losing touch with the product. Rinehart foresaw the trend of women in beer continuing long into the future of craft brewing. No stranger to hiring women in the brewery, he also noted the many economic development programs for female-owned businesses and credits them with recognizing the growing number of women in the brewing industry. Rinehart desired further participation in more collaborations with other brewers like DOG brewing, Flying Dog, and DuClaw, but he never got the chance.

Sadly, after five years in business, Rinehart closed his doors on March 26, 2016. The brewery was too small to meet the demands of distribution and recognition in a field of larger craft breweries in Maryland. In addition, the space and temperature issues were just too much to overcome. Operating with a predominantly volunteer workforce was also not sustainable over the long haul. What will remain is a legacy of devotion to craft, creativity, and quadrupeds.

Prince Georges

Franklin's is a wonderfully quirky brewpub located just over the Washington, D.C., line in Hyattsville, Maryland. Built in the 1880s as a blacksmith and carriage shop it eventually became a hardware store. Mike and Debra Franklin purchased the Hyattsville Hardware Store in 1992 and converted it into a general store and deli.[30] During the first decade of operation, Franklin's sold beer and wine in the store in addition to the other accoutrements. Franklin noticed that the majority of consumers purchased craft beer, not Budweiser, as the 1990s drew to a close. This was the impetus for him to build a brewpub. In 2002, after quite a bit of construction, Franklin's became Franklin's Restaurant and Brewery. The brewpub was a two-story addition, but the heart of the general store remained, including the craft beer and wine sales. The 10-barrel Bohemian system was installed on the upper level of the pub.

The first brewer was an experienced bloke with a brewer's certification from the

American Brewer's Guild. Charles Knoll brewed for a (now defunct) brewery in California before taking the Franklin's job. He helped install the Bohemian system and created all of the recipes, getting the very first brewpub in Prince Georges County off to a grand beginning. There was a quite a draw, due to location and the novelty. In part the novelty revolved around the kitschy little items still offered in the general store along with the beer, including fun little children's toys, candy, and sassy adult-themed items like fridge magnets. Franklin's has also been known for giving back to the supportive community through charitable events, like hosting fundraisers, from which Mike Franklin turns over 20 percent of the profits for the cause. This endears him to the community, and further cements his ties to the neighborhood.

Knoll continued to brew good, reliable beer for eight years at Franklin's, growing the business and the profitability. In 2010 he departed for New York, and Mike Roy, an experienced brewer from IncrediBrew in Nashua, New Hampshire, was brought in as a replacement. As soon as Roy arrived changes were made to the brewery. Not only did Roy begin regular blog postings in order to keep consumers informed of upcoming beers but a new hopper was also installed capable of holding 1,000 pounds of grain to prepare for the new Belgian style offerings that he created. Roy kept some of Knoll's recipes and intermingled his own in an effort not to alienate the favorites of regular customers. Seasonal brews like a pumpkin beer were introduced for the fall, drawing in a whole new crowd of craft beer lovers. In addition, a host of medals from various beer festivals began to make their way to Franklin's, affirmation of the quality brews. Franklin's certainly is poised for the future, and willing to expand or adapt as needed to meet the demands of the consumers. In 2014, they added a bottling line to place their product in liquor stores and appeal to the non-growler patrons. To date, it is considered the place to be for family friendly meals and craft beer aficionados alike. That is also why Franklin's is opening a sister location in College Park that will have Franklin's on tap, spreading the malty love.

Prince Georges County played host to another brewery in 2016. Calvert Brewing Company is an industrial brewery located in Upper Marlboro. The brewery started as a farm brewery in Prince Frederick. Mike Scarborough and his wife, Barbara, owned a winery, Running Hare, when the realization came to them that beer was the direction in which the business should head. Once the farm brewery bill was passed, they diversified, planting hop acreage and beginning the brewing process. Soon enough they were over their production limits and looked for broader horizons, with eight other partners, to open an industrial brewery. Upper Marlboro provided the perfect location, an untapped market nestled between commercial and residential areas just beginning to thrive.

The facility was extensive and would want for nothing, including a stunning taproom. The brewery also has the most advanced technology available, including the rare IDD Mash Filtration System, one of the most efficient "green" systems available, reducing water, energy, and grain needed to brew. They have ten fermentation tanks (six 60, and four 120-bbl) for the flagship and seasonal offerings.[31] The vast production facility is more than Calvert currently needs for demand although they have expanded distribution across the state and into Washington, D.C. With additional unused capacity, they also operate as contract brewers, like many new industrial breweries, brewing both Greenspring and Smoketown beers. Time will be the determinant to success, but they have left their mark already. The Friday night flip game at the taproom bar has drawn quite a regular crowd of craft beer drinkers. Calvert has, like so many breweries today, saturated social media to spread the brand to potential drinkers. The distinctive and easily recognizable label can be found in most liquor stores. Recognition is slowly coming for the taste of the beers as well, significantly the Cream ale, which garners much local praise. For now the transition from farm brewery (which remains operational) to industrial brewery has been a promising one.

Farm Breweries, or Shall We Say Breweries on a Farm?

So, you ask, just what is a farm brewery? In 2012 Maryland passed the farm brewery bill, creating a class-eight license that allowed farms to not only produce up to 15,000 barrels of beer for sale per year but also to serve pints on premises. Cheaper than a class-five license, this opened the door for many farms already dabbling in the agricultural end of the brewing business to use their own hops, and the like in their own beers instead of just selling them to local breweries. Some farms quickly took advantage of this change, and others opted to stick with the class-five industrial license and open an industrial brewery on their farms.

Adam Fry attended McDaniel College as an English major, earning his degree in 1996. Even at that point in his life he knew he wanted to open a brewery. This instinct ran in the family; Frey's uncle was a home brewer. Frey didn't begin home brewing until he was discharged from the United States Air Force. While serving in the air force he was stationed in Germany, in 1990, with time spent in Frankfurt and Bavaria, which turned him onto weissbier. After he returned home Frey branched into multimedia and in 2004 he used the family farm to film *Hunting Dragonflies*, his feature-length independent movie with local actors playing convicts (which included a hunt for beer).[32] Frey longed for something else, however, and began to brew in 2008. His first brew was a stout with lager yeast (he likes beer dry). By his fifth batch he was making all-grain beers and was motivated toward industrial production.[33]

Frey purchased the farm together with his brothers in 1995 after the death of his mother. His brother's farm adjoins the property and totals 800 acres. This is where Frey created his brewery on a hill. This is not a farmhouse brewery (class 8) but an industrial brewery (class 5) on a working farm. Although registered as a "Class 5" brewery with the state, Frey's is still classified as a farm brewery as far as Frederick County zoning law. Frey started Frey's Brewing Company in a one hundred year old milk house for less than $30,000. He started with a two-barrel system and two plastic fermenters with hopes of producing around 100 barrels annually to start. All beers openly ferment with no temperature control, which, as Frey says, defines a farm brewery by using the same ingredients every time and getting occasionally differing results. Frey's wife, Debbie, was also a home brewer, increasing both experience and knowledge evidenced in the quality beers they produce. Frederick County was quite helpful and easy to work with in establishing the brewery. One exception was a "gentlemen" who prevented Frey

Adam Frey, proprietor of Frey's Brewing, brewmaster and U.S. Air Force veteran.

from pouring tastings for consumers without paying a $5,000 fine for not having a site-two plan. He paid the fine and the health department signed off. This "gentleman" also wanted other restrictions put in place, but Frey was able to go forward without them.[34]

All beers are significantly named based upon military themes. Frey is proud of all of our service men and women and honors them with his brews. This is also the foundation of the logo, based upon a Bolling Air Force Base mockup of stripe patterns for the fledgling United States Air Force from 1948. Debbie's brother was a graphic artist and finalized the design for the brewery. The names intrigue and may seem familiar, like Backwoods Brigade, Pussy Pilot Parade, and the Recruit, or sound cacophonous to catch your ear and lure you in, like Whack Truck McDonkey. The seasonal offerings are just as much fun in name and taste.[35] Frey currently uses no water treatment, and all water comes from a well on the farm. There is some minerality in the water but not enough to compromise the beer. Occasional calcium deposits in the liquor tank occur and are easily remedied. At thirty gallons per minute the well is enough for the brewery at its current size but not enough for the hop farm. The name of Frey's farm is Libertytown Hop. He has been growing hops since 2010. When he opened the brewery in 2013 he understood the hop growth was not enough to sustain the brewery. A second well, three hundred feet deep, was drilled in July of 2013 for hop irrigation to accommodate the growth. Frey grows Chinook, Nugget, Centennial, Brewer's Gold, Mount Hood, Magnum, Willamette, Zeus, and Spalter Select hop varieties. He has also become integral in the start of a Maryland hop farmers meeting, to help foment growth of local hop farms and plan for the future of craft beer. In 2012 Frey produced enough hops to sell to Heavy Seas and Flying Dog for their seasonal beers (Harvest Porter and Secret Stash).[36]

Frey also possesses a W-4 wholesale distributor's license and self-distributes. Although extremely beneficial, since Frey gets his beers in the venues and in the manner that he prefers, it is also time consuming. He averages over 80 hours per week among the farm, the brewery, and the distribution. He has made full-time hires incrementally as business increased to ease his workload. One thing that has helped is the change in growler laws. Growlers are now reusable instead of returnable. When consumers would come to fill growlers, they were by law not allowed to wash them but just return them for a sanitized growler filled with the beer of their choice. The sanitization of the growlers took an entire day every week, a day Frey did not have to spend on the process. With the new law, he has his day to use for the multitude of other duties he faces. He also was relieved at the ability to sell pints to consumers, as the farm is family friendly and a pint may lead to extra income, increased growler sales, and increased demand for his product.[37]

Soon he would like to upgrade to a five-barrel system. Within five years he hopes to graduate to building a separate brewery up the hill from the milk house. This would encompass a 20-barrel system, a bottling line, and a tasting room. This might also require an adjustment to the current well-water system he has in place. Frey is interested in the malting business as a means to become self-sustaining. Currently there are only a few maltsters in the state, but others have begun the process. Frey noted the vast acreage he has available and the possibilities of malting on premises.[38] The difficulty comes with the expense of the malting equipment and United States Department of Agricultural regulations.[39] What does Frey want to leave as his legacy? A quality family-run business passed down through the generations. He has created craft beer that is local, with local ingredients (as much as possible) and always involved the human element (not just pushing buttons). Frey's is a craft brewery that supports the military through beer and happens to be situated on a farm.

Ruhlman Brewing is a true family business in the greatest sense of the word. This also was not the anticipated family business. The Ruhlman family of Hampstead had always farmed. When the senior Ruhlman passed away in 2010, the land was inherited by the children. In addition to the inheritance, adjacent lands were already held by the family. Henry Ruhlman made a decision to begin hop farming on the property in 2007. He did not know where this would take him or for how long, but he forged ahead. In 2011 the hop production reached 1,500 ounces. Ruhlman was excited to see what would become of hops in the future. In 2005 Henry's three sons bought an extract brewing kit for his birthday. Henry delved in immediately and produced three extract brews fairly quickly. The next two included specialty grains. After that, every beer he made was all grain. With the success of the hop growth Henry consulted his siblings and requested that the inherited family land be used for continued hop farming and an industrial brewery. Everyone jumped quickly on board when Carroll County approved the preliminary plans.[40]

The Ruhlman family joined together to make the brewery a reality. In 2012 the brewery opened with brand new equipment at a cost of $300,000. The brew house and

Ruhlman's Brewery, Our Ales on the Carroll County Farm of Henry Ruhlman and family.

10-barrel fermenting tanks were only the beginning. Ruhlman insists that the learning curve was minimal on the professional equipment due to his use of a professional pilot system to work out his brews while the brew house was put on order. The one curve he was thrown was to operate without a filter because it was damaged in transit. All of his beers are unfiltered. Ruhlman uses well water from his property without adjusting the pH, which averages around 5.8 percent. This is ideal for his ESB (a tavern ale) due to the high mineral content. His production includes ales for the time being, as lagers take up too much space and time (in the fermenting tanks). Ruhlman did plan for expansion; there is room for four more fermentation tanks in the 28 × 40-foot brewery. With the exception of his IPA (which requires too many hops) he uses only his own full-flower hops for all of his ales. Extra hops are sold to DOG Brewing for special brews.[41]

The entire Ruhlman family works in the business, Ruhlman's sister runs the retail store and hop fields, and his nephew Jesse is the assistant brewer. Matt is responsible for disc golf, and has since gotten into brewing. This is where Ruhlman is a pioneer and truly thinks outside of the box, with a little help from his predecessors. He believes in family and created none other than a family friendly brewery. Much like those breweries before Prohibition, coming out to the brewery and spending the day should be a family event. This also meant that there must be something to engage in to occupy your time at the brewery. Ruhlman has created a beer garden, a concert hall, horseshoes, corn hole, and a disc golf course (with league play). All of this is accompanied by food

George Humbert and Henry Ruhlman sharing their collaboration brew for the Historical Society of Carroll County.

The hop farm at Ruhlmans Brewery

trucks and, of course, Our Ales, which are crafted by Ruhlman Brewing Company. Those who want to enjoy the summer or fall on the farm can bring tents and stay the night. This truly is a unique experience in the Maryland (and perhaps the national) craft brewing community. This is a treat for the thirsty beer adventurer—a place where families and quadrupeds are welcome and encouraged. Ruhlman keeps things interesting by changing the disc golf course periodically and hosting weddings and special events. The farm truly is a multifunctional business with long term growth potential.[42]

Ruhlman has also reached out through Carroll County events like the Microbrew Festival at Union Mills each September to access a wider audience of craft beer consumers. His historic beers, like the North & South Rebel Rye, based on the Civil War and the Shriver family fighting on both sides. The Shriver family has owned Union Mills since the eighteenth century and they were called upon for grain milling for both Union and Confederate troops in the region when the war broke out. Ruhlman honored their place in history by creating an ale using only hops from his farm and local rye milled at Union Mills. The brew was a hit and really demonstrates what the brewery on a farm is all about: honoring legacy and using local.

Surprisingly, this vision of a brewery on a farm has not culminated in Ruhlman's dream just yet. He not only plans to expand as demand allows, he also envisions growing all of his own grain for his brews on the farm and malting his own. The goal is to be completely self-sustaining. This also extends, at least for now, to distribution. Ruhlman self-distributes in Carroll County and Washington, D.C. His production in 2013 hovered around 200 barrels. For wider distribution he would need to increase production. The current changes in the law favor his ability to self-distribute and he has taken advantage of that. Our Ales has gone ahead with a bottling line for 12-ounce bottles—the most saleable packing for consumers. This will aid Ruhlman in reaching his future goals, which include a full return on the startup investment and distribution throughout Maryland and into neighboring regions like Pennsylvania. To carve out his legacy Ruhlman would like to see production at the brewery increase to full time, instead of the part-time operation he now runs. This is also a legacy he wants to pass down to his sons and nephew to carry on when he retires. As always, Ruhlman keeps it in the family.

So who truly operates a farm brewery in Maryland as opposed to a brewery on a farm? That would be Tom Barse and Carolann McConaughy at their Stillpoint Farm in Mt. Airy, on forty-seven acres.[43] Their farm brewery bears the distinction of being the very first farm brewery under the class-eight license in the state of Maryland. They built the Milkhouse Brewery to not only bring in the rural audience available to them but also to complement the vast hop growth the farm started before the farm brewery license was even available. Barse supplied hops to local brewers like Eric Gleason, when he was with Growlers, and Flying Dog. It seemed a natural progression to open a brewery; after all, there cannot be beer without farmers, and why not have it all in one place? The farm was once a dairy farm, and the scenic views are beyond tranquil. A visit will not only offer the lovely combination of scenery and great brews from a country comfort taproom but also a cornucopia of delightful foods, crafts from local artisans, and a chance (if one so desires) to aid in the harvesting of hops. It's all family friendly and the mirror image of a pre–Prohibition beer garden where one could literally spend the day. It certainly is part of the draw, something that is not lost on Barse and McConaughy.

They have produced quality beers that annually take home at least one award from the touted Brewer's Association of Maryland Comptroller's Cup, which does not hurt in the savvy Maryland craft beer community.

Maryland beer drinkers are not only interested in getting back to locally sourced ingredients, they are also interested in getting back to nature and understanding where things are coming from and how they get from the soil to the glass or table. This brings an educational component to the farm breweries that standard industrial breweries and brewpubs often lack. Milkhouse takes advantage of this aspect as well. They are supported in the community by neighbors but also by one another in the brewing community. Flying Dog, for example, allows small breweries like Milkhouse to use their lab for the development of recipes.[44] Supporting the farmers that supply local ingredients to the breweries is always a good thing. Every brewery has to start somewhere, but all beer starts on the farm.

Another farm brewery in Mt. Airy under a class-eight license opened one year after Milkhouse, Red Shedman's Farm Brewery & Hop Yard. Frederick farmland has been extremely conducive to the growing of hops and planting of malting grains. Like Milkhouse, Shedman's celebrates the beer from soil to glass in one place. With more than two hundred acres, the hop harvest is incredible, with five different varieties to supplement the selection of brews. The Aellen family is perhaps best known for their winery, Linganore Cellars, which many people in the region have frequented for decades. What few knew of them was that Vic Aellen had become a head brewer at a Michigan brewery for several years before returning home to Maryland when the new farm brewery bill passed in 2012.[45] Aellen's background had been in chemistry, which cultivated a perfect marriage in beer. Since the Shedman brewery had the added advantage of an experienced industrial brewer at the helm, it made for a smoother transition from the 15-barrel brew house to the lips of the consumer. The brewery and winery operating on one farm is a draw for every palate. Known for the frequent festivals at the vineyard bursting with music, food, and local craftspeople the brewery has a built-in regular audience to draw from. Additionally they have gotten their kegs into local bars and restaurants to reach more consumers. The brewery has gotten off to a great start and hopes to be a staple of the community just as its sister the winery has been for decades.

The first farm brewery to open in Howard County was Manor Hill. The farm brewery was a project of love, and a complement to the farm-to-table mentality of the owner's first venture, Victoria Gastro Pub. The Marriner family purchased Manor Hill Farm in 2011 to supplement the pub with their own locally grown vegetables and meats. In addition they decided to plant four different kinds of hops. If there be hops, then beer naturally follows. With the new farm brewery license, the Marriner family decided to start producing their own beers to complement the gastro pub local offerings. They snatched experienced brewer Ben Little (formerly of Push and Flying Dog) to helm the operations and the farm brewery was on its way. They settled on a 15-barrel brew house that they situated in a converted barn on the property. By 2015 the first beer was available for purchase at the farm and of course the gastro pub. Within months Manor Hill cans were stocked in liquor stores across the Baltimore-Howard region, becoming a household name. The brewery draws quite a crowd and commonly hosts events at the farm, even ranking among the top "destination wedding" sites in the state. Manor Hill has gotten off to a sprint out of the gate!

Whether it's farm brewery, brewpub, or industrial operation, Maryland is firmly established as a beer destination and continues to grow her ranks of breweries. The quality of the product continues to climb, making a strong challenge to some of the best in the world. She is only getting started on her revival.

BREWERY LISTINGS FOR CHAPTERS 10 AND 11

(Chain brewpubs originating out of state are not included on the list)

Anne Arundel County

BREWERY	PROPRIETOR	LOCATION/ NEIGHBORHOOD	YEARS	PEAK PRODUCTION (IF KNOWN)
Chesapeake Brewing Company	Carolyn & David Marquis	114 West Street	2014– present	400 bbls/yr

Baltimore

BREWERY	PROPRIETOR	LOCATION/ NEIGHBORHOOD	YEARS	PEAK PRODUCTION (IF KNOWN)
Sisson's	Craig & Tracy Stuart-Paul, Paul Morrissey, Tom Cizauskas (Pelion LLC)	36 Cross Street Federal Hill	2000–2002	
Ryleigh's Brewpub & Oyster Bar	Brian McComas, Tom Strawser, Craig Stuart-Paul	Same	2002–2007	750 bbls/yr
Bawlmer Craft Beers	John O'Melia	4401 Eastern Avenue Highlandtown	2010– present[46]	
Stillwater Artisanal Ales	Brian Strumke	Baltimore/contract brewing through-out U.S.	2010– present	5,000 bbls/yr
Dempsey's Brewpub	Rick Dempsey	Camden Yards	2012– present	800 bbls/yr
Peabody Heights	Co-op (Demczuk, Bielle, Albert)	401 East 30th Street Waverly	2012– present	
	Richard O'Keefe	Same	2014– present	24,000 bbls/yr[47]
Full Tilt Brewing	Nick Fertig & Dan Baumiller	Same (contract brewing)	2012– present	2,750 bbls/yr
Monument City	Ken & Matt Praay	Same (contract brewing)	2014– present	300 bbls/yr
Union Craft Brewing	Jon Zervitz, Kevin Blodger, Adam Benesch	1700 Union Avenue Union Mills	2012– present	7,100 bbls/yr

BREWERY	PROPRIETOR	LOCATION/ NEIGHBORHOOD	YEARS	PEAK PRODUCTION (IF KNOWN)
DuClaw Brewing Company	Dave Benfield	8901 Yellow Brick Road Rosedale	2013– present	31,842 bbls/yr
Brew house No. 16 (brewpub)	Harry, Ian, Sophea Hummel	831 N. Calvert Street Baltimore	2015– present	
Key Brewing	Mike McDonald & Spike Owen	2500 Grays Rd Dundalk	2015– present	700 blls/yr
Oliver's Brewing Company	Justin Dvorkin, et al.	Shannon Drive Baltimore	2015– present	2,500 bbls/yr
Waverly	Roy Fisher & Bill Stevenson	1625 C Union Avenue Hampden	2015– present	130 bbls/yr

Carroll County

BREWERY	PROPRIETOR	LOCATION/ NEIGHBORHOOD	YEARS	PEAK PRODUCTION (IF KNOWN)
Clay Pipe	Greg Norris	1203 New Windsor Road Westminster	2002–2006	1,500 bbls/yr
DOG Brewing	George Humbert	Same	2006– present	Unavailable
Clay Pipe	Greg Norris	36 Carroll Street Westminster (Contract Brewing out of Flying Dog)	2006–2010	

Calvert County

BREWERY	PROPRIETOR	LOCATION/ NEIGHBORHOOD	YEARS	PEAK PRODUCTION (IF KNOWN)
Ruddy Duck	Carlos Ynez & Michael Kelly	13200 Dowell Road Dowell	2009– present	630 bbls/yr
Mully's Brewery	Jason & Cindy Mullikin	141 Schooner Lane #15 Prince Frederick	2013– present	563 bbls/yr
Calvert Farm Brewery	Scarboroughs, et al.	150 Adelina Road Prince Frederick	2014– present	257 bbls/yr
Scorpion Brewing	Brian Dailey	929 Skinners Turn Owings	2014– present	175 bbls/yr
Greenspring Brewing Company	Karl & Kerry Puttlitz	2309 Greenspring Chesapeake Beach (contract brew— Calvert)	2015– present	75 bbls/yr

Dorchester County

BREWERY	PROPRIETOR	LOCATION/ NEIGHBORHOOD	YEARS	PEAK PRODUCTION (IF KNOWN)
RaR (Reale Revival)	Chris Browhan & J.T. Merryweather	504 Poplar Street Cambridge	2013– present	3,500 bbls/yr

Frederick County

Brewery	Proprietor	Location/ Neighborhood	Years	Peak Production (if known)
Flying Dog	Jim Caruso	4607 Wedgewood Blvd. Frederick	2006– present	97,330 bbls/yr
Monocacy Brewing	Philip Bowers	1781 North Market Street Frederick	2012– present	1,150 bbls/yr
Frey's Brewing (farm)	Adam Frey	8601 Mapleville Road Mt. Airy	2013– present	150 bbls/yr
Milkhouse Brewery Stillpoint Farm	Tom Barse	8253 Dollyhide Road Mt. Airy	2013– present	500 bbls/yr
Red Shedman Farm Brewery	Vic, Anthony, & Eric Aellen	13601 Glissans Mill Road Mt. Airy	2014– present	750 bbls/yr
Barnwerks Brewery	Maureen Flynn & James Luther	Thurmont	2015–	
Olde Mother Brewing	Nick Wilson & Keith Marcoux	911 E Patrick Street Frederick	2015– present	
Mad Science Brewing Company (farm)	Brian Roberts	1619 Buckeystown Pike Adamstown	2015– present	37 bbls/yr
Smoketown Brewing Station	Davis Scott Blackmon	223 West Potomac Street Brunswick	2015– present	
Barley & Hops Brewery	Lori Lee Keough	5473 Urbana Pike Frederick	2016– present	800 bbls/yr

Harford County

Brewery	Proprietor	Location/ Neighborhood	Years	Peak Production (if known)
Falling Branch Farm Brewery	Alex Galbreath	825 Highland Road Street	2015– present	50 bbls/yr
Independent Brewing Company	Phillip Rhudy	418 North Main Street Bel Air	2015– present	231 bbls/yr

Howard County

Brewery	Proprietor	Location/ Neighborhood	Years	Peak Production (if known)
Jailbreak Brewing	Kasey Turner & Justin Bonner	Washington Blvd. Laurel	2014– present	4,076 bbls/yr
Frisco Taphouse/ Push Brewing	Adam Carton	6695 Dobbin Road Columbia	2012– present	50 bbls/yr
Manor Hill Farm Brewery	Randy & Mary Marriner	4411 Manor Lane Ellicott City	2014– present	1,000 bbls/yr
Black Eyed Susan Brewing Company	Matthew & Susan Levine	9570 Berger Road Columbia	2014	NP
Black Flag	Bryan Gaylor	9315 Snowden River Parkway Columbia	2016–present	
Bulkhead Brewing	Josh Matthews	8980 State Road 108 Columbia	2016	NP

Kent County

BREWERY	PROPRIETOR	LOCATION/ NEIGHBORHOOD	YEARS	PEAK PRODUCTION (IF KNOWN)
Chester River Brewing	Michael Schultz	519 Morgnec Road Chester River	2016	

Montgomery County

BREWERY	PROPRIETOR	LOCATION/ NEIGHBORHOOD	YEARS	PEAK PRODUCTION (IF KNOWN)
Hook & Ladder[48]	Rich & Matt Fleischer	2231 Distribution Circle Silver Spring	2005–2013	
Growlers Brewpub[49]	KB Summit Land LLC	277 East Diamond Avenue Gaithersburg	2006–2015	1,150 bbls/yr
	David Sellman, Carl Verstandig, et al. (227 East Diamond LLC)	Same	2015– present	1,000 bbls/yr
Baying Hound Aleworks	Paul Rhinehart	1108 Taft Street Rockville	2010–2016	240 bbls/yr
Tuppers Hop Pocket Brewing	Bob & Ellie Tupper	Bethesda (Contract via St. George Brewing)	2010–2013	
Denizen's Brewing Company	Julie Verratti, Emily Bruno, & Jeff Ramirez	1115 East West Highway Silver Spring	2014– present	1,140 bbls/yr
7 Locks Brewing (Sligo Mill Brewing LLC)	Jim Beeman & Keith Beutel	12227 Wilkins Ave. Rockville	2015– present	Unavailable
Waredaca Brewing (farm)	Robert & Grechen Butts	4015 Damascus Road Laytonsville	2015– present	20 bbls/yr

Prince Georges County

BREWERY	PROPRIETOR	LOCATION/ NEIGHBORHOOD	YEARS	PEAK PRODUCTION (IF KNOWN)
Franklin's Restaurant & Brewery	Mike Franklin	5123 Baltimore Ave Hyattsville	2007– present	700 bbls/yr
Calvert Brewing Company	Scarboroughs, et al.	15850 Commerce Court Upper Marlboro	2016–present	

Somerset County

BREWERY	PROPRIETOR	LOCATION/ NEIGHBORHOOD	YEARS	PEAK PRODUCTION (IF KNOWN)
Chesapeake Brewing Company	Carolyn & David Marquis	8th Street Crisfield	2009–2014	

Talbot County

Brewery	Proprietor	Location/ Neighborhood	Years	Peak Production (if known)
Eastern Shore Brewing	Adrian Moritz	605 South Talbot St. St. Michaels	2008– present	1,200 bbls/yr
National Brewing Company	Tim Miller	Port Street Easton	2012– present	250 bbls/yr

Washington County

Brewery	Proprietor	Location/ Neighborhood	Years	Peak Production (if known)
Antietam Brewery/Pub	Bill Skomski	37 Eastern Blvd. Hagerstown	2012– present	330 bbls/yr

Wicomico County

Brewery	Proprietor	Location/ Neighborhood	Years	Peak Production (if known)
Evolution Craft Brewery	Southern Boys Concepts (Tom & John Knorr)	201 East Vine Salisbury	2012– present	13,216 bbls/yr
Rubber Soul Brewing Company	Jesse Prall & Frank Hrestak	1930 Northwood Drive Salisbury	2015– present	110 bbls/yr
Tall Tales Brewing Company	Jason Hearne	Parsonsberg	2011– present	

Worcester County

Brewery	Proprietor	Location/ Neighborhood	Years	Peak Production (if known)
Burley Oak	Bryan Brushmiller	10016 Old Ocean City Blvd. Berlin	2011– present	2,200 bbls/yr
Backshore Brewing (former Shorebilly)	Danny Robinson	913 Atlantic Ave. Ocean City	2013– present	600 bbls/yr
Fin City	Vince Wright	Hoopers Crab House Ocean City	2012– present	
Costa Ventosa Winery & Farm Brewery	Jack & Kathryn Lord	9031 Whaleyville Rd. Whaleyville	2014– present	50 bbls/yr
De Lazy Lizard Brewpub	Todd Hayes & Wayne Odachowski	25 Philadelphia Ave. Ocean City	2014–2015	320 bbls/yr
OC Brewing Company[50]	Joshua Aaron Shores	5509 Coastal Highway Ocean City	2014– present	2,000 bbls/yr
Assawoman Bay Brewing Company	Jason Weissberg	4435 Coastal Highway Ocean City	2015– present	330 bbls/yr

12

What the Future Holds

As the future of brewing in Maryland is pondered it is evident that things have improved substantially due in part to medical research touting the health benefits of America's favorite repast. Scientific evidence supports the range of benefits derived from regular consumption of beer, from mitigating the symptoms of rheumatoid arthritis in women to faster rehydration after exercise. Many of these "new" findings actually support the claims of doctors prior to Prohibition. Beer taken daily aids in digestion by stimulating gastric acid secretion and lowers the risk of developing kidney stones by 41 percent.[1] A daily brew or two has also shown substantial benefit in lowering the risk of Type II diabetes, osteoporosis, and heart disease.[2] It seems there is nothing beer isn't good for. Perhaps the most significant finding with respect to the overwhelming medicinal value of beer comes from xanthohumol, a compound found in hops (humulus lupulus). Xanthohumol has been proven to protect brain cells from damage and slow the development of brain disorders such as dementia and Parkinson's disease.[3] Xanthohumol appears to be a super compound, as it is shown to contain anticarcinogenic properties, aiding in the prevention of liver cancer and other types of cancers.[4] It has become common knowledge to marinate meat in beer before grilling to prevent the carcinogenic effects of polycyclic hydrocarbons that often result. Beer as a tool to improved wellbeing is resonating across the globe, and craft breweries are spotlighted in a resoundingly positive way.

Despite the medical benefits of beer, craft breweries of today face many challenges just to remain operational, much less generate a profit. Breweries set up in areas that do not have any local breweries yet established can achieve the greatest success in a short time. A look at the Brewers' Association of America statistics on population and breweries has Maryland near the bottom in the United States with their 2015 analysis. Maryland averages 1.4 breweries per capita, achieving the dismal rank of 34th in the nation. By contrast, consumption of beer per legal adult in Maryland leaves it ranked 26th in the nation, a vast improvement. The result here is that Maryland still has room for growth compared to some states that are almost fully saturated like Oregon and Colorado.[5] With 61 breweries in production and over a dozen more scheduled to open in the next sixteen months, Maryland will still rank near the lower quarter in the country. Room, however, does not always equate to success.

Several breweries have failed in Maryland since the resurgence in the 1980s as detailed in previous chapters. There is no hard and fast rule to success. Mismanagement is often a culprit in failure, along with rapid overexpansion and large debt. The other catalysts toward closure include owners who are not passionate about craft beer. Consumers are discerning and know when the brewer's heart isn't in the brew. That is when they find another brewery that truly believes in its product. With passionate, invested breweries, consumers are willing to forgive and remain loyal even when they occasionally don't care for a product. Every palate is different and that is why so many breweries can succeed—if they offer something different and in demand. Even with loyal customers, quality matters. If a brewery is not consistently producing a superior product, it will not stay in business very long, regardless of loyalty. These, however, are all the standard expected pitfalls of any manufacturing business. Dedication and a great business plan can preempt most of these issues. It is difficult to predict when we will reach the zenith, but for now Maryland is not considered a saturated market and is self-correcting. Breweries that are not turning out a quality competitive product are either adjusting or closing. Breweries that have not invested in sufficient planning are not opening. This allows room for sustained growth.

What is more difficult and threatening to the existence of craft breweries can be found in the internecine legal feuding that has been fomented by the increase in the number of breweries in the nation (over 4,200 as of 2015).[6] The figure is continuing to climb despite a raft of closures. This increase comes with its own set of difficulties to maneuver in the form of legal hurdles. With the craft beer resurgence of the new century, there were necessary legal expenses breweries anticipated, including the retention of trademark attorneys to file paperwork and secure naming rights. Some breweries did not even bother with the trademark of their individual beer names, just the brand. As the industry has crossed into the teens of the new millennium, breweries find themselves in dire circumstances for labeling and naming both annual and seasonal brews if not already trademarked, making it difficult to release the beers at all.

Trademark infringement has become the centrifugal force in closing down breweries, from the legal expenses alone, not only to protect the trademark or to prove a lack of infringement but also to fight onerous trademark enforcement of truly generic terms that became proprietary (and perhaps never should have been). In the early years of the craft beer boom, most infringement issues were resolved with a phone call (brewery to brewery) or even a letter. This solved the issue the majority of the time and all was settled without the involvement of lawyers. Today, however, things have taken a decidedly different turn. Candace Moon, Esq., known as the "craft beer attorney," operates out of California. Her specialty is trademark filings and trademark dispute resolution. Moon has noted that there are only so many beer-related names to go around, and at any given time breweries are infringing upon a trademark—often unwittingly.[7] In his article for the *Salt*, Alastair Bland noted that almost every large city name and weather pattern has been trademarked by breweries, leaving little room in this growing industry.[8] What is more disturbing is the attempted trademarking of generic beer terms like "nitro."

In September of 2013, Lefthand Brewing Company of Colorado, which is one of the most saturated beer markets in the nation, filed for a trademark of the word "nitro." Nitro is not a term that could be exclusive to a single brewery, as the technique using nitrogen to carbonate the beer instead of just CO_2 is used throughout the world to produce a smother, creamier beer. Lefthand claimed it was the first to do this in a bottle, although many breweries have engaged in the process of nitrogenating beer prior to this, not necessarily in a bottle. The term "nitro" is a descriptor indicating that carbonation was not strictly CO_2 and the consumer should expect the creamier mouth feel. If Lefthand won the patent, how the labelling of the process would be indicated on a bottle, label, or draft for other breweries would be the point of contention. Although the trademark had been owned by a brewery in British Columbia it was cancelled in January 2014. Lefthand fought the trademark for years to install the term "nitro" on their bottles. Thus it was baffling that they would then apply for that trademark. Eventually they abandoned the trademark pursuit, in November 2014, after several months of backlash in the industry, including legal challenges from Anheuser-Busch and Boston Beer Company.[9] Common sense prevailed. The question is, will it remain?

In Maryland, the Brewer's Art was fighting an infringement claim in 2014 for their Ozzy beer label with the Osbourne family. Although the beer was limited to the Mid-Atlantic regional market, and the family was well aware of and had enjoyed the beer for years, Sharon Osbourne decided to send a cease and desist for trademark infringement in 2014. Instead of the legal wrangling that would potentially shut down the brewery, Stewart chose to rename the beer. Brewer's Art held a contest, allowing patrons to choose the new name via popular vote. The winner was Beazly, after beloved bartender Marcus Barcus, who worked at the establishment for seventeen years. Although the name was changed, the labelling remained nearly identical, allowing quick recognition for consumers. Other trademark infringement cases are handled on an almost daily basis by Maryland breweries. That is one reason new breweries in the state have to plan for an extraordinary monthly expense for trademark attorneys who regularly fetch $720 per hour. The golden rule with all trademarks is to use them or lose them. If you stop using it you will lose the trademark, and documentation is key to keeping it. Other than producing great beer, trademarks have become a priority concern.

One of the newest trends in Maryland is brewery consulting. Buzzed Brewery Consulting has set up shop specifically to help with some of the aforementioned branding difficulties in addition to a host of other services. For many brewers, they are exceptional at their craft but not at the paperwork, tax filings, and the tangled web of regulatory hoops that must be jumped through to actually produce and sell that liquid malt. Buzzed was founded in 2016 by Sam Riley, former operations manager at Calvert Brewing. Riley was integral to getting the brewery running, from construction to regulatory pitfalls to taxation and the all-important branding and trademark issues. Riley, a native Marylander, wanted to use her experience to help transition other new breweries from concept to implementation and beyond. It is the first consulting company of its kind in the state, capable of serving new and already established breweries. For many this will be the difference between actually opening a brewery and just conceptualizing the idea. The critical factor not to overlook is that Riley is a woman, and she has become an example of how the industry is changing—or perhaps returning to its colonial roots where beer was the purview of the female of the species.

The great benefit of the craft beer explosion is the increasing number of women in the industry. The days of the Swedish bikini models are (predominantly) a thing of the past. Although admittedly some breweries will still provide buxom women to pour the beer at festivals, it is no longer a necessary component to achieve sales goals. The role that women are occupying in the industry ranges from positions in sales and marketing to brewers, quality analysts, trademark attorneys, operations managers, and food pairing specialists among many other roles. This growth of females in the industry has been fomented by the Pink Boots Society, started by Teri Fahrendorf, a brewmaster in the industry for over twenty-five years. As a road brewer who traveled between breweries across the country collaborating with a variety of brewers, she often met young female brewers who felt a bit isolated as the only women in the brewery. Fahrendorf determined there was a need for a society that would provide a sense of community where women in the industry could connect, share, and inform one another. Since the foundation of the society in 2007, the membership has exceeded 1,590 members and includes chapters throughout the United States and the world. Fahrendorf has also established an annual scholarship program to Siebel Institute and other brewery education institutions for members.[10] Pink Boots has changed the culture and the conversation around craft beer.

A more recent Maryland brewery that opened in Silver Spring is helmed by women. Denizens Brewing Company was opened in 2014, after a few hiccups with branding, specifically a naming dispute with a Washington, D.C.–based brewery. The brewpub was the brainchild of partners in both life and business, Emily Bruno and Julie Verratti. The couple were LGBT political activists together and wanted to branch out into the next step of their lives, which was often centered on quality beer. After Verratti earned her law degree from George Washington University, Bruno devoted herself full time to the opening of the brewery while Verratti navigated the corridors of the legal profession.[11] Neither woman had real experience brewing beer, but both knew one thing that was a certainty: beer was everyman's (or woman's) drink. Montgomery County, with its antiquated alcohol regulations and unyielding liquor board, was not ideal, but the population was. Located near the metro, in the heart of Silver Spring a shake from Washington, foot traffic was undeniable. All they needed was a little regulatory help and a brewer. Enter Jeff Ramirez, Bruno's brother-in-law, who also happened to be a graduate of the Seibel Institute. At the time, Ramirez was working as a brewer in Colorado for Mountain Sun. A little convincing brought him to Maryland as a third partner in Denizens. The beer is excellent, as one would expect from a Seibel graduate, and the food creations pair quite well. The atmosphere is most welcoming, whether one is bringing the dog for a brew and snack in the beer garden or enjoying the flurry of activity and joyous chatter of patrons eagerly sampling the new Born Bohemian pilsener. It has become what Bruno and Verratti hoped it would, and expanded distribution will only ameliorate their brand.

Another notable female in the industry, Chris Anderson, began brewing more than fifteen years ago. It was a natural fit for her as a cook used to working with herbs in a variety of formats. Most of her home brewing ingredients were purchased at Maryland Homebrew, one of only a handful of places in the state to purchase brewing ingredients on a less than industrial scale. After years of brewing, Anderson noticed a "help wanted" sign in the shop and thus began her tenure at Maryland's largest home-brew store. Over the course of several years, she was given greater responsibility. Eventually she was running the shop.[12] This was a normal progression for focused, talented employees, but in the case of Anderson the road was much more challenging. In what has been a predominantly male culture of home brewing (roughly 80 percent are men), Anderson had to earn the respect of each and every customer. She was repeatedly overlooked and ignored with comments like, "What does SHE know about brewing?"[13] Individuals and industrial brewers alike frequented Maryland Homebrew and Anderson demonstrated her extensive knowledge of the brewing process and expertise in brewing. Over time even the most hardened skeptics were won over by her talent and prowess.

To date, Anderson is an active participant in several home brewer's guilds in Maryland, from CRABS (Chesapeake Real Ale Brewer's Society) to Cross Street Irregulars (Hugh Sisson's former club), to SPBW (Society for the Preservation of Beers from the Wood). This keeps her involved with home brewing on every level and her finger on the pulse of what is coming out for beer. Industrial brewers know and respect Anderson for her acumen, in part because many of them started as home brewers and worked their way into industrial positions through contacts made at Maryland Homebrew.[14] This is also indicative of a burgeoning culture. Many people are more interested in home brewing during a recession when money is tight and people are staying home. This coincides with the uptick in beer consumption during difficult financial times, as beer provides great flavor and often greater volume for a price that is less than a bottle of wine.[15] Maryland Homebrew has become a place to exchange ideas, recipes, tips,

Chris Anderson, general manager at Maryland Homebrew, standing in the Push American Brewery. She makes better brewers out of everyone she comes in contact with.

and information. Anderson often receives visitors to the store bringing in samples of their home brews wondering what went wrong or how it can be improved. This community atmosphere is one Anderson would not trade. She has often been asked to work for industrial breweries in Maryland but has repeatedly turned down those offers, stating that her heart belongs to Maryland Homebrew, where she is now the sole proprietor.[16]

Often industrial brewers have used the thirty-gallon system at Maryland Homebrew to test batches for flavor profiles before creating them on an industrial scale. Sometimes they are completely new recipes; other times they are simply new hop profiles for an established recipe. Breweries regularly buy supplies from Anderson due to the accessible pricing and seemingly endless variety of goods for brewing. Anderson has witnessed changes, including the push for locally grown grains and hops. This is prohibitive currently due to the limited production, but she sees this becoming a reality in the future as Maryland experiences an increase in the number of hop and barley growers. She also foresees an increase in organic products, which has been restrictive due to cost and availability. On the horizon, she suggests, the winds of change will bring more legalized home distilling to Maryland, providing yet another avenue for her to demonstrate her skills and gain greater respect in another male-dominated enterprise.[17] Anderson notes that home distilling may be a bit in the future for most Maryland counties due to the dangerous nature of the process and the extremely small window one has to get it just right.

Anderson has been a champion not only for home brewers but also for women in the brewing industry. She is cofounder of a group of women called the Baltimore Beer Babes who are involved in the brewing trades in various capacities. The purpose of the group is to educate women about beer, letting them know there is more for them than just wine and macro beers. Ultimately Anderson would like to not only introduce them to new tastes, and styles but also get them interested in home brewing. Her sister members include Judy Neff, scientist and avid home brewer who also founded "pints and plates" pairing food and beer. Neff is slated to open her own brewery in 2017, Checkerspot, in Baltimore. Another founder, Kelly Zimmerman, was a marketing and sales manager for Heavy Seas until opening her own promotions company focused on the

Judy Neff, cofounder of Checkerspot Brewing Company, and Joe Gold, sales manager, Heavy Seas Beer, enjoying a toast to Hugh Sisson on his 20th anniversary.

beer industry. The remaining founders are Lisa Lawson, who is a sergeant at arms for the Society for the Promotion of Beers from the Wood, and Erin Tyler, general manager at Legends, a craft beer-focused distributor in Maryland. The Baltimore Beer Babes began the modern trend of bringing women and beer together in a new way, and other groups have since followed suit. Lady Brew Baltimore is a chapter of the local Pink Boots Society in Maryland focusing on women home brewers who are establishing and refining their craft. That is only one of the ever-growing number of female craft beer clubs across Maryland.

Will Anderson one day have her own label like Neff is attempting to do with Checkerspot? Many who know Anderson have commented on her exceptional abilities in brewing and flavor profiles, and they support her opening one of the few female-owned breweries in Maryland.[18] Over the years Anderson has been contracted to teach people how to brew, and many of her students are now employees in Maryland and other regional industrial breweries. The root of Anderson's success is derived from her willingness to make mistakes and try again. There is always another opportunity to try again according to Anderson. This she says is also the secret to keeping women interested in brewing.[19] Anderson has been referred to as a "cheerleader for home brewing" but prefers the moniker "mother of beer" due to her great concern for each brewer and the beers they produce. Whatever title she takes, Anderson will remain a stalwart of women brewers in Maryland. All of these ladies represent just a few of the myriad options for women in the brewing industry and provide an example of just how much the culture has changed and will continue to change in the future as more women establish themselves among the ranks of the industry.[20]

An important step forward in the industry also involves embracing the legacy of past brewers across Maryland through philanthropy. It is universally understood by breweries that there is a need to support their communities, not just with finely crafted liquid and jobs but also with charity. Many of the breweries, even the contract breweries, work exceptionally hard to find their footing and carve their niches in the industry, often at a loss for the first few years. Despite that, all of the breweries of Maryland give back, even when the funds and the logic don't support it. Many breweries support charities like BARCS (the Baltimore Animal Rescue and Care Shelter) or another local incarnation of animal rescue. It is uncanny how craft beer and quadrupeds go together, and many of the breweries not only support the rescues but also welcome quadrupedal friends of every persuasion, whether dog, cat, rabbit, or even more exotic beings. That is not where the charity stops, however.

The Chesapeake Bay is the lifeblood of Maryland, and every brewer understands that. In addition to malting grains and agriculture, there is also a push for aquaculture. Sustainable harvesting of the fish and shellfish in the fragile ecosystem of the Chesapeake Bay is something that serves everyone in the region, and breweries across the state always support this. The myriad oyster festivals held at the breweries highlight not just the cornucopia of delicacies that come from the Bay, but also demonstrate how to protect them.[21] Spent oyster shells are all collected and returned to the Oyster Recovery Partnership (ORP) for placement in the Bay, where over time the shells will create a reef supporting more oysters and thus protect the ecosystem, as each mature oyster filters fifty gallons of water per day.[22] In addition to the shells, breweries like Flying Dog create oyster stouts, donating proceeds to ORP annually. These efforts help clean the Bay, keeping it habitable for all native organisms.

Much of the philanthropy comes in the form of helping humans, whether a cancer charity or something more personal. When Ellicott City suffered the devastating flood in 2016, breweries across the state pitched in. They not only offered jobs to suddenly homeless and unemployed victims, they also raised money to help them pay their bills, find a home, and rebuild the city. It was an incredible outpouring of support that was desperately needed. Heavy Seas, Jailbreak, Oliver's, Flying Dog, and so many more turned on the taps to support the community that had supported them over the years. This philanthropy builds communities and makes Maryland strong and is why craft beer has become a cornerstone of industry in the state. The breweries mobilize to take care of their own, and that means every one of us. To quote Kevin Blodger of Union Craft, "Beer unites. We all come together with beer."[23] Never has that sentiment held more true than today.

Brewers also know how to take care of one another. One of the largest craft breweries in the nation, Boston Brewing Company, AKA Sam Adams, started a program to not only reach out to aid other brewing businesses by holding classes and offering coaching for startup breweries but also to provide loans to help new breweries and businesses get off the ground. The program is called Brewing the American Dream, and it has had a marked effect on those participants, preparing them for success and supporting every step of the process until they are standing on their own. The comradery among craft brewers is substantial, not just within the state but beyond the borders as well. Regionally, the breweries help one another often. Sometimes it is through collaborations to further the success of the breweries, and sometimes it can be as simple as borrowing malt when a shipment doesn't arrive. They may be competitors but they are all in it together, and support is key. That is also why the Brewer's Association of Maryland has been revamped, to better serve the needs of all members of the craft brewing community. BAM, as it is referred to now, serves as a beacon to new breweries while constantly assessing the course for established breweries, whether that be via legislation, competition, festivals, or charitable causes. A new man at the helm as of 2015, Kevin Atticks leads the way. BAM also recognizes and supports the most critical aspect of the brewing industry, without which it could not exist: farming, specifically local agriculture.

The craft beer industry in Maryland, as mentioned previously, has reexamined the role of agriculture in the state. According to noted economist Darius Irani, at the Regional Economic Studies Institute conference in November of 2014, Maryland was far slower at climbing out of the economic recession than surrounding territories and still has work to do. One notable area of loss is agriculture, which continues to lose ground each year. This could be helped tremendously by one of the only manufacturing industries in the state that has demonstrated steady growth: the brewing industry. The buy local/use local trend discussed in previous chapters is part of the solution. Consumers want to know where the grains for their beers came from, particularly when they are locally sourced.

Barley has a long history of harvest in Maryland. Prior to Prohibition Maryland had a fine six-rowed, bearded winter barley crop that was used for malting and at one time was considered the only barley profitable in the state.[24] It was sown in September and harvested in June and sent to local malting facilities. When enough barley was not harvested within Maryland to supply the maltsters' demand, barley supplements came from the west and local malt houses like H. Straus Bros & Bell malted the barley for the breweries that did not malt their own.[25] Prior to Prohibition there was quite a bit more farmland in Maryland; in fact, 80 percent of the state was farmland in 1900.[26] By 2007 only 31 percent of Maryland was farmland, despite thirty years of preservation efforts by MAPLF (Maryland Agricultural Land Preservation Foundation) and substantial tax breaks geared toward the conservation of farmland.[27] In 2014 the Regional Economic Studies Institute report on the economy noted that the farming industry in Maryland has shown a loss of 3.4 percent, while all other industries in Maryland demonstrated stability or growth after the recession ended. Today barley and rye grown in Maryland that is suitable for malting is limited. The small amount produced is not nearly enough to supply the demand by breweries, but attempts are being made to rectify that.

Humanim remodeled the American Brewery Building (Wiessner's tuetonic pagoda) at the turn of the millennium. The history of the structure was taken fully into account, from the preservation of the grain elevator to the brew kettles to the stained glass. This stands as a shining light reminding Baltimore of her former glory, while bringing hope to depressed neighborhoods through job training, tutoring, and community outreach. The Wiessner family would be most proud.

Amber Fields, a local farm and malting facility in Frederick, Maryland, partnered with Brewer's Alley and Monocacy Brewing Company to supply local malted barley and rye to the brewery for production. Tom Flores, brewmaster at Monocacy and Brewer's Alley (and the newest member of the board of directors for the Brewers Association of America) worked hand in hand with Greg Clabaugh, the founder of Amber Fields, to create a facility for the malting of his barley and rye. In 2001 Flores and Clabaugh produced the first Maryland beer since Prohibition brewed with local malts. After ten years of tweaking the process, Clabaugh and Flores have consistent production of malted grains for the breweries, including Monocacy Riot Rye, a flavorful pale ale.[28]

Bryan Brushmiller, founder of Burley Oak Brewing Company,

also partnered with local farmer Brooks Clayville to begin a malting venture with local grains. As with Amber Fields, it took several attempts to get the barley and malting perfected. The series of Burley Oak brews that contain locally grown and malted grains are known as "Home Grown Ales." The first in the series was produced in 2013 and named Local, a pale ale embodying everything Brushmiller and Clayville were striving for. Both worked in conjunction with the University of Maryland and its Agricultural Sciences Department to plan the best malting grains for the soil.[29]

Burley Oak and Monocacy engender the pervasive buy local/use local mentality. Other breweries would like to follow in the footsteps of Flores and Brushmiller but are finding it difficult due to a lack of local grains suitable for malting. Scorpion Brewing out of Calvert is attempting to set up barley malting operations in conjunction with Swann Farms in Owings. The funding was raised for the malting vessel but malting has not yet begun.[30] This may be what swings the trend back toward growth for a struggling farming industry. The most significant aspect of the expansion of barley and rye farming for malting is the effect on the Chesapeake Bay. Barley and rye are both considered cover crops and have the added benefit of storing nitrogen in their plant tissue instead of allowing it to run off into the soil, which eventually pollutes the fragile ecosystem of the Bay.[31] Drinking more beer made from local grains could literally save the Chesapeake Bay. It may also save many Maryland farms struggling under the weight of heavy EPA burdens and the push toward land development. A return to the soil for Maryland may be in order. If more farmers in Maryland can plant suitable grains for malting to

The National Brewing Company complex. This, too, was completely remodeled in the new century. The history of Brewer's Hill was honored, complete with Mr. Bohemian winking at the beer lovers of Baltimore. Although it houses condominiums, businesses, and shops it stands as a reminder of Baltimore's past brewing legacy and her resurgence as force in the industry once again.

supply the breweries, everyone benefits. An increase in farming specifically for Maryland breweries not only foments the growth of Maryland's lagging agricultural industry but also allows for that development without compromising the health of the Bay. An increase in regionally grown and malted grains is in high demand by other Maryland breweries that would love to produce a regular offering of brews made from local grains.

This all supports the greater economic picture for the brewing industry in Maryland. Maryland craft breweries have demonstrated an annual growth of 35 percent over five years. The active brewing companies in the state created 24,575 jobs in 2015 (including affiliated industries), with a total economic contribution of $2,875,479,400. In tax revenues alone the industry generated $628,734.700 in 2015.[32] With the growth of the breweries in the state, these numbers will continue to climb, as will the agricultural industry in both job creation and positive economic impact. All it takes is one. One brewpub, one brewer, one taphandle, one row of barley, one hop vine, one cooper, and the world has changed. It is a ripple, a ripple created by a tradition steeped in malt and hard work, a tradition that is neither lost nor forgotten, but present, honored, and embraced.

Breweries in Planning

Brewery	Proprietor	Location	Opening	Planned Capacity
7th State Brewing		Bethesda Montgomery County	2017	
Attaboy Beer Company	Brian & Carly Ogden	400 Sagner Avenue Frederick County	December 2016	1,200 bbls/yr
Black Locust Farm Brewery	Che & Lisa Carton	Baltimore County	2017	
Bull & Goat Brewery	Jeff Putman	206 Banjo Lane Centreville Queen Anne's County	October 2016	
Checkerspot	Judy & Rob Neff, Stephen Marsh	Baltimore City	2017	
Cushwa Brewing	Marcus Thomas, Garrett Chambers, Scott Coleman	10212 Governor Lane Boulevard Williamsport Washington County	2017	
Diamondback Brewing	Colin Marshall, Tom Foster, Francis Smith	1215 E Fort Avenue Baltimore	2016	2,000 bbls/yr
Federal Brewing Company	Gayle Galbraith	102 N. Main Street Federalsburg Caroline County	2017	
Grail Point Beer Co.	Jeff Kusterbeck	Emmitsburg Frederick County		
Hysteria Brewing Company	Rich Gue, Geoff Lopes, Jordan Baney	9570 Berger Road Columbia Howard County	February 2017	
Idiom Brewing Co.	Michael Clements	Frederick County	2017	
Maryland Beer Company	Kevin Taylor, Scott McCardle, Jessica Fincham	41 Cherry Hill Road Elkton Cecil County	2016	
Midnight Run		Frederick City		
Monument City Brewing	Ken & Matthew Praay	1 North Haven Street Highlandtown	2017	20,000 bbls/yr
Paradiddle		Baltimore County		
Skipjack	Steve States & Max Fleming	Baltimore County		
SOMD Brewing	David Jones & David Mahoney	St. Mary's County	2017	
Steinhardt Brewing	James & Daria Steinhardt	Braddock Heights Frederick County	2016	
Suspended Brewing	Josey Schwartz, Yasmin Karimian	Baltimore City	2017	
True Respite Brewing Co	Brendan & Bailey O'Leary	Rockville Montgomery County	2017	
Wet City	Josh & P.J. Sullivan	223 West Chase Street Baltimore	2017	Brewpub Limit 22,500 bbls/yr

Chapter Notes

Introduction

1. Edward Emerson, *Beverages, Past and Present: A Historical Sketch of Their Production, Together with a Study of the Customs Connected with Their Use* 1 (New York: G.P. Putnam's Sons, 1908), 500; John Ashton and James Mew, *Drinks of the World* (London: Leadenhall Press, 1892), 16–17.

2. Emerson; Michael Homan, "Beer Production by Throwing Bread into Water: A New Interpretation of Qoh XI 1–2," *Vetus Testamentum* 52, no. 2 (April, 2002): 255–258. Also of note here is that an understanding of the role yeast played in fermenting sugar into alcohol was not salient until the modern era and Louis Pastuer in the 1870s.

3. Delwan Samuel, "Bread Making and Social Interactions at the Amarna Workmen's Village, Egypt," *World Archaeology* 31, no. 1 (June 1999): 121–144.

4. Merryn Dineley, "Who Were Our First Maltsters? The Archaeological Evidence for Floor Malting," *Brewer and Distiller International* (February 2016): 34–36.

5. Jeremy Black, et al. *The Literature of Ancient Sumer* (Oxford: Oxford University Press, 2004), 297.

6. Sarah Hand Meacham, *Every Home a Distillery: Alcohol, Gender, and Technology in the Colonial Chesapeake* (Baltimore: Johns Hopkins University Press, 2009), 9–13.

7. Amelia Simmons, *American Cookery* (Hartford: Simeon Butler, 1798), 48.

8. *Ibid.*; Stanley Baron, *Brewed in America: The History of Beer and Ale in the United States* (Boston: Little, Brown, 1962), 16–17, 85–86.

9. Gervase Markham, *The English Housewife*, ed. Michael R. Best (London: Hannah Sawbridge, 1615; McGill-Queen's University Press, 1994), 204–208; Margery Kempe, *The Book of Margery Kempe*, ed. Lynn Staley (New York: Oxford University Press, 1940; Kalamazoo: Medieval Institute Publications, 1996), 208–210.

10. Gregg Smith, *Beer in America: The Early Years—1587–1840* (Boulder: Siris Books, 1998), 12, 16.

11. Hewson L. Peeke, *American Ebrietatis* (New York, 1917), 20–21.

12. Michael Combrune, *Theory and Practice of Brewing* (London: Vernor and Hood, 1804), 235, 286; Baron, *Brewed in America*, 107–108.

13. Combrune, *Theory and Practice*, 4, 21, 110, 152; James Baverstock, *Hydrometrical Observations and Experiments in the Brewery* (London, 1785).

14. Henry Dunster, 1640–1654, *Memorandum of Henry Dunster*, December 1653 (typewritten transcription, October 2007), UAI 15.850 Box 1, Folder 17, Harvard University Archives.

15. Baron, *Brewed in America*, 38.

16. Peeke, *American Ebrietatis*, 44.

17. Ibid., 127–128.

18. Baron, *Brewed in America*, 16.

19. *Beer in Britain,* compiled by the London Times (London: London Times Publishing Co., April 1958), 85–87.

20. J.R. Ainsworth-Davis, *Cooking Throughout the Centuries* (London: J.M. Dent and Sons, 1931), 93.

21. Gallus Thomann, *Liquor Laws of the United States: Their Spirit and Effect*, 4th ed. (New York: United States Brewer's Association, 1885), 104.

22. Baron, *Brewed in America*, 34.

23. Thomann, *Liquor Laws*, 16; Peeke, *American Ebrietatis*, 29.

24. *Virginia Gazette*, April 1, 1775.

25. *Boston Evening Post*, September 10, 1750.

26. Baron, *Brewed in America*, 88–89; *Virginia Gazette*, April 1, 1775.

Chapter 1

1. "The Charter of Maryland: 1632," in *The Federal and State Constitutions, Colonial Charters, and Other Organic Laws of the States, Territories, and Colonies Now and Heretofore Forming the United States of America*, ed. Francis Newton Thorpe (Washington, D.C.: Government Printing Office, 1903); Father Andrew White, S.J., "An Account of the Colony of the Lord Baron of Baltimore, in Maryland, Near Virginia: In Which the Character, Quality and State of the Country, and Its Numerous Advantages and Sources of Wealth are Set Forth" (1633), in *Narratives of Early Maryland, 1633–1684*, ed. Clayton Colman Hall (New York: Charles Scribner's Sons, 1910), 6–7.

2. Meacham, *Every Home A Distillery*, 64–67.

3. Maryland General Assembly, "Proceedings and Acts of the General Assembly, September 1704–April 1706," *General Assembly Upper House Proceedings 1704–1706* 26, 314–315, Maryland State Archives.

4. Anne Arundel County Land Records, Liber WT 2, Folio 327.

5. Jane W. McWilliams, *Annapolis, a City on the Severn: A History* (Baltimore: Johns Hopkins University Press, 2011), 25–26.

6. Benjamin Fordham, *Last Will and Testament*, Prerogative Court Wills 14, 501–504, MDHR 1292–2, 1–11 to 1–16.

315

7. *Maryland Gazette*, February 25, 1746; February 18, 1746.

8. Harry W. Newman, *The Lucketts of Port Tobacco* (Washington, D.C.: self published, 1938), 4. This also appears to be the same John Muschett mistakenly noted to have a brewery in Charlestown from 1845 to 1848.

9. *Maryland Gazette*, June 1, 1748.

10. Norman K. Risjord, *Builders of Annapolis: Enterprise and Politics in a Colonial Capital* (Baltimore: Maryland Historical Society, 1997), 24, 99; Robert Atwell and Alan Tully, *Cultures and Identities in Colonial British America* (Baltimore: Johns Hopkins University Press, 2015), 192.

11. *Maryland Gazette*, October 4, 1749; December 2, 1756.

12. Risjord, *Builders of Annapolis*, 24; United States Department of the Interior, "Patrick Creagh House, AA-654," *National Register of Historic Places*, 1972.

13. *Maryland Gazette*, March 4, 1773.

14. *Maryland Gazette*, November 3, 1774; December 7, 1774.

15. *Maryland Gazette*, March 1, 1764.

16. Dale P. Van Wieren, *American Breweries II* (West Point: Eastern Coast Breweriana Association, 1995), 128; William J. Kelley, *Brewing in Maryland*, (Baltimore: William J. Kelley, 1965), 35, 39.

17. Jacob M. Price, ed., *Joshua Johnson's Letterbook 1771–1774: Letters from a Merchant in London to His Partners in Maryland* (London: London Record Society, 1979), 321. Accessed January 6, 2014. http://www.british-history.ac.uk/report.aspx?compid=38795.

18. *Maryland Gazette*, September 10, 1772.

19. Charles B. Clark, *The Eastern Shore of Maryland and Virginia* 2 (New York: Lewis Historical Publishing Company, Inc., 1950), 963.

20. John Beale Bordley, *Essays and Notes on Husbandry and Rural Affairs* (Philadelphia: Budd and Bartram, 1799), 85, 411.

21. *Ibid.*, 1058.

22. *Ibid.*, 475, 481, 500.

23. Dr. William H. Wroten, Jr., "John Bordley: One of America's Foremost Agriculturalists," *The Salisbury Times* (Salisbury, MD), May 22, 1958.

24. Col. J. Thomas Scharf, *History of Western Maryland: Being a History of Frederick, Montgomery, Carroll, Washington, Allegany, and Garrett Counties from the Earliest Period to the Present Day; Including Biographical Sketches of Their Representative Men* (Philadelphia: L.H. Everts, 1882), 114.

25. C.E. Schinldknecht, *Monocacy & Catoctin: Some Early Settlers of Frederick and Carroll Counties, MD and Adams County, PA also Descendants c. 1725–1985* 1 (Shippensburg, PA: Beidel Printing House, 1985), 338.

26. Maryland Calendar of Wills 13, 1764–1767; James A. Helman, *History of Emmitsburg, Maryland: With a Prelude of Historical Facts of Frederick County, and a Romance Entitled Disappointed, or, the Recluse of Huckle's Field* (Frederick: Citizen Press, 1906), 10; Thomas John Chew Williams and Folger McKinsey, *History of Frederick County, Maryland* 1 (Frederick: Genealogical Publishing Co., 1979), 286, 314, 431, 511.

27. William Hand Browne and Louis Henry Dielman, "Extracts from the Carroll Papers," *MD Historical Magazine* 14, no. 3 (September 1919): 284.

28. *Maryland Gazette*, June 8, 1774.

29. Earl Leon Werley Heck, *The History of the Heck Family of America: With Special Attention Given to Those Families Which Originated in Indiana, Kentucky, Maryland, Ohio, Pennsylvania, Virginia* (Madison: University of Wisconsin Press, 1959), 6.

30. Honorable William T. Brantley, et al., *The History of Baltimore* (Baltimore: S.B. Nelson, 1898), 13.

31. Clarence P. Gould, "The Economic Causes of the Rise of Baltimore," in *Essays in Colonial History: Presented to Charles McLean Andrews by His Students* (New Haven: Yale University Press, 1931), 232–239.

32. Robert McIlvaine, *The Barnitz Family* (Baltimore, 1961), 9.

33. Bernard Penner, *Zion in Baltimore 1755–1955 History Book Supplement 1955–2005* (Baltimore: Zion Church of the City of Baltimore, 2008), 9.

34. Klaus G. Wust, *Zion in Baltimore 1755–1955; the Bicentennial History of the Earliest German-American Church in Baltimore, Maryland* (Baltimore: Zion Church of the City of Baltimore, 1955), 2.

35. Penner, *Zion in Baltimore*, 10.

36. Wust, *Zion in Baltimore*, 5–7.

37. *Ibid.*, 8–11.

38. McIlvaine, *The Barnitz Family*, 11. John Leonard died in 1749.

39. Kelley, *Brewing in Maryland*, 54–55. Granshet has several variations and is most often spelled "Granshed."

40. *Ibid.*

41. Col. J. Thomas Scharf, *The Chronicles of Baltimore: Being a Complete History of Baltimore Town and Baltimore City from the Earliest Time to the Present* (Baltimore: Turnbull Brothers, 1874), 53, 168, 230.

42. *Ibid.*, 261. Scharf does not mention why the fire was intentionally set or who was responsible.

43. *Ibid.*, 171, 210; *1790 Census*, Baltimore Town, 4.

Chapter 2

1. Although the Townsend Acts were repealed in 1770, the tea tax was left in place as a method of continuing to draw revenue from the colonies.

2. "Documents from the Continental Congress and the Constitutional Convention, 1774 to 1789," *Library of Congress*. June 10, 1777: Resolved for Supplying the Army of the United States with Provisions; April 22, 1782: A System on Which Provisions Are to Be Issued; October 23, 1782: Regulations for the Quarter Master General's Department: By the United States in Congress Assembled.

3. Tucker F. Hentz, *Unit History of the Maryland and Virginia Rifle Regiment (1776–1781): Insights from the Service Record of Capt. Adamson Tannehill.* (Richmond: Virginia Historical Society, 2007), 3, 10–12.

4. Many of the historical records pertaining to the Maryland 400 were lost. Attempts to recover the names of those men and tell their stories has become an ongoing collaborative project between the Maryland State Archives, the Maryland Military Department, the Maryland Historical Society, the Moss Family Foundation, and the Office of the Adjutant General.

5. McIlvaine, *The Barnitz Family*, 11.

6. *Baltimore Directory*, 1802.

7. *Maryland Journal*, December 18, 1795; November 23, 1796.

8. Kelley, *Brewing in Maryland*, 68–69.

9. *The Maryland Journal and Baltimore Advertiser*, October 2, 1789.

10. Wust, *Zion in Baltimore*, 30–31.

11. James Dissette, "The Chester River Brewing Company Finds a Home," *The Chestertown Spy* (Chestertown, MD), January 9, 2014.

12. *Maryland Gazette*, April 13, 1775.

13. *Pennsylvania Gazette*, October 19, 1785.

14. Maryland Historical Trust, Historic Sites Inventory PG 82A-041.

15. Fred Shelley, ed., "Ebenezer Hazard's Travels Through Maryland in 1777," *Maryland Historical Magazine* 46, no. 1 (March 1951): 44–54.

16. Thomas Peters, "A Scrap of Troop History," *The Pennsylvania Magazine of History and Biography* 15, no. 2 (1891): 226–227.

17. *Maryland Journal*, August 24, 1792; Kelley, *Brewing in Maryland*, 78–79. Edward Johnson was Peters' brother-in-law. By 1796, the third and silent partner was ousted and the brewery was strictly called *Peters and Rom Johnson*.

18. Kelley, *Brewing in Maryland*, 80–88; Scharf, *The Chronicles of Baltimore*, 294–296, 306.

19. *The Baltimore Sun*, November 23, 1812; Col. J. Thomas Scharf, *History of Baltimore City and County from the Earliest Period to the Present Day: Including Biographical Sketches of Their Representative Men* (Philadelphia: L.H. Everts, 1881), 261.

20. *The Maryland Journal*, June 17, 1791.

21. *The Baltimore Daily Repository*, December 1, 1792; Richard J. Cox, ed., *A Name Index to the Baltimore City Tax Records, 1798–1808, of the Baltimore City Archives* (Baltimore City Archives and Records Management Office, 1981), 79.

22. Richard J. Cox, ed., 97.

23. Thomas Sullivan, *A Treatise of Practical Gauging* (Baltimore, 1795–1797), Maryland Historical Society.

24. Thomas L. Purvis, *Colonial America to 1763* (New York: Facts on File, 1999), 90, 107.

25. Amy Reed, "Chronology of Glass Making in Frederick County, Maryland," in *In and Out of Frederick Town: Colonial Occupations* (Frederick, MD: LDS Church, 1985).

26. Dwight P. Lanmon and Arlene M. Palmer, "Amelung In Europe," *Journal of Glass Studies* 18 (1976): 20–24. http://www.jstor.org/stable/24190009.

27. Dwight P. Lanmon and Arlene M. Palmer, "The New Bremen Glassmanufactory," *Journal of Glass Studies* 18 (1976): 25–38. http://www.jstor.org/stable/24190010.

28. *Ibid.*; Schildknecht, *Monocacy & Catoctin: Some Early Settlers of Frederick and Carroll Counties, MD and Adams County, PA also Descendants c. 1725–1985* 1 (Shippensburg, PA: Beidel Printing House, 1985), 266–267.

29. Lanmon and Palmer, "The New Bremen Glassmanufactory."

30. *Maryland Chronicle or The Universal Advertiser*, November 15, 1786.

31. Lanmon and Palmer, "The New Bremen Glassmanufactory."

32. *Ibid.*; Jos D. Weeks, *U.S. Census Report on the Manufacture of Glass* (Washington, D.C.: Government Printing Office, 1884), 95.

33. Helen McKearin and Kenneth Wilson, *American Bottles and Flasks and Their Ancestry* (New York: Crown, 1978), 229–231.

34. Scharf, *The Chronicles of Baltimore*, 291; *Baltimore American*, November 5, 1800.

35. *Federal Gazette*, September 23, 1801.

36. *Baltimore Directory*, 1819; Charles Varle, *Complete View of Baltimore*, 1833.

37. *Federal Gazette*, May 16, 1804.

38. Kelley, *Brewing in Maryland*, 119–120. Kelley assumed Saumenig to have been a brewmaster in Germany prior to his arrival in Baltimore, but I cannot support that with documentary evidence at this time.

39. Van Wieren, *American Breweries II*, 138; Scharf, *History of Western Maryland*, 1051, 1172. It is speculated that the brewery was located near city hall on Franklin and Potomac Streets, as it was near the marketplace; Thomas J.C. Willliams, *A History of Washington County, Maryland, from the Earliest Settlements to the Present Time, Including a History of Hagerstown* 1 (Salem, MA: Higginson Book Co., 1990), 59. Hager's Fancy was also known as Hager's Choice.

40. Scharf, *History of Western Maryland*; Williams, *A History of Washington County*; Mary Vernon Mish, *Jonathan Hager, Founder* (Hagerstown, MD: Hagerstown Bookbinding & Print Co., 1937), 66.

41. Mish, *Jonathan Hager*; Williams, *A History of Washington County* 2, 963; Thomas J.C. Williams, *A History of Washington County, Maryland* 163, 23.

42. Scharf, *History of Western Maryland*, 1061.

43. *Ibid.*, 1063.

44. Gaius Marius Brumbaugh, *Genealogy of the Brumbach Families* (New York: F.T. Hitchcock, 1913), 151, 171.

45. Williams, *A History of Washington County* 2, 631. Gravestone records from Rose Hill Cemetery also list Louisa Gelwicks Brumbaugh as wife of George Brumbaugh dating to this period.

46. Scharf, *History of Western Maryland*,1225.

47. James A. Helman, *History of Emmitsburg*, 46.

48. *Ibid.*, 65–66.

49. *Ibid.*, 61, 26, 76.

Chapter 3

1. "Commodore Barron's Inquiry into the Presence of Deserters Aboard the *Chesapeake*," *The Mariner's Museum*, Accessed January 27, 2014, https://www.marinersmuseum.org/sites/micro/usnavy/08/08e.htm. Commodore James Barron of *Chesapeake* on June 22, 1807, regarding the inquiry results of four alleged deserters from the British vessels *Melampus* and *Halifax*. Two of the four were born and raised in Maryland and Commodore Barron refused to surrender them. His ship was subsequently fired upon and so damaged that he was forced to surrender them.

2. *An Act to Establish an Executive Department to be Denominated the Department of the Navy* 1, chap. 35, 553 (April 30, 1798).

3. David S. Heidler and Jeanne T. Heidler, *The War of 1812* (Westport: Greenwood Press, 2002), 164–165.

4. Isaac Hull, *Commodore Hull: Papers of Isaac Hull, Commodore, United States Navy* (Boston: Boston Athenaeum, 1929).

5. Christopher T. George, *Terror on the Chesapeake: The War of 1812 on the Bay* (Shippensburg, PA: White Mane Books, 2000), 91.

6. Frederick M. Colston, "The Battle of North Point," *Maryland Historical Magazine* 2, no. 2 (1997): 2.

7. Brig. Gen. John Stricker, Baltimore, to Maj. Gen. Samuel Smith, "Report on the Battle of North Point," September 15, 1814; George, *Terror on the Chesapeake*, 142–145. NARA.

8. Major George Armistead to Secretary of State James Monroe, September 24, 1814. Congreve Rockets were the first rockets to use liquid fuel. They were notoriously unreliable but could achieve longer distances based upon the amount of liquid fuel added. Thus they were quite useful (when accurate) during the bombardment of Fort McHenry.

9. *The Baltimore Directory and Register* (Baltimore: Edward Matchett, 1816), 33.

10. "Ordnance Voucher no. 26, James Calhoun, Deputy Commisary, for Mary Pickersgill for One American Ensign and One Garrison Flag, 1 February 1815." *Maryland State Archives*. Accessed March 30, 2014. http://msa.maryland.gov/megafile/msa/spec col/sc3500/sc3520/012400/012457/pdf/voucher.pdf.

11. Steve Vogel, "Q&A: The Star Spangled Banner, Francis Scott Key and the War of 1812," *The Washington Post* (Washington, D.C.), May 6, 2013.

12. Fred Hopkins, "For Flag and Profit: The Life of Commodore John Daniel Danels of Baltimore," *Maryland Historical Magazine* 80, no. 4 (Winter 1985): 392–401.

13. *1850 U.S. Census of Manufacturers*, Baltimore, Maryland, 131.

14. *The Baltimore Sun*, March 21, 1849.

15. *1860 U.S. Census of Manufacturers*, Baltimore, Maryland, 3.

16. *The Baltimore Sun*, October 7, 1842; *Matchett's Directory* 1855–1856, 383; *Wood's Directory* (Baltimore: John W. Woods, 1859), 444. Both men were listed as brewers in the colored directory. Eli set forth in his will that his slaves would be freed shortly after his death. Danels apparently had similar feelings toward free Blacks.

17. "Claggett's Brewery Damage Case: Verdict for the City," *The Baltimore Sun* (Baltimore, MD), December 3, 1878.

18. *Matchett's Directory 1816*, 102.

19. Kelley, *Brewing in Maryland*, 127.

20. *Federal Gazette*, February 15, 1820.

21. *Matchett's Directory 1827*, 100. It was previously believed that Freinscht opened the Camden brewery in 1829, but Matchett's directory has him listed as already operational at that location.

22. "Maryland Indexes: Baltimore County & Baltimore City Equity Papers, Index," *Maryland State Archives*, November 9, 1830.

23. Kelley, *Brewing in Maryland*, 120, 135.

24. *Laws of the State of Maryland* (Annapolis: Department of Legislative Reference, 1829), 40.

25. *The Baltimore Sun*, February 20, 1838.

26. *The Baltimore Sun*, June 20, 1842; "Interesting Examination," *The Baltimore Sun* (Baltimore, MD), October 10, 1842.

27. *The Baltimore Sun*, October 22, 1842.

28. *The Baltimore Sun*, November 26, 1842.

29. *Matchett's Directory 1829*, 200.

30. *Matchett's Directory 1833–1834*, 78. The Washington Brewery changed hands from John Krouse to Andrew Graham and his partner Silvey. They advertised in the *Matchett's Directory* of 1831 as operating

the Washington Brewery. By 1834 they are no longer operating the brewery, nor is Lucas operating on Holliday. Due to the frequent flooding of Jones Falls, it is not surprising that Lucas relocated.

31. *Matchett's Directory 1837*, 23.

32. *Matchett's Directory 1842*, 253.

33. *1860 U.S. Census*, Baltimore, Maryland, Francis Dandelet, Maryland State Archives, 486.

34. Index to the Naturalization Petitions for the U.S. Circuit and District Courts of Maryland, 1797–1951. NARA M1168; *Matchett's Directory*, 1849–1850, 96.

35. *The Baltimore Sun*, March 26, 1855.

36. *Woods' Directory*, 65.

37. *1860 U.S. Census*, Baltimore, Maryland, Francis Dandelet, 486, MSA.

38. John C. Gobright, *City Rambles, or Baltimore as It Is: Being a Series of Notices Originally Published in the Baltimore Patriot and Commercial Gazette, in Which Is Given Descriptive Notices of New Buildings, Prominent Houses in Trade, the Public Drives from the City, Descriptions of Machinery, Inventions, &c. &c* (Baltimore: John W. Woods, 1857).

39. *Matchett's Directory*, 1842, 273.

40. *Matchett's Directory*, 1837, 23; *U.S. Census of Manufacturers* Maryland, 1850, 263.

41. *A Brief Outline of the Rise, Progress, and Failure of the Revolutionary Scheme of the Nineteen Van Buren Electors of the Senate of Maryland: In the Months of September, October, and November, 1836* (Baltimore: Sands and Neilson, 1837), 50.

42. *The Baltimore Sun*, March 12, 1838; "The Visit To Baltimore," *The Baltimore Sun* (Baltimore, MD), May 11, 1839; Hezekiah and William Niles, *Niles' Weekly Register* 37 (Baltimore: Franklin Press, 1830), 122.

43. *Craig's Business Directory and Baltimore Almanac* (Baltimore: J. Robinson, 1842), p 99; "Riot," *The Baltimore Sun*, March 1, 1841.

44. *1850 U.S. Census of Manufacturers*, Baltimore, Maryland, Maryland State Archives, 241, 263; *The Plan of the City of Baltimore Map* (Baltimore: Sidney & Neff, 1850); *Matchett's Directory*, 1849–50, 438.

45. Kelley, *Brewing in Baltimore*, 154–155; *Baltimore Wholesale Directory* (Baltimore: J. Craig, Book & Job Printer, 1852), 165.

46. "The Burning of the Saratoga Brewery," *The Baltimore Sun* (Baltimore, MD), March 17, 1859.

47. *Matchett's Directory*, 1847, 194; *Matchett's Directory*, 1849–1850, 243. Lekauf is listed in the 1850 census as operating his brewery out of Ward 1, which coincides with *The Plan of the City of Baltimore Map*.

48. *Matchett's Directory*, 1851, 168.

49. *1850 U.S. Census of Manufacturers*, Baltimore, Maryland, Maryland State Archives, 85, 130, Lekauf is noted by a few sources as moving to the Little Italy region of the city in 1849. He was still located in Ward 1 (Fells' Point) as of June 1850 when the census was taken. Although Lekauf is listed as operating at 30 Fell Street (Kelley) or 10 Fell Street (Van Wieren), 30 Fell Street was not the location of his brewery in Fell's Point. That was a rooming house. *Matchett's* directories for 1847, 1849–1850, and 1851 clearly have several gentlemen living at 30 Fell street at the same time. They are all of differing occupations and conflict with supposed breweries operating at those locations at that time. Adam Lurz is also noted to have breweries at 10, 30, and 24 Fell Street as well. 24 Fell Street was

a famous boarding house and tavern in the mid–19th century. The introduction to the directories addresses the fact that many addresses are homes, not places of business, as information provided to the directory often gets mixed. Many properties on the wharves were rented to businessmen catering to the incredible and continually migrating population of Fell's Point at this time.

50. *The Baltimore Sun,* May 19, 1860. Berlinerweisse Beer is a sour wheat beer common to Northern Germany. It was not widely popular, but Berlinerweisse brewers in Baltimore had a readymade and very loyal patronage to their brewery for the "taste of home."

51. *The Baltimore Sun,* September 23, 1853; *The Baltimore Sun,* May 3, 1867.

52. *Matchett's Directory,* 1851, 125; *1850 Census of Manufacturers,* Baltimore, MD, 99.

53. *1850 Census of Manufacturers.*

54. *Woods' Directory,* 156.

55. Kelley, *Brewing in Maryland,* 210.

56. *Matchett's Directory,* 1853–1854, 268; *1860 Census,* Baltimore, 128.

57. *Matchett's Directory,* 1855–1856, 302.

58. Baltimore City Land Records, Liber GES 153, Folio 23–24.

59. *Woods' Directory,* 1858–1859, 343.

60. *1860 U.S. Census,* Baltimore, Maryland, John Ramming, Maryland State Archives, 513; *1860 U.S. Census of Manufacturers,* Baltimore, Maryland, Maryland State Archives, 4.

61. Kelley, *Brewing in Maryland,* 309–310.

62. *Baltimore Wholesale Directory,* 165.

63. *1850 U.S. Census of Manufacturers,* Baltimore, Maryland, Maryland State Archives, 268; *The Baltimore Sun,* April 18, 1859.

64. Baltimore City Land Records, Liber 131, Folio 144.

65. *The Baltimore Sun,* February, 27, 1864. Baltimore County Land Records, Liber HMF 9, Folio 3.

66. *1860 U.S. Census of Manufacturers,* Baltimore, Maryland, Maryland State Archive, 4; *The Baltimore Sun,* April 18, 1859. Kelley suggests that Zwansger had the first lager beer brewery in Baltimore, but there is no verification of this theory in the historical record. Kelley also reports George Rossmarck as the first lager beer brewer in the same work.

67. *The Baltimore Sun,* June 24, 1850.

68. *The Baltimore Sun,* June 13, 1860.

69. *Ibid.;* Baltimore County Land Records, Liber G.H.C. 29, Folio 208. The lease was granted for a term of 13 years beginning on October 2, 1859, ending October 1, 1872.

70. *The Baltimore Sun,* October 20, 1870.

71. Kelley, *Brewing in Maryland,* 275.

72. *1850 U.S. Census of Manufacturers,* Baltimore, Maryland, Maryland State Archives, 99.

73. *Ibid.; Matchett's Directory,* 1851, 260, 278. Granff was pulling in $6500 per year with one additional employee over Röst.

74. *Woods' Directory,* 1856–7; 1864. Ruppert, *National Geneological Society Quarterly* 82 (December 1994), 269–291.

75. "German Rifelmen," *The Weekly Clipper,* April 15, 1854.

76. Richard Edwards, ed., *Industries of Maryland: A Descriptive Review of the Manufacturing and Mercantile Industries of the City of Baltimore* (Baltimore: Historical Publishing Company, 1882), 278.

77. *1860 U.S. Census of Manufacturers,* Baltimore, Maryland, Maryland State Archives, 10.

78. *Baltimore American,* December 5, 1871.

79. *The Baltimore Sun,* July 20, 1846.

80. *Matchett's Directory,* 1849, 430; *The Baltimore Sun,* July 11, 1882; Kelley, *Brewing in Maryland,* 160.

81. *Matchett's Directory,* 1855–1856, 378.

82. *The Baltimore Sun,* December 11, 1849; *Matchett's Directory,* 1851, 20.

83. *Matchett's Directory,* 1855, 32. John opened his tavern on 114 N Howard in 1853 while Frederick opened his tavern on 43 N Frederick in the same year.

84. *Matchett's Directory,* 1853–4, 182.

85. George Wetzel, *Baltimore Subterranean* (Baltimore: Wetzel, 1954), 14.

86. *Ibid.,* 15. Wetzel, having explored the tunnels, noted the mark of General Butler with the date 1861 inside the Covington Street tunnel. Wetzel also observed that when the sewer was constructed in Federal Hill in 1891, workers dug at Cross Street all the way to the Harbor and never encountered the vaults or tunnels. Covington Street sank two feet in 1902, and many chalked it up to "quick sand." The brewers knew, however, it was due in no small part to the subterranean lagering cellars.

87. *Baltimore Wholesale Directory,* 1852, 166; *Matchett's Directory,* 1853–1854, 259.

88. *Woods' Directory,* 1856–7, 290.

89. *The Baltimore Sun,* October 26, 1858.

90. Scharf, *History of Baltimore,* 786–788.

91. *Ibid.*

92. *The Baltimore Sun,* May 9, 1859; *The State Gazette and Merchants and Farmers' Directory for Maryland, and the District of Columbia* (Baltimore: Sadler, Drysdale & Purnell, 1871), 459–484.

93. *1880 U.S. Census of Manufacturers,* Catonsville, Baltimore County, Maryland, 5.

94. H. Rich, *One Hundred Years of Brewing: A Complete History* (Chicago: H.S. Rich and Co., 1903), 180.

95. Baier has several spellings including Baer (most famously), Byer, and Bayer (as in the Woods' Directory of 1865 where Baier and Bayer are both provided). The names were somewhat bastardized (as with most German immigrants) once translated into English. Several spellings for the same individual has been seen in the record and is a common occurrence.

96. Kelley, *Brewing in Maryland,* 199. Records Baier as owning the brewery at Fell Street. All records including the 1850 census and subsequent directories have Herzog as the owner. It is clear Baier was a brewer for Herzog at this location, not an owner.

97. *Special Report of the President and Directors of the Canton Company of Baltimore Made to the Stockholders, March 10, 1871* (Baltimore: John Murphy & Co., 1871), 5–10.

98. National Register of Historic Places, B-996, November 14, 2002.

99. *Matchett's Directory,* 1853–1854, 21.

100. *Woods' Directory,* 1865, 22 ad, 28, 521.

101. *Baltimore City Court of Common Pleas, Marriage Index for Males,* 1851–1885, Maryland State Archives, CM 205–1, Film CR 1663.

102. Headstone of Johann Baier, Baltimore Cemetery plot 137, center section 3.

103. *Woods' Directory,* 1868–69, 23, 32, 681.

104. *1870 U.S. Census,* Baltimore City, Maryland, George Pabst, 114.

105. *Woods' Directory*, 1860, 295; Kelley, *Brewing in Maryland*, 277.
106. *1870 U.S. Census*, George Pabst, 114.
107. "E. Sachse, & Co.'s Bird's Eye View of the City of Baltimore, 1869," *Library of Congress*, https://www.loc.gov/resource/g3844b.pm002540/.
108. Wetzel, *Baltimore Subterranean*, 18; *1850 U.S. Census of Manufacturers* Baltimore, Maryland, 263; *Baltimore Map*, 1850, Sidney and Neff.
109. *The Baltimore Sun*, July, 23, 1851.
110. *The Baltimore Sun*, June 30, 1853.
111. *The Baltimore Sun*, December 13, 1853.
112. *The Baltimore Sun*, January 11, 1855; March 15, 1855.
113. *The Baltimore Sun*, March 16, 1855.
114. *The Baltimore Sun*, October 28, 1857; Wetzel, *Baltimore Subterranean*, 18. Wetzel contends that due to two deaths that took place in the vaults below Brandel's Saratoga brewery, the vaults were haunted as recently as 1954.
115. *Woods' Directory*, 1858–1859, 97.
116. Kelley, *Brewing in Maryland*, 207.
117. Scharf, *History of Baltimore*, 423; *The Baltimore Sun*, January 21, 1839.
118. Baltimore City Land Records, Liber ED 31, Folio 441.
119. *Woods' Directory*, 1864, 355. *1858*, 357.
120. John C. Gobright, *The Monumental City, or Baltimore Guide Book, Being a Reliable Directory for Citizens and Strangers to the Prominent Objects of Interest, Together with a Description of the Prominent Mercantile and Manufacturing Houses* (Baltimore: Gobright & Torsch, 1858), 207–208.
121. Scharf, *History of Baltimore*, 423.
122. Gobright, *Monumental City*, 208; *Ibid.*
123. *1850 Census*, Baltimore City, Maryland, Thomas Beck, Maryland State Archives, 85; *Matchett's Directory*, 1853–1854, 29.
124. Kelley, *Brewing in Maryland*, 252.
125. *1860 U.S. Census*, Baltimore City, Maryland, Thomas Beck, Maryland State Archives, 172. It is worth noting that Kelley claimed Beck only produced ale and porter, but no lager. The primary focus of Beck's brewery was lager, as is verified in the voluminous advertisements at the Thomas Beck Rock Spring Lager Beer Brewery.
126. *1860 U.S. Census*, Baltimore City, Maryland, George Neisendorfer, Maryland State Archives, 1011.
127. *Woods' Directory*, 1856–1857, 249.
128. *Ibid.*
129. *Woods' Directory*, 1858–1859, 251.
130. Kelley, *Brewing in Maryland*, 215–216.
131. *1860 Census*, George Neisendorfer, Maryland State Archives, 1011.
132. *Ibid.*, 31.
133. *1860 U.S. Census of Manufacturers*, Baltimore, Maryland, Maryland State Archives, 3.
134. *Ibid.*
135. George W. Howard, *The Monumental City: Its Past History and Present Resources* (Baltimore: J.D. Ehlers & Co, 1873), 83–85, 129.
136. "Campbell-Barnitz House: 211 East Main Street," Inventory Form For State Historic Sites Survey, *Maryland Historical Trust*, https://mht.maryland.gov/secure/medusa/PDF/Carroll/CARR-132C.pdf.
137. *Carrolltonian*, December 20, 1834.
138. Scharf, *History of Western Maryland*, 930.
139. *Democrat and Carroll County Republican*, August 9, 1838.
140. *Ibid.*
141. Scharf, *History of Western Maryland*, 935, 947.
142. "Chrisman-Barnitz House: 227 East Main Street," Inventory Form For State Historic Sites Survey, *Maryland Historical Trust*, https://mht.maryland.gov/secure/medusa/PDF/Carroll/CARR-134B.pdf.
143. Scharf, *History of Western Maryland*, 959.
144. *The State Gazette and Merchants*, 502–528.
145. Williams & McKinsey, *History of Frederick County* 1, 168.
146. Frederick County Land Records, Liber WBT 3, Folio 100.
147. *Frederick [Maryland] Directory City Guide and Business Mirror 1859–1860* (Frederick, MD: C.S. Williams, 1859–1860).
148. Land Records Frederick County, Liber 12, Folio 240–241; Dieter Cunz, *The Maryland Germans: A History* (Princeton, NJ: Princeton University Press, 1948), 918.
149. *1850 U.S. Census*, Frederick County, Maryland, John G. Lipps, *Maryland State Archives*, 12A.
150. *1860 U.S. Census*, Frederick County, Maryland, John G. Lipps, Maryland State Archives, 578.
151. Frederick County Land Records Liber 3, Folio 466; Liber 14, Folio 470.
152. *1880 U.S. Census of Manufacturers*, Frederick County, John G. Lipps, *Maryland State Archives*, 3.
153. *1850 U.S. Census*, Frederick County, Maryland, Jacob Markell, *Maryland State Archives*, 42B.
154. Williams and McKinsey, *History of Frederick County* 1, 169.
155. Thomas John Chew Williams and Folger McKinsey, *History of Frederick County, Maryland, from the Earliest Settlements to the Present Time, Including a History of Hagerstown* 2 (Baltimore: Regional Pub. Co., 1967), 710, 715, 770.
156. Frederick County Land Records, Liber ES 5, Folio 268.
157. *1860 Census*, Frederick County, Maryland, Jacob Markell, Maryland State Archives, 581; Frederick County Land Records, Liber BGF 4, Folio 213; Liber BGF 4, Folio 292.
158. Williams and McKinsey, *History of Frederick County* 2, 962.
159. *Ibid.*
160. *1860 Census of Manufacturers*, Frederick County, Maryland, 1.
161. Williams and McKinsey, *History of Frederick County* 2, 962–963; *1860 Census*, Frederick County, Maryland, 586. *1870 Census*, Frederick, Maryland, Ward 2, 36.
162. Schildknecht, *Monocacy & Catoctin*, 222, 259.
163. Frederick County Land Records, Liber WBT 3, Folio 234–246.
164. Scharf, *History of Western Maryland* 1, 580.
165. *The Gettysburg Times*, December 29, 1937.
166. Allegany County Land Records, Liber DD, Folio 83.
167. Kelley, *Brewing in Maryland*, 629.
168. *1860 U.S. Census of Manufacturers*, Allegany County, Maryland, 10.
169. Allegany County Land Records, Liber 8, Folio 318–319; Liber 7, Folio 508; Liber 17, Folio 596; *1850 U.S. Census*, Allegany County, Maryland, 466.

170. Allegany Land Records, Liber 7, Folio 508; Liber 17, Folio 596; Liber 14, Folio 176, Folio 208. The brewery was located on North Centre Street, which was called Broad Street at the time of Hodel's original purchases, and was changed in 1856.

171. *1860 Census of Manufacturers*, Allegany County, Maryland, Maryland State Archives, 10.

172. *1850 Census*, Allegany County, Maryland, Bartholomew Himmler, Maryland State Archives, 461.

173. Allegany County Land Records, Liber 5, Folio 738.

174. *1850 Census*, Allegany County, Maryland, Bartholomew Himmler, Maryland State Archives, v457.

175. Allegany County Land Records, Liber 17, Folio 133.

176. *1860 Census of Manufacturers*, Allegany County, Maryland, Maryland State Archives, 10.

177. *1860 Census*, Allegany County, Maryland, John Zink (name misspelled as 'Sink'), Maryland State Archives, 56.

178. *1860 Census*, Allegany County, Maryland, James McNulty, Maryland State Archives, 456; Kelley, *Brewing in Maryland*, 712; *Maryland Gazetteer & Business Directory* (Baltimore: George W. Hawes, 1867), 123.

179. *1870 Census*, Alleghany County, Pennsylvania, James McNulty, Maryland State Archives, 7.

180. Kelley, *Brewing in Maryland*, 712.

181. *Ibid.*, 12. The census and directories have the name spelled as both "Haneykamp" and "Hamkamp." The correct spelling is listed in the text above.

182. *1860 U.S. Census*, Allegany County, Maryland, Hamkamp, Maryland State Archives, 432.

183. Kelley, *Brewing in Maryland*, 709.

184. *1860 U.S. Census of Manufacturers*, Allegany County, Maryland State Archives, 12.

185. Kelley, *Brewing in Maryland*, 709; *Boyd's Business Directory*, 331.

186. *1860 U.S. Census*, Washington County, Maryland, Margaret Butz, Maryland State Archives, 286.

187. *Ibid.*; *Maryland Gazetteer*, 1867, 493.

188. Washington County Land Records, Liber IN 2, Folio 280.

189. Washington County Land Records, Liber YY, Folio 226–229.

190. *1850 U.S. Census of Manufacturers*, Washington County, Maryland, Gelwicks, Maryland State Archives, 389.

191. *Herald of Freedom and Torch Light*, July 12, 1854.

192. *Herald of Freedom and Torch Light,* September 19, 1855; Washington County Land Records, Liber IN 16, Folio 389; Liber IN 10, Folio 267.

193. *Herald of Freedom and Torch Light*, October 10, 1855; November 21, 1855.

194. *1850 U.S. Census*, Washington County, Maryland, Peter Middlekauf, Maryland State Archives, 205A; *1860 U.S. Census*, Washington County, Maryland, Peter Middlekauf, Maryland State Archives, 15.

195. Washington County Land Records, Liber IN 13, Folio 602–603.

196. Washington County Land Records, Liber LBN 1, Folio 71.

197. *1850 U.S. Census of Manufacturers*, Washington County, Maryland, Maryland State Archives, 391;

1850 *U.S. Census*, Washington County, Maryland, Andrew Leibold, Maryland State Archives, 124A.

198. *1850 U.S. Census of Manufacturers.*

199. *Maryland Gazetteer*, 1867, 493.

200. *1880 U.S. Census*, Washington County, Maryland, William Witzenbacher, Maryland State Archives, 342B.

201. Kelley, *Brewing in Maryland*, 688.

202. Washington County Land Records, Liber IN 18, Folio 9.

203. *Boyd's Business Directory*, 331.

204. *1880 U.S. Census*, Washington County, Maryland William Witzenbacher, Maryland State Archives, 342b.

205. Williams and Folger, *History of Washington County* 2, 949–951.

206. Brantz Mayer, *Baltimore As It Was and As It Is: A Historical Sketch of the Ancient Town and the Modern City* (Baltimore: Richardson & Bennett, 1871), 87, 95, 97.

207. Frederick Ludwig died in 1852 and his brewery was left for sale by trustees of his estate. The property was still unsold as of 1854. Frederick Weber does not appear in the census or any directory until 1860 when he is operating the former Ludwig plant on Belvedere (*Woods' Directory*, 1860, 402.) Deutschen Literarische Bureau, *Baltimore: Seine Vergangenheit und Gegenwart* (Baltimore: Druck und Satz von C.C. Bartgis & Bro., 1887), 335–336, states that Weber married the Ludwig widow sometime after Ludwig's death and continued operations. If this were the case, it was operated while the family still held ownership, and the property was in the hands of trustees until the sale. Land records do not support Weber until 1856 when he enters into a mortgage agreement on Hollins Street, which is paid in 1861 (Liber GES 203, Folio 328). The state of the brewery is unclear in those intervening years.

208. Christopher Hitzrodt was not included in this list as a brewery proprietor. The correct spelling of his name is "Hitzroth," and he is listed in one directory: *Matchett's*, 1855–1856, as a beer brewer at 40 Thames Street. There is no Hitrodt or Hitzroth in the census for Baltimore, but there is a Hitzroth family in the 1870 census in Pennsylvania. There is not substantial information to include him as he was most likely a brewer for another brewery during his time in Baltimore. There were no land records bearing his name at the time, nor advertisements found in newspapers for a brewery owned by Hitzroth.

209. John Bodenschatz of Bavaria was not included in this list as a brewery proprietor. Not only does he not appear in the census of 1860, he is listed as a laborer and retired liquor dealer in the census of 1870. Bodenschatz is listed in the 1863 *Woods' Directory* as a liquor dealer at 44 Camden. He is listed in the *Woods'* 1870 and 1880 directories as a tavern owner on Pratt. There is insufficient evidence to consider him a brewery owner during his time in Baltimore. The land records of the time (1873) indicate Bodenschatz and his wife paying off a mortgage on the property located at West Pratt (where his tavern was located) and immediately mortgaging that row of brick homes and adjacent lots to John Bauernschmidt, Jr. on the same day (Liber GR 634 Folio 320, 326). There were no advertisements in newspapers of the time for a brewery owned by Bodenschatz.

Chapter 4

1. Frederick Douglass, *Narrative of the Life of Frederick Douglass, an American Slave* (Boston: The Antislavery Office, 1845), 34–35.

2. T. Stephen Whitman, *The Price of Freedom: Slavery and Manumission in Baltimore and Early National Maryland* (New York: Routledge, 2000), 8–14.

3. "An Act Concerning Negroes and Other Slaves," *Proceedings and Acts of the General Assembly January 1637/8-September 1664* 1, 533–534.

4. Benjamin Banneker, *Benjamin Banneker's Pennsylvania, Delaware, Maryland and Virginia Almanack and Ephemeris for the Year of Our Lord, 1792; Being Bissextile, or Leap-Year, and the Sixteenth Year of American Independence* (Baltimore: Goddard & Angell, 1797); Silvio Bedini, *The Life of Benjamin Banneker* (New York: Charles Scribner's Sons, 1972).

5. *Proceedings and Acts of the General Assembly January-June 1692* 13, 451–457, 546–549; *Proceedings and Acts of the General Assembly January-June 1711–1729* 30, 65–66, 177–179.

6. Peter Kolchin, *American Slavery 1619–1877* (London: Macmillan, 2003), 82, 253–257.

7. Washington County Land Records, Liber IN 9, Folio 248. Lipps home was later known as the Steiner House, which is now a confirmed stop on the Underground Railroad tour in Frederick, Maryland.

8. Harry Ezratty, *Baltimore in the Civil War: The Pratt Street Riot and a City Occupied* (Charleston, SC: The History Press, 2010), 44.

9. Daniel Carroll Toomey, *The War Came by Train: The Baltimore & Ohio Railroad during the Civil War* (Baltimore: Baltimore & Ohio Railroad Museum, 2013), 18–19.

10. *Ibid.*, 20.

11. *Ibid.*, 58–62.

12. Ezratty, *Baltimore in the Civil War*, 67.

13. Toomey, *The War Came by Train*, 33.

14. *The Constitution of the United States of America* (Washington, D.C.: Government Printing Office, 2007).

15. "An Act for Enrolling and Calling Out the National Forces, and for Other Purposes," *Congressional Record*, 37th Congress, 3d Session Ch. 74, 75, March 3, 1863.

16. Deutschen Literarische Bureau, *Baltimore: Seine Vergangenheit*, 335–336.

17. *1880 U.S. Census*, Baltimore, Maryland, Maryland State Archives, 140D.

18. Deutschen Literarische Bureau, *Baltimore: Seine Vergangenheit*, 335–336. Berger installed a Von Linde Refrigeration machine.

19. *The Baltimore Sun*, October 6, 1896.

20. *The Baltimore Sun*, December 26, 1898.

21. *The Baltimore Sun*, August 13, 1863.

22. *The Baltimore Sun*, March 23, 1881.

23. Index to the Naturalization Petitions for the U.S. Circuit and District Courts of Maryland, 1797–1951, NARA M1168, John F. Wiessner of Bavaria Naturalized 1860, Witness John Kinzey, Baltimore Maryland.

24. Kelley, *Brewing in Baltimore*, 294.

25. A. Von Degen, *Baltimore; Its Past and Present* (Baltimore: The Baltimore Brewers and Maltsters Association, 1887), 38.

26. *The Baltimore Sun*, August 30, 1866; Library of Congress, "E. Sachse, & Co.'s."

27. Aaron Packard, "Baltimore's Schuetzen Park and Its Tokens," *NOVA Numismatics: The Historical Pursuit of Exonumia*, January 23, 2012.

28. "Local Matters," *The Baltimore Sun* (Baltimore, MD), May 28, 1878.

29. Samuel Berry, "The Wiessners and Their Horses," *The Baltimore Sun* (Baltimore, MD), July 3, 1960.

30. Robert Wahl, "John Frederick Wiessner," *American Brewer's Review* 20, (1906): 573.

31. R.L. Polk & Co., *Baltimore City Directory 1892* (Baltimore: R.L. Polk, 1892), 1306.

32. Kelley, *Brewing in Maryland*, 300–301.

33. Wahl, "John Frederick Wiessner," 573.

34. Polk & Co., Baltimore City Directory, 1306.

35. Library of Congress, "E. Sachse, & Co.'s."

36. *The Baltimore Sun*, May 28, 1878.

37. *The Baltimore Sun*, March 3, 1870.

38. James Bauernschmidt, phone interview with author, Baltimore, Maryland, September 29, 2014.

39. Kelley, *Brewing in Maryland*, 311.

40. Bauenschmidt, phone interview, 2014.

41. "Buried $14,000 in Gold Coins: Late George Bauernschmidt Put Coin Under Front Steps," *The Baltimore Sun* (Baltimore, MD), November 19, 1904.

42. Kelley, *Brewing in Maryland*, 243–244, 246.

43. Bauernschmidt, phone interview, 2014.

44. Kelley, *Brewing in Maryland*, 247.

45. "John J. Bauernschmidt Jr. Obituary," *The Baltimore Sun* (Baltimore, MD), June 30, 1879.

46. Kelley, *Brewing in Baltimore*, 472.

47. Deutschen Literarische Bureau, *Baltimore: Seine Vergangenheit*, 335–336.

48. *1880 U.S. Census* Baltimore, Maryland, John Von der Horst, 429A, MSA.

49. Scharf, *History of Baltimore*, 931.

50. Deutschen Literarische Bureau, *Baltimore: Seine Vergangenheit*, 335–336.

51. William Stump, "The Man in the Street," *The Baltimore Sun* (Baltimore, MD), January 14, 1951.

52. *The New York Times*, July 29, 1905.

53. Fred Lieb, *The Baltimore Orioles: The History of a Colorful Team in Baltimore and St. Louis* (Carbondale: Southern Illinois University Press, 2005), 63–78, 81.

54. Baltimore City Land Records, Liber 1776, Folio 35.

55. *The New York Times*, July 29, 1905.

56. *The Baltimore Sun*, February 26, 1904.

57. *1870 U.S. Census*, Baltimore, Maryland, George Brehm, Maryland State Archives, 758; "Marriage Reference: Gertrude Neis M George Brehm," Maryland State Archives, May 3, 1866, http://msa.maryland.gov/megafile/msa/stagsere/se1/se27/000100/000112/pdf/se27-0112.pdf.

58. *The Baltimore Sun*, November 1, 1867.

59. *The Baltimore Sun*, October 15, 1906.

60. *Ibid.*

61. *The Baltimore Sun*, September 10, 1889.

62. *The Baltimore Sun*, December 5, 1898.

63. George Washington Englehardt, *Baltimore City, Maryland: The Book of Its Board of Trade* (Baltimore: George Washington Englehardt, 1895), 179–180.

64. Kelley, *Brewing in Maryland*, 216–219.

65. *1880 U.S. Census*, Baltimore, Maryland, Louis Muth, Maryland State Archives, 15.

66. *The Baltimore Sun*, November 3, 1880.

67. Sherrif, *Polk Directory*, 1888, 810.

68. Kelley, *Brewing in Maryland*, 398–399; Edwards, *Industries of Maryland*, 373.

69. *1870 U.S. Census*, Baltimore, Maryland, Philip Odenwald, Maryland State Archives, 272.

70. Kelley, *Brewing in Maryland*, 281–283.

71. *1870 U.S. Census*, Baltimore, Maryland, Philip Odenwald, Maryland State Archives, 272; *Woods' Directory*, 1870, 776; *The Baltimore Sun*, November 21, 1884.

72. *1870 U.S. Census*, Baltimore, Maryland, John Summerfield, Maryland State Archives, 252.

73. *The Baltimore Sun*, January 11, 1881.

74. Von Degen, *Baltimore: Its Past and Present*, 36.

75. *The Baltimore Sun*, August 16, 1894.

76. Edwards, *Industries of Maryland*, 239.

77. *The Baltimore Sun*, February 6, 1891.

78. Baltimore City Land Records, Liber 1780, Folio 20.

79. Loudon Cemetery Plot P 197 and 199, Headstone/Grave of August Beck Senior and Son Adolph, *1870 Census*, Baltimore, 39.

80. *The Baltimore Sun*, May 24, 1865.

81. *The Baltimore Sun*, June 10, 1868.

82. *1870 U.S. Census*, Baltimore, Maryland, August Beck, Maryland State Archives, 39.

83. *The Baltimore Sun*, October 17, 1871.

84. *The Baltimore Sun*, December 5, 1876.

85. Maryland Historical Trust, Site Survey B-1058.

86. *The Baltimore Sun*, March 11, 1872; December 6, 1872.

87. *The Baltimore Sun*, February 22, 1876.

88. *The Baltimore Sun*, November 12, 1880.

89. *The Baltimore Sun*, December 2, 1880.

90. *The Baltimore Sun*, September 10, 1881.

91. Baltimore County Land Records, Liber WMI 123, Folio 19.

92. Von Degen, *Baltimore; Its Past and Present*, 38.

93. *1880 U.S. Census*, Baltimore, Millington, Maryland, John Shultheis, Maryland State Archives, 318.

94. Baltimore County Land Records, Liber EHA 48, Folio 57; Liber EHA 48, Folio 62; Liber EHA 33, Folio 416.

95. Baltimore County Land Records, Liber EHA 48, Folio 61; Liber EHA 33, Folio 416.

96. Edwards, *Industries of Maryland*, 283.

97. *The Baltimore Sun*, April 17, 1885.

98. *Woods' Directory*, 1886, 1521.

99. Morton Mcl. Dukehart, *A Collection of Authenticated Biographical Sketches of the Author's Ancestors Dating from the Thirty Years War (1618–1648) and Continuing Unbroken Sequence to the Date of Publication (1947)*, 2nd ed. (Baltimore: Morton Dukehart, 1947), 79–81.

100. *Ibid.*, 105–110.

101. Edwards, *Industries of Maryland*, 373.

102. *The Brewer's Guide to the United States, Canada, and Mexico 1898* (Chicago: American Brewers Review, 1898), 35.

103. Baltimore County Land Records, Liber 181, Folio 426, 507, 509, 513.

104. Sherrif, *Polk Directory*, 1890–1891, 63.

105. Baltimore City Land Records, Liber EHA 73, Folio 265.

106. Edwards, *Industries of Maryland*, 229.

107. *The Baltimore Sun*, January 20, 1885.

108. Von Degen, *Baltimore; Its Past and Present*, 28.

109. *The Baltimore Sun*, June 20, 1889; *The Baltimore Sun*, September 11, 1891.

110. *The Chicago Journal of Commerce and Metal Industries* 61, 1892, 27.

111. Kelley, *Brewing in Maryland*, 521–522.

112. *The Brewer's Guide 1898*, 36.

113. Baltimore City Land Records, Liber 1780, Folio 468.

114. Baltimore County Land Records, Liber JHL 50, Folio 331.

115. Kelley, *Brewing in Baltimore*, 359.

116. *The Baltimore Sun*, November 12. 1874.

117. Isidor Blum, *The Jews of Baltimore: An Historical Summary of Their Progress and Status as Citizens of Baltimore from the Early Days to the Year Nineteen Hundred and Ten* (Baltimore: Historical Review Pub. Co., 1910), 133–137.

118. Von Degen, *Baltimore; Its Past and Present*, 27.

119. Sherrif, *Polk Directory*, 1890, 64.

120. Baltimore City Land Records, Liber 1804, Folio 237; Liber 1819, Folio 498.

121. Deutschen Literarische Bureau, *Baltimore: Seine Vergangenheit*, 342.

122. *The Baltimore Sun*, March 30, 1880.

123. Deutschen Literarische Bureau, *Baltimore: Seine Vergangenheit*, 342.

124. *1870 U.S. Census*, Baltimore, Maryland, Sebastian Helldorfer, Maryland State Archives, 305.

125. *The Baltimore Sun*, January 30, 1893.

126. *1900 U.S. Census* Baltimore, Maryland, George Guenther, Maryland State Archives, 252. Guenther is spelled in various incarnations. Guenther is the correct German spelling. It was later adjusted to Gunther, a more easy and Americanized version. Both are acceptable.

127. Deutschen Literarische Bureau, *Baltimore: Seine Vergangenheit*, 326.

128. Bradford Rhodes, *The Bankers Magazine* 60, (January–June 1900): 625.

129. *Ibid.*

130. Deutschen Literarische Bureau, *Baltimore: Seine Vergangenheit*, 326.

131. *Ibid.*; Von Degen, *Baltimore; Its Past and Present*, 26.

132. Baltimore City Land Records, Liber JB 1069, Folio 202; Liber JB 1069, Folio 497; Liber JB 1073, Folio 319; Liber 1166, Folio 367.

133. *Ibid.*

134. *The Baltimore Sun*, February 15, 1894.

135. Kelley, *Brewing in Maryland*, 258.

136. Baltimore County Land Records, Liber JB 69, Folio 257; Liber JB 83, Folio 464.

137. Baltimore County Land Records, Liber JB 83, Folio 464; Liber WMI 118, Folio 434.

138. *Woods' Directory* 1881, 465.

139. "Tuberculosis and Its Prevention," *Journal of the American Medical Association* 23 (August 25, 1894): 302. This is also why there is a TB epidemic among miners in South Africa: close quarters, no sunlight and stagnant air for bacteria to thrive and spread.

140. *1880 U.S. Census*, Baltimore, Maryland, 1st Ward, Henry Beck, Maryland State Archives, 18.

141. *Brewers Guide to the United States*, 35.

142. *Woods' Directory*, 1867, 167, 638; *The Baltimore Sun*, June 21, 1883.

143. *Woods' Directory*, 1868, 167, 681.

144. *Ibid.*, 1870, 775–776.

145. *The Baltimore Sun*, October 22, 1881.

146. Baltimore City Land Records, Liber GR 1118, Folio 556, Liber GR 720, Folio 351.

147. *The Baltimore Sun*, December 15, 1887.

148. Kelley, *Brewing in Maryland*, 393–4.

149. *Journal of the Institute of Brewing* 8 (1903): 623–624; *International Brewer's Journal* 36 (1900): 578–579.

150. Kelley, *Brewing in Maryland*, 393.

151. Frank H. Sandkuhler, "I Remember ...Wiess Beer Being Bottled in the Basement," *The Baltimore Sun* (Baltimore, MD), May 12, 1974.

152. *1870 U.S. Census*, Baltimore, Maryland, John Nagengast, Maryland State Archives, 361.

153. *Woods' Directory*, 1877, 461.

154. F.W. Salem, *Beer: Its History and Economic Value as a National Beverage* (New York: Arno, 1972), 213.

155. *The American Engineer* 22, no. 3 (July 18, 1891): 21; Von Degen, *Baltimore; Its Past and Present*, 31.

156. Deutschen Literarische Bureau, *Baltimore: Seine Vergangenheit*, 331.

157. Salem, *Beer: Its History*, 212.

158. Sherrif, *Polk Directory*, 1890–1891, 62.

159. *Woods' Directory*, 1864, 53, 103, 384.

160. Mayer, *Baltimore As It Was and As It Is*, 118.

161. Howard, *The Monumental City*, 139.

162. *Woods' Directory*, 1871, 818; *Woods' Directory*, 1877, 109.

163. Salem, *Beer: Its History*, 213.

164. *Williams' Wheeling Directory, City Guide, and Business Mirror* (Wheeling: A.W. Paul & Co, 1868), 61.

165. *1870 U.S. Census*, Wheeling, West Virginia, 5th Ward, John Butterfield, Maryland State Archives, 39.

166. *West Virginia State Gazetteer and Business Directory* (Wheeling: Standard Printing Co.,1877), 364.

167. *1870 U.S. Census*, New York, NY, 20th Ward, Gottleib, 77.

168. Deutschen Literarische Bureau, *Baltimore: Seine Vergangenheit*, 331; Edwards, *Industries of Maryland*, 194.

169. Henry Elliott Shepherd, *The History of Baltimore, Maryland, from Its Foundings as a Town to the Current Year 1729–1898* (Baltimore: S.B. Nelson, 1898), 703–704.

170. *1880 U.S. Census of Agriculture & Manufacturers*, Baltimore City, Maryland, Maryland State Archives, 5.

171. Shepherd, *The History of Baltimore, Maryland*, 700.

172. *The Baltimore Sun*, June 25, 1889.

173. Baltimore City Land Records, Liber 1794, Folio 409.

174. Eleanor Bruchey, "The Industrialization of Maryland 1860–1914," in *Maryland: A History 1632–1974*, ed. Richard Walsh and William Lloyd Fox (Baltimore: Maryland Historical Society, 1974), 444.

175. Hermann Schlüter, *The Brewing Industry and the Brewery Workers' Movement in America* (New York: B. Franklin, 1970), 129–131.

176. Kelley, *Brewing in Maryland*, 529.

177. *1870 U.S. Census*, Carrol County, Westminster, Maryland, William Liedlich, 540b. The spelling also has incarnations that include "Liedlick."

178. *The Democratic Advocate*, September 2, 1869.

179. *The Democratic Advocate*, January 26, 1871; *Ibid.*

180. *1870 U.S. Census*, Carroll County, Westminster, William Liedlich, Maryland State Archives, 540b.

181. *The Democratic Advocate*, September 11, 1871.

182. *The State Gazette and Merchants and Farmers' Directory for Maryland and District of Columbia*, 1871 (Baltimore: Sadler, Drysdale & Purnell, 1871), 485–501.

183. *Washington DC City Directory*, 1873, 507.

184. *Maryland Gazetteer*, 1867, 533.

185. *1880 U.S. Census of Agriculture & Manufacturers*, Fredrick City, Maryland, Maryland State Archives, 3.

186. Schildknecht, *Monocacy & Catoctin* 2, 1096.

187. *1900 U.S. Census*, Frederick City, Maryland, John Kuhn, 6.

188. Kelley, *Brewing in Maryland*, 674.

189. Toomey, *The War Came by Train*, 117–121.

190. Washington County Land Records, Liber LBN 1, Folio 71.

191. *The Daily Mail*, February 23, 1939.

192. *Boyd's Business Directory*, 316, 331; Washington County Land Records, Liber IN 8, Folio 586.

193. *The Daily Mail*, 136.

194. *An Illustrated Atlas of Washington County, Maryland: Drawn and Published from Actual Surveys* (Philadelphia: Lake, Griffing & Stevenson, 1877), 10; Scharf, *History of Western Maryland* 1, 1100.

195. Washington County Land Records, Liber GBO 76, Folio 532.

196. *The Washington Post*, September 10, 1894. Scharf, *History of Western Maryland* 1, 1181.

197. Washington County Land Records, Liber 96, Folio 309; Kelley, *Brewing in Maryland*, 698.

198. *1880 U.S. Census* Washington County, Hagerstown, Maryland, Robery Shuster, Maryland State Archives, 22.

199. *1870 U.S. Census*, Washington County, Hagerstown, Maryland, William Wagner, 86, MSA.

200. Salem, *Beer: Its History*, 214.

201. *1860 U.S. Census*, Allegany County, Frostburg, Maryland, Peter Hinckle, 99; *1900 U.S. Census*, Allegany County, Mount Savage, Maryland, Hinckle, 10. There are a few incarnations of Hinkle, including "Hinckle," "Henckel," and "Henkel."

202. *1870 U.S. Census*, Allegany County, Mount Savage, Maryland, Hinckle, Maryland State Archives, 5.

203. Allegany County Land Records, Liber 26, Folio 293. Liber 27, Folio 45. Liber 38, Folio 170.

204. Allegany County Land Records, Liber 28, Folio 628.

205. Kelley, *Brewing in Maryland*, 713.

206. Salem, *Beer: Its History*, 214.

207. *1870 U.S. Census*, Allegany County, Cumberland, Maryland, Bartholomew Himmler, Maryland State Archives, 34. Himmler originally relocated to West Virginia, then moved on to Virginia to farm.

208. Allegany County Land Records, Liber 42, Folio 509; Liber 45, Folio 526.

209. *Boyd's Business Directory*, 1875, 331.

210. *Cumberland City Directory* (Cumberland; John Fulton & Co, 1884), 52.
211. Salem, *Beer: Its History*, 213.
212. *Cumberland City Directory*, 1884, 52.
213. *1870 U.S. Census*, Allegany County, Cumberland, Maryland, William Himmler, 34; *1880 U.S. Census*, Allegany County, Maryland, Cumberland, Maryland State Archives, 106A.
214. *Sanborn Fire Insurance Map from Cumberland, Allegany County, Maryland* (Colorado Springs: Sanborn Map Co., 1887), section 2.
215. *Sanborn Fire Insurance Map from Cumberland, Allegany County, Maryland* (Colorado Springs: Sanborn Map Co, 1892), section 12.
216. *1880 U.S. Census*, Allegany County, Cumberland, Maryland, John H. Zink, Maryland State Archives, 96 A.
217. *1900 U.S. Census*, Allegany County, Cumberland, Maryland, John H. Zink, Maryland State Archives, 8 B.
218. *Sanborn Fire Insurance Map*, 1892, section 12.
219. *1910 U.S. Census*, Allegany County, Cumberland, Maryland, John H. Zink, Maryland State Archives, 4A.
220. Kelley, *Brewing in Maryland*, 630.
221. *1880 U.S. Census*, Allegany County, Cumberland, Maryland, Paul Hugo Ritter, Maryland State Archives, 124 C.
222. *Cumberland Directory*, 1884, 126; *Cumberland Directory*, 1890, 127.
223. Salem, *Beer: Its History*, 213.
224. James Wolf, "The Breweries of Cumberland, Maryland," *The Keg* (Summer 2006): 6.
225. Allegany County Land Records, Liber 37, Folio 148.
226. *Cumberland Directory*, 1884, 108.
227. Land Records, Allegany County, Maryland, Liber 78, Folio 320.
228. *Sanborn Fire Insurance Map*, 1892, section 9.
229. *1860 U.S. Census*, Allegany County, Cumberland, Maryland, Michael Fesenmeier, Maryland State Archives, 196.
230. Allegany County Land Records, Liber 18, Folio 393; Allegany County Land Records, Liber 20, Folio 685.
231. *1870 U.S. Census*, Allegany County, Cumberland, Maryland, Michael Fesenmeier, Maryland Land Records, 94.
232. Salem, *Beer: Its History*, 213.
233. *Cumberland Directory*, 1884, 35.
234. Kelley, *Brewing in Maryland*, 644.
235. Wolf, "The Breweries of Cumberland, Maryland," 6.
236. Allegany County Land Records, Liber 77, Folio 617, 620.
237. *Cumberland Directory*, 1890, 270.
238. Wolf, "The Breweries of Cumberland, Maryland," 6.
239. *Sanborn Fire Insurance Map*, 1910.
240. *The Daily News Directory of the City of Cumberland*, 1876, 23.
241. William Leonard gave up the brewery within a year, but continued to operate as a Malthouse on the site until 1897, supplying malt to the local breweries in Allegany County. It was a much more lucrative option for Leonard. *Cumberland Directory*, 1884, 69.

Chapter 5

1. Orrin Chalfant Painter, *William Painter and His Father Dr. Edward Painter: Sketches and Reminiscences* (Baltimore: The Arundel Press, 1914), 7, 23.
2. *Ibid.*, 8,14.
3. *Ibid.*, 20.
4. *Ibid.*, 28, 31.
5. *Ibid.*
6. *Ibid.*, 49, 51.
7. Delbert B. Lowe, *History of the Consolidated Gas, Electric, Light, and Power Company of Baltimore* (College Park: University of Maryland, 1928), 1–5.
8. Werner Troesken, "Regime Change and Corruption: A History of Public Utility Regulation," in *Corruption and Reform: Lessons from America's Evonomic History*, ed. Edward L. Glaeser and Claudia Goldin, (Chicago: *National Bureau of Economic Research*, March 2006), 259–281.
9. *Ibid.* As expected, this caused many other problems with rate and utilities.
10. Sherry H. Olson, *Baltimore: The Building of an American City* (Baltimore; Johns Hopkins University Press, 1980), 251.
11. *Ibid.*, 250.
12. *Ibid.*, 246–248.
13. National Fire Protection Association Standards, 1905.
14. "City of Baltimore United Breweries, Limited" *Brewer's Guardian* 25, no. 632 (January 1, 1895): 14; Mira Wilkins, *The History of Foreign Investment in the United States to 1914* (Cambridge: Harvard University Press, 1989), 325–325.
15. Baltimore City Land Records, Liber 1776, Folio 039.
16. Baltimore City Land Records, Liber 1800, Folio 257.
17. "News of the Courts: Suit Instituted for the Dissolution of the Brewers' Exchange and the Sale of its Assets. Action Caused by Formation of Maryland Brewing Company," *The Baltimore Sun* (Baltimore, MD), December 30, 1898.
18. "The Brewery Combine: The Maryland Company Formally Launched—Large Savings Expected by Promoters," *The Baltimore Sun* (Baltimore, MD), March 2, 1899.
19. "Maryland Brewing Company," *The Baltimore Sun* (Baltimore, MD), November 2, 1899.
20. "Maryland Brewing Company Employees," *The Baltimore Sun* (Baltimore, MD), July 17, 1899; "Asks For A Receiver: A Bill Against the Maryland Brewing Company, Raymond H. Whiting Files It—Alleges Company Is Insolvent and Is About to Default Its Interest—Officials Decline to Talk," *The Baltimore Sun* (Baltimore, MD), February 28, 1901.
21. "The Temperance Cause: An Advocate for it Among the Ranks of the Brewer's Association," *The Baltimore* Sun (Baltimore, MD), March 15, 1900.
22. "New Brewery Plan: Trust Plants to Be Bought in Under Foreclosure Proceedings Then Leased to New Concern—The Financial Plan Provides for Reducing the Fixed Charges and Getting More Working Capital," *The Baltimore Sun* (Baltimore, MD), April 27, 1901.
23. "Big Buisiness in Beer: Showing Made by Gottlieb-Bauernschmidt-Straus Company," *The Baltimore Sun* (Baltimore, MD), May 13, 1905; Gottlieb-Bauernschmidt-Straus, *Eigenbrot Ledgers* 1, Baltimore

Museum of Industry Rare Book Collection; "A Great
Bottling Plant: GBS Brewing Company Has One of
the Finest in the World," *The Baltimore Sun* (Baltimore, MD), September 30, 1905.

24. Baltimore City Land Records, Liber 1776, Folio
039.

25. Bauernschmidt, phone interview, 2014.

26. "Retired from the Firm: Frederick Bauern-
schmidt Has Sold His Interest in the Well Known
Brewing Company," *The Baltimore Sun* (Baltimore,
MD), July 15, 1898.

27. "A New Brewery: Frederick Bauernschmidt's
Large Building Completed," *The Baltimore Sun* (Baltimore, MD), January 24, 1900.

28. *American Brewer's Review* 28 (1914): 312;
American Brewer's Review 12 (1899): 322.

29. *American Brewer's Review* 30 (1916): 327;
American Brewer's Review 31 (1917): 97, 365.

30. *American Brewer's Review* 31 (1917): 157.

31. "Maryland Historical Trust State Historic Site
Inventory Form: Planter's Paradise," *Maryland Inventory of Historic Properties.* BA 263. https://mht.mary-
land.gov/secure/medusa/PDF/Baltimore%20County/
BA-263.pdf.

32. "Buried $14,000 in Gold Coins," *The Baltimore
Sun*, November 19, 1904.

33. *The Baltimore Sun*, August 14, 1899.

34. *Bauernschmidt vs. Bauernschmidt*, 101 Md.
148, 149 (Court of Appeals, 1905).

35. Bauernschmidt, phone interview, 2014.

36. *Ibid.*

37. *The Baltimore Sun*, May 24, 1899; June 16, 1913.

38. *The Baltimore Sun*, Obituary: J. Frederick Wiessner, March 8, 1904.

39. University of Maryland, *Bulletin of the School
of Medicine* 25, no. 1 (July 1940).

40. "About Weissner," *The Wiessner Foundation for
Children, Inc.*, http://wiessnerfoundation.org/About.
html.

41. *Wegefarth vs. Wiessner*, 134 Md. 555 (Court of
Appeals, 1919).

42. "Mr. J.F. Wiessner Dead: Was for Many Years
Head of Big Brewing Company," *The Baltimore Sun*
(Baltimore, MD), September 23, 1906.

43. *Wegefarth v. Wiessner*, 1919.

44. *Ibid.*

45. *Das Neue Baltimore, 1729–1905* (Baltimore:
The German Publishing Company, 1905), 194–195.

46. Charles Stalfort, Jr., "Grosspapa Frank Steil
Family History," Unpublished manuscript (Baltimore:
Zion Church Archives, 2009).

47. *Das Neue Baltimore*, 194–195.

48. Isidor Blum, *The Jews of Baltimore*, 412.

49. "The Call of the States," *American Brewer's Review: A Monthly Journal Devoted to the Science and
Practice of Brewing* 31 (1917): 155.

50. Kelley, *Brewing in Baltimore*, 536–537.

51. *American Brewer's Review* 20 (1906): 296.

52. *American Brewer's Review* 28 (1914): 65.

53. *American Brewer's Review* 19 (1905): 145.

54. U.S. Congress, Senate, "Brewing and Liquor In-
terests and German Propaganda: Hearings Before a
Subcommittee on the Judiciary," 65th Congress, 2nd
Session, Pursuant to SR 307 2 (Washington, D.C.:
Government Printing Office, 1919), 908.

55. R.I. Polk, *Baltimore City Directory 1906*, 1291.

56. *American Brewer's Review* 19 (1905): 498.

57. "Brewer's Case in Court: The Mount Vernon

Company Enjoins Chesapeake Company," *The Baltimore Sun* (Baltimore, MD), October 26, 1907.

58. *American Brewer's Review* 10 (1906): 622; *American Brewer's Review* 22, (1908): 492; *The Baltimore
Sun*, August 16, 1908.

59. New York Bar Association, *New York Supreme
Court Appellate Division, 2nd Dept* 733, 30–64, 86.

60. "Messrs. Eurich Go to Jail: Officials of Mount
Vernon Brewery Unable to Obtain Bail," *The Baltimore Sun* (Baltimore, MD), January 9, 1909.

61. "Big Brewery is Sold: New Owner Will Operate
Mount Vernon Plant on Large Scale," *The Baltimore
Sun* (Baltimore, MD), April 15, 1909.

62. *The Baltimore Sun*, April 12, 1900.

63. *The Baltimore Sun*, January 6, 1902.

64. *The Baltimore Sun*, October 5, 1904.

65. Sherrif, *Polk Directory*, 379.

66. *The Brewer's Handbook 1918* (Chicago: H.S.
Rich, 1918), 43; *American Brewer's Review* 30 (1916):
323.

67. *The Baltimore Sun*, March 6, 1908.

68. *American Brewer's Review* 30 (1916): 286.

69. *American Brewer's Review* 31 (1917): 204;
American Brewer's Review 24 (1910): 213.

70. Schlüter, *The Brewing Industry*, 72.

71. *American Brewer's Review* 12 (1899): 294–297.

72. Washington County Land Records, Liber 112,
Folio 527.

73. Clarence E. Weaver, *The Story of Hagerstown
1911* (Hagerstown: Mail Publishing Company, 1911),
19.

74. *American Brewers Review* 27 (1913): 285.

75. *American Brewer's Review* 30 (1916): 368.

76. *American Brewer's Review* 31 (1917): 404; Washington County Land Records, Liber 152, Folio 440.

77. *American Brewer's Review* 21 (1907): 325,
271.

78. Kelley, *Brewing in Maryland*, 681.

79. *American Brewer's Review* 22 (1908): 528.

80. *American Brewer's Review* 29 (1915): 19, 307.

81. *American Brewer's Review* 30 (1916): 361, 98.

82. *The Brewer's Journal and Barley Malt and Hop
Trades Reporter* 41 (1917): 498.

83. "Mayoralty Election Contest in the City Of
Cumberland 'Coulehan Against White' Republican
Mayor Called Upon to Defend Returns—Lack of Sys-
tem Alleged in Counting of Ballots," *The Baltimore
Sun* (Baltimore, MD), June 1, 1902.

84. *The Baltimore Sun*, December 23, 1902, 10.

85. "Abstracts of Corporations," *Governor's Message Submitted to the Legislature of 1903 with the Accompanying Reports and Documents of Fiscal Years
October 1, 1900 to September 30, 1902* (Charleston:
The Tribune, 1903) 1, 304; *The Baltimore Sun*, July 9,
1903, 5.

86. "City Official Indicted: Charges of Malfeasance
Against Mayor White of Cumberland, Maryland," *The
Baltimore Sun* (Baltimore, MD), April 22, 1904.

87. "How it All Ended: How Mayor White Was Not
Guilty of Nonfeasance," *The Baltimore Sun* (Baltimore, MD), May 9, 1904.

88. *American Brewer's Review* 31 (1917): 249.

89. "Brewery to Drop German," *The Baltimore Sun*
(Baltimore, MD), December 7, 1917.

90. "Marketing and Communications," *Printer's
Ink: A Journal for Advertising* 86, no. 1 (1914): 39.

91. *American Brewer's Review* 30 (1916): 323.

92. *American Brewer's Review* 31 (1917): 97, 400.

Chapter 6

1. "John Anderson to His Dearest Love," December 11, 1850, *Anderson Family Papers,* Maryland Historical Society Archives.

2. "John Anderson to His Dearest Love," January 25, 1851, *Anderson Family Papers,* Maryland Historical Society Archives.

3. "Early History," *Women's Christian Temperance Union.* Accessed July 11, 2014, https://www.wctu.org/history.html.

4. "The Temperance Movement in Cecil County," *The Baltimore Sun* (Baltimore, MD), February 12, 1874.

5. "The State Temperance Alliance," *The Baltimore Sun* (Baltimore, MD), May 7, 1874.

6. Edward Behr, *Prohibition: Thirteen Years That Changed America* (New York: Arcade, 1996), 67–71.

7. U.S. Congress, Senate, *Brewing and Liquor Interests,* 14–16.

8. Wust, *Zion in Baltimore 1755–1955,* 99–100.

9. Thomas R. Pegram, *One Hundred Percent American: Rebirth and Decline of the Ku Klux Klan in the 1920's* (Lanham: Rowan and Littlefield, 2011), 90–91, 101–103, 113; Hiram W. Evans, *The Klan: Defender of Americanism* (New York: Forum, 1925).

10. "Series 1: Minutes, 1923–1925," *Knights of the Ku Klux Klan, Klan No. 51, Mt. Rainier, Maryland Archives* (Special Collections: University of Maryland Hornbake Library).

11. Pegram, *One Hundred Percent American,* 3–5, 113; Knights of the Ku Klux Klan, series 2: Publications.

12. U.S. Congress, House, "The Volstead Act," 66th Congress, 1st session, H.R. 6810, Record Group 11, *General Records of the United States Government,* NARA (16 October 1919). The Volstead Act was named after the senator who penned it—Andrew Volstead.

13. *Ibid.*

14. *The Anti-Prohibition Manual: A Summary of Facts and Figures Dealing With Prohibition* (Cincinnati: National Wholesale Liquor Dealers Association of America, 1917), 49–51.

15. *Ibid.,* 41, 12.

16. *Ibid.,* 7.

17. *Ibid.,* 2, 56.

18. Wesley C. Mitchell, Chairman of President's Research Committee on Social Trends, *Prosperity and Thrift: The Coolidge Era and the Consumer Economy, 1921–1929* (New York: McGraw-Hill, 1933), 29–30, 32.

19. Mark Thornton, "Alcohol Prohibition was a Failure," *CATO Policy Analysis,* no. 157 (July 17, 1991).

20. George W. Liebmann, ed., "The Battle of Franklin Farms," in *Prohibition in Maryland: A Collection of Documents* (Baltimore: Calvert Institute for Policy Research, 2011), 12–16.

21. *Ibid.,* 17–18.

22. *Ibid.,* 20.

23. *Ibid.,* 174.

24. "A. C. Ritchie to Chandler P. Anderson," April 26, 1926, *Governors Correspondence: Albert Cabell Ritchie 1920–1935,* Maryland Hall of Records, Annapolis, MD f.d. 24-c.

25. U.S. Congress, Senate, Committee on the Judiciary, *The National Prohibition Law: Hearings before the Committee on the Judiciary,* 69th Congress, 1st Session, *Committee on the Judiciary,* 1926, 649–52.

26. Liebman, "The Battle of Franklin Farms," 12–16; Dana Kester-McCabe, "Fisherman by Day-Bootleggers by Night," *Delmarva Almanac,* n.d., http://delmarva-almanac.com/index.php/content/article/fishermen_by_day_-_bootleggers_by_night/.

27. *Delmarva Almanac.*

28. Thornton, "Alcohol Prohibition was a Failure," 1991.

29. "Twenty Freed in Bail After Raid on Brewery," *The Baltimore Sun* (Baltimore, MD), November 21, 1931; "Frederick Brewing Company Brewmaster Arrested," *The Washington Post* (Washington, D.C.), August 17, 1928.

30. Bauernschmidt, phone interview, 2014.

31. Michael V. Lardner, "Memoirs," (2013), 46–49.

32. *Ibid.*

33. *Ibid.,* 51–52, 57.

34. *Ibid.,* 50.

35. Liebman, "The Battle of Franklin Farms," 175.

36. H.L. Mencken, "Journal," Enoch Pratt Mencken Collection, September 3 and 23, 1932, 18.

37. "H.L. Mencken to Harry Rickel," March 27, 1933, *The New Mencken Letters,* edited by Carl Bode (New York: The Dial Press, 1977), 285–286.

38. H.L. Mencken, *Newspaper Days 1899–1906* (New York: Alfred A. Knopf, 1955), 180–181.

39. *Citizenship Declaration of John Fitzgerald,* State of Maryland, City of Baltimore, September 2, 1892.

40. Anne (Fitzgerald) Lansinger, interview with author, September 19, 2012. All family history has been obtained from the interview with Anne Lansinger, granddaughter of John Fitzgerald, where documents, photographs and unpublished family memoirs were provided for information and verification.

41. *Marriage Certificate: John Fitzgerald and Bridget McCormick,* State of Maryland, September 19, 1904.

42. Anne (Fitzgerald) Lansinger, interview with author.

43. Hobby Distiller's Association, *The Distillation of Spirits for Personal and Private Use: A Proposal to Amend Federal Law Title 26 of the United States Code (Internal Revenue Code) to Legalize Hobby Distilling* (Keller: HAD, 2013).

44. Herbert Asbury, *The Great Illusion: An Informal History of Prohibition* (New York: Doubleday, 1950), 279; *Oil, Paint, and Drug Reporter* 99, 1921, 29, 84.

45. Asbury; Lardner, 47, 57, 60.

46. Frank Farrell to John Edgar Hoover, January 28, 1935, "St. Valentines Day Massacre Confession," Federal Bureau of Investigation, http://vault.fbi.gov/St.%20Valentines%20Day%20Massacre/St%20Valentines%20Day%20Massacre%20Part%201%20of%202/view.

47. "Maryland Women Pledge Reform in Prohibition," *The Enterprise* (Brockton, MA), June 16, 1930, 4.

48. Pauline Sabin, "Declaration of Principles," in *Women and Repeal: The Story of the Women's Organization for National Prohibition Repeal,* Grace Cogswell Root (New York: Harper and Bros., 1934), 161–164.; U.S. Congress, House, "The Prohibition Amendment: Hearings Before the Committee on the Judiciary," 71st Congress, March 12, 1930, 41–43.

49. "Prohibition: United Wets," *Time* (New York, NY), November 7, 1932.

50. Maryland, *State of Maryland Session Laws* 421, Maryland State Archives, January 4–April 3, 1933 Session.

51. H.L. Mencken, *The Evening Sun* (Hanover, PA), September 17, 1923.

52. Picture and documentation provided by family member of Walter Samuel, William Janyska, July 2013.

53. Larry Handy, "The Arrow Beer Nudes," *Eastern Coast Breweriana Association,* n.d.

54. "Prohibition Repeal is Ratified at 5:32 PM; Roosevelt Asks Nation to Bar the Saloon; New York Celebrates with Quiet Restraint," *The New York Times* (New York, NY), December 5, 1933.

55. *Inaugural Addresses and Legislative Messages of Governor Albert C. Ritchie of Maryland 1920–1935* (Baltimore: n.d.), 3–15.

56. Erich Wagner, "Liquor Legislation is Complicated, Confusing and Very Local," *The Maryland Reporter* (Columbia, MD), March 16, 2010.

Chapter 7

1. "Power Pictorial," May 1935 (Baltimore: Consolidated Gas, Electric, Light and Power Company, 1935); "Century Roll of Honor Firms," *Baltimore Magazine* (Baltimore, MD), April 1940, 24–25.

2. "Power Pictorial," May 1935 (Baltimore: Consolidated Gas, Electric, Light and Power Company, 1935).

3. "Power Pictorial" June 1934 (Baltimore: Consolidated Gas, Electric, Light and Power Company, 1934).

4. Dori Whitney, "Salute to MBAA-100 Years," *Brewer's Digest,* August 1987, 18.

5. C.D. Heiser, "Educational Program Eliminates Beer Complaints," *Beer Distributor*, July, 1935, 20.

6. Robert B. Smith, Federal Housing Authority, "Modernization Loans Available to Distributors and Taverns," *Beer Distributor,* July 1935, 18.

7. "What Are the Prospects for Small Breweries?" *Brewery Age* 7, no. 1 (January 1939): 38.

8. Bart Potts, "The Principal Cause of Brewery Mortality," *Brewery Age,* January 1938, 22–23.

9. Dr. George Parrish, "The Health and Temperance Value of Beer," *Beer Distributor*, November 1935, 15–18.

10. Morris Pozen, "Can Good Beers Be Made with Domestic Hops?" *Brewery Age* 7, no. 6 (June 1939): 56.

11. "Latest Fiscal Year Stats for Maryland," *Brewery Age: Buyers Guide and Brewery Directory 1939,* table 5, 185.

12. "1939 Barley Acreage Up," *Brewery Age* 7, no. 4 (April 1939): 79.

13. Seibel Institute of Technology, "Adjuncts-Then and Now," *Brewery Age,* September, 1938, 64–65; R.B. Zimmerman, "Malted Rice as a Brewing Material," *Communications on the Science and Practice of Brewing*, no. 4 (December, 1938): 7–8.

14. *Miracle of the Can,* Caravel Films, Inc (American Educational Films, 1956); National Park Service, *American Can Company: Historic American Buildings Survey* (Philadelphia: Department of the Interior, 1988).

15. *Beer Distributor* (Chicago: Beer Distributor Publishing Co.), June 1935, 18.

16. *Beer Distributor* (Chicago: Beer Distributor Publishing Co.), November 1935, 21.

17. *Nineteenth Annual Report of Bureau of Statistics and Information of Maryland 1910* (Annapolis: Kohn & Pollack Printers, 1911), 57, 251.

18. *Maryland in World War II: Industry and Agriculture* 2 (Baltimore: War Records Division of Maryland Historical Society, 1951), 103–104.

19. *Ibid.,* 24.

20. *Ibid.,* 140.

21. Judy Barnett Litoff and David C. Smith, "United States Women's Land Army," in *The American Experience in WWII: The American People at War: Minorities and Women in the Second World War* 10 (New York: Taylor & Francis, 2003), 275–289.

22. *Maryland in World War II,* 2–6.

23. *Baltimore African American,* May 14, 1955; *The Virgin Islands Daily News,* July 14, 1941.

24. *Baltimore African American,* June 30, 1953.

25. "Black Moon Mysteries," *Database of Old Time Radio Programs and Peoples,* Accessed August 24, 2015.

26. Gilbert Sandler, "The Quiz of Two Cities," *The Baltimore Sun* (Baltimore, MD), May 4, 1993.

27. *The Washington Post,* April 18, 1940.

28. Bob Lemke, *Vintage Baseball Cards* (Iola: Krause Publications, 2011), 191.

29. Gilbert Sandler, "Beers and Breweries Have a Long History Here," *The Baltimore Sun* (Baltimore, MD), January 24, 1995; Burt Solomon, *Where They Ain't: The Fabled Life and Untimely Death of the Original Baltimore Orioles, the Team That Gave Birth to Modern Baseball* (New York: Simon & Schuster, 1999), 262.

30. "Gunther Brewing Co. Acquired Fort Pitt Brewing of Pittsburgh," *Washington Post* (Washington, D.C.), November 18, 1957.

31. Gilbert Sandler, *Glimpses of Jewish Baltimore* (Charleston: History Press, 2012), 68.

32. *Brewery Age,* January 1936, 76; *Brewery Age,* October 1936, 94; *Brewery Age,* December 1937, 61.

33. Stuart Shea, *Calling the Game: Baseball Broadcasting from 1920 to the Present* (Phoenix: SABR, 2015), 26–27.

34. American Brewery, Inc. v. United States of America 223F, 2d. 43, 48 (C.C.A. 4, 1955).

35. *Brewery Age,* May 1936, 36.

36. *Power Pictorial* (Baltimore: Consolidated Gas Electric Light and Power, 1933).

37. "Leaders Take Hockey Games," *The Baltimore Sun* (Baltimore, MD), February 16, 1936.

38. *Brewery Age,* 1935, 139.

39. *Brewery Age* 7, no. 3 (1939): 48.

40. *Brewery Directory and Supplies Index* (New York: Atlas Publishing Co., 1934), 35.

41. "Free State Brewery Sold: Name Now Wiessner Brewing," *Wall Street Journal* (New York, NY), July 14, 1950.

42. *The Milwaukee Sentinel,* November 23, 1952.

43. "Says Firm Here Made High Test Beer 3 Years Ago," *The Baltimore Sun* (Baltimore, MD), October 12, 1932.

44. *Brewery Age Buyers Guide,* 1935, 139; *The Baltimore Sun,* February 22, 1935.

45. *Brewery Age Buyers Guide,* 1939, 139.

46. *Brewery Age,* March 1939, 48–49.

47. *The Baltimore Sun,* April 5, 1939.

48. "Brewery Asks Receiver for Gay Street Tavern," *The Baltimore Sun* (Baltimore, MD), July 9, 1937.

49. *The Baltimore Sun,* April 21, 1940.

50. *Brewery Directory and Supplies Index* (New York: Atlas Publishing, 1934), 34–35.

51. *Brewery Age Buyer's Guide,* 1939, 139.

52. *Brewery Directory and Supplies,* 34–35.

53. *The Baltimore Sun,* October 20, 1939; *Brewery Age,* January 1938, 17.

54. *The Baltimore Sun,* July 23, 1934; *Brewery Directory and Supplies,* 34–35.

55. *The Baltimore Sun,* January 22, 1934; .July, 15, 1934.

56. *The Baltimore Sun,* February 1, 1937.

57. *Modern Brewery,* July 1935, 22.

58. Washington County Land Records, Liber 192, Folio 645; Washington County Land Records, Liber 195, Folio 636.

59. *Brewery Directory and* Supplies, 34–35.

60. *Brewery Age,* January 1936, 76; *Brewery Age,* July 1936, 16.

61. Washington County Land Records, Liber 203, Folio 150.

62. Kelley, Brewing in Maryland, 707. This was a private correspondence between William Kelley and Betty Winn in 1941.

63. *Morning Herald,* May 10, 1935.

64. "Near Beer Stolen at Frostburg," *The Baltimore Sun* (Baltimore, MD), June 16, 1921.

65. *Brewery Directory and Supplies,* 34–35.

66. Wolf, "The Breweries of Cumberland Maryland," 6–14.

67. *The Cumberland Evening Times,* March 20, 1936.

68. *Brewery Age Buyer's Guide,* 1939, 139.

69. Wolf, "The Breweries of Cumberland, Maryland," 6–14.

70. "No Coal, No Ice, No Beer-Is Threat" *The Baltimore Sun,* April 19, 1946. "Breweries Deny Use of Sugar," *The Washington Post* (Washington, D.C.), August 2, 1945.

71. "Brewery Bought in Cumberland," *The Baltimore Sun,* January 1, 1959.

72. *Brewery Age,* February 1938, 18.

Chapter 8

1. Stanley N. Vlántes, "The Changing Aspects of the Negro Market-1967," *Beer Distributor* 34, no. 3 (May 1967): 7–18.

2. *Ibid.*

3. Baltimore City Land Records, Liber 792, Folio 347; "Hamm's Purchases Gunther Brewery; 10 Million Dollar Expansion Starts!" *The Baltimore Sun* (Baltimore, MD), December 15, 1959.

4. "Hamm's To TV Oriole Games," *The Baltimore Sun* (Baltimore, MD), December 18, 1959.

5. Bill Janeska, interview with author, October 21, 2013.

6. Tim Hampson, "Green Beer," *Oxford Companion to Beer* (Boston: Oxford University Press, 2011), 406–407.

7. Janeska, interview with author, 2013.

8. Baltimore City Land Records, Liber 1505, Folio 226; Jesse Glasgow, "Hamm Plant Sold to Schaefer," *The Baltimore Sun* (Baltimore, MD), June 18, 1963.

9. Jesse Glasgow, "Gunther Tag Purchased by Schaefer: Hamm Announces the End of the Eastern Division," *The Baltimore Sun* (Baltimore, MD), April 19, 1964.

10. Jesse Glasgow, "Arrow Beer Pushes West: Cumberland Plant to Brew Globe Product," *The Baltimore Sun* (Baltimore, MD), October 11, 1963.

11. "New Markets Added as Gunther Returns," *The Baltimore Sun* (Baltimore, MD), August 14, 1973.

12. Bob Leasure, "A Beer Man's Journal: My Life's Work," 2012.

13. *Ibid.*

14. *Ibid.*

15. Charles G. Whitford, "5 Brewers Take Fight to Governor," *The Baltimore Sun* (Baltimore, MD), March 17, 1956.

16. *Ibid.*

17. Siegal, Eric, "Jerry Hoffberger," *The Baltimore Sun* (Baltimore, MD), January 21, 1979.

18. "Brewing Firm Buying Another," *The Baltimore Sun* (Baltimore, MD), September 18, 1954; Harold Roberts, "National Brewing Sets Growth Program Here: New Packaging Center is First Part of Big Five-Year Expansion," *The Baltimore Sun* (Baltimore, MD), July 18, 1965.

19. Jesse Glasgow, "Brewing Firm Plans Boost in Capacity," *The Baltimore Sun* (Baltimore, MD), September 6, 1964.

20. *The Pittsburgh Courier,* January 28, 1967.

21. Jesse Glasgow, "City's Biggest TV Advertisers Vary Approach to Reach Market," *The Baltimore Sun* (Baltimore, MD), July 6, 1969.

22. National Brewing Company, "Colt 45 Malt Liquor Commercial (1967)," filmed (1967), YouTube video, 1:02, posted September 14, 2015, https://www.youtube.com/watch?v=CJ_mtRc3WwU; National Brewing Company, "1960's Colt 45 Malt Liquor Beer Commercial⊠," filmed (1960), YouTube video, 1:25, posted December 6, 2009, https://www.youtube.com/watch?v=FBqq27rDucs.

23. "National Expands Brewing," *The Baltimore Sun* (Baltimore, MD), June 2, 1975.

24. Baltimore City Land Records, Liber 3312, Folio 081; Jesse Glasgow, "Carling Seeks to Purchase National Beer," *The Baltimore Sun,* September 11, 1975.

25. James Gutman, "Brewing Firm Hops to It to Help Carling's Aleing Business," *The Baltimore Sun* (Baltimore, MD), July 13, 1980.

Chapter 9

1. Howard, *The Monumental City,* 940.

2. Edwards, *Industries of Maryland,* 259, 349.

3. Howard, *The Monumental City,* 940, 941.

4. *Ibid.,* 942

5. Hugh Sisson, interview with author, January 17, 2011.

6. SB 418, *Session Laws of Maryland 1988* 770, 1525.

7. Sisson, interview with author, 2011.

8. *Ibid.*

9. *Ibid.*

10. Kevlin C. Haire, "McHenry Brewing Founder Prepared to Dive Right on in," *Baltimore Business Journal* (Baltimore, MD), August 18, 1994.

11. Baltimore City Land Records, Liber 2269, Folio 001.

12. Baltimore City Land Records, Liber 6225, Folio 264; Baltimore City Land Records, Liber 6761, Folio 375; "Maryland Pub Brewers Say Archaic Laws Are Driving Them Out of the State," *Modern Brewery Age,* May 6, 1996.

13. John Hendren, "Brewpubs Bemoan Law Limiting Production," *The Washington Post* (Washington, D.C.), April 25, 1996.

14. Craig S. Ey, "A Really Big Weekend," *Baltimore Business Journal* (Baltimore, MD), April 20, 1998.

15. *The Washington Post,* September 14, 1998.

16. Baltimore City Land Records, Liber 3666, Folio 155.

17. Baltimore City Land Records, Liber 1365, Folio 530.

18. Baltimore City Land Records, Liber 3327, Folio 211, 232.

19. Julie Johnson, "Pull Up a Stool with Jason Oliver of Devil's Backbone," *All About Beer Magazine* 32, no. 6 (January 1, 2012).

20. Mike Stein, "District Chophouses Barrett Lauer Discusses All Manner of Beer Topics," *DC Beer,* January 8, 2015.

21. Mark Stevens, "Brimstone Brewing Company—Rekindling Brewing Traditions on Brewery Hill," *Brewing Techniques,* September, 1997.

22. *Ibid.*

23. "Frederick Brewing Company Finalizes Mergers with Wild Goose and Brimstone Brewing Co." *The Baltimore Business Journal,* January 29, 1998.

24. Volker Stewart, interview with author, June 11, 2013.

25. *Ibid.*

26. Steve Frazier, interview with author, June 11, 2013.

27. Mike McDonald, interview with author, July 27, 2012.

28. *Ibid.*

29. Bill Blocher, interview with author, July 27, 2012.

30. McDonald, interview with author, 2012.

31. Bill Blocher, interview with author, 2012.

32. Stephen Demczuk, interview with author, March 23, 2011.

33. *Ibid.*

34. Anne Arundel County Land Records, Liber 4712, Folio 745.

35. Thomas Cizauskas, "Farewell to a Maryland Tradition," *thomascizauskas.net,* 2000, Accessed March 15, 2016, http://thomas.cizauskas.net/articles/oxford.html.

36. Michael Jackson, *Pocket Guide to Beer* (NY: Simon & Schuster, 1997), 138.

37. Cizauskas, "Farewell."

38. Cheryl Lu-Lien Tan, "Microbreweries Learn to Ferment Interest," *The Washington Times* (Washington, D.C.), September 29, 1997.

39. Matt Hahn, interview with author, November 21, 2014.

40. Ellen Gamerman, "Plans for Microbrewery in Full Swing," *The Baltimore Sun* (Baltimore, MD), June 11, 1995.

41. Dave Gulliver, "Brewpub Bill too Late for Ram's Head," *The Capital,* January 10, 1997.

42. Kristen Seal, "Dogfish Head," *The Cape Gazette* (Lewes, DE), May 17, 1996.

43. Todd Karpovich, "Johansson's Hopes to Brew Up Some Tourism for Main St.," *Carroll County Times* (Westminster, MD), November 8, 1999.

44. Dail Willis, "Shore's Own Microbrewery," *The Baltimore Sun* (Baltimore, MD), August 8, 1995.

45. *Ibid.*

46. Dorchester County Land Records, Liber 326, Folio 796.

47. "Frederick Brewing Company Finalizes Mergers with Wild Goose and Brimstone Brewing Co.," *The Baltimore Business Journal* (Baltimore, MD), January 29, 1998.

48. *The Baltimore Sun,* November 28, 1998.

49. Frederick County Land Records, Liber 2208, Folio 733.

50. Frederick County Land Records, Liber 2207, Folio 857.

51. Kristine Henry, "Significant Loss Indicated By Frederick Brewing Co., 6 Managerial Jobs, Executives' Pay Cut," *The Baltimore Sun* (Baltimore, MD), July 21, 1998.

52. Kristine Henry, "Brewer Sidles Up to Buyer: Frederick Gives Snyder Until July 25 to Buy Majority Stake. A Bittersweet Adjustment," *The Baltimore Sun* (Baltimore, MD), July 1, 1999.

53. Kristine Henry, "Brewery Seeks Merger-Would Increase Output," *The Baltimore Sun* (Baltimore, MD), January 10, 2001.

54. Frederick Land Records, Liber 4586, Folio 121.

55. Frederick County Land Records, Liber 2182, Folio 1361, 1391.

56. Hahn, interview with author, 2014.

57. *Ibid.*

58. Tom Flores, interview with author, July 10, 2012.

59. *Ibid.*

60. *Ibid.*

61. Dave Benfield, interview with author, July 23, 2013.

62. Jim Wagner, interview with author, July 23, 2013.

63. Howard County Land Records, Liber 3605, Folio 0001.

64. Dan Morse, "New Restaurant to Offer 4 Theme Rooms, Plans to Brew Beer on Premises," *The Baltimore Sun* (Baltimore MD), October 17, 1996.

65. Hahn, interview with author, 2014.

66. Larry Carson, "Eclectic Ellicott Mills Brewing Company Lends Itself to a Little Uniqueness," *The Baltimore Sun* (Baltimore, MD), April 6, 2000.

67. Montgomery County Land Records, Liber 12116, Folio 0413; SBA loan #CDC-L 603–290–30–00-DC, August 30, 1994.

68. *U.S. v. Tavern Breweries, Inc,* Case # 99-bk-17692, Greenbelt, MD, 1999.

69. Montgomery County Land Records, Liber 16972, Folio 420–570.

70. Bill Turque, "Montgomery County Liquor Monopoly May Be Facing Last Call," *The Washington Post* (Washington, D.C.), November 28, 2015.

71. Montgomery County Land Records, Liber 21319, Folio 0439.

72. Montgomery County Land Records, Liber 32459, Folio 044.

73. Castle Bay, beginning in 2008, cut back the production of their own beers in favor of macro beers. By 2011 they were occasionally serving one Castlebay Brew. After 2011 they no longer brewed their own, although the pub remains open.

74. Globe Brewing took the name of the former Globe Brewery in Baltimore. The young cousins teamed

with Siarcloth, head brewer from the Wharf Rat, to open the Brewpub/Brewing School in South Baltimore. Althouth the food was considered quite good and the beer was drinkable (but needed tweaking), and it became nationally known due to the "Homicide: Life on the Street" 100th episode party held there by NBC, the brewery/school could not stay above water. The doors were open for less than two years when it went belly up. In part, the trademark was abandoned by December of 1997, creating great difficulty in maintaining the brand the following year.

75. Deep Creek Founders seemed to have a successful enterprise when located in Oakland where the investment was paid off relatively quickly (Garrett County Land Records Liber792, Folio 439). This was buttressed by Mortimer's diverse real estate interests. The move to the three acre property in McHenry seemed to usher in the death knell. Squabbles over shoddy construction by contractors resulting in lawsuits combined with a bust in the real estate market. The brewery was scrapped and the restaurant was called Santa Fe Grille beginning in 2004. Shortly thereafter, Deep Creek Brewing Company LLC was filing for Chapter 11 with 51 creditors (U.S. Bankruptcy Court, Case # 0:14-bk-13189).

76. The Tuppers are world renowned for their beer tastings. In 1994 they chose to create their own. They had neither experience brewing nor the necessary equipment and gave the rudimentary components (hops, yeast, process desired) to Old Dominion who contract brewed the Tupper's *Hop Pocket Ale*. It went on to win several medals, including gold at the 1997 GABF. They also contract brewed a pilsener out of Old Dominion, which also went on to win gold at the 2001 GABF.

77. Although this was only a contract brewing operation, it appeared to be rather widespread, at least for a time through Ocean City (Theresa Humphrey, "A Following Is Brewing for Ocean City Beer," *The Washington Post* (Washington, D.C.), May 18, 1989). It is unclear when operations stopped, but the company switched over to strictly distribution as a wholesale beer distributor.

Chapter 10

1. Sisson, interview with author, 2011.
2. *Ibid.*
3. Linda Strowbridge, "Coming About," SmartCEO. com, October 2014; Christine Shaffer, "New Brewhouse at Heavy Seas Beer," craftbeer.com, Accessed September 6, 2014, http://www.craftbeer.com/news/brewery-news/new-brewhouse-heavy-seas-beer.
4. Sisson, interview with author, 2011
5. Strowbridgel, "Coming About"; Shaffer, "New Brewhouse."
6. Sisson, interview with author, 2014.
7. *Ibid.*
8. Strowbridge, "Coming About."
9. Sisson, interview with author, 2011.
10. Wesley Case, "Q&A, Brewmaster on Heavy Seas First New Year-Round Beer Since 2003, Crossbones," *The Baltimore Sun* (Baltimore, MD), November 25, 2014.
11. Brewer's Association of Maryland, *Awards List*, accessed September 10, 2014 http://www.maryland beer.org/default.asp?iId=MGFHD.

12. Stephen Demczuk, interview with author, August 16, 2012.
13. Jacques Kelly, "Surveyors Locate Site of Home Plate of Old Oriole Park," *The Baltimore Sun* (Baltimore, MD), May 1, 2015.
14. Demczuk, interview with author, 2012.
15. *Ibid.*
16. Mark Supik, interview with author, March 6, 2013.
17. Stephen Demczuk, interview with author, September 20, 2014.
18. Demczuk, interview with author, 2014.
19. Edgar Allen Poe, *Eleonora* (North Charleston: BookSurge, 2004), 1.
20. James Briggs, "DuClaw Brewing Picks Baltimore County for New HQ," *Baltimore Business Journal* (Baltimore, MD), September 13, 2013.
21. Benfield, interview with author, 2013.
22. *Ibid.*
23. *Ibid.*
24. *Ibid.*
25. Wagner, interview with author, 2013.
26. "GABF Awards-Maryland," accessed August 17, 2014 http://www.marylandbeer.org/default.asp?iId=MDEGF.
27. Benfield, interview with author, 2013.
28. *Ibid.*
29. *Ibid.*
30. Wagner, interview with author, 2013.
31. Steve Jones, Interview with author, November 18, 2015.
32. Stewart, interview with author, 2012.
33. "Green Peppercorn Triple Is First Brewer's Art Beer Brewed And Packaged at Sly Fox Royersford," *Sly Fox News* October 11, 2007, Accessed June 25, 2014 http://www.slyfoxbeer.com/index.php/front/news_archive/14.
34. Brian Strumke, interview with author, February 14, 2015.
35. Emily Hutto, "Breakout Brewer: Stillwater Artisanal Ales," *Craft Beer and Brewing Pro*, January 26, 2015.
36. Joe Tucker, "Best Brewers in the World," *Rate Beer*, 2011, Accessed September 8, 2015 https://www.ratebeer.com/ratebeerbest/bestbrewers_012011.asp.
37. "State Craft Beer Production and Data," *The Brewer's Association*, ND.
38. Jon Zervitz, interview with author, July 26, 2012.
39. *Ibid.*
40. *Ibid.*
41. Kevin Blodger, interview with author, July 26, 2014.
42. *Ibid.*
43. Ryan McDonald, "Union Craft Brewing Expands in Clipper Mill, Plans to Double Production," *Baltimore Business Journal* (Baltimore, MD), March 20, 2014.
44. Anna Weaver, "Union Craft Brewer Stands Out in Largely White Industry," *Capital News Service*, ND, http://cnsmaryland.org/maryland-brewers-put-state-on-craft-beer-map/.
45. Nick Fertig, interview with author, June 4, 2013.
46. Max Weiss and Jesse Peterson, "The Great Berger Cookie Debate: Baltimore Sure Loves Them. But are Berger Cookies Really All That? An Unscientific Debate," *Baltimore Magazine* (Baltimore, MD),

February, 2014, Accessed June 22, 2014, http://www.
baltimoremagazine.net/2014/1/are-berger-cookies-
really-all-that.

47. John K. Ross, "The FDA Wants to Ban Berger
Cookies, the World's Most Delicious Dessert," Rea-
sonwww, November 23, 2013, Accessed June 22, 2014,
http://reason.com/blog/2013/11/23/the-fda-wants-
to-ban-berger-cookies-the.

48. *Ibid.*

49. Fertig, interview with author, 2013.

50. Nick Fertig, interview with author, October 11,
2014.

51. *Ibid.*

52. Supik, interview with author, 2013.

53. *Ibid.*

54. Adrian Moritz, interview with author, June 26,
2012.

55. *Ibid.*

56. *Ibid.*

57. *Ibid.* Moritz eventually sold the defunct bottling line to another brewery and focused instead on
growler and keg sales.

58. Brewer's Association of Maryland, *Awards*, Accessed September 15, 2014, http://www.maryland
beer.org/default.asp?iId=LGMEJ.

59. Moritz, interview with author, 2012.

60. Brewer's Association of Maryland, *Awards.* Accessed September 15, 2015, http://www.marylandbeer.
org/default.asp?iId=MGFHD; Kathy Bosin, "Cheers!
Eastern Shore Brewery Wins Again," *Talbot Spy* (Easton, MD), November 26, 2013.

61. Bryan Brushmiller, interview with author, June
18, 2013.

62. *Ibid.*

63. *Ibid.*

64. Jon Bleiweis, "Loakal Pays Homage to Burley
Oaks Roots," *USA Today* (McLean, VA), March 28,
2014; Brews Travelers 365, *#87 Burley Oak*, http://
brewstravelers365.com/2014/04/06/87-burley-oak-
brewing-company-in-berlin-md/.

65. Jeremy Cox, "Laurel Plant to Make Malt for
Brewers," *Delmarva Now* (Salisbury, MD), February
10, 2016.

66. Tom Knorr, interview with author, July 9, 2013.

67. D.E. Ferraris, "The Evolution of an Easton-
Based Brewmaster," *Eastern Shore Savvy* (Easton,
MD), March 22, 2012.

68. Knorr, interview with author, 2013.

69. *Ibid.*

70. Geoff DeBisschop, interview with author, July
9, 2013.

71. *Ibid.*

72. *Ibid.*

73. *Ibid.*

74. Danny Robinson, interview with author, June
19, 2013.

75. *Ibid.*

76. Lisa Capitelli, "Shorebilly Brewing Company
Beers a Big Hit," *Ocean City Today* (Ocean City, MD),
June 21, 201Bi.

77. Robinson, interview with author, 2013.

78. Capitelli, "Shorebilly Brewing Company."

79. Syd Nichols, "Shorebilly's Swill," *Ocean City
Blogs*, www.oceancityblogs.com.

80. Robinson, interview with author, 2013.

81. "Fraud Alleged in Civil Suit Over Shorebilly
Term," *Maryland Coastal Dispatch* (Berlin, MD), July
24, 2014.

82. Robinson, interview with author, 2013.

83. *Ibid.*

84. "Fraud Alleged in Civil Suit," *Maryland Coastal
Dispatch.*

85. Robinson, interview with author, 2013.

86. *Teal Bay Alliances LLC v. Southbound One
Inc.*, 1:13-cv-02180-MJG (4th Circuit Court of Appeals).

87. Vince Wright, interview with author, June 30,
2013.

88. Sam Calgione, *Dogfish HeadPunkin Ale*, Accessed August 24, 2014, http://www.dogfish.com/bre
ws-spirits/the-brews/seasonal-brews/punkin-ale.htm

89. Wright, interview with author, 2013.

90. Wagner, "Liquor Legislation is Complicated."

91. Patrick Brady, interview with author, June 18,
2013.

92. Wright, interview with author, 2013.

93. Brady, interview with author, 2013.

94. Wright, interview with author, 2013.

95. Brady, interview with author, 2013.

96. *Ibid.*

97. *Ibid.*

98. Wright, interview with author, 2013.

99. *Ibid.*

100. Anthony Towey, "A New Craft Beer Legacy is
Brewing at Tall Tales," OceanCitywww, November 21,
2013, Accessed September 2, 2014, www.oceancity.
com.

101. *Ibid.*

102. Brushmiller, interview with author, 2013.

103. Towey, "A New Craft Beer Legacy."

104. Brooke Feichtl, "Tall Tales Brewing Company:
Second Stop on the ShoreBread Beer Tour," *Shore-
Bread*, (Berlin, MD), November 20, 2013.

105. *Ibid.*

106. Wesley Case, "Brewers Aim to Add Eastern
Shore to Craft Beer Map," *The Baltimore Sun* (Baltimore, MD), May 16, 2014.

107. Jimmie Sharp, *LinkedIn Profile*. Accessed September 3, 2014, https://www.linkedin.com/profile/
view?id=237119186&authType=NAME_SEARCH&
authToken=PXST&locale=en_US&srchid=543943
111409759625231&srchindex=1&srchtotal=21&trk=
vsrp_people_res_name&trkInfo=VSRPsearchId
%3A543943111409759625231%2CVSRPtargetId%3A
237119186%2CVSRPcmpt%3Aprimary.

108. Chris Browhan and J.T. Merryweather, interview with author, July 24, 2013.

109. *Ibid.*; Choose Dorchester, "Reale Revival Cuts
Ribbon to Cambridge Brewery," *Dorchester County
Economic Development Department*, August 13, 2013.

110. Browhan and Merryweather, interview with
author, 2013.

111. *Ibid.*

112. *Ibid.*; The Statistics Portal, *Frequency of Craft
Beer Consumption in the United States in 2012 by Age
Group*, http://www.statista.com/statistics/289590/
us-frequency-of-craft-beer-consumption-by-age-
group/; Chris Crowell, "Craft Beer Consumer Stats:
How Will They Affect Your Business Plan?" *Craft
Brewing Business*, May 20, 2013. Although numbers
vary slightly, the theory of a large percentage of older
craft beer drinkers is supported. An additional point
is that 35 to 54-year-olds comprise approximately 44
percent of craft beer consumers in the United States
and should also be a part of all marketing plans.

113. Browhan and Merryweather, interview with
author, 2013.

114. *Ibid.*

115. Mitchell Northam, "RAR: Big Time Brewery with a Small-Town Mentality," *Delmarva Now* (Salisbury, MD), July 18, 2015.

116. Browhan, and Merryweather, interview with author, 2013.

117. Tim Miller, interview with author, June 26, 2012.

118. *Ibid.*

119. *Ibid.*

120. *Ibid.*

121. Miller, interview with author, June 18, 2013.

122. *Ibid.*

123. Hahn, interview with author, 2014.

124. *Ibid.*

125. Ray Andreassen, interview with author, May 2, 2012.

126. *Ibid.*

127. Alex Taylor, interview with author, August 17, 2012.

128. "Push American," BeerAdvocatewww, Accessed October 11, 2016, https://www.beeradvocate.com/beer/profile/12648/.

129. Taylor, interview with author, 2012.

130. Kasey Turner, interview with author, June 3, 2014.

131. *Ibid.*

132. *Ibid.*

133. *Ibid.*

134. *Ibid.*

135. *Ibid.*

136. Sarah Meehan, "Jailbreak Brewing is Doubling Its Capacity After Running Out of Beer," *Baltimore Business Journal* (Baltimore, MD), March 31, 2015.

137. Kasey Turner, interview with author, June 4, 2016.

138. *Ibid.*

Chapter 11

1. Carlos Ynez, interview with author, January 18, 2013.

2. *Ibid.*

3. Matt Glass, interview with author, January 18, 2013.

4. Ynez, interview with author, 2013.

5. *Ibid.*

6. Jason Millikins, interview with author, January 18, 2013.

7. *Ibid.*

8. *Ibid.*

9. Marc Moore, interview with author, June 5, 2014.

10. Lew Bryson, *Virginia, Maryland, and Delaware Breweries* (Mechanicsburg: Stackpole Books, 2005), 172–175.

11. Dave Johansson, interview with author, June 14, 2013.

12. Jay Lampart, interview with author, June 14, 2013.

13. Drew Holcomb and the Neighbors, Good Light, Dualtone Records, 4, 2013, CD.

14. "Brewmaster: After Learning from Some of the Biggest in the Beer Business, Greg Norris is Making a Splash with His Clay Pipe Brewing Company in Carroll County," *The Baltimore Sun* (Baltimore, MD), June 24, 2003.

15. *Washington Post* (Washington, D.C.), September 24, 2008.

16. Flores, interview with author, 2012.

17. *Ibid.*

18. *Ibid.*

19. "Brewer's Association Seats Board of Directors," *Brewer's Association of America*, February 24, 2016, Accessed May 24, 2016, https://www.brewersassociation.org/press-releases/brewers-association-seats-2016-board-of-directors/.

20. Fritz Hahn, "In with the New at Gaithersburg's Growlers," *The Washington Post* (Washington, D.C.), May 4, 2007.

21. "Quirky Brewing Pays Off for Growler's of Gaithersburg," *The Washington Post* (Washington, D.C.), April 17, 2012.

22. Eric Gleason, interview with author, July 31, 2013.

23. *Ibid.*

24. "Comptroller's Cup 2013," *Brewer's Association of Maryland*, Accessed August 24, 2014, http://www.marylandbeer.org/default.asp?iId=MGFHD.

25. Eric Gleason, interview with author, September 20, 2014.

26. The Governor's Cup was retitled the Comptroller's Cup in 2013 as an homage to Comptroller Peter Franchot and his dedicated work helping breweries open across the state.

27. Paul Rinehart, interview with author, May 30, 2013.

28. Brewers Association of America, Member Directory, *Lindsey Miller Profile*, accessed August 16, 2014, http://www.brewersassociation.org/category/profile/?tag=Maryland.

29. Jerry Miller, *10 Mid-Atlantic Brewmasters to Watch*, Scoutology, n.d., Accessed November 12, 2014, http://nashville.scoutology.com/10-mid-atlantic-brewmasters-to-watch/.

30. Prince George's County Land Records, Liber 8500, Folio 389.

31. Crista Dockray, "Calvert Brewing Co. is Md's First Designated Farm Brewery," *Southern Maryland Online*, April 8, 2016, Accessed September 25, 2016.

32. Dickson Mercer, "Adam Frey Believes in Keeping it Simple, yet Creating Havoc," *Frederick News Post* (Frederick, MD), June 16, 2005.

33. Adam Frey, interview with author, July 30, 2013.

34. *Ibid.*

35. *Ibid.*

36. *Ibid.*

37. *Ibid.*

38. *Ibid.*

39. USDA, *United States Standards for Barley* (Washington, USDA, 1997), §810.202, 810.204–810.206.

40. Henry Ruhlman, interview with author, June 14, 2013.

41. *Ibid.*

42. *Ibid.*

43. Frederick County Land Records, Liber 8284, Folio 0179.

44. Lizzy McClellan, "From the Dirt to the Glass," *Tribune Business News*, August 21, 2013.

45. Sarah Meehan, "Red Shedman Farm Brewery to Open its Taproom in Frederick County," *Baltimore Business Journal* (Baltimore, MD), November 7, 2014.

46. It is unclear if Bawlmer Craft Beer is still operational, as the website is gone and the products have not been on the market in at least two years as of

2016. There is, however, a "new" Bawlmer product— *Lean* IPA, suggesting Mr. O'Melia is not done. He may have an infringement case as New Belgium Brewery also has a new beer released this year called *Bawlmer*.

47. This total includes all contract brewed beer in addition to Peabody Heights own brand.

48. The Fleischers initially teamed with Jeremy Gruber to open Hook & Ladder Brewing with a plan to open in the Historic Fire Station #1 on Georgia Avenue in Silver Spring. They contract-brewed out of Wilkes Barr, PA, until they could open the brewpub. Unfortunately, the parties went their separate ways, with Gruber opening a restaurant in the historic fire house now called Firestation 1. The Fleischers eventually opened a brewery at the above listed address. Unfortunately, they filed for Chapter 7 bankruptcy in 2013 with over 262 creditors (U.S. Bankruptcy Court, Greenbelt, MD case # O-13-bk-14841).

49. KB Summit LLC went into receivership, forcing the sale of Growler's brewpub in January, 2015. Montgomery County Land Records, Liber 49743, Folio 250.

50. Joshua Aaron Shores was charged with and plead guilty to $2.5 million in wire fraud for obtaining and selling counterfeit sports memorabilia in February of 2016. As of September 2016, Ocean City Brewing added three more restaurants to infiltrate Baltimore and Western region. It is unclear how that plea deal will affect the future of the brewing company (Department of Justice, "Former Owner of Internet Sports Memorabilia Businesses Charge with $2.5 Million Fraud Scheme," *Federal Information & News Dispatches*, January 29, 2016).

Chapter 12

1. Jessica Walkert, et al., "Identification of Beer Bitter Acids Regulating Mechanisms of Gastric Acid Secretion," *Journal of Agriculture and Food Chemistry* 60, no. 6 (2012): 1405–1412; P.M. Ferraro, et al., "Soda and Other Beverages and the Risk of Kidney Stones," *Clinical Journal of the American Society of Nephrology*, no. 8 (August 8, 2013): 1389–1395.

2. Charles T. Price, Kenneth Koval, and Joshua Langford, "Silicon: A Review of Its Potential Role in the Prevention and Treatment of Postmenopausal Osteoporosis," *International Journal of Endocrinology* 2013 May. Article ID 316783, Accessed September 13, 2016, https://www.hindawi.com/journals/ije/2013/316783/; C. Barry, "Alcohol Answer?" *Science News* 171, no. 26 (June 30 2007): 405.

3. Juan Yao and Baoxm Zhang, et al., "Xanthohumol, A Polyphenol Chalcone Present in Hops, Activating NIFZ Enzymes to Confer Protection Against Oxidative Damage in PCIZ Cells," *Journal of Agriculture and Food Chemistry* 63, no. 5 (2015): 1521–1531.

4. V. Lamy and S. Roussi, et al., "Chemopreventive Effects of Lupulone, a Hop {Beta} Acid on Human Colon Cancer-Derived Metastatic SW620 Cells and in a Rat Model of Carcinogenesis," *Carcinogenesis* 2007 28, no. 7 (July 2007): 1575–1581; F. Ferk, et al., "Xanthohumol, a Prenylated Flavonoid Contained in Beer, Prevents the Induction of Preneoplastic Lesions and DNA Damage in Liver and Colon Induced by the Heterocyclic Aromatic Amine Amino-3-Methyl-Imidazo[4,5-f] Quinolone (IQ)," *Mutation Research/Fundamental and Molecular Mechanisms of Mutagenesis* 691, no. 1–2 (September 10, 2010): 17–22.

5. Brewers Association of America, "Maryland," *State Craft Beer Sales and Production Statistics, 2015*, Accessed September 16, 2016, http://www.brewersassociation.org/statistics/by-state/.

6. Brewers Association of America, *Brewery Production Statistics 2011–2015*, Accessed September 16, 2016, http://www.brewersassociation.org/statistics/brewery-production/?type=success&msg=You%20have%20been%20logged%20in%20successfully.

7. Allastair Bland, "Craft Brewers Are Running Out of Names and into Legal Spats," *The Salt*, January 5, 2015.

8. *Ibid.*

9. Timothy Geigner, "About Face: Lefthand Brewing Abandons Attempt to Trademark 'Nitro,' Invites Other Breweries to Their Nitro Fest Instead," *TechDirt*, November 17, 2014.

10. Pink Boots Society, Accessed January 22, 2015, http://pinkbootssociety.org/; Teri Fahrendorf, *Biography*, Accessed January 22, 2015, http://www.terifahrendorf.com/.

11. Justin Peligri, "Bold Brews," *The Washington Blade* (Washington, D.C.), July 23, 2014.

12. Chris Anderson, interview with author, May 24, 2012.

13. *Ibid.*

14. *Ibid.*

15. Mike Esterl, "After Long Downturn, Beer Sales are Back," *Wall Street Journal* (New York, NY), October 2, 2012.

16. Anderson, interview with author, February 23, 2015.

17. *Ibid.*

18. Stephen Marsh, interview with author, September 20, 2014.

19. Anderson, interview with author, 2012.

20. *Ibid.*

21. Rona Kobell, "Aquaculture Most Likely Future for Chesapeake Bay's Oysters," *Chesapeake Bay Journal*, October 2010, 1–8.

22. Oyster Recovery Partnership, "Shell Recycling Alliance," Accessed September 28, 2016, http://oysterrecoverypartnership.squarespace.com/about-the-shell-recycling-alli/.

23. Blodger, interview with author, 2012.

24. *American Brewer's Review* 27 (1913): 181–182.

25. *Baltimore American*, May 2, 1870, 5.

26. James DiLisio, *Maryland Geography* (Baltimore: Johns Hopkins Press, 2014).

27. *Ibid.*; *Farmland Preservation Report 2014*, Accessed February 2, 2015, http://www.farmlandpreservationreport.com/.

28. Caryl Velisek, "Amber Fields Brewing Beer with Maryland-Grown Barley," www.AmericanFarm.com, 2012, Accessed February 7, 2015.

29. Brushmiller, interview by author, July 2013; "Burley Farming," BurleyOak.com 2015, Accessed February 7, 2015.

30. "Scorpion Brewing Company Malting Expansion," *Kickstarter*, August 2, 2014.

31. Velisek, "Amber Fields"; Stephen Ausmus, "Chesapeake Bay Clean Up Revs Up," *Agricultural Research*, August 2010, 16–17.

32. "Economic Impact: State Data at A Glance: Maryland," 2015, *Beer Institute*, Accessed September 25, 2016, http://www.beerinstitute.org/assets/map-pdfs/Beer_Economic_Impact_MD.pdf.

Bibliography

"Abstracts of Corporations." *Governor's Message Submitted to the Legislature of 1903 with the Accompanying Reports and Documents of Fiscal Years October 1, 1900 to September 30, 1902.* Charleston: The Tribune, 1903, vol. 1.

"A.C. Ritchie to Chandler P. Anderson." April 26, 1926, *Governor's Correspondence: Albert Cabell Ritchie 1920–1935.* Maryland Hall of Records, Annapolis, MD f.d. 24-c.

"All Counties, 1653–2016." *Maryland Land Records.* https://mdlandrec.net/main/index.cfm.

American Brewers Gazette and Malt and Hop Trades. Chicago: Tovey, 1876–1917.

Anderson, James. James Anderson to Mary Anderson, December 11, 1850. In *Anderson Family Papers* at Maryland Historical Society Archives.

Anderson, Sonja, and Will Anderson. *Anderson's Turn of the Century Brewery Directory: A Complete Listing of All U.S. Breweries in Operation in 1890, 1898, 1904 and 1910, as Listed in the Original Brewers' Hand-Books for Those Years.* Carmel, NY: Sonja and Will Anderson, 1968.

The Anti-Prohibition Manual: A Summary of Facts And Figures Dealing with Prohibition. Cincinnati: National Wholesale Liquor Dealers Association of America, 1917.

Asbury, Herbert. *The Great Illusion: An Informal History of Prohibition.* New York: Doubleday, 1950.

The Baltimore Business Journal. Baltimore, 1985–present.

The Baltimore Clipper. Baltimore, 1839–1865.

The Baltimore Daily Advertiser. Baltimore, 1786–1792.

The Baltimore Daily Repository. Baltimore, 1791–1793.

The Baltimore Sun, Baltimore, 1837.

Banneker, Benjamin. *Benjamin Banneker's Pennsylvania, Delaware, Maryland and Virginia Almanack and Ephemeris for the Year of Our Lord, 1792; Being Bissextile, or Leap-Year, and the Sixteenth Year of American Independence.* Baltimore: Goddard & Angell, 1797.

Baron, Stanley. *Brewed in America: The History of Beer and Ale in the United States.* Boston: Little, Brown, 1962.

Barron, James, Commodore of *Chesapeake.* Commodore James Barron letter. Accessed via the Mariner's Museum. June 22, 1807.

Barry, C. "Alcohol Answer?" *Science News* 171, no. 26 (June 30, 2007): 405.

Bedini, Silvio. *The Life of Benjamin Banneker.* New York: Charles Scribner's Sons, 1972.

Beer Distributor. Chicago, 1935–present.

Behr, Edward. *Prohibition: Thirteen Years That Changed America.* New York: Arcade, 1996.

Black, Jeremy, Graham Cunningham, Eleanor Robson, and Gabor Zolyomi. *The Literature of Ancient Sumer.* Oxford: Oxford University Press, 2004.

"Black Moon Mysteries." *Database of Old Time Radio Programs and Peoples.* Accessed August 28, 2015.

Blum, Isidor. *The Jews of Baltimore: An Historical Summary of Their Progress and Status as Citizens of Baltimore from Early Days to the Year Nineteen Hundred.* Baltimore: Historical Review Publishing Company, 1910.

Bordley, John Beale. *Essays and Notes on Husbandry and Rural Affairs.* Philadelphia: Budd and Bartram, 1799.

Brantley, Honorable William T., et al. *The History of Baltimore.* Baltimore: S.B. Nelson, 1898.

Brewer's Digest. Chicago, 1937–present.

The Brewer's Guide to the United States, Canada, and Mexico 1898. Chicago: American Brewers Review, 1898.

The Brewer's Handbook 1918. Chicago: H.S. Rich, 1918.

The Brewers' Journal and Barley, Malt and Hop Trades Reporter 41, (1917): 498.

Brewery Age. Chicago: Brewery Age Publishing, 1936–1939.

Brewery Directory and Supplies Index. New York: Atlas Publishing, 1934.

A Brief Outline of the Rise, Progress, and Failure of the Revolutionary Scheme of the Nineteen Van Buren Electors of the Senate of Maryland: In the Months of September, October, and November, 1836. Baltimore: Sands and Neilson, 1837.

Briggs, D.E. *Malts and Malting.* New York: Springer, 1998.

Brumbaugh, Gaius Marius. *Genealogy of the Brumbach Families.* New York: F.T. Hitchcock, 1913.

Canton Co. of Baltimore. *Special Report of the President and Directors of the Canton Company of Baltimore Made to the Stockholders, March 10, 1871.* Baltimore: J. Murphy & Co., 1871.

Caravel Films, Inc. prod. *Miracle of the Can.* New York: American Educational Films, 1956.

"The Charter of Maryland: 1632." In *The Federal and State Constitutions Colonial Charters, and Other Organic Laws of the States, Territories, and Colonies Now and Heretofore Forming the United States of America,* edited by Francis Newton Thorpe. Washington: GPO, 1909.

The Chicago Journal of Commerce and Metal Industries Vol. 61 (1892): 27.

"Citizenship Declaration of John Fitzgerald." State of Maryland, City of Baltimore. September 2, 1892.

"City of Baltimore United Breweries, Limited." *Brewer's Guardian* 25, no. 632. (January 1, 1895).

Clark, Charles B. *The Eastern Shore of Maryland and Virginia,* vol. 2. New York: Lewis Historical Publishing Company, Inc., 1950.

Cunz, Dieter. *The Maryland Germans: A History.* New Jersey: Princeton University Press, 1948.

Deutschen Literarische Bureau. *Baltimore: Seine Vergangenheit und Gegenwart.* Baltimore: Druck und Satz von C.C. Bartgis & Bro., 1887.

Digital Sanborn Fire Insurance Maps, Maryland. Sanborn Map Company, 1867–1970.

DiLisio, James. *Maryland Geography.* Baltimore: Johns Hopkins University Press, 2014.

Dineley, Merryn. "Who Were the First Maltsters? The Archaeological Evidence for Malting." *Brewer and Distiller International.* February, 2016.

"Documents from the Continental Congress and the Constitutional Convention, 1774 to 1789." *Library of Congress.* June 10, 1777: Resolved for Supplying the Army of the United States with Provisions; April 22, 1782: A System on Which Provisions Are to Be Issued; October 23, 1782: Regulations for the Quarter Master General's Department: By the United States in Congress Assembled. https://www.loc.gov/collections/continental-congress-and-constitutional-convention-from-1774-to-1789/.

Douglas, Frederick. *Narrative of the Life of Frederick Douglass, an American Slave.* Boston: The Antislavery Office, 1845.

Dukeheart, Morton Mcl. *A Collection of Authenticated Biographical Sketches of the Author's Ancestors Dating from the Thirty Years War (1618–1648) and Continuing Unbroken Sequence to the Date of Publication (1947),* 2d ed. Baltimore: Morton Dukeheart, 1947.

"Economic Impact: State Data at a Glance: Maryland," 2015. *Beer Institute.* Accessed September 25, 2016. http://www.beerinstitute.org/assets/map-pdfs/Beer_Economic_Impact_MD.pdf.

Edwards, Richard, ed. *Industries of Maryland: A Descriptive Review of the Manufacturing and Mercantile Industries of the City of Baltimore.*

Baltimore: Historical Publishing Company, 1882.

Englehardt, George. *Baltimore City Maryland: The Board of Its Book of Trade.* Baltimore: George Englehardt, 1895.

Evans, Hiram W. *The Klan: Defender of Americanism.* New York: Forum, 1925.

Ezratty, Harry A. *Baltimore in the Civil War.* Charleston: The History Press, 2010.

"Farmland Preservation Report 2014." *Farmland Preservation Report.* Accessed February 7, 2015. http://www.farmlandpreservationreport.com/.

Farra, Jody, and Phil Meyers. *Post Prohibition Brewery Guide 1933–1983: The 50th Anniversary Edition.* New York: 1983.

Farrell, Frank. "St. Valentine's Day Massacre Confession." Frank Farrell to John Edgar Hoover, January 28, 1935. *Federal Bureau of Investigation.* https://vault.fbi.gov/St.%20Valentines%20Day%20Massacre/St%20Valentines%20Day%20Massacre%20Part%201%20of%202.

Ferk F., et al. "Xanthohumol, a Prenylated Flavonoid Contained in Beer, Prevents the Induction of Preneoplastic Lesions and DNA Damage in Liver and Colon Induced by the Heterocyclic Aromatic Amine Amino-3-Methyl-Imidazo[4,5-f] Quinolone (IQ)." *Mutation Research/Fundamental and Molecular Mechanisms of Mutagenesis* 691 no. 1–2 (September 10, 2010): 17–22.

Ferraro, P.M., et al. "Soda and Other Beverages and the Risk of Kidney Stones." *Clinical Journal of the American Society of Nephrology,* no. 8 (August 8, 2013): 1389–1395.

First Records of Baltimore Town and Jones Town 1729–1797. Baltimore: Mayor and City Council of Baltimore, 1905.

Fordham, Benjamin. *Last Will and Testament.* Prerogative Court Wills 14, 501–504. MDHR 1292-2, Accessed January 11, 2016.

"Free State Brewery Sold: Name Now Wiessner Brewing." *Wall Street Journal* (New York), July 14, 1950.

Freidrich, Manfred, and Donald Bull. *The Register of United States Breweries 1876–1976.* Trumbull, CT: D. Bull, 1976.

Glasgow, Jesse. "Carling Seeks to Purchase National Beer." *Baltimore Sun* (Maryland), September 11, 1975.

Gobright, John C. *The Monumental City, or Baltimore Guide Book, Being a Reliable Directory for Citizens and Strangers to the Prominent Objects of Interest, Together with a Description of the Prominent Mercantile and Manufacturing Houses.* Baltimore: Gobright & Torsch, 1858.

Groeninger, W.J. *Groeninger's New Baltimore.* Baltimore: Jones & Groeninger, 1906.

Hampson, Tim. "Green Beer." In *The Oxford Companion to Beer.* Boston: Oxford University Press, 2012.

Heck, Earl Leon Werley. *The History of the Heck Family of America: With Special Attention Given to Those Families Which Originated in Indiana, Kentucky, Maryland, Ohio, Pennsylvania, Virginia.* Madison: University of Wisconsin, 1959.

Helman, James A. *History of Emmitsburg, Maryland: With a Prelude of Historical Facts of Frederick County, and a Romance Entitled Disappointed, or, the Recluse of Huckle's Field.* Frederick, Maryland: Citizen Press, 1906.

Hentz, Tucker F. *Unit History of the Maryland and Virginia Rifle Regiment (1776–1781): Insights from the Service Record of Capt. Adamson Tannehill.* Richmond: Virginia Historical Society, 2007.

Hobby Distiller's Association. *The Distillation of Spirits for Personal and Private Use: A Proposal to Amend Federal Law Title 26 of the United States Code (Internal Revenue Code) to Legalize Hobby Distilling.* Keller: HAD, 2013.

Homan, Michael. "Beer Production By Throwing Bread Into Water: A New Interpretation of Qoh XI 1–2." *Vestus Testamentum* 52, no. 2 (April 2002): 255–258.

Hopkins, Fred. "For Flag and Profit: The Life of Commodore John Daniel Danels of Baltimore." *Maryland Historical Magazine* 80, no. 4 (Winter 1985).

Hornsey, Ian. *A History of Beer and Brewing.* London: Royal Society of Chemistry, 2003.

Howard, George Washington. *The Monumental City: Its Past History and Present Resources.* Baltimore: J.D. Ehlers & Co., 1873.

Hull, Isaac. *Commodore Hull: Papers of Isaac Hull, Commodore, United States Navy.* Boston, MA: Boston Athenaeum, 1929.

Illustrated Atlas of Washington County. Philadelphia: Lake, Griffing & Stevenson, 1877.

Inaugural Addresses and Legislative Messages of Governor Albert C. Ritchie of Maryland 1920–1935. Baltimore, n.d.

Industries of Maryland: A Descriptive Review of the Manufacturing and Mercantile Industries of Baltimore. New York: Historical Publishing Co., 1882.

International Brewers Journal and Malt and Hops Trade Review. London: w. Reed, 1865–1915.

John Fitzgerald and Bridget McCormick: Marriage Certificate. State of Maryland. September 19, 1904.

Journal of the Institute of Brewing. London: Harrison & Sons, 1895–present.

Kaufmann, Donald M., and June Kaufmann. *The United States Brewer's Guide 1630–1864.* Cheyenne, 1967.

Kelley, William J. *Brewing in Maryland: From Colonial Times to the Present.* Baltimore: William J. Kelley, 1965.

Kolchin, Peter. *American Slavery 1619–1877.* New York: Hill and Wang, 2003.

Lamy, V., et al. "Chemopreventive Effects of Lupulone, a Hop {Beta} Acid on Human Colon Cancer-Derived Metastatic SW620 Cells and in a Rat Model of Carcinogenesis." *Carcinogenesis* 28, no. 7 (July 2007): 1575–1581.

Lanmon Dwight P., and Arlene M. Palmer. "Amelung in Europe." *Journal of Glass Studies* 18 (1976): 20–24. http//www.jstor.org/stable/24190009.

Lardner, Michael V. "Memoirs." 2013. Unpublished manuscript.

Leasure, Bob. "A Beer Man's Journal: My Life's Work." 2012. Unpublished manuscript.

Lieb, Fred.. Carbondale: Southern Illinois University Press, 2005.

Liebmann, George, ed. "The Battle of Franklin Farms." In *Prohibition in Maryland: A Collection of Documents.* Baltimore: Calvert Institute for Policy Research, 2011.

Litoff, Judy Barnett and David C. Smith. "United States Women's Land Army." In *The American Experience in WWII: The American People at War: Minorities and Women in the Second World War* vol. 10, edited by Walter L. Hixon. New York: Taylor and Francis, 2003.

Lowe, Delbert B. *History of the Consolidated Gas, Electric, Light, and Power Company of Baltimore.* College Park: University of Maryland, 1928.

Lutz, Henry Frederick. *Viticulture and Brewing in the Ancient Orient.* Carlisle, MA: Applewood Books, 2008.

"Marketing and Communications." *Printer's Ink: A Journal for Advertising* 86, no. 1 (1914).

Markham, Gervase. *The English Housewife,* Edited by Michael Best. Montreal: McGill-Queen's University Press 1994.

Maryland Chancery and Land Commission Papers. 1785–1908.

Maryland Gazette. Annapolis, 1731–1800.

"Maryland Historical Trust State Historic Site Inventory Form: Planter's Paradise." *Maryland Inventory of Historic Properties.* https://mht.maryland.gov/secure/medusa/PDF/Baltimore%20County/BA-263.pdf.

Maryland in World War II: Industry and Agriculture, vol. 2. Baltimore: Maryland Historical Society, War Records Division, 1950.

Matchett's Directory for Baltimore. Baltimore: Matchett, 1816–1855.

Mathias, Peter. "Agriculture and the Brewing and Distilling Industries in the 18th Century." *The Economic History Review* 5, no. 2 (1952).

Mayer, Brantz. *Baltimore As It Was and As It Is: A Historical Sketch of the Ancient Town and the Modern City.* Baltimore: Richardson & Bennett, 1871.

"Mayoralty Election Contest in the City Of Cumberland 'Coulehan Against White' Republican Mayor Called Upon to Defend Returns-Lack Of System Alleged In Counting Of Ballots." *Baltimore Sun* (Maryland), June 1, 1902.

McKearin, Helen, and Kenneth Wilson. *American Bottles and Flasks and their Ancestry*. New York: Crown Publishers, 1978.

McWilliams, Jane W. *Annapolis, A City on the Severn: A History*. Baltimore: Johns Hopkins University Press, 2011.

Meacham, Sarah Hand. *Every Home a Distillery*. Baltimore: Johns Hopkins University Press, 2009.

Menken, H.L. H.L. Mencken to Harry Rickel, March 27, 1933. In *The New Mencken Letters*, edited by Carl Bode. New York: Dial Press, 1977.

Mencken, H.L. *Journal September 3, & 23, 1932*. Enoch Pratt Mencken Collection. 18.

Mencken, H.L. *Newspaper Days 1899–1906*. New York: Alfred A. Knopf, 1955.

Mencken, H.L. *The New Mencken Letters*, edited by Carl Bode. New York: Dial Press, 1977.

Mish, Mary Vernon. *Jonathan Hager, Founder*. Maryland: Hagerstown Bookbinding & Print Co., 1937.

Mitchell, Wesley C. *Prosperity and Thrift: The Coolidge Era and the Consumer Economy, 1921–1929*. New York: McGraw-Hill, 1933.

Modern Brewery Age. Norwalk, 1937–1954.

National Park Service. *American Can Company: Historic American Buildings Survey*. Philadelphia, PA: Department of the Interior, 1988.

Das Neue Baltimore, 1729–1905. Baltimore: The German Publishing Company, 1905.

"The New Bremen Glassmanufactory." *Journal of Glass Studies* 18 (1976): 25–38.

"The New Brewer." *Journal of the Brewers Association*. Colorado, 2014.

New York Bar Association. *New York Supreme Court Appellate Division, Second Judicial Department*, vol. 733.

19th Annual Report of Bureau of Statistics and Information of Maryland 1910. Annapolis: Kohn & Pollack Printers, 1911.

Olson, Sherry H. *Baltimore: The Building of an American City*. Baltimore: John's Hopkins University Press, 1980.

Packard, Aaron. "Baltimore's Schuetzen Park and Its Tokens." *NOVA Numismatics: The Historical Pursuit of Exonumia*. January 23, 2012.

Painter, Orrin Chalfant. *William Painter and His Father Dr. Edward Painter: Sketches and Reminiscences*. Baltimore: Arundel Press, 1914.

Pegram, Thomas R. *One Hundred Percent American: Rebirth and Decline of the Ku Klux Klan in the 1920's*. Lanham: Rowman & Littlefield, 2011.

Penner, Bernard. *Zion in Baltimore 1755–1955 History Book Supplement 1955–2005*. Baltimore: Zion Church of the City of Baltimore, 2008.

Peters, Thomas. "A Scrap of Troop History." *The Pennsylvania Magazine of History and Biography* 15, no. 2 (1891).

Polk's Baltimore City Directory. Baltimore: R.I. Polk, 1887–1964.

Power Pictorial June 1934. Baltimore: Consolidated Gas, Electric, Light and Power Company, 1934.

Price, Charles T., Kenneth Koval, and Joshua Langford. "Silicon: A Review of Its Potential Role in the Prevention and Treatment of Postmenopausal Osteoporosis." *International Journal of Endocrinology* (May 2013).

Price, Jacob M., ed. *Joshua Johnson's Letterbook 1771–1774: Letters from a Merchant in London to His Partners in Maryland*. London: London Record Society, 1979. Accessed January 6, 2014. http://www.british-history.ac.uk/report.aspx?compid=38795.

Reed, Amy Lee Huffman, and Marie LaForge Burns. "Chronology of Glass Making in Frederick County, Maryland." In *In and Out of Frederick Town: Colonial Occupations*. Frederick, Maryland: LDS Church, 1985.

Rich, H. *One Hundred Years of Brewing: A Complete History*. Chicago: H.S. Rich and Co., 1903.

Richard J. Cox, ed. *A Name Index to the Baltimore City Tax Records, 1798–1808, of the Baltimore City Archives*. Baltimore: Baltimore City Archives and Records Management Office. 1981.

Risjord, Norman K. *Builders of Annapolis: Enterprise and Politics in a Colonial Capital*. Baltimore: Maryland Historical Society, 1997

Sabin, Pauline. "Declaration of Principles." In *Women and Repeal: The Story of the Women's Organization for National Prohibition Repeal*, by Grace Cogswell Root. New York: Harper and Bros., 1934.

Salem, F.W. *Beer, Its History and Its Economic Value as a National Beverage*. New York: Arno, 1972.

Samuel, Delwan. "Bread Making and Social Interactions at the Amarna Workmen's Village, Egypt." *World Archaeology* 31, no. 1.

Scharf, Col. J. Thomas. *The Chronicles of Baltimore: Being a Complete History of Baltimore Town and Baltimore City from the Earliest Time to the Present*. Baltimore: Turnbull Brothers, 1874.

Scharf, Col. J. Thomas. *History of Baltimore City and County from the Earliest Period to the Present Day: Including Biographical Sketches of Their Representative Men*. Philadelphia: L.H. Everts, 1881.

Scharf, Col. J. Thomas. *History of Western Maryland: Being a History of Frederick, Montgomery, Carroll, Washington, Allegany, and Garrett Counties from the Earliest Period to the Present Day; Including Biographical Sketches of Their Representative Men*. Philadelphia: L.H. Everts, 1882.

Schildknecht, C.E. *Monocacy & Catoctin: Some Early Settlers of Frederick and Carroll Counties, MD and Adams County, PA also Descendants c. 1725–1985*, vol. 1. Shippensburg, PA: Beidel Printing House, 1985.

Schlüter, Hermann. *The Brewing Industry and the Brewery Workers' Movement in America.* New York: B. Franklin, 1970.

Seibel Institute of Technology. "Adjuncts—Then and Now." *Brewery Age*, September 1938.

"Series 1: Minutes, 1923–1925." *Knights of the Ku Klux Klan, Klan No. 51, Mt. Rainier, Maryland Archives.* Special Collections: University of Maryland Hornbake Library.

Shea, Stuart, and Gary Gillette. *Calling the Game: Baseball Broadcasting from 1920 to the Present.* Phoenix: SABR, 2015.

Simmons, Amelia. *American Cookery.* Hartford: Simeon Butler, 1798.

Smith, Gregg. *Beer in America: The Early Years, 1587–1840: Beer's Role in the Settling of America and the Birth of a Nation.* Boulder: Brewer's Association of America, 1998.

Smith, Robert B. Federal Housing Authority. "Modernization Loans Available to Distributors and Taverns," *Beer Distributor.* July 1935.

Solomon, Burt. *Where They Ain't: The Fabled Life and Untimely Death of the Original Baltimore Orioles, the Team That Gave Birth to Modern Baseball.* New York: Free Press, 1999.

Stalfort, Charles Jr. *Grosspapa Frank Steil Family History.* Unpublished Manuscript. Baltimore: Zion Church Archives, 2009.

"State Craft Beer Sales and Production Statistics, 2015: Maryland." *Brewers Association of America.* http://www.brewersassociation.org/statistics/by-state/.

Toomey, Daniel Carroll. *The War Came by Train: The Baltimore & Ohio Railroad during the Civil War.* Baltimore: Baltimore & Ohio Railroad Museum, 2013.

Tremblay, Victor J., and Carol Horton Tremblay. *The U.S. Brewing Industry: Data and Economic Analysis.* Cambridge, MA: MIT Press, 2009.

Troesken, Werner. "Regime Change and Corruption: A History of Public Utility Regulation." In *Corruption and Reform: Lessons from America's Evonomic History.* Edited by Edward L. Glaeser and Claudia Goldin. Chicago: *National Bureau of Economic Research,* March 2006.

"Tuberculosis and Its Prevention." *Journal of the American Medical Association* 23. (August 25, 1894): 302

United States Brewers Association. *The History of Brewing and the Growth of the Unites States Brewers' Association.* New York: United States Brewers Association, 1937.

United States Census Records, 1790–1930.

U.S. Congress, House. "The Prohibition Amendment: Hearings Before the Committee on the Judiciary." 71st Congress. March 12, 1930. 41–43.

U.S. Congress, House. "The Volstead Act." 66th Congress, 1st session, H.R. 6810, Record Group 11. *General Records of the United States Government.* NARA. October, 16 1919.

U.S. Congress, Senate. "Brewing and Liquor Interests and German Propaganda: Hearings Before a Subcommittee on the Judiciary." 65th Congress, 2nd Session, Pursuant to SR 307. *Subcommittee on the Judiciary.* 1919.

U.S. Congress, Senate. "The National Prohibition Law: Hearings before the Committee on the Judiciary." 69th Congress, 1st Session. *Committee on the Judiciary.* 1926. 649–52.

Van Wieren, Dale P. *American Breweries II.* West Point, PA: Eastern Coast Breweriana Association, 1995.

Varle, Charles. *Complete View of Baltimore.* 1833.

Vlántes, Stanley N. "The Changing Aspects of the Negro Market—1967." *Beer Distributor* 34, no. 3. (May 1967).

"Volume 421: General Assembly January 4–April 3, 1933 Session Laws." *Maryland State Archives.* http://slavery.msa.maryland.gov/megafile/msa/speccol/sc2900/sc2908/000001/000421/html/index.html.

Von Degen, A. *Baltimore; Its Past and Present.* Baltimore: The Baltimore Brewers and Maltsters Association, 1887.

Walker, Jessica, et al. "Identification of Beer Bitter Acids Regulating Mechanisms of Gastric Acid Secretion." *Journal of Agriculture and Food Chemistry* 60, no. 6. (2012): 1405–1412.

The Wall Street Journal. New York, 1889–present.

The Washington Post. Washington, D.C. 1877–present.

Watson, Bart. "U.S. Brewery Count Tops 3,000." *Brewers Association of America: Insights and Analysis.* July 9, 2014.

Weaver, Clarence E. *The Story of Hagerstown 1911.* Hagerstown, MD: Mail Publishing Company, 1911.

Weeks, Jos D. *U.S. Census Report on the Manufacture of Glass.* Washington: Government Printing Office, 1884.

White, S.J., Father Andrew. "An Account of the Colony of the Lord Baron of Baltimore, in Maryland, Near Virginia: In Which the Character, Quality and State of the Country, and its Numerous Advantages and Sources of Wealth Are Set forth." (1633). In *Narratives of Early Maryland, 1633–1684,* Edited by Clayton Colman Hall. New York: Charles Scribner's Sons, 1910.

Whitman, T. Stephen. *The Price of Freedom: Slavery and Manumission in Baltimore and Early National Maryland.* (New York: Routledge, 2000), 8–14.

Whitney, Dori. "Salute to MBAA—100 Years." *Brewer's Digest.* (August 1987): 16–29.

Wiebe, Gustav A., Cowan, et al. "Yields of Barley Varieties in the United States and Canada 1932–36," no. 735. *USDA.* (1940).

Wilkins, Mira. *The History of Foreign Investment in the United States to 1914.* Cambridge, MA: Harvard University Press, 1989.

Williams, Thomas J.C. *A History of Washington County, Maryland, from the Earliest Settlements to the Present Time, Including a History of Hagerstown*, vol. 2. Baltimore: Regional Pub. Co., 1968.

Williams, Thomas John Chew, and Folger McKinsey. *History of Frederick County, Maryland*, vol. 1. Frederick: Genealogical Publishing Co., 1997.

Williams, Thomas John Chew, and Folger McKinsey. *History of Frederick County, Maryland: With a Biographical Record of Representative Families*, vol. 2. Baltimore: Regional Pub. Co., 1967.

Wolf, James. "The Breweries of Cumberland Maryland." *The Keg.* Summer 2006.

Woods Baltimore City Directory. Baltimore: John W. Woods, 1856–1886.

Wust, Klaus G. *Zion in Baltimore 1755–1955; the Bicentennial History of the Earliest German-American Church in Baltimore Maryland.* Baltimore: Zion Church of the City of Baltimore, 1955.

Yao, Juan, et al. "Xanthohumol, A Polyphenol Chalcone Present in Hops, Activating NIFZ Enzymes to Confer Protection Against Oxidative Damage in PCIZ Cells." *Journal of Agriculture and Food Chemistry* 63, no. 5 (2015): 1521–1531.

Zimmerman. "Malted Rice as a Brewing Material." *Communications on the Science and Practice of Brewing*, no. 4 (December, 1938).

Index

341